T0270673

# Dr. Linda's
## Comedy Marriage Boot Camp

Otherwise Known As:
## "How to Stay Happily Married for 25 Years or More From A to Z"

# DR. LINDA MARIE WATSON

The stories you are about to see are based upon true scenarios. The names have been changed to protect the innocent.

FIRST EDITION

Printed in the United States of America

Watson, Dr. Linda Marie

Print ISBN: 979-8-35092-131-1
eBook ISBN: 979-8-35092-132-8

# DEDICATION

First off, this book is meant to be taken very lightly. It's all in fun. We don't need serious, now do we? Heck, no!

I'm dedicating this book to my husband Robert, and my daughter Andrea. Thank you both for everything! There's no way to express my appreciation. I love you both so much.

I also wish to express my deepest gratitude to Andrea Watson for editing and proofreading this book. Thank you Christopher Capp and Lois Winters for your endless support, encouragement and friendship.

Let's now salute those couples who've maintained strong marriages long-term. Hey, it ain't easy! Their lives aren't perfect with everyday bursts of rainbows and glitter. But they've defied the odds by staying happy together, and not becoming another divorce statistic.

Please feel free to skip around here, but do read the "Alien" chapter first! You will be nodding in agreement within seconds.

So where does the 25 years' time limit come in? Well, seems miserable married folks can tolerate just about 20 years max. Then they "suddenly" split up after about two decades. If you and your spouse can be happy at the 25-year mark, chances are decent you'll stay together for good.

While researching this book, I spoke with hundreds of married folks. In addition, for close to 12 years I worked for a very large company, where I encountered many individuals with interesting and weird situations. All names in this book have been changed, including the success story couples.

We shall give real-life scenarios throughout this book to illustrate the concept behind each section. Some narratives are compilations of more than one story and all are based on actual situations.

Quite a few men were interviewed for this book and their answers will often really surprise you.

Please laugh and enjoy this book, dear reader! Don't take any of it seriously; we're just gonna poke fun at a whole lot of stuff!

I'm donating 50 percent of the proceeds from this book to my non-profit, Nimchuk Equine Foundation. 100 percent of all monies donated to this 501(c)(3) non-profit go directly to help horse rescues and sanctuaries.

I'm including lots and lots of my own past screw-ups to make you feel better about your own.

We'll poke fun at some of the gold standard marital advice you've had shoved down your throat for decades. We shall replace that tired wisdom with what really works for real-life couples. Nothing is too wild and crazy to be included.

There are also some food, movie and TV references throughout this book just to make it entertaining.

Intimacy is an important part of marriage, so we've got a glorious sex chapter and an incredible orgasm chapter coming up. Oh, *yes we do*. No one will judge you in the *least* if you decide to skip and jump on ahead and read those fun sections first. Please feel free to do so!

Thank you so much for your support in buying this book, and please do check out our website, Nimchukequinefoundation.org

# FOREWORD

Robert and I were married on June 25<sup>th</sup> of 1988. This year, we celebrated our 35th wedding anniversary. "Where has the time gone?" is a constant theme.

At one time, celebrating 25 years or more of marriage was no unusual accomplishment. Sadly, this is no longer the case. The current rate of divorce is so high that more couples end up splitting up than staying together. As of this writing, the rate of divorce in the U.S. is over 50 percent.

So, why do some folks stay together, while others break up? They're madly in love at the start, but a few years later, can't stand so much as the sight of one another. Over 20 percent of divorces happen in the first five years. There are so many statistics on this topic, but they're depressing, so we won't cover them too much here.

What works for one couple won't work for another. That's why we've included diverse tips.

So here, in the following 26 chapters, one for each letter of the alphabet, we've compiled stories to entertain you and maybe help improve your marriage.

As for our success stories, they're narratives of couples who've stayed happily married for a long time (at least 25 years). Each had struggles to overcome, but they did it together and their stories are inspiring.

Maybe your marriage is happy, fantastic, incredible, and you want to keep it that way. You don't even need this book, you lucky sucker! Maybe then still read it just for sheer entertainment value.

Perhaps your union has become uber stale, kind of like that miniature piece of cinnamon raisin bread that somehow got shoved to the back of the fridge three or four months ago. If your sex life has gotten drab, no one will give you judgy looks if you skip right on over to that section.

Or, worst case scenario: things between you and your spouse are in the Freddy Krueger boiler room basement. You are 99 percent sick of one another. Maybe you've already consulted a luxury divorce attorney.

In this case, skip directly to the Dr. Linda one-month comedy marriage boot camp. Begin to employ the steps therein *immediately*. Don't delay... just try it!

Thank you again, dear reader, for taking the time to purchase this book. I hope you like reading it as much as I enjoyed writing it.

# TABLE OF CONTENTS

# A

---

## Alien

If you motor through Roswell, New Mexico, you'll see billboards everywhere with pictures of UFO's and cute little tiny aliens. What on earth does this have to do with a long and happy marriage, you may ask?

Well, get ready. Here goes... it's stranger than fiction, but it's all true! Envision the beautiful Kate Hudson in "Skeleton Key," sobbing on the phone, "It's real...it's all real!"

Yep, in this context, it's your very own horror movie! Because, dear reader... take our word for it! When you *very* least expect it, you will innocently go to sleep one night, then wake up the next day in panic and dread, because you'll realize that you are married to a bona fide alien.

Never mind that you and your beloved grew up in the same town, perhaps you are both the same race and religion, the same approximate age, plus you share similar ideological beliefs... *none* of this matters! None.... muahahahah!

Don't even think you're above it, because *no one is!* Even the Queen went through this. Which queen, you ask? All of 'em! Every queen in history, that's who! All the royalty, and common folks as well. It's unbelievably tragic, yet comical, and it would be even funnier if it just happened to other people, not to you as well!

Here's the full scenario: You first meet your beloved. They are wonderful, handsome, beautiful, sexy, kind, and interesting. You then fall madly, passionately in love with this most glorious creature. You are so dang crazy about them, it's as though heaven and earth conspired to bring them directly into your life. You aren't merely on cloud nine, nope, you're on cloud ten trillion!

Your beloved is the most perfect, insightful, considerate, romantic, adorable, incredible, lovable, sexy person on the entire planet. You're in such lust and such love it's a wonder you can even sleep at night. You then get married and you're living on a radiant, puffy cloud of sheer joy and ecstasy.

Then, a few years go by. Maybe your partner's creepy little habits have gotten to you, or perhaps they did something really big and idiotic. Either way, at some point in your marriage, you sadly come to realize with utmost chagrin that your partner is dumb, strange, weird, or all three.

You then look at them in horror and you think miserably to yourself, "Oh dear God, I married an alien!"

If, in reading this, you're nodding knowingly, with a resigned, tragic expression on your face, chances are excellent you've been married for a little while.

If you have no idea what we're talking about whatsoever, you're adorable, and you're probably fresh-faced and haven't yet even unpacked from your honeymoon.

Something your spouse does or says will make you *truly* believe you're living with a creature who originated from *another planet* entirely! Like in one of those B+ horror movies from the 50s, you are actually wed to an extra-terrestrial!

Here are a few possible statements a husband or wife might make when they become excruciatingly aware they've joined forces with someone from outer space.

For the sake of convenience, let's just use the pronoun "he."

"He's an alien!"

"He's so Goddamn weird! Where'd he get such a crazy idea? Not on planet earth, that's for sure!"

"What kind of a space invader did I marry anyways?"

"What the hell was he thinking? He must be from Planet Mars."

Or, my personal favorite: "What fucking planet is he from anyways?"

No matter how many similarities you and your spouse may share, nonetheless, the harsh reality is this: you both grew up in totally dissimilar households, with different parents and distinctly separate lifestyles.

No matter how much you love someone, these facts are as inescapable as "The Creature From the Black Lagoon."

Then, to further complicate matters, there may be many more cultural differences to overcome. Your spouse may have also grown up with substantially more or less money than you did, or different beliefs about money. These all can also cause major challenges.

Hundreds of married folks were interviewed for this book. When the pathetic and sorry topic of being wed to an alien arose, everyone, without exception, admitted that they had encountered planet Mars sometime during their years of wedded bliss.

So just know with absolute certainty, that one day you'll look at your beloved and you will see an Android or if you're not so lucky, maybe even a little Martian. By the time you've celebrated your second wedding anniversary, you may, in fact, think you are driving through Area 51 every sad sack day.

But just stick it out, and the feeling shall pass, well, at least until next time.

No one can promise that you will really ever get over that "wed to an alien" feeling.

So, be realistic about your differences. Know going into it that you two are from entirely different planets.

Also, be pragmatic. If you ditch your spouse when you discover their space invader status, you will then spend a virtual fortune on divorce. One day, you're likely to remarry, only then after awhile, to discover in horror that your new spouse is an extraterrestrial too, just in new, *state-of-the-art* ways.

Without a doubt, finances are one of the most challenging "Area 51" zones that married folks must navigate just like a loaded mine field.

Here's a case in point. Becky and Tyler had been married for three years; they were in their late 20s, and had meticulously planned out their lives together. Their objectives and goals for the future were perfectly in sync. They'd known one another since high school. Tyler felt he understood Becky better than anyone in the entire galaxy.

This couple dreamed of owning their own home. They'd been saving since their wedding day, and were only one year away from reaching this monumental goal. Once they'd bought a house, they'd immediately begin trying to have a baby. Their goal was for Becky to have all of their 2.5 planned children before she turned 34.

Both Becky and Tyler drove modest, practical cars. Tyler didn't care what he drove, but Becky did especially admire flashy sports cars.

One weekend, Tyler left early Saturday morning for a fishing trip. Becky planned to spend the day with her single girlfriend, Rachel. Rachel was very spontaneous, quite a sharp contrast to Becky, who'd always been so sensible. Two months earlier, Rachel had quit her job on impulse and had traveled throughout Asia for six weeks.

Rachel planned to take Becky along with her to look at a new Mustang she wanted to buy. Becky casually mentioned this to Tyler when they spoke on the phone as he was driving to the lake, but he didn't think anything of it. After all, Becky was just going along for moral support; to prevent Rachel from buying something she couldn't afford.

Imagine, if you will, Tyler's shock and dismay when he returned home Sunday night. There on their driveway, in all its gleaming splendor, was a brand-new, top-of-the-line, bright red Mustang GT. Scarlett (for Becky had already christened her) had all the bells and whistles and was absolutely beautiful. Every gleaming inch displayed luxury and speed.

Apparently, Rachel had been turned down for poor credit; Becky had not. Becky had zoomed off the dealership lot in her new $65,000.00 ride because a) her credit was impeccable and b) she'd written a check from their house savings account for $9,000.00.

Tyler was speechless... he was beyond livid. She'd taken the money out of their house account, and saddled them with five years' worth of $954 per month car payments.

Tyler couldn't believe his practical, frugal wife would have gone and done something like this. Furthermore, Becky adamantly refused to even consider returning the car.

"You do realize," Tyler told her furiously, "this means now it will take us at least two more years, maybe three, before we can buy a house."

Becky said that now she wasn't in that big of a hurry to buy a house. She also told Tyler she'd decided not to have kids so young. Plus, she wanted the two of them to go to Asia and Europe before starting a family.

Becky stated all of this with absolute calm and certainty. However, it must be said that her eyes were slightly glazed over as she stroked Scarlett's leather interior and began talking about personalized license plates.

To say that Tyler was experiencing shock would be to put it quite mildly. He was now entering what is commonly known in married circles as "the alien nation."

Tyler became short of breath and felt a strange buzzing in his ears. He had the eerie sensation that over the weekend, while he was obliviously fishing for marlin, his dependable little Becky had been transformed by weirdo body snatchers into an Android.

There was actually a very reasonable explanation for Becky's sudden alien behavior. Every minute of every day, she'd always done the practical thing. She'd lived at home and commuted to college, even though she'd wanted desperately to live on campus, because her folks had said it was too expensive. She'd missed out on studying abroad because her grandma had been elderly and her mom had needed help caring for her. She'd wanted desperately to go to interior design school, but had become a nurse instead, because Tyler had told her it was the more practical career.

Her entire life, Becky had subjugated her dreams for practicality, and in the process, had missed out on so much. So, it's no small wonder that she finally turned into an extraterrestrial.

The red Mustang meant much, much more than a car to Becky. Tyler finally understood where she'd been coming from and they were able to compromise. They worked in a trip to Europe before buying their first house, and planned to go to Asia for Becky and Ireland for Tyler before starting a family.

Becky's extraterrestrial behavior had more to do with not missing out on experiences and learning not to agree to things that she didn't want.

Sometimes, as in the case of Becky, alien exploits do not just come out of nowhere, although that's how it seems at first.

At any rate, know that you've been warned... and you're not alone if one day you look at your spouse and see some sort of green alien creature!

## Affection

Traditionally, it was believed that only women craved affection and men could do without it, so long as they had sex. It's pretty much a known fact that women resent it if their husbands don't display affection other than when making sexual advances.

We've all known couples who are not affectionate at all; you can't even tell they're together. When they're walking, he's easily 20 paces ahead. You often see couples like this at the airport. He's 10 feet in front of her as he shouts over his shoulder, "Edna, where are our passports?" and she screams, "Fred, you've got them!"

So, it came as a real surprise when researching this book, to hear over and over from men how much they craved not just sex (though that is very important as well) but also good old-fashioned affection.

This can be a hug, a kiss, or a kind touch. The guys mentioned they love to have their hand held. Couples who've been happily married a long time aren't always too demonstrative in public. No one is exactly telling them to "go get a room," but they often hold hands, or show other signs of affection.

So, what do you do if you and your spouse have not shown much (or maybe any) physical affection for years? How do you turn this around?

Perhaps start with little steps, such as a touch on the shoulder or holding your spouse's hand for even a couple of minutes. Even small progress can improve a stale relationship.

Either the husband or the wife can take the initiative; someone has to "break the ice," and then ideally, both partners will become warmer in time.

One of our success story wives relayed that her husband always makes her coffee in the morning. This type of little action means a lot. Or they give each other a couple quick squeezes when they hold hands. No is aware of this but them, and it contributes to their closeness as a unit.

Even baby steps can be worth so much toward increasing connection.

## Apologize

Most of us have seen the classic film "Love Story" with Ali McGraw and Ryan O'Neal. In this beautiful movie, there's a famous line where McGraw's character says to O'Neal, "Love means never having to say you're sorry."

Not to sound disrespectful toward a cinematic masterpiece, but what a total load of crap. Adam and Beth were married for close to 20 years when he abruptly (or so it seemed to her) left her and moved out on his own. Within weeks, he had filed for divorce. Beth, who is a very bright, articulate person, was stunned and heartbroken. She told friends she'd known they had problems, but never to the extent where she thought Adam would actually leave her.

You see, Beth loves to be right and absolutely refuses to admit when she's in the wrong. As Adam explained to friends, much as he loved Beth, he'd grown extremely weary over the years of being told he was wrong every time they had a disagreement. He'd also become completely fed up with her insulting him when she became angry. Adam is somewhat overweight, and when they fought, Beth mocked him about his extra pounds.

This couple sought help from an array of expensive marriage therapists over the years, but nothing really improved. Beth always made excuses to the therapists for her outbursts, citing her difficult childhood and verbally abusive mother. However, Adam made the observation that Beth never lashed out at clients or co-workers. He knew that she could control her temper when she wanted to. So there was something of a bullying component at work here as well.

But what really compounded the misery was that when Beth lashed out at Adam, she never apologized afterwards. Once they'd split up, Adam told friends that if Beth could have apologized even just once in a while, he probably could have stayed married to her forever.

Here's another possible way to look at the "Love Story" quote. Perhaps what the line from the movie could mean is this: in a good relationship, you shouldn't *need* to be apologizing all the time to your spouse.

If you continually have to mop up your messes, so to speak, perhaps you need to take an honest assessment of yourself. Do you make a lot of tactless comments? Do you say things which offend your partner? Do you take it out on your partner when you've have a bad day?

## Arguments

Ah, arguments. If a couple absolutely never argues, it could be they're some kind of zombies. One or both of them may be holding in anger, hostility or resentment.

If so, perhaps one partner believes everything is going along swimmingly until one day "out of nowhere," he or she is served with grisly divorce papers, and is shocked and devastated.

If a couple argues from time to time, and it's done constructively, this can actually be a very healthy way to clear the air.

Number one rule: no hitting below the belt, meaning no personal insults made toward your partner when you're angry. You can count on this behavior to damage your relationship, and ultimately your wallet.

That's because divorce lawyers will readily accept a very large percentage of your cash.

Steve and Caroline were madly in love and had been married for three years. They enjoyed camping, hiking and spending time with friends. Steve said that Caroline was the best thing that had ever happened to him.

Unfortunately, Steve had a very nasty temper, which caused him to lash out with bitter and insulting comments. When angry, he insulted Caroline, calling her names such as "dumb," "stupid idiot," and "bimbo." This bothered Caroline very much, but she kept thinking he would change.

Over the next two years, Caroline forgave Steve repeatedly, as he was usually so wonderful to her. He always said he was just kidding, and would apologize afterwards. But she didn't see his comments as jokes, rather as nasty insults.

As time went on, Caroline became more and more angry at this treatment, and their marriage began to deteriorate very rapidly.

After one particularly nasty argument, during which Steve called her a "stupid bitch," Caroline began moving out. She made a deposit on a new apartment and began packing her things. Steve begged her to reconsider; she told him unless they went for counseling, she was done and wanted a divorce.

Luckily, this couple went for counseling and the therapist taught Steve techniques how to calm down, quiet his thoughts and fight fair without lashing out. This eventually put a complete end to his name-calling and insults.

During therapy, Steve revealed for the first time that his alcoholic father, who had passed away five years before, had been very verbally abusive toward him. He had regularly insulted him, often in front of others, when Steve was growing up. This was a source of great embarrassment to Steve, something he'd always kept hidden.

Therapy was very painful for Steve.

He realized he was replicating this same awful treatment with his wife, whom he loved very much, and did not want to lose.

Steve had a significant breakthrough as a result of therapy. He'd always had a major disconnect between hearing those words himself and being hurt by them, to realizing how emulating his father's behavior could inflict hurt and pain on someone he loved.

Once Steve was able to truly comprehend what he'd been doing, he completely transformed his communication style. He learned how to pause before speaking, particularly when he was angry, and to never "hit below the belt."

Steve also learned to stop making excuses for his own behavior and to own up to his past mistakes. He made himself accountable for his actions. We shall discuss accountability here in just a bit.

Fortunately, Steve and Caroline worked out their problems and are still happily married. They do argue from time to time, but their disagreements are constructive and completely devoid of that toxic component called verbal abuse.

## Aging

No book about long-term marriage should exclude the sadly inevitable topic of aging. Until we discover the true fountain of youth, growing old is inescapable for us all. Those who pity themselves for maturing may recall that the only true alternative to aging lies about six feet under their Keds, Vans, high heels or espadrilles!

Aging gracefully is something we all aspire to, but there's just no way your body, metabolism, eyesight, physical stamina and so forth will be the same in your 60s as they were in your 20s or even your 40s. The clever and witty writer Fran Lebowitz expressed this beautifully and somewhat comically. She said it was amusing when people lamented that they no longer looked like their younger selves, because face it, maybe when they were young, they didn't look so great then either!

This is not to say give up, throw in the towel, be old before your time! It's important to keep up your health and appearance throughout your 30s, 40s, 50s, 60s, 70s, 80s, and God willing, beyond!

Unfortunately, some men and women (both are guilty of this, although it still seems more prevalent with men) maintain that picking a much younger partner will miraculously infuse them with the many joyful attributes of youth.

Sometimes it works. An acquaintance of mine had been divorced for 10 years when she married a new guy 15 years her junior. They are one of the cutest couples ever. He loves her wisdom and "smarts" and he's gotten her to go zip lining, skiing and traveling to places she'd never before considered.

Going to the gym, taking vitamins, eating healthy, staying active, doing fun things, planning trips, keeping up a regular sex life, reading the news or novels, these are all things which help one stay young. Louise, one of my very dearest friends for over 30 years, is now in her 70s. She stays ultra-sharp by reading the Wall Street Journal cover to cover every single day. She's done this for over 40 years.

So there are two numbers: one's the number of your age, say 45. The other is your actual age, based upon things like health and fitness levels. So you could be a 45-year-old living in the body of a 70-year-old if you eat crappy, smoke, drink like a fish, and sit in front of the computer all day and the TV all night.

Or, if you take good care of your health, it can be quite the opposite. We have a neighbor who walks miles up and down our long road every day. He is in his 70s and looks 50. He's so strong and fit.... just amazing. He also doesn't smoke or drink and eats incredibly healthy.

## Alcohol

Alcohol is the devil that has destroyed relationships, marriages and families for centuries.

Alcohol is wonderful; a fun, enjoyable hobby. Wine and spirits such as bourbon and tequila are true art forms. The great vineyards of France and Italy are spectacular and distilleries in places like Ireland are absolutely beyond compare.

So it's not fair to say that alcohol is evil in and of itself, just when consumed in excess and out of control.

Before we hit the bad news, let's just make this statement: some couples love to drink together, and this actually brings them closer. They are not alcoholics; they are not problem drinkers. They enjoy alcohol and perhaps may even be very knowledgeable about wine, beer, bourbon or other spirits. They are what we would call connoisseurs.

But ah, of course, there's the flip side.

Drugs are also tough to quit, but unlike drugs, which are not as easily accessible, alcohol is EVERYWHERE... and we mean everywhere. It's even in food. Restaurant menus typically offer more alcohol options than food; this of course is inspired by a need to make a good profit.

Alcohol's a depressant, so it should make folks mellower, but instead makes many individuals more aggressive.

It's often said, "There's no fairness in fertility." The same holds true for alcohol. Two people can drink exactly the same amount; one carries on with their work and personal life intact, while the other falls apart. Some alcoholics are very high-functioning and are able to maintain careers and relationships for an extremely long time. Others hit bottom rather quickly. There does seem to be a correlation between food and alcohol; those alcoholics who continue to eat regularly appear to function better. Those who drink heavily and barely eat any food seem to hit that bottom of the pond more quickly.

One of my favorite uncles was a very high-functioning alcoholic. He never missed a day at the office, worked his entire life, and was fairly successful, staying married to my aunt until he passed away in his 70s.

But, that's not to say that my uncle was a nice drunk. When sober, he was brilliant, kind and personable. But when he drank, he became obnoxious, loud, sometimes belligerent — another person entirely. His wife, my aunt, covered for him in countless ways, and also eventually began drinking to keep him company. This too, is common behavior in couples where one is a drinker- their partner begins to drink as well.

A difficult dynamic is when both partners are alcoholics, then one manages to become sober, but the other refuses to stop drinking.

This was portrayed in the Jack Lemmon and Lee Remick film "Days of Wine and Roses." At the film's beginning, Jack Lemmon was an established alcoholic and Lee Remick was sober. She didn't even like alcohol; she drank to keep him company. He pressured her because he didn't want to drink alone. But in the end, they split up when he became sober and sadly, she would not.

Jean is a 34-year-old Los Angeles wife and mom who just spent an hour in traffic driving to her office. It should have only taken her 25 minutes, but there was an accident on the 10 freeway and the three right lanes were blocked.

It also took far longer for Jean to drop off her two-year-old son Thomas at day-care. His caregiver Molly had complained how yesterday Thomas had bit Hannah, another child at the day-care.

This was not the first time Thomas had taken a bite out of another child. The pint-sized Hannah was a deeply obnoxious toddler, so Jean secretly applauded Thomas for his action, but now unfortunately he was in hot water at the day-care.

Molly stressed that Hannah's parents had not been too upset, but that if Thomas bit one more child, Jean would need to find another day-care. Stuck in traffic, Jean is filled with dread and anxiety, because Molly's day-care is far cheaper than any others and is a good program. Jean simply doesn't have the extra $200 a month that another day-care would charge.

The whole time Jean's driving to work, she's also anticipating the reaction of her smug boss Phil when she walks in late. Phil lives a stone's throw away from the office, doesn't care that the traffic in Los Angeles is unpredictable, and recently wrote up one of Jean's co-workers for tardiness. Phil is a bachelor five years younger than Jean and doesn't have kids; the situation with the day-care is of no interest to him. When Jean rushes into the office, he says loudly, "So glad you could finally join us." When she tries to explain about the traffic, Phil rolls his eyes and does not reply.

Jean works all day long at a job she doesn't like, but it pays the bills—sort of. Her husband Kevin's job is pretty much the same. He's looking for a better job, but with no college degree, his prospects are limited. Last year, he was laid off from his job of nine years and it took five months for him to find a new one.

Jean and Kevin have been a financial mess ever since.

After work, Jean wants to go to the gym to unwind, but has a headache, so skips it. Kevin had already picked up Thomas from day-care; Jean heads home to fix dinner, before realizing she'd forgotten to go to the market last night for bread and a few other essentials.

When she finally gets home close to 7 p.m., Kevin helps her unload the groceries. Kevin's a good guy; he loves Jean and Thomas, and unlike many of her friends' husbands, does way more than his share around the house. But then he asks Jean irritably, "Did you pay the cell phone bill? We've got to pay it tomorrow or they will disconnect us."

After dinner is Thomas's bath and bedtime; when Thomas is finally asleep, it's nearly 9:30 p.m. Jean and Kevin settle in on the couch to watch some TV. This is supposed to be their time together, but Kevin has been up since 5:15 a.m. and drives all day for work. He's so exhausted, within minutes he's asleep in front of the TV.

Jean is worn out also, but she is so tense... she's always anxious. She can't stop worrying about her complacent boss Phil and the sassy comment he'd made when she'd walked into work late. She's not really seeing the TV show; she's picturing the pile of unpaid bills in the kitchen drawer, and the fact that she may have to find a new day-care for Thomas.

Jean now wishes that she'd gone to the gym. Her neck and shoulders are in knots and her stomach feels like it is being squeezed from the inside. She knows she will never be able to fall sleep. She will just lie there awake. She is afraid...she's always afraid. Anxious she will lose her job, nervous Thomas will somehow get hurt, and scared they won't make the rent.

But most of all, she's terrified that Kevin will discover how much she's been drinking.

Somehow, Jean finds herself in the kitchen. There's a bottle of red wine hidden in the back of the pantry and she opens it. She originally plans to drink just one glass, but that won't do anything for her at all. Two glasses used to be perfect, but not anymore. She drinks three, and then four glasses. At last, the familiar warmth flows through her. It feels wonderful. She can finally relax.

Jean never drinks hard alcohol. She tells herself, "It's just wine." In the past, she never drank more than an occasional glass of wine when out with the girls, or maybe just one beer at a party.

But last year, when Kevin lost his job, the stress never ended. The only way she got through those dark days was the thought of a nice glass of wine in the evenings. She has no idea how it got to be every night. She always keeps a couple of bottles of wine in the trunk of her car now so she can fetch one when Kevin is asleep in front of the TV.

Kevin, easygoing about most everything, adamantly hates alcohol. His mom was an alcoholic who passed away from cirrhosis of the liver when he was 17.

Kevin has no problem with marijuana, which Jean would love to have instead. She knows it would relax her just as well, but her company does random drug testing so she can't risk it.

Jean has a fifth glass only on the weekends, polishing off the entire bottle, but during the week she sticks to four glasses. Even though she's a bit tipsy, she carefully washes out her wineglass, dries it and puts it away, then places the near-empty bottle in the back of the fridge where Kevin won't see it.

The next morning, Jean's alarm wakes her at six a.m. She has a rotten headache, an awful taste in her mouth, and is so sodden she thinks she'll never get out of bed, but once she's up, two cups of coffee do the trick.

On her way to work, she calls the cell phone company to ask for an extension. Focusing on her phone call, Jean misses her freeway exit, has to take side streets, and arrives late to work a second day in a row. Predictably, the disagreeable Phil writes her up for tardiness.

Does any of this sound familiar? For nearly 12 years I worked for a large company; most of us employees seemed to be facing significant stress in our lives. We all dealt with it in different ways... some healthy, and some not. Alcohol has no charm for me, but even though I ate healthy during the daytime, I never lost any weight during those years because I usually "snacked away my stress" in the late evenings.

Annette and Martin have been married for nine years and have two daughters, Amelia and Diana. Martin has a good job in the insurance business, but hates being tied to a desk all day. He and his buddy Ralph opened a restaurant a few years back, but they struggled and it closed within 15 months. Martin is very outgoing, and loves to go to bars to drink and socialize.

Annette had no idea how much he was drinking; he'd become quite sophisticated at hiding it. Martin's tolerance level had also had increased to a point where he never actually appeared inebriated.

This all ended when he received his first DUI driving home from the bar two years ago. Annette was furious. He told her he hated his job and that was why he drank. Then last year Martin was at happy hour with friends and got a second DUI on the way home. The legal and court fees, as well as other expenses, cost over $30,000.00. Annette was furious about the cost, but also that he was putting other drivers at risk. She brought up the excellent fact that their daughters would be driving in a few years and her main worry was they would be out on the road with the drunks.

Annette threatened to leave him and told Martin he'd better get help or she would find a divorce attorney. Martin begged her to reconsider. He loved his wife and daughters. Before he went to DUI court, his lawyer recommended he attend Alcoholics Anonymous. Initially, Martin began attending meetings only because it helped him in court. However, as he told Annette, the program turned out to be the best thing that could have happened.

Fortunately, this story has a very happy ending. Not only has Martin stayed sober since joining AA, the friends he's made there have helped fill his need to socialize. He and a few AA pals meet at a local coffeehouse at least twice a week to talk and drink coffee, plus give one another encouragement and support.

Some of his new friends have been sober for many years; being able to relate to other alcoholics and derive strength from them has been a lifesaver for Martin. His relationship with Annette has also improved immensely because he no longer has to lie to her to hide his drinking. Martin now looks upon the DUI's as a blessing, because he feels otherwise he would have kept drinking until he died.

So, let's say you're not a drinker, but your spouse is. What do you do when you realize your partner is drinking heavily? If they're coping well with their job, life in general, and treating you well, it may be extremely easy to pretend that nothing is wrong.

But then, maybe something terrible happens and ignoring the problem becomes impossible.

Maybe your spouse gets a DUI, they wreck the car, lose a job, or you can see their personality is changing... and not for the better. Perhaps they're becoming more argumentative and belligerent. They may say or do things and then not remember later. They may make irrational decisions.

What should you do? How can you help?

This topic is not simple; in fact, it's far, far beyond the scope of this book.

However, I asked this question of several friends who used to drink to excess, and who are now sober. Some classified themselves as alcoholics, and some maintained that at one time, they'd had a drinking problem.

Their answers varied. Most stated that support from their spouse helped them get sober. Some observed that their partner giving them an ultimatum, such as in the above example with Martin, was crucial. Still others claimed nothing their spouse could have said or done would have made the slightest bit of difference had they themselves not wished to quit drinking.

The one common denominator was this: everyone I spoke to said that it was not an easy journey by any means, but ultimately was well worth the struggle.

The subject of denial came up frequently. When their spouse pretended there was not a problem, this was very convenient, as it allowed them to keep drinking, but did not contribute to their becoming sober. An interesting fact: one individual expressed a great deal of resentment that his wife ignored his drinking problem for so many years. "Didn't she see I was killing myself?" he said. But as he progressed further along on his path of sobriety, he realized this kind of thinking was unfair to his wife. It placed the blame on her, when in fact it was his responsibility to stop drinking.

Alan and Denise, a couple in their late 30s, had been wed for seven years when his drinking became excessive. When this couple had first met, Alan was already a drinker, "just a social drinker," as he put it. He was also a successful sports agent; much of his time was spent entertaining clients over food and drink.

A superstar at his large company, Alan loved to go to lunches, dinners and happy hours with co-workers, clients and friends. He had a generous expense account and a beautiful company car. He and his wife also had a large circle of friends; he was usually the life of the party. Alan was fun, generous, witty and kind. Most everyone adored him. He was also quite an aficionado of whiskey and bourbon and in recent years had become quite knowledgeable about both.

Alan's drinking didn't concern Denise because she saw it as his hobby and after all, he never missed a day of work. Alan also never became aggressive or rude like some drinkers she'd known. Denise herself enjoyed a glass or two of wine on occasion but that was the main extent of it.

One night Alan drove home after dinner with some colleagues, and his left wheel hit the center divider on the road. Except for a flat tire, his car wasn't damaged. A policeman stopped by to see and to help change the tire and realized that Alan was drunk.

Alan was then arrested for a DUI and spent the night in jail. He had to pay to get his car out of impound and his license was suspended for 30 days. His attorney helped Alan get his driver's license back again after 60 days. This was also over ten years ago, when DUI penalties weren't as strict as they are today.

Denise vented to her mother on the phone. "Alan was right around the block from home and he's gone the same way for years without any problem." Denise added that if the cop hadn't shown up when he did, Alan could have just changed the tire and they wouldn't have to deal with this "big headache."

Denise's mom disagreed. "Seems to me Alan has been drinking and driving for years and has gotten away with it." This infuriated Denise, who ended the conversation with her mom as quickly as possible. Denise then called her sister Cynthia. Much to Denise's exasperation, Cynthia agreed with their mom. She observed that Alan had been drunk driving for years. And instead of hitting the center divider on the road, he could have instead struck a pedestrian.

Alan's employer was not amused by the situation. His wife's best friend had lost her youngest son to a drunk driver. Alan could now use his company car only during the daytime; he had to park it at the office lot overnight and on weekends. For several days, until Alan bought himself a personal car, Denise had to drive him to and from work.

Two years passed. During this time, Alan tried to quit drinking numerous times, but after a couple days, would always begin again. However, he was very careful to take a taxi or get someone else to drive when he'd "had a few," as he put it.

The following summer, Alan and Denise visited Bora Bora on holiday with two other couples, and he passed out in the hotel lobby on the third night. He admitted to Denise that he had begun blacking out on occasion. When they returned home, Denise insisted that he go to their doctor to talk about his "problem."

Thankfully, this couple's story had a happy ending, but it took two more years, and Alan losing his job and hitting bottom before he sought help. With the assistance of a support group, Alan regained his career and has now been sober for six years. He attends a support group meeting twice a week. He didn't like all of the aspects of Alcoholics Anonymous, so found another support group that worked well for him.

Dylan and Claire met in their late 30s; it was a second marriage for both of them. This couple worked in real estate and were quite successful; they loved wine tastings and trips involving wineries. Their honeymoon was spent in Tuscany, Italy at a vineyard.

Claire also enjoyed going out with her girlfriends for drinks after work. She loved martinis, wine, spritzers, any kind of mixed drinks, but she never had more than two. Claire was also a "foodie," and she loved food as much as she did alcohol.

When she became pregnant with their first child, Claire stopped drinking, but Dylan continued his habit of opening a bottle right after work, finishing it during dinner, and then uncorking a second bottle in the late evening.

Claire no longer was helping him to drink the wine, and so Dylan now began drinking two bottles most evenings.

After their tiny daughter Melanie was born, Claire told Dylan he needed to stop drinking so much – she felt it was affecting him more and more. Dylan loved his wine and didn't want to give it up. He did not agree that his drinking was a problem.

Over the next three years, Dylan began to drink more and more heavily and often passed out in the evenings. Claire demanded he get help; he continued to insist he did not have a problem.

The irony was Dylan's father had been an alcoholic and Dylan had sworn to never become like his dad.

Dylan began to wake up with terrible hangovers. He began having a drink or two in the mornings, "just to take the edge off." Although frustrated, Claire insisted she was in it for the long haul; she loved Dylan and wanted to stay married.

The turning point came one Saturday afternoon when Claire went to the gym. Dylan was supposed to be watching Melanie, who was now four years old. Instead, he got drunk and passed out. When Claire returned home three hours later, Melanie was in their backyard alone. She'd stood on some phone books to unlatch the back door. This couple lived in the Hollywood Hills, and from time to time, mountain lions and coyotes roamed their neighborhood.

At this point, Claire began telling friends she was for the first time considering divorce.

Increasingly, Dylan cancelled meetings to show houses to clients, or simply forgot to show up for appointments. When Melanie turned five years old, Claire filed for divorce and asked Dylan to move out.

Dylan moved to a small apartment, which was all he could afford. He found that friends he'd known for years no longer returned his phone calls. Many of them had sided with Claire in the divorce.

One day Dylan called his former college roommate Keith, and before he realized it, he was sobbing on the phone. Keith had been a heavy drinker in college- they both had - but with the help of a therapist and AA, Keith had stopped drinking more than 10 years before.

Keith offered to take him to Alcoholics Anonymous- Dylan refused. "Those people are drunks, I just have a little too much sometimes," he said.

Keith kept calling him and offering to take him to AA.

One day, Dylan passed out at the grocery store and someone called an ambulance. He was sober at the time. The emergency room doctor was very concerned about Dylan's vitamin deficiencies, dehydration and overall very poor health. Dylan ended up spending eight days at the hospital. The doctor there explained to him that he had become allergic to alcohol; that for him, it had become like poison.

Dylan finally began attending AA meetings and is sober to this day. There he feels he has the support and friendship he's lacking elsewhere.

Keith supported him throughout this process. Dylan began selling real estate through another broker and was able to revive his career. He also made amends with many friends whom he'd alienated during his drinking years.

Sadly, his attempts to reconcile with Claire have not been successful, but he has a close and loving relationship with his daughter Melanie, who is now 12 years old.

# Attention
## (as in Pay Attention to your partner)

If you're feeling out of sync with your husband or wife, perhaps you aren't connecting, or have lost that "special spark," please, please read this section twice. Lest I sound the least bit "judgy," I've been as guilty as anyone in *all* of the following areas, but somehow have managed to improve dramatically.

Okay, here goes: there's absolutely no substitute for you looking at your marriage partner when they speak, and completely focusing on what they say. It could be a "play by play" of the last football game he watched, including a detailed description of the touchdown. It might even be her relaying critical details of her girlfriend Mandy's lipo success, and how she's now fitting into jeans from the 90s.

Focusing on your partner is more challenging than ever these days. This is seen everywhere... couples sitting in restaurants together, but not focused on one another at all. Not in the slightest.

Instead, they're gazing into the wee miniature face of their beloved, adored, true significant others... their mobile phones. Maybe it's Facebook, Instagram, Twitter, or TikTok. Perhaps they're reading their emails or looking at the stock market.

Lord knows, there's so much fantastic stuff on your phone. Let's just call it the "Instagram Daze." You go on there to wish someone happy birthday. That's your sole intention. Somehow, 120 minutes later, you're still on there looking at film stars, pictures of London, Rome, Singapore, how to repaper your dining room... how did this happen?

Heavens to Betsy, where did the past two hours go?

The term "crack-berry" isn't really heard anymore, but that word didn't just come out of nowhere!

Several birthdays ago, my daughter treated me to a fabulous sushi dinner at Sasabune restaurant in Glendale, California. It was one of the best surprises of my life. We had "omakase" sushi, which for those who haven't tried it, is an incredibly special adventure difficult to find outside of Japan.

We briefly chatted with the couple at the table next to us, who said they'd been married for three years. They seemed like such nice people. However, the wife was on her phone throughout the entire dinner, either checking her Facebook or texting.

Her phone was placed in the seat of honor next to her plate, or she held it in her left hand as she smoothly maneuvered the chopsticks in her right. I had to hand it to this lady; she was super coordinated. Not one single drop of soy sauce or ponzu landed on her gorgeous white blouse.

This couple exchanged a few sentences, but 99 percent of the time the husband looked around the restaurant, studied the soy sauce bottle, or just appeared to be plain bored. By the end of the meal, he looked annoyed. He kind of listened in on our conversation, not in a creepy way, but more wistfully, as though he would have loved to actually been conversing with someone during the beautiful meal. He paid the check and they left; she was still looking at her phone when she got up from the table.

As these two were a married couple, perhaps it doesn't matter that he paid the check. But from a purely practical standpoint, had he been there alone, he'd have only paid for one expensive sushi dinner, and not two!

I managed to "stay in my lane," but I felt like saying to this woman, "For the love of God, you clearly have a nice husband there; he brought you to this wonderful restaurant, so put your freaking phone away!"

If this sounds oddly familiar, and you have G for guilty stamped on your forehead, don't feel bad: we've all been guilty as sin. Never fear, cuz you can turn this around. The very next time you and your partner are at dinner, whether at home or at a restaurant, put your phone on mute so you can't hear it ring or buzz, and put it *completely* away.

Place it in your purse or your pocket, and not on the table. If you've been a confirmed "phone-aholic" for quite awhile, this may seem super creepy! You may even be extremely uncomfortable, as though you're missing a limb.

Carry on; it can be done. Friends who've transitioned attest it's easier than quitting cigarettes and just a bit tougher than ending a cocaine habit.

Your partner may be stunned at first, but most likely in a pleased way.

Here's a comical tale: Madeleine and her husband Thomas recently went for dinner at a popular Mexican joint.

A couple was seated at the next table, only nine inches away. Let's dub them Thelma and Louie. Their close proximity is the reason Madeline and Thomas noticed them. This restaurant was designed similarly to those in Europe. You know the layout: tiny tables placed so closely together that it's deeply challenging to squeeze into that back booth if you sport any kind of booty *whatsoever*.

In random news, I myself over the years have perfected a special patented "tiptoe booty shuffle." If I stand on absolute tiptoe whilst creeping sideways over to the booth side of the table, I then narrowly avoid banging into the next table with my booty. I thus avoid the humiliation of clam linguine or worse yet, chicken marengo plastered drippingly onto my backside.

Now, let's get back to Thelma and Louie. They were in their early 30s, but we're not just picking on the younger folks – we middle-aged ones are just as guilty!

Thelma and Louie gazed intently at their phones throughout their entire meal. You had to hand it to them: their concentration was absolute. They did not speak to one another AT ALL. Not one word. They glanced at their menus, rapidly gave their order to their server, whom they treated like a robot, then immediately went back to their tiny transistor loved ones.

In due course, their waiter brought the charming duo enormous margaritas. They didn't acknowledge him in any way, and began sipping while looking at their phones.

Next, Thelma accidentally knocked over her entire giant margarita. It careened, spilled and sloshed gloriously everywhere, even onto the Spanish tile floor. Here in San Diego, one of these "monsta margaritas" is a whopping 24 ounces, not including the miniature umbrella and lime slices.

The waiter raced over and he, Thelma and a busboy began to sop up the mess. Now, here's the kicker: Louie never once looked up from his phone, not when Thelma spilled the margarita, not when they all were mopping it up, NOT ONCE.

A friend once joked to me that her husband's phone should have its own little tiny pillow to sleep on at night.

If you and your spouse are "#phone-addicted," perhaps your partner is unhappy about it, but has gotten into the habit themselves because you're always on your phone. Some time ago they decided, "If you can't beat 'em, join 'em!"

When the cards are on the table, however, often one partner admits this has bugged the bejeez out of them for a long time, but they never said so.

Next step: come up with some sort of compromise (you will see much more about compromise later in this book, by the way). Perhaps put your phones away when eating meals at home or at a restaurant. When hanging out in your den or living room, keep your phones in another room... easier to ignore them that way.

These are just a couple ideas.

It's crucial to put your phone on mute and entirely out of sight, so you won't hear its seductive little siren song- that tiny blinking light or that little beeping sound. Both the light and sound scream the words "exciting and fun!" to your brain's prefrontal cortex.

If your phone is muted, out of range –then to use a "huevos" term, perhaps we can then call it a free range phone!

At restaurants, give it a whirl! Set your phone to mute and place it in your purse or pocket. Many ladies don't carry purses nowadays, so perhaps a pocket is one option. There are also those mini purses for just carrying a phone and a few credit cards — I say, most popular with the millennial crowd.

Daniel, an avid sports fan, found a way to outfox his clever wife Marjorie. She'd become fed up with him for constantly checking sports scores on his phone when he was supposed to be spending time with her. So, his admittedly clever ruse was to wear shorts with deep pockets, and keep his phone on mute. Darn her, Marjorie is gifted with supersonic hearing and she would have easily heard a vibrate tone.

Daniel then periodically dashed into the powder room to check football and basketball scores to see if he was winning various bets. Wonder if Marjorie has begun to fear her young husband has developed some weirdo digestion issues?

But as of this telling, Daniel has never yet been found out.

Have you got that friend who always texts you back and forth like a ping-pong match, expecting an immediate reply?

"Serial texters" aren't as dangerous as serial killers, but are perhaps even a tad more annoying. They message you to the point of sheer exhaustion, often including several questions. Who has time to answer these questions? If you enjoy this, do partake. On the other hand, if it's become one more chore, wean them off and show no mercy.

# Always
## (See also: Never)

"Always" is a most powerful word. When used in a positive light, it can be a wonderful thing for your partner to hear. For example, a wife overhears her husband telling their small daughter, "Your mother always looks so beautiful." Or a husband listens to his wife telling their son, "Your dad always works so hard at his job."

Human beings simply adore hearing wonderful things about themselves. I guess we're all a little conceited deep down. They especially love compliments joined with the word "always."

Now, here's the flip side to this: in an argument, the word "always," just like the word "never," can have very destructive results. Here are some examples:

"You're always such a nag."

"You always mess things up with my parents."

"You always ruin holiday parties with your dumb jokes."

"You always buy the wrong thing at the market."

"You always drive too slow (or too fast)."

The word "always," like the word "never," is one of those words best avoided, unless it's used in a positive context.

When tossed into an argument or angry confrontation, the word "always" will *always* cause resentment "budumch."

It's de-motivating to your partner; they aren't likely to improve.

Since they've been made to feel like they "always" do things wrong, they get an attitude of "why fucking bother?"

If you do use the word "always," say it in the context of a positive, affirming statement or a compliment.

# Arrogance
## (see also Humility)

When interviewed for this book, Mary described humility as an important trait in her long and happy marriage. She emphasized it's crucial for both husbands and wives to be humble in their relationship.

Conversely, the arrogant individual behaves as though they are superior to others. Deep down, they may actually suffer from low self-esteem, which they attempt to cover up. Either way, the end result is the same...they act like they are "better than."

To toss in an equine reference, they act as if they're on a "high horse."

What if you suspect you've gone and gotten hitched to an arrogant person? What are some of their un-charming character traits?

Well, here's a Whitman's sampler:

- They interrupt others and pay little attention to conversations unless they're doing the talking.

- They insist they're right, even if a chubby-cheeked toddler could easily tell they're mistaken.

- They're frequently annoyed with waiters, waitresses, taxi drivers and hotel employees, and embarrass the hell out of you when you're with them.

- They're impatient when waiting, even if they're not busy that day — or *any* day, for that matter.

- They can't seem to apologize, and if they do, it's half-assed.

- They speak of others as lesser than themselves.

- They make disparaging comments about those whom they consider weak or inferior.

- They're charming when they choose to be, but can be quite cruel, particularly toward those who don't fight back.

- Yep, Miss Fargo, "you betcha" ... arrogance and bullying are two nasty little friends who often stroll down the boulevard or "la playa" hand-in-hand.

- They give unsolicited advice; it's actually criticism under the guise of being "helpful."

- They love to be center of attention.

- They use words like "disgusting" to describe people they view as different or inferior.

Many arrogant people can be charming when they want to be, especially if they need something from you, as in our next example.

Abigail and Mark worked together and dated for several years. Mark was admittedly very handsome, and boy, did he ever know it. He constantly flirted with other girls and treated Abigail like "second fiddle." Then, when she'd finally become fed up, he'd treat her better just long enough to ensure she was still under his spell.

He waited until last minute to ask her out, and frequently cancelled plans last-minute. But Abigail was absolutely crazy about Mark, and made endless excuses for his crapola behavior.

Abigail came from a very rich family, and had lent large sums of money to Mark in the past. When he got what he wanted, Mark could be incredibly charming, and would give Abigail all kinds of wonderful attention.

After they'd dated for two years, he unexpectedly broke up with her, saying he just didn't know why. Abigail was heartbroken, but her close friends and family felt she was far better off.

Six months later, Mark and Abigail got back together, against the advice of all her girlfriends as well as her parents. He presented her with a huge engagement ring (most people assumed she'd paid for it) and they began planning their lavish wedding.

However, Mark still treated her as lesser than, breaking plans at the last minute and flirting with other girls. Abigail still lent him cash regularly, which he never paid back. One of her girlfriends saw him at a bar with another girl hanging all over him; Abigail made excuses for this and all of his other bad behavior.

After a few months, Mark dumped Abigail yet again. Interestingly enough, she wasn't nearly as upset as she'd been the first time. She told her girlfriends she suspected the breakup was because she'd begun refusing to lend him any more money. Also, she'd told Mark that her father had insisted she obtain a prenuptial agreement.

About this time, Abigail began casually dating another fellow named James. He was not nearly as handsome as Mark. James was actually rather shy and quiet, but was obviously crazy about Abigail and made much more effort to be with her. He also didn't cancel their plans last-minute. Abigail's family and friends all liked James far better than Mark. Mark tried to get Abigail back after a few months, but fortunately, she was smarter this time. The nice ending to this story is that Abigail and James have been happily married now for eight years.

What's the scoop with our friend Mark? Well, he's still single and still just as arrogant. He's what's commonly referred to as a "serial dater," getting very serious about a girl, but also taking her for granted, using her financially, then eventually breaking up with her. This wicked syndrome isn't just restricted to men, by the way.

An interesting psychological fact: the arrogant person and the narcissist are what we call "ugly ishkebibble twins." They have several unsavory traits in common. One is that they are super charming when you first begin dating them. They're wonderful, attentive, and complimentary; they seem to understand you better than anybody. They go out of their way to be thoughtful and kind. You feel like it's a dream come true.

But it's just an act. It won't last for long. The more comfortable they feel with you, the lousier they become. They also become unpredictably insulting as they try to "cut you down" to make themselves feel better. You pray they'll revert back to their original charming self, but alas! That was all just for show.

Robert and I socialized with a couple named Alan and Holly when we lived in Los Angeles. About five years older than us, they'd been married for seven years. Alan had a decent enough job as an English teacher. Well, to be candid, his job was mediocre, quite like those that Robert and I had at the time.

Holly, on the other hand, had a fantastic, huge, very high-powered career. She was exceedingly well-paid, a fact of which she never grew weary of reminding *everyone*. As the four of us sat over our cocktails or our sushi dinners, she frequently referred to herself as the "breadwinner of the family." This has nothing to do with gender, by the way. It sounds just as creepy and conceited coming from the mouth of a husband. Now, Holly did earn more than Alan, actually, five times more, because she told us in sordid detail, but really, who has to know?

Holly usually interrupted Alan when he was speaking; in other words, she treated him like he was beneath her. It was tough to witness this because Alan was a great guy, very bright, with lots of interesting things to say.

But good ol' Holly just steamrolled right over him like one of those big round asphalt paving machines. Alan got squashed just like a little bug.

Holly always brought up law school. She was adamant that Alan become Alan Smith, Esq., and then make some "real money," although he'd stated numerous times he had no interest whatsoever in law.

In those days, I myself was underpaid and overworked at a second-rate job, and I adored griping about it. I was only 24 at the time; I didn't really want to make a change.

Maybe I was right where I needed to be back then. Maybe at 24 I wanted to stagnate, be underpaid and then bitch about it. Maybe I liked my crummy job, in some sick sort of way.

But Holly was chock-full of unsolicited advice how I could step it up, get my resume together, and land that better job.

Hey, Holly, maybe I don't want to step it up! Maybe I'm happy being super mediocre right now!

A few years later, Alan unexpectedly left Holly for a new gal Trisha. It wasn't a celebration, but nobody really felt terrible for Holly. We'd all seen how arrogantly she'd treated him all those years.

Trisha, the new girlfriend, accepted Alan the way he was. She didn't treat him as "lesser than" because of his average job. She encouraged him in what he really loved, which was the written word, and ironically, Alan eventually ended up with a hugely successful career as a book editor.

So, what do you do if *you* are the arrogant one in your relationship?

First off: kudos for admitting it, if only to yourself.

A good therapist can help you identify the source of your insecurity, which is one deeply gnarled root of the arrogance tree. Recognizing the source of the problem is only part of the solution, however. It's also important to identify your behaviors (see the list above) and work on changing them.

Now, if your partner is the arrogant one in your relationship, read this section to him or her in its entirety and ... best of luck!

Keep in mind, if you've been allowing your partner to treat you as "less than," time to bring a new sheriff to town. It's time to turn that cruise liner around. In this situation, couples therapy might be helpful as well.

And, as Eleanor Roosevelt coined it best: "No one can make you feel inferior without your consent."

## As Good As It's Gonna Get

Here we shall present a super practical, somewhat pathetic, and frankly, very unromantic section of this book. Newlyweds, or couples who've been together for only a few years may be squeamish, may even cringe at looking at this...but please ... do so anyways!

By forcing yourself to read this gut-wrenching section, you won't be caught with your pants down, so to speak, when, one day, you painfully realize that maybe, just maybe, things with your marriage partner are just about as good as they're ever gonna get.

This dreadful epiphany is akin to that sinking feeling that will hit you one day when you realize your spouse is an alien, as we miserably relayed in our first segment. When we refer to "as good as it gets," this signifies that no matter how many wonderful qualities your spouse possesses, and there may be simply oodles of them, some of their other traits will always be massive, colossal, horrific disappointments.

You may already have observed these shortcomings before the wedding bells pealed, depending upon your individual level of sheer denial.

We've all heard that saying, "No one is perfect until you fall in love with them." When you're in the first throes of adoration, you gaze upon the perfection of your beloved through gossamer, sheer, billowing, rose-colored curtains. You worship and adore them. You are so enraptured with your partner; you believe they are utterly perfect. You think about them all the time and how glorious they are.

But most of all, you love, love, love how wonderful they make you feel. Because, as we all know, that glorious, magnificent feeling of being in love is a totally narcissistic experience.

You love the way it makes *you* feel. It's mostly about... you guessed it! *You*. Does this sound just like a character in "Peaky Blinders?"

At first, you're so thoroughly "head over heels," it's a miracle you can even sleep at night. For an eternity, usually about two years, the sun rises and sets directly above your beloved's head. It's as if the entire world was created for you two alone.

The object of your devotion can do no wrong. At this stage, if they're guilty of any offense, such as robbing a convenience store, grand theft auto, or even throwing recycling in the trash, you hasten to make excuses for them. Your adoration knows no bounds.

Then, it's unavoidable...real life and time take their evil toll. Perhaps the day-to-day grubbiness of living together sets in. You've got bills to pay, dirty laundry, screaming munchkins, whatever it is ... suddenly, your spouse starts to *really* bug you. *Really, really, really get on your nerves.*

You may then feel deceived and betrayed when you suddenly comprehend just how far from perfect they truly are.

Please fill in your own blanks. Perhaps she snores, plus viciously bends the toothpaste tube in half, he enjoys being babied by mommy, she procrastinates, he drives terribly, she eats peanut butter out of the jar, or he parks his Harley in the living room smack dab in front of your stone fireplace. Now, any of these items may seem quite trivial, well, maybe not the Harley, as it steadily leaks oil onto your beige and white rug, but never fear, divorce attorneys are relentlessly kept busy due to peanut butter and toothpaste tubes.

By the way, the Harley scenario was a reality for one very lucky lady. Their romance was short-lived, as you may have already suspected.

So, you may be asking yourself, why didn't these things bother me before? Possibly, you were in denial, plus, you didn't have to live with them every dang day. Amazingly, living together before marriage is no guarantee this sad disillusionment still won't take place.

Perhaps one or both partners were auditioning for marriage and therefore on their Sunday best behavior for the duration of the "living together" process.

Now, this doesn't mean you have to throw in the towel, or think that you are "settling." It does mean, however, that at some point you'll realize, much as you love your spouse, he or she will always do some things you can't stand.

Here's a crucial notion to remember. You yourself possess some horrendously irritating, disappointing qualities which your spouse has to put up with as well. Do not think for a single moment that you don't! We human beings are amazing creatures, but we all have imperfections and inadequacies.

Every one of us is super annoying, when you come right down to it. That's an inescapable aspect of our humanity.

I myself am personally so flawed that I resemble a piece of Swiss cheese with of all those little tiny holes. Sadly, I can imagine myself as a perfect pairing with ham for a toasty sandwich.

Folks anticipating sheer magnificence day in and day out from their spouse will find it challenging to stay married longer than four and a half months.

If you're hypercritical of your spouse, look inwards. Counseling can assist, but remember that your therapist only knows as much as you tell them. If you lie or paint a rosy picture to look better, you won't improve nearly as much. Face it, many sad sacks, tragically myself included, have sugar-coated with their therapist. You want them to think you are blameless, so cool... I totally get it!

One handy exercise for that early, idyllic stage of your marriage: write down every positive attribute your spouse possesses. Write 'em all down...every single last item. Don't leave out *anything.* Keep this piece of paper "at the ready." Xerox extra copies for your pocket, wallet, purse, car and office. You're gonna need 'em later.

That way, in the coming years, when you overhear your husband telling mommy lotsa confidential stuff, or your wife tailgates as she drives whilst spooning peanut butter directly from the jar, or he smart-mouths his boss and gets fired *again,* or you get home and find she's left the garage door open *one more time,* you can refer to your list, breathe deeply, and carry on, just as the English have done beautifully for centuries.

This goes hand-in-hand with humility, which we shall discuss later. If you humbly accept the fact that you, too, are chock-full of flaws, you are more likely to cut your partner some slack.

And here's the beautiful payoff for your patience: after you've been married awhile longer, you will then come full circle. Time will have broken you down just like an old mattress with no springs, and those irritating traits of your spouse won't bother you any longer... or at least, they will *annoy you less.*

One day, you may actually become so desensitized that you find your spouse's most tiresome little habits quite endearing.

## Ask Not What Your Spouse Can Do For You, But What You Can Do For Your Spouse

As former President John F. Kennedy said, "Ask not what your country can do for you, but what you can do for your country."

There are a multitude of possible meanings for this. Some are: Be grateful for what you have, be a contributor, a giver, and not just a "taker."

This concept also applies to a successful marriage. How often do we long-wedded folks complain, either to ourselves or to others that our spouse doesn't do enough for us?

Perhaps they don't earn enough money, they spend too much, procrastinate, spend too little time at the gym, don't bring you gifts or flowers like they used to, have gotten lazy about sex, ignore their share of housework, allow bills to go unpaid, are cranky in the morning, or don't text you back.

Gheesh, I'm out of breath!

We could go on all day here, since the ways in which a spouse can disappoint you are virtually *endless*.

It's sad and sick, but you will never be able to change some of these. However, you do have a great deal of control over your own mindset.

Let's first address a real "biggie:" money.

If your spouse doesn't earn enough of that wondrous green stuff, can you possibly earn more yourself? Perhaps you can take on a second job, or search for a better one. After Robert and I bought our first house in 1990, we were as broke as two eggs that had been flung off the Cliffs of Moher. Every penny had gone toward the house, plus our mortgage payment was pretty high. Frankly, so were we, since we had deal with all that stress somehow!

We both worked full-time, but it just wasn't enough. So, I got a part-time job at a local pharmacy store on the weekends. I therefore worked seven days a week, so it didn't last long, but it kept our boat afloat that first year of home ownership.

In 1993, I got a second job babysitting an elderly rich lady. God bless her, she took a shine to me and gifted me with beautiful, voluptuous cash tips. This helped us take our first trip to Europe.

Then, in 2000, Robert got a second job doing a paper route job five days a week and he stuck it out for an entire year. This permitted us to continue paying Andrea's private school tuition and at the same time, actually buy groceries.

If your spouse spends too much, take an honest gander at your own habits before addressing theirs. Sebastian resents it that his wife Chloe complains whenever he goes to the bar with his buddies, as she conveniently forgets how much she spends on her hair, nails, makeup, and high heels. Sebastian is an electrician and hasn't bought new clothes in over two years, unless you count those work boots he got last December at Sears.

He gets his hair cut at Super Cuts. So, can Chloe honestly say that he's overspending in comparison to her? She hasn't got a high-heeled leg to stand on!

Now, if your spouse isn't pulling their share around the house, are these big jobs, or things that be done in a matter of moments?

The "Dr. Linda song technique," created by one of our success story husbands and ruthlessly appropriated by this author, can be quite useful. If you're exasperated with your spouse for not taking out the recycling, for example, take a stab at doing it yourself. Simultaneously, sing one of your favorite songs. Sing it loud. Really belt it out. You may be surprised to find an annoying task takes less than three minutes to complete, or about the length of an average Billy Joel or Springsteen song.

Perhaps the task is a bit lengthy, but after all, that's why they wrote "Stairway to Heaven." By the way, notice here we never employ the word "chore." That's because we have an upcoming section on "unsexy words and phrases," and "chore" tops the list, alongside its dreary cousins "budget," "coupon," and the ever-drab "portion control."

Stella had been deeply annoyed with Ricardo since 1992, because he frequently neglected to make their bed in the mornings. He got up later than her, so it was supposed to be *his* job. But if rushed, Ricardo bypassed the bed-making and sashayed merrily out of the house while the unsuspecting Stella was still warbling her favorite song in the shower.

She then, upon emerging from the shower, viewed the unmade bed in absolute horror.

Now, Stella worked from home, so, as she complained bitterly to friends, she then was virtually trapped almost "round the clock" with the unmade bed. Sometimes, she was exasperated about the bed all the live-long day.

Then, when Ricardo returned home in the evening, acting all innocent, you'd better believe there was a spirited argument.

Does it seem perhaps life is far too short for this kind of nonsense? One possible suggestion is that Stella actually makes the bed herself, and simultaneously sings a song. She could belt out the Eagles classic "Take it Easy," and have spare time to comb her hair as well.

Stella, even if you have two duvets on your bed, plus lots of fluffy pillows and stuffed animals, it can't possibly take you longer than the lyrics of "The Sound of Music."

"The hills are alive....!"

## Actions Speak Louder Than Words

So, let's say you're reading this book during a time that you and your spouse are just not getting along. We're not merely talking about a couple of arguments. Unfortunately, the entire fabric of your relationship has become as frayed as an old pair of Levi's 501's.

Most married couples go through this at some point, possibly even several times over the years. Perhaps your relationship is in a slump or on the skids, maybe you're fighting a lot, you don't feel "in love" or even "in like," so what do you do?

What do you do? Remember that line from the movie "Speed?"

Of course, we've all heard 'til the cows come home, communicate. *Just communicate.* This is the Holy Grail, the magic secret, all the advice you'll ever need. And it does play a big part in a healthy relationship. But when a relationship is kinda in the dumpster, maybe it's just not enough.

It's very likely that popular, vivacious, sparkling tidbit of wisdom to "just communicate" isn't serving you right now. Not a little bit, not even at all. Maybe you've tried it and things have become worse: you just ended up with ugly arguments.

So, let's present an unconventional idea. "Just communicate" is not what's recommended here *at all.*

Let's explore the concept of "actions speak louder than words." Instead of talking to improve your relationship, take concrete, positive actions towards your spouse and see what results you get.

An added plus is that you have a gigantic advantage here, a real edge on the situation. If you've lived with your spouse for at least a few years, you know better than anyone on earth exactly how to butter their toast.

You know if they adore gifts or surprises, if they love having their door opened, or other gallant gestures, or if the best path to their heart is through their stomach. Maybe it's respect and admiration, or hearing compliments that makes them come alive.

In short, you know what floats your partner's boat. Therefore, you're in a unique position to understand better than anyone else on the planet how to make them feel appreciated, loved, cherished and respected.

However, since right now you unfortunately can't even stand them, of course you don't want to do any of those nice things... I get it.

But take a moment to reminisce and get sentimental.

Close your eyes and relax. Try to remember when the two of you were madly in love. How did it feel? It felt just great, didn't it?

Next, take a step back and recall what first made your relationship slide downhill. It might have been a large event, or perhaps their creepy little annoying habits or personality traits just got to you over the years.

Now once again, reminisce about how wonderful it was when you got along great. Wasn't everything easier then? Life is tough enough without dealing with a relationship that's in the crapper, to use a most inelegant term.

Next, here's where we get to be creative. Think of some inventive ways to butter the toast of your partner. Lots and lotsa butter; no worries about cholesterol! Maybe throw some peanut butter on that sourdough toast as well.

Ben and Cassandra had been married for 12 years; they had a nine-year-old daughter and a seven-year-old son. This couple was perpetually frazzled, short on money, stressed out, and bickered constantly. They were broke from paying private school tuition for both kids. As public schools in their area sucked, for lack of a better term, they felt they had no real choice. But after paying their mortgage, car payments, kids' tuition and utilities, there was almost nothing left over. Each believed the other spent too much money.

We shall address money millions of times more throughout this book. It's often one of the largest sources of tension for married couples.

At one time, Ben and Cassandra had been super romantic. He'd bought her flowers at least once a week, plus other little gifts like her favorite chocolates. She'd cooked his favorite foods all the time, especially her glorious chili con carne, which he especially loved. They'd held hands, laughed at nothing whatsoever, and had sex at least a couple times a week. They'd loved to spend time together; in short, they'd found one another *irresistible*.

We'll elaborate on the concept of "irresistible" later, but suffice to say it's one of the most important components of a happy relationship.

Sadly, over the past few years, disagreements about money and spending, plus general irritation with one another had caused their relationship to descend to basement level. It was pretty low, to be sure, but not yet in the Freddy Krueger boiler room, so there was still some hope for this couple.

Lately, however, whenever Cassandra saw Ben or heard his voice, she sighed and rolled her eyes. She was weary of his mother, his frequent colds, and his driving. He spent too much money on himself when their finances were already stretched to the breaking point. Ben never did thoughtful things for her anymore, little romantic gestures such as buying her flowers or candy, or making her a pot of coffee in the morning. He used to surprise her by meticulously washing and waxing her car on the weekends; he hadn't done this in ages. His overall lack of attention had made her bitter and in turn, far less likely to want to please him.

Ben was super sick of Cassandra as well. In his opinion, she was bossy and argumentative. She told him how to do everything better, from the way he drove to how he stirred pasta in a pot. His biggest beef, though, was that she criticized him in front of their kids. Their nine-year-old daughter Emily was spoiled and disrespectful, but when Ben tried to discipline her by sending her to her room, Cassandra always butted in and said he was too strict. The result was that Emily had no respect for him and was becoming a little punk. She had sworn at him only last week. When Ben told her to sweep the floor as punishment, Cassandra had laughed and said he was making a big deal out of nothing.

Ben and Cassandra never held hands anymore, didn't laugh together, when they did talk they disagreed, and their sex life was below mediocre, while it used to be great.

To condense, Cassandra doesn't feel pampered or spoiled by Ben. She isn't receiving romantic attention, and this makes her feel unloved. Ben does not feel valued or respected by Cassandra and this makes him feel unloved as well.

So, how can Ben and Cassandra turn their marriage around? Conventional wisdom says they need to communicate. If you view their relationship as a hotel, it's in basement mode, folks. Communication alone is not the answer.

Instead, let's find a way for this couple, so much in love a few years ago, to once again find each other *irresistible*. This can whisk them to the 12th floor of the hotel, with hopes of someday again reaching the pinnacle, that penthouse suite with lots of windows, luxury room service, plus a fantastic view of the bay.

A surprisingly easy fix could just be the answer.

How about Ben initiates the turnaround by bringing home beautiful flowers for Cassandra twice a week, without fail? Twice a week, you say? Didn't we just mention this couple was broke? Well, Ben brings his lunch to work every day to save money. But he walks across the street from his office each morning with his co-workers Ted and Amanda for a Starbucks. Ben's iced coffee and snack run about nine dollars a day. We're not talking about fancy florist bouquets here, just those cute ones from the market. If just three times a week Ben skips the Starbucks snack, he can show up at home Monday and Thursday evenings with lovely flowers for his wife. He can still join Ted and Amanda in their beloved ritual of escaping their office for

20 minutes each morning to drink coffee standing up and complain about their respective spouses.

Ben, don't just leave that bouquet on the counter. Earn yourself bonus points by cutting the stems, and placing the flowers into a vase with water, one aspirin tablet and a shiny penny to make them last longer. Alternate days; Monday and Thursday one week, Tuesday and Friday the next week, and so forth.

In this way, the flowers will actually last all week. Ergo, every single day of the week, Cassandra can gaze upon beautiful and fragrant flowers.

Next, how about Cassandra cooks Ben's favorite chili every other week like she used to? This chili smells wonderful... he adores it. He can also eat the leftovers the next day at the office, once again being the envy of his co-workers, because Cassandra's chili is really an art form in itself.

There's another priceless skill Cassandra can employ, which is to make her husband look like a king in the eyes of his children. Next time sassy little Emily is disrespectful toward Ben, Cassandra should scold her. Cassandra needs to support Ben and back him. This will make him feel respected and not minimized.

The bonus is that Emily won't grow up to be a snotty, bratty little punk whose future college roommates detest her and make her freshman year utterly miserable.

Every few days Cassandra and Ben can do something nice for one another, without being asked. When they go places, one of them can reach for the other's hand, so they'll start holding hands again. We shall discuss later the benefits of a couple holding hands.

Now, at this point, things will ideally have warmed up so that Cassandra and Ben can have some productive discussions. As they feel more romantic, their sex life should improve. One of them might also sacrifice by getting a second job. The two can even take turns with this. Yes, it's tiring, but perhaps it's better to be weary than to be broke.

Just like "It's better to look good than to feel good!" Ah, Billy Crystal!

For more on actions speaking louder than words, please skip ahead to our "Dr. Linda Comedy Marriage Boot Camp" section.

## Ask for What You Want

This is one arena where the tired platitude "just communicate" actually *does* hold a full pony of bourbon. If you're not getting what you want from your partner, try asking.

We all go through stages when we think our partners should be mind readers. It's probably a blessing they aren't, because you don't want them knowing everything you're thinking, now do you?

Here are some things married folks say they want to ask their partner:

"Don't just sit there looking at me when I say I've had a crappy day, get up and give me a big hug."

"When you hear Maxwell (Maxwell is a terrier) barking and annoying the neighbors, I know you're pretending that you don't hear him. Get up and let him in the house; don't wait for *me* to always do it."

"Let me know you appreciate it when I've mowed the lawn and spent three hours in our yard in the hot sun."

"When we get together with your sister for dinner, don't make excuses for her rude-ass comments."

"Don't mumble when I'm trying to talk to you. Don't call out important things from the other room and expect me to hear you."

"When it's your turn to put away the laundry, don't leave three socks on the bed. They will not magically get up and stroll into the drawer."

"Compliment my cooking. I mean, you're gobbling it down so fast I know you like it, but words would be nice to hear also."

Somehow many of these sound a trifle sarcastic, don't they? You can absolutely modify the delivery however you want.

Anyways, these are just a few. You can probably supply a few dozen of your own!

# B

## Boredom

One of the top reasons proclaimed by someone who's filing for divorce is "boredom." Their spouse used to be fun and life was exciting, but no more.

Nowadays, they find they're married to a crashing bore and they are planning a quick getaway.

A very wise friend of mine told me many years ago: "Only boring people get bored."

Boredom can be the kiss of death for a relationship. But you definitely can take steps to stave it off. If you continually do new and fun things, and have novel experiences to look forward to, there's less chance you'll become weary of life in general, and then by association, your marriage partner.

Some married folks believe that sticking to their "same old, same old" is the key to happiness. Let's observe Eleanor and James. They eat out at the same few restaurants. The movie theatre is too much of a hassle. Better to stay home and watch from their Barca loungers. Friends invited them to Paris last year, but they skipped it – too impractical. They rarely drive to the beach, only 20 minutes away. There's a park five minutes from their home, so that's where they walk the dog, every time. Since Covid, they both work remote; each week they get groceries and run a few errands. Speaking of the market, they shop at the same Trader Joe's every week; their market list remains unvaried. I'm dozing off now... reading this out loud has put me to sleep! Zzzzzzz

Now, here's the gruesome surprise! Eleanor and James are not retirement-age. They aren't in their 50s, or even their 40s! This couple is in their mid-30s. So, I ask you this, how are the lives of Eleanor and James any different than your average 75-year-old's?

It's quite easy, even when young, to get into a bit of a "rut." You're comfortable with your same old, reliable routine. You believe this makes you happy.

However, studies have shown that engaging in novel activities is actually much more conducive to happiness than repetition of old favorites. Learning new things and trying novel activities improves brain function and the actual health of your brain.

There are also psychological advantages to engaging in novel experiences. When you try something new, you feel a sense of accomplishment and your confidence increases. It doesn't have to be climbing Mount Kilimanjaro. It could be trying a new restaurant, hobby or sport, or traveling someplace you've always wanted to go.

My husband's late, beloved Uncle Bob took a computer class when he was in his 80s. This helped him sharpen his mind and gain confidence by going light years out of his comfort zone, as he was born in the early 1930s.

Alan and his husband Jonathan always have a trip or excursion planned, even if it's six months in the future, so they have something to talk about and have fun planning together. Both of these men have huge, very high-pressure careers. Arranging exciting trips takes them away from the day-to-day grind of their stressful jobs, traffic, difficult co-workers, and so forth. Alan and Jonathan make it a point to actively plan and talk about their next adventure on an almost-daily basis. If they're saving to go to Italy, for example, they go to an Italian restaurant to plan. This is fun and gives them something positive to discuss, besides their respective careers. Most of all, it gives Alan and Jonathan something to look forward to.

If cost is an issue, a day trip can be fun and a way to shake up things a little. It's all in your mindset. Here in San Diego, we visit Coronado Island and hang out at the very lovely Hotel del Coronado. Sometimes when we do this, I pretend we're tourists. No matter where you live, there are always fun things to do and see. Look up travel destinations in your town; there may be amusing places you never even knew existed.

We've all heard of the "Eiffel Tower Phenomenon." It's when someone lives near a fantastic landmark or building, and since it is right there and they could go anytime, they never actually go. Tourists visiting a town may see more than the locals, as they have limited time and may never visit again.

So to reiterate, boredom is a dangerous thing for a marriage. When one partner wants to try new things and enjoy life but their partner is "kinda duddy," this can cause untold frustration.

Harold worked as an accountant for a small company in San Francisco. He'd never actually been diagnosed with depression, but every day said how bored and depressed he was. If someone suggested, "Hey, Harold, maybe you could volunteer at the animal shelter? You love dogs and they're desperate for people to walk them," Harold would reply, "Yeah, but I'm tired after work." If someone suggested Harold join a weekend social club, since his wife worked both Saturdays and Sundays, Harold would answer, "Yeah, but you meet weird people at those things."

"Yeah, but," was Harold's go-to reply.

Harold's wife Ruth, a realtor, always joined him for his company's summer picnics and Christmas parties. One year, after a couple drinks, with Harold out of earshot, she confessed that he was a boring fella. Of course, Harold's co-workers already knew this intimately. Ruth claimed that at one time, Harold had been fun and open to trying new things, but for the past nine or ten years, only went to work and ran necessary errands. He always had excuses for not going anywhere, including travel, which was Ruth's favorite activity.

Consequently, over the past several years, Ruth had built an entire social life that did not include her husband. She ate out, saw movies, went to museum openings, and traveled with her sister and three other women friends she'd met through work. Two of these women were married and suggested double dates; whenever Ruth asked Harold, he made excuses or refused outright.

Ruth felt that Harold had stopped trying. He refused to go to marriage counseling and maintained it was her fault he was unhappy. Ruth told friends she could have stayed married had Harold made any effort at all, but she felt he'd just given up on life and on her as well. Perhaps the most important aspect was that Harold refused to compromise.

After Ruth filed for divorce, she told friends she looked forward to enjoying life as a single person, because for all practical purposes, she'd been single for nearly a decade.

Now, if both enjoy a more leisurely lifestyle, that's not necessarily a bad thing. Brad and Joanne, both self-proclaimed "homebodies," prefer relaxing at their ranch-style home in the Houston suburbs. Brad's father was in the military, so as a child, he'd moved 12 times before finishing high school and so has little desire to travel. Joanne is fearful of flying and is not too crazy about road trips. However, from time to time they do try new restaurants, go visit their son who lives in another state, and they both have fun hobbies. Brad plays chess on the weekends and Joanne takes painting classes. Both are very content with their lives and their marriage. Neither one would describe themselves as being "bored."

Some married folks don't know why they feel bored and dissatisfied with their lives. They often then assume that it's their partner's fault.

Since possibly they interact with their partner more than anyone, it's easy to point the finger at them. The partner may then become a virtual scapegoat for everything that's wrong in their life.

Bonnie and Ted had been married for 14 years. Their two children would be teenagers soon, and Bonnie was feeling very restless. She may have been going through a bit of a mid-life crisis, which could have ended on its own...who knows? She only knew that she was restless, dissatisfied with her life, and bored.

Bonnie then began blaming Ted. She could recite a litany of his shortcomings. Ted always liked the same foods. He had nothing interesting to say anymore. He agreed with her too much and didn't make her feel super-charged with energy, like her entertaining co-worker Greg. Bonnie mentally compared Ted to the guys she worked with, and he fell short every time. Greg, for example, liked to debate and to challenge her – this was very exciting for Bonnie. She was also sick of Ted's wardrobe. He wore a shirt and tie to work because he had to, but otherwise still dressed like the surfer he'd been in his adolescence. Bonnie told her girlfriends she'd outgrown Ted.

Whenever Bonnie criticized Ted, most of her girlfriends were sympathetic and took her side. This is, after all, the traditional role of girlfriends. A couple girlfriends pointed out that Ted was a really decent guy and a wonderful father. Bonnie certainly couldn't disagree with this. At parties, Ted did all the barbecuing, most of the cleanup, and attended every sporting event with their kids. He wasn't a drinker, didn't do drugs, and held down a good job. He did lots around the house, all the cooking and most of the cleaning. Their two kids absolutely adored him.

Nonetheless, Bonnie became increasingly restless and whenever she socialized with her group of girlfriends, this was her main topic of conversation. Every sentence began with another example of how Ted was falling short.

A few months later, Bonnie informed Ted that she was just tired of being married to him and wanted a divorce. Ted was extremely upset; he wanted to work on their relationship and marriage. At first Bonnie agreed, then changed her mind a week later...she told Ted she'd hired a divorce attorney. Their two kids, preteens at the time, wrote a long letter to Bonnie and Ted begging them not to divorce.

Here's a crucial element for any married person to remember: if you're feeling dissatisfied with your spouse, be extremely careful whom you talk to. When you confide in your single or divorced friends, they have every good intention, but may steer you in the direction of divorce.

Instead, if you're really bored with your spouse and just want to throw in the towel, seek out a married friend, preferably someone who's been wed for ten years or more. By the way, talk to a *happily* married friend. Several friends whom Bonnie asked for advice were either divorced or unhappily married.

Her two happily married friends both tried to dissuade her from leaving Ted. They suggested her restlessness was a passing thing, and to wait before doing anything irrevocable. They encouraged her to see a marriage counselor, and to at least delay any divorce proceedings.

But Bonnie was strongly influenced by those friends who told her to "go for it." One of them said, "There's a whole exciting world out there and you deserve to experience it."

Bonnie proceeded with the divorce, although Ted and their kids tried to change her mind. Here is the end result: Their divorce was very amicable. Ted never tried to turn their kids against her. Unfortunately, her lawyer encouraged her to be more aggressive about money, so in the end, it was a long, costly and painful process.

Ted was heartbroken over the divorce, but never spoke badly about Bonnie to anyone. He floundered for awhile, six years later marrying a very nice lady who adores him, loves his kids, and really appreciates his fine qualities.

Guess what? Ted's new wife, Meredith, doesn't find him boring. Another plus: Meredith happens to be extremely well-off. Ted and his kids have benefited in many ways, including frequent trips to Europe, Asia and the Bahamas.

As for Bonnie, she dated quite a bit, starting with Greg at her office. She'd believed Greg walked on water, especially compared to Ted. But when she actually began dating him, she realized Greg was quite cheap, plus he often cancelled their plans with little notice. She came to realize she had been much more desirable to Greg when she'd been married. She then also dated some other fellows, but none for long, and one guy took financial advantage of her.

Bonnie now tells friends that if she could do it over again, she would have stayed with Ted. She realized that it wasn't really him, but that she'd been going through a restless and difficult phase of life. Had she waited before making a major decision, she would have saved herself, Ted and her kids a lot of emotional pain and misery.

If you're feeling disgruntled with your partner and dissatisfied with your life, first take stock of your own situation. Are you tired of your career? Were you always home with the kids and now that they're older you're floundering? Do you regret not having gone to college? Are you not as physically fit as you could be? Do you feel remorse over not having done more fun things earlier in life?

Most importantly, drumroll please! Are you blaming your spouse for your unhappiness instead of working to fix it yourself?

Once you take inventory of the things that are eating at you, look to see if these items are fixable. If you're sick of your job, put your resume out there... maybe a better career awaits. If you regret not having finished your education, thanks to technology, there are opportunities to complete a degree online that were impossible even two decades ago.

If you're feeling frumpy and a tad out of shape, consider joining a gym and improving your eating habits.

So – presenting Lucy and Ricky. Rather than Lucy saying, "Ricky is driving me nuts, I'm so sick of him, I need a change, I'm so bored with that guy," perhaps Lucy can take a long hard look at...guess who...*Lucy*. Lucy might take self-inventory, and see which things she can improve.

This ain't easy, folks. This involves personal growth and change, both of which are challenging if not downright excruciating.

It's so much more convenient for Lucy to just point her finger at Ricky, sick of him always playing those dang conga drums, and blame it all on him. That way, she doesn't have to make any tough adjustments herself.

Next time your partner is bugging you more than usual, pause. Take a personal inventory of your own life. Are you sick of your boring humdrum job? Is your boss mean or creepy? Do your bratty, ungrateful kids drive you nuts? Did you blame the dry cleaners for shrinking your suits when it's really those extra Dorito's? Have you postponed a personal goal, such as a degree? Are finances tight? Money is always a stressor. Believe me, I've been there. Coming up soon is our "broke" section.

We human beings are inherently leisurely. We shall always choose the path of least resistance, unless we push ourselves to do otherwise.

It takes concerted effort to resist the tempting urge to make a scapegoat out of your partner.

Stop for a moment, and look at yourself. Take a long, hard, honest look. For lack of a better term, what sucks? What can you change or improve? Have you gotten into the habit of taking out your frustrations and disappointments on the person (aside from your kids) who is closest to you?

Maybe it's time to alter this pattern once and for all. Determine what you can change and improve. After all, you can't *really* change your partner, but you do have control over that person who goes through life with you every day, 100 percent of the time... and that is *you.*

Perhaps also ask a trusted friend what they think. We're not talking about a "yes friend." You know the kind of friend we're talking about. This is the buddy who will call you out when you need it. They admit you shouldn't have yelled out your car window at the creep who cut you off in traffic. They will acknowledge that your new hair shade is...well, wrong. In short, they will level with you and not just tell you what you want to hear. But be prepared for the truth! This friend may bluntly tell you that you have become a massive complainer, that you're blaming it all on your spouse, when it's yourself you need to improve.

This is tough! For one thing, it is very difficult to transform. It can be painful to look at one's own life, take oneself firmly in hand, and work on those things which need improvement.

Once you start, it's difficult to stop that pattern of blaming your spouse. Ernie says that he's heavy because his wife is such a good cook. Unless Millie holds a loaded revolver to his head as she force-feeds him her famous mac and cheese, this does seem unrealistic. Angie complains she's never able to exercise because she's too busy working and watching her kids. But she's on the phone with best girlfriend Cindy an hour every night. Nothing's stopping her from getting one of those headsets and walking around the house as she chats.

Many folks, rather than changing, updating, improving, or adding more joy, instead condemn their spouse for their drab life.

Let's now imagine this person is you. You've been married for quite awhile... maybe it seems *too long*. You're unhappy, perhaps even miserable, and you're positive it's your tedious spouse who is to blame.

You then begin to fault them for everything: unhappiness, dissatisfaction with life, all your dreams put by the wayside. Once you begin to do this, your partner then becomes the fall guy. Everything you dislike about your life is their fault.

In due course, you begin to view your spouse with dislike, contempt and resentment, for who wouldn't feel this way about the one person who's creating unhappiness in your life? Ultimately, you become convinced that if you can just get rid of your spouse, this will solve all your problems. By the way, the "get rid of" part sounded terrible, didn't it? We're not talking murder here, just divorce.

We're devoting a lot of time to this scenario, because I've personally seen this phenomenon played out countless times with friends and co-workers.

If you're experiencing this, perhaps there's merit to what you're seeing. It may be absolutely true that your spouse is annoying, a spendthrift or a penny-pincher, tedious, sloppy around the house, too much of a neat freak, talks too much, says the wrong things, doesn't talk enough, so on and so on.

However, chances are excellent they have some really good qualities you've just forgotten about. Perhaps your spouse has become a punching bag for all your disappointments, frustrations and failures.

Sometimes just becoming aware of this can totally boost your outlook toward your spouse. After all, they had so many wonderful qualities when you met them, and that's probably why you married them in the first place.

If you're at any stage in this process, one helpful exercise is as follows: write down 15 things you appreciate, like or love about your spouse. If your marriage has hit a very rough spot, you may initially have trouble coming up with even two.

Keep at it; don't give up until you list 15 items. Don't feel guilty if you can only list miniscule things, such as how he remembered to turn on the porch light last night or that she still churns out a fabulous lasagna. Stick to the list until you think of 15. The next step is to list just three things which you dislike about your partner.

You can also ask your spouse to do the same, so that the two of you are doing this exercise together. Warning: If your marriage is in trouble, your partner may stare at you like you're mainlining heroin when you ask them to list 15 good things about you.

But sometimes it's easy to forget over the years why you fell in love in the first place, and this exercise is great because it helps you to remember.

Robert and I have done this many times over the years. A premarital counseling workshop we attended with about 20 other couples included this exercise.

Here's the funny thing: most of the little pieces of paper we wrote our lists on have been lost over the years, but what I recall most are the good things we said about one another. A few years after we'd married, we had had a huge argument, over something silly I'm sure, and Robert and I did this exercise. I vividly remember some positive things we wrote. He said I was a "great mom to the critters," "nice to his friends," and "a lot of fun." I said he had a "great sense of humor" and was "always so wonderful to my dad" and "made great pasta." Pasta, as I recall, was the only thing Robert knew how to cook at this stage of our marriage.

Try doing this and see if it helps. Also, if you're going through a boredom phase with your spouse, try doing lists for this as well. Each of you lists five things you think will add fun and spice to your marriage. Just be prepared in advance in case your spouse suggests something like "couples swapping" that you're not really cool with!

We shall actually see more about couples swapping in the "Do's and Dont's" and "Sex" sections at the end of this book.

## Baggage

It's a tragedy, no less; we're all hauling around some baggage. And it's not those modern, graceful, rolling suitcases available nowadays... no siree Bob! We're talking those retro-hefty, cumbersome, unwieldy Samsonites with one handle and sticky wheels!

This is precisely what I lugged to our honeymoon in 1988. It's a burden that throws your back out because it's just so dang heavy as you haul it up and down stairs, with no moving sidewalks in sight.

In a Kevin James comedy stand-up show, he says that on the moving walkway at the airport, there should be an off-ramp for the "Cinnabon" shop!

Baggage can originate from our parents, siblings, other family members, childhood traumas or painful experiences. Let's also not forget the hideous emotional weight we're hauling around from past romantic disasters.

For sure, we all have baggage. Do we hide it in a closet behind some old college sweatshirts, pretending it doesn't exist? Or, at other end of the spectrum, do we focus on it constantly? To what extent does it affect our everyday life? Past experiences do influence our present reality, no doubt about it. But, how can we keep from clobbering our spouse over the head with our old gnarly baggage?

Here's an example of how this hurts a marriage: Becky's husband Martin had a very critical mother named Lillian. Martin never did anything right as far as Lillian was concerned, beginning when he was a young boy. No matter how hard he tried, even with simple chores like raking leaves in the yard, Lillian would heap verbal abuse upon him. She struck him frequently when she was drinking, which was most of the time. Martin wore glasses, and she'd laugh as she knocked his glasses off his face.

Lillian vastly preferred Martin's younger sister Eloise, and lavished love and affection upon her. To the same extent that Martin could do no right, Eloise could do no wrong as far as Lillian was concerned.

Martin was a baby of the 60s, and as you young readers may have heard, there was nothing remotely resembling Child Protective Services back then. In those days, most folks believed parents should raise their kids how they saw fit. Even if a parent was clearly abusive, friends and neighbors rarely got involved. The only recourse was to call the police, and most folks didn't take it that far.

When Martin became a teenager, Lillian stopped hitting him physically, because his sister intervened, but the verbal abuse worsened. You may wonder: where was Martin's father in all this? Well, Albert was a weak man and he was cowed by his wife. He never spoke up or defended his son. The only lifeline for Martin was his little sister Eloise, who staunchly defended him.

So, here's the nasty baggage Martin was hauling around every dang day when he married Becky. Whenever Becky tried to discuss anything with him, no matter how diplomatically she did so, he became very defensive. Martin also became angry quite easily. Eventually, Becky became weary of this, and their relationship suffered as a result.

Becky finally suggested they go see a counselor together. Martin was very reluctant, but she insisted. In addition to couples' counseling, Martin began individual therapy. It took five years, but he was finally able to heal the painful roots of his insecurity and anger. He was able to find compassion for himself as a boy because he now realized that at the time, he couldn't defend himself. Martin was also able to forgive his father (now deceased) for not being strong enough to help him.

Becky and Martin's relationship improved so much that she was amazed. "He's like another person entirely. It's like this huge burden he's been carrying around just evaporated," she told friends.

To share my own "Samsonite story," I was hauling around some hefty luggage when Robert and I married. My mom had died when I was 18;

I had never dealt with it. Therapy was rarely utilized back then. You just dealt with whatever happened the best way you could. The phrase used back then was "suck it up, buttercup."

However... better late than never! From 2010 to 2016, I had regular sessions with my wonderful therapist Laurie, which made all the difference.

At the time, I was ashamed I needed a therapist, so I mainly kept it a secret. Very few people knew. There continues to be a stigma about therapy, which is precisely why I'm now very open about it. I'm so grateful for those six years. Therapy transforms you into a nonchalant baggage handler, hurtling your own suitcase off the plane onto that little ground transportation cart. Guess what, if your baggage lands on the runway by accident; well, what the fuck!

I'm now the person I was meant to be, had nothing bad ever happened in my life.

Your individual process may include multiple steps, such as group therapy and hypnosis.

Possibly foremost of all is a desire to better yourself, not just for the sake of your marriage, but to become the person you were always meant to be.

As George Eliot (aka Mary Ann Evans) wrote so beautifully, "It is never too late to be what you might have been."

## Blame

Heidi kept track of each and every mistake, both major and minor, made by her hapless husband, Brett.

So, how did I know this?

Well, each morning at work, while the rest of us were trying to (variously) check our emails, wake up, or nurse our hangovers, Heidi would waltz into the office and treat us to her litany of woes. Most were Brett's failures from the day before (including the decade before).

No one, but no one, wanted to hear it! But we lucky ducks got treated on a Monday through Friday basis.

No matter what transpired, it was always Brett's fault. Heidi tallied a laundry list of transgressions and f-ups she'd been compiling religiously since they'd first married in 1993.

Heidi complained each day about Brett's mistakes and how "dumb" he was. As you may imagine, this became excruciatingly boring in no time. But here's the kicker: Brett didn't know a thing. Heidi faulted him for everything wrong in her life, and shared it with everyone except the one person who could have improved things: that's right ...you guessed it...good ol' Brett, her husband.

Although hers is an extreme example, little Havarti Heidi does not stand alone. With some couples it's reciprocal: both keep a running tally against each other. It's like a volleyball game with that giant scoreboard on the wall.

Bonus points are earned by tattling to friends and co-workers; this garners sympathy and attention. It may be weary, bored attention. So it's like a tennis match, but no one wins... in the long run, both partners lose.

This damages your marriage in two distinct ways. First, your spouse has no idea what's bothering you, so it's unlikely they will change. Second, if this continues, you may begin to view your partner with contempt. Contempt is the kiss of death for a relationship. Contempt is a particular type of scornful disdain... looking down on someone with disrespect.

We're not talking about selective grumbling to a trusted pal, by the way. In order to save their sanity, most married folks do vent to one or two trusted friends from time to time.

Otherwise, they run the risk of totally losing their minds.

If you're "doing a Heidi," how do you turn this habit around? One way is to extend grace to your partner. Extending grace is one of the most powerful gifts you can give to your marriage.

What exactly does it mean to extend grace? Next time your spouse makes a dumb or annoying mistake, change your response. Instead of reacting with anger, annoyance, scorn, or irritation, pause, and breathe deeply. Then, say something kind and affirmative to reassure your partner.

The beauty of extending grace is that rather than pointing the harsh finger of blame at your partner, you let them off the hook.

They realize that you've done this, and they are pathetically grateful.

This can be highly contagious. The phrase "highly contagious" isn't usually a good thing! But when your partner screws up, particularly if you've been quick to blame them in the past, they'll expect you to be angry, upset, or annoyed. When you instead respond with loving kindness, your spouse will be amazed, happy and relieved.

And, don't we want a happy marriage partner? Yes, indeed we do! A happy spouse helps keep you married, and prevents divorce attorneys from getting all of your money.

I repeat this: prevents divorce attorneys from getting all of your money!

Another positive result is your partner will likely be more compassionate when you yourself flub up.

Robert gets bonus points as he began this dynamic with us. Several years ago, I left our garage door wide open and innocently gallivanted off to work. We live on top of a 500' driveway and thieves are generally lazy, so our chances of getting robbed are less than average.

Nonetheless, it can always happen!

When I returned home that evening, Robert didn't say a thing. After dinner, he casually mentioned, "Be sure to close the garage door when you leave tomorrow."

Later here, we'll talk more about timing as it is super important. For example, how often have we "pounced" on our partner at the door when they've barely set down their car keys to inform them about their latest screw-up?

The habit of extending grace didn't come naturally to me, but with peer pressure, I began to follow suit. Some years ago, Robert updated our medical coverage while watching "Sons of Anarchy." He was so engrossed in the escapades of Jax and the bikers, he accidentally checked the "HMO" box instead of the "PPO" box.

A few days later, Robert received an email confirming his medical benefits and realized what he'd done. When he first told me, I won't lie; I was really annoyed. Earlier in our marriage, this would have caused a huge fight with lots of drama. Instead I asked him, "Is there any way out of it?" "No," he answered, "looks like we're stuck." I calmly replied something along the lines of "Oh, well, it's just for one year."

In this way, I didn't blame him. I extended grace by not making a big deal out of something he couldn't change. Then, the next time I myself did something dumb, and let's face it, folks, we are ALL going to do foolish stuff from time to time, he was, in turn, laid-back about it.

Try this, folks! You'll be glad you did. The opposite is to constantly blame your partner for every single screw-up. This eventually does so much damage, I cannot adequately express it here. The partnership spirals downwards as each one keeps score of the other's mistakes. The couple either divorces or stays together for financial or other reasons, but if they do this, they're generally miserable together.

## Besties

This scenario sometimes occurs with men, but far more often is a "girlie syndrome."

This is the "bestie" phenomenon. Many women have a best friend, "bestie," or BFF. This is generally a good thing, unless it becomes an "extreme sport."

Nothing wrong with having girlfriends; I for one adore mine, and they are sacred to me.

But what I'm describing here is a grown-ass woman who simply can't do anything without her "bestie." This may hurt her marriage and other relationships as well.

Madeleine and Joan were "besties" and worked at the same company. They carpooled to the office every day and took coffee breaks and lunches together. Not just often... folks, *every day.*

Madeleine was delightful, but Joan was rather abrasive. But everyone at their office knew that if they invited Madeleine for coffee, lunch or happy hour, it would be a package deal 100 percent of the time. Joan would show up just like a rusty little penny.

Joan was an appendage on Madeleine, just like her boobs and arms. Unfortunately, Joan was very opinionated and dominated every conversation. When Joan was around, Madeleine couldn't get in two words edgewise.

Everyone really liked Madeleine. If you could get her by herself, she was funny, witty and a great conversationalist. Once, I bolstered my courage and ventured, "Hey, Madeleine, let's go to lunch just the two of us, so we can really catch up." Madeleine agreed, but then when we met downstairs at our building's fountain, guess who should be standing right there with her?

You guessed it ...the inescapable, the unavoidable, the terrifying ...*Joan.*

Come on, ladies! You're grown women, not 6th graders! (Hope this doesn't offend anyone!) If a married person has a "bestie" like this, the "bestie" is really their significant other. Their spouse...ummm...perhaps *not*.

Eventually, this can take a toll on a marriage. However, that's not always the case. Let's dash back to that cozy duo, Joan and Madeleine. Joan is single; Madeleine has been married to Brad for five years. Joan texts Madeleine a dozen times every evening, after having been in one another's pockets all the live long day at work. Yep, no surprise: this annoys Brad.

But here's the kicker: Amazingly, Brad is quite fond of Joan, even though he finds her personality as abrasive as a brillo pad. Brad's younger brother Matthew is special needs and lives two hours away at their parents' home. Brad is devoted to Matthew and spends every weekend visiting him there. Madeleine doesn't care for Brad's mom, so she dislikes accompanying him on these visits.

So, in this case, the "bestie" situation is actually a fantastic convenience. Brad knows Joan will keep Madeleine busy on the weekends, so he is able to take much of the responsibility for his brother's care off his elderly parents' shoulders. Madeleine and Joan spend every weekend happily brunching, shopping, getting their nails done, and seeing movies. It's a very agreeable situation for everyone.

This same dynamic with men has a most delightful and glam title: "bromance." Perhaps "bromance" partners watch ball games together, or go camping or fishing. I'm eternally grateful for my husband's desert buddies, because my idea of "roughing it" is a hotel without room service, so God bless them. They get me off the hook.

In certain scenarios, a "bromance" can harm a marriage in much the same way a "bestie" can. If one guy is married and one is single, perhaps if the married guy is going through a slump with his wife, he may increasingly envy his friend's carefree lifestyle. His single "bromance" buddy might not place as high a value on marriage, and might encourage him to leave his wife.

Kevin and Joyce were in their mid-30s and had been married for two years with a one-year-old son, Aidan. Kevin worked in the mortgage industry and Joyce was a stay-at-home mom. Both were adamant that Aidan not attend day-care, so they were living on one income. Kevin's best buddy Richard was in his late 40s and part owner of the company where Kevin worked. Their "bromance" had been going strong for over 15 years.

Richard was single and had no children, and his company brought in massive profits, so his disposable income far exceeded Kevin's.

Richard loved the finer things in life: imported cigars, bourbon, first-class restaurants, his magnificent sports car, and lots of traveling, including deep-sea fishing trips. Richard always had a new leggy blonde girlfriend; these relationships generally lasted a year. He'd been married and divorced twice and had entirely sworn off marriage.

Richard frequently invited Kevin on outings that Kevin could no longer afford now that he was supporting a wife and a son. Richard usually grabbed the check, and although Kevin didn't mind this, Joyce felt it wasn't right.

Richard and Joyce heartily disliked one another. This had culminated on Joyce and Kevin's wedding day, when Richard had slept with one of Joyce's bridesmaids. Joyce viewed Richard as selfish and narcissistic; Richard saw Joyce as uptight and bossy.

Joyce confided in her best friend Amy (not the bridesmaid who'd slept with Richard, by the way) that Richard was ruining her marriage. She believed Richard missed the "good old days" when both guys had been single. The majority of arguments between Kevin and Joyce were over Richard.

What should Joyce do in this situation? The reality is Richard and Kevin were friends long before she and Kevin had even met. Richard is Kevin's *best friend*. So when the two guys are out together, if Richard picks up the tab, not to put too fine a point on it, but maybe it's none of Joyce's concern.

To some extent, it's immaterial whether Joyce even likes Richard; it's not as though she has to put up with him very often. Usually this "bromance duo" goes to sporting events, takes fishing trips and so forth.

On those rare occasions they double-date, one possible compromise might be that Richard picks up the tab at restaurants, and then Joyce and Kevin invite him and his current girlfriend over for dinners or barbecues.

If Joyce is gracious to Richard, Kevin will likely be grateful, and their relationship will then be strengthened rather than diminished.

These are just a couple scenarios: every circumstance is different. And of course, if your husband's "bromance" partner leads him into unsavory habits such as doing drugs, robbing convenience stores, or even wearing over-the-calf argyle socks, that's a whole other thing. You'll be well within your rights to protest the friendship.

## Bla Bla Bla
### (also known as over-communication)

When people talk about maintaining a successful marriage, communication is nearly always mentioned. Oh, you can count on this! "Communication, communication, communication!"

There's nothing wrong with communication in and of itself. However, if it only took this to make a successful marriage, would we be seeing such a gigantic proportion of couples splitting up?

Communication can be positive for sure, but *over*-communication is another thing altogether. Folks think they're coming across just grand, then are puzzled and disheartened when they get bad results.

Lily and Pablo had been married for 14 years. Lily was often frustrated because she felt Pablo didn't really listen to her.

Sadly, this was absolutely, positively, 100 percent... the truth.

Lily talked so much, endlessly repeating herself, that Pablo had earned three Michelin stars at tuning her out.

Now here's the kicker: Pablo was great at faking it. He nodded at the appropriate times. At regular intervals, he added, "Um-hmm."

But, in reality, he barely heard anything she said.

Pablo was either looking at his phone or thinking about the stock market (he was a day trader). Sensing this, Lily redoubled her efforts to get his attention by talking even more ... and Pablo increasingly tuned her out.

Lily is pouring her heart out about her feelings; she's telling Pablo really important stuff. He appears to be interested, and in agreement. However, in reality, he's telling himself, "Geez, I'm starving. I wish she would stop talking so we could go and get some Thai food!"

Timing is critical for effective communication. Also, being able to express yourself in a concise manner; in other words, don't talk too much. Now, I'm not referring to fun conversations. Nope, I'm talking about when you've got something very important to tell your spouse.

In the mid-80s, my boss Kip taught me the importance of timing in communication. Kip was an alcoholic. In the mornings he'd drag himself, hostile and hung over, into our small office. It was just like sharing space with a snarling, caged bear. I avoided Kip until late morning, at the earliest. Before his three cups of coffee, anything said to him was taken badly. The choice time to interact with Kip was when he'd return from lunch, drunk and jovial. This was when I'd ask for time off, or confess I'd screwed up something.

Whether he was drunk or sober, Kip became impatient when I "beat around the bush." I learned to state my point clearly, using as few words as possible. If I dared to interrupt him, he would immediately stop talking and belligerently demand, "Are you going to talk, or am I?"

I must admit, this was harsh but effective.

Clear communication can be challenging for women. When we express ourselves bluntly, we may feel we're being rude. We're trained from an early age to be "nice" and "polite." For example, we may say something like "Oh, I feel bad when you're late to the movies; we might miss the beginning." That might work better with a girlfriend. But with men, it's generally more effective to state clearly, "Please be on time tomorrow. I don't want to miss the beginning of the movie."

Another valuable skill for both men and women is to say your piece and then *stop.* Stop talking entirely, and then really listen to your partner. Let them finish their thought completely. Don't interrupt or start talking right at the end of their sentence. Pause before you reply.

Julie, one of our success story wives, says that before you say something important, insist on your partner's full attention. Her advice: make a statement to your partner to get their complete focus: say "let's talk" and mean it. Be sure to commit to being a good listener. If your partner is looking at their phone when you want to say something crucial, remind them you need their full attention.

Julie's tip: don't start talking until they have set their phone aside.

Larry, one of our success story husbands, maintains that it takes courage to have high expectations for your spouse. He adds that if you don't strive for excellence in how you expect to be treated, and in turn, how you will treat your spouse, you are accepting low standards and will be treated accordingly.

Many of us, especially when angry, only "kinda" listen to our partner when they're talking. This is because we're already formulating our own response. Does this sound familiar? Don't worry! I too, am guilty as sin!

If we're busy formulating an angry or clever response, we don't focus on what our spouse is saying. If we reply right on the heels of their last sentence, this is the conversational equivalent of tailgating whilst driving in the saloon car. And nobody really likes someone riding up on their hindquarters, do they? It's like that bumper sticker that says, "If you're going to ride my ass, at least pull my hair."

At any rate, I recall hearing somewhere, no matter how interesting you think you are, if you're doing all the talking, you're boring *somebody*!

Michael, another past boss, but this one kind and sober, used to place a "post it" note on my desk when I was on the phone with a client. It said simply "70/30." This meant to listen 70 percent and talk 30 percent. He said 80/20 was ideal, but if I could average 70/30, that would be sensational.

# Broke
## Otherwise Known as "Two Dimes"

So... this was an extremely painful section to write. For starters, it's embarrassing. But maybe reading my story will comfort some of you if you're going through a similar miserable situation.

Robert and I have gone totally broke not just once, but twice. When she was a toddler, our daughter Andrea needed six surgeries on her leg to correct a birthmark (the surgeries were successful, thank God). Insurance refused to cover the procedures, claiming they were cosmetic. The hospital wouldn't schedule the next surgery until we'd paid for the last, and we had to complete all the surgeries while she was still small. Otherwise, the birthmark would return, meaning a lifetime of surgeries. We therefore had no choice but to pay out-of-pocket for six surgeries within one and a half years. We adamantly wished to pay for everything ourselves, and not accept help from family.

Right after Andrea's final surgery, at possibly our lowest financial point ever, she and I were out and about on a Monday, and my car was nearly out of gas. I literally had no cash, no credit card to put it on, zilch. Robert would get paid on Friday, but until then there was nothing. I had 53 cents in my wallet. So I put that 53 cents' worth of gasoline into the car so I could get home, put Andrea down for her nap, sat down on the living room carpet and just cried. After all these years, I can still remember that feeling.

So, to insert a little comedy, using one of my mom's favorite sayings, I can now recall with absolute certainty, we did not have two dimes to rub together!

Sitting there on the floor, I stopped crying, because number one, I'm Ukrainian, and number two, crying gives you wrinkles. Even mid-tragedy, it can't hurt to be practical. Suddenly, I recalled that I used to hide cash in books...odd, isn't it?

I was a literature major in college...so you know I'm gonna have a lot, a lotta books. I pulled down every book from our shelves... hundreds of them.

I found $184. Honestly, to this very day, that $184 was the best money of my entire life.

I called Robert and screamed, "We're rich!"

We had a glorious taco dinner that night at Rubio's to celebrate, gassed up both cars and bought some groceries. At that point, we finally agreed to get a little help from family, and things slowly turned around. But there's no denying it was just an excruciating time.

We were still embarrassingly broke when Andrea first began attending private school. Somehow we managed to scrape together her tuition. We still were broke as sin, but had the joy of daily contact with families who were literally dripping money.

One day on the playground, another mom vented to me about the stress of juggling her kitchen remodel with trips to Jamaica and Tahiti. As I stood there listening, I was mentally strategizing how to delay our SDGE payment just one more time so that our lights would not get shut off.

Like I say, if you've never been really broke, I do envy you.

Then, in 2008, the year of predatory lenders, we made the mistake of signing up for a terrible home loan. We'd used this company before, and trusted the loan guy. He was so charming and fun. I even made up special goody bags for this total schmuck.

Imagine then how foolish we felt, as we considered ourselves to be educated and fairly intelligent people, when our mortgage ballooned (we had not read all the smallest teeny-tiny print). Overnight, we found ourselves facing a $6,500 mortgage payment.

We weren't alone, although it seemed that way at the time. 2008 was the year so many Americans lost their homes and their life savings. Lori and Eugene, a success story couple at the end of this book, did lose their home. We hung onto our house, but it was horribly stressful.

Financial trouble either brings you closer or tears you apart. Another success story couple, Claire and Sam, feel that financial challenges contributed to their closeness and to being a strong team.

Both times we went broke it took tons of work, energy and misery to extricate ourselves. Robert did a paper route for an entire year. If I live to be 100, I'll never forget he did that for me and Andrea. He would sleep until 3 a.m., do the paper route, come back home, sleep one hour, then get up and work all day.

We got lucky in 2008; I got a great job right after we received a loan modification on our mortgage.

Getting approved for the loan modification was a miserable process. For months, I spent every break and lunch hour on the phone with the mortgage company. Each time we were on the verge of approval, some demon at the mortgage company would lose our paperwork and the entire process would begin again.

The Great Recession that started in 2008 caused a housing crisis in which more than six million American households lost their homes to foreclosure.

If you've been married for a while and have never gone broke, again, I envy you. It is hell... there's no other word for it.

Going broke is like stuffing rocks into a dam that is geysering water from every hole. It's making late payments on your credit cards while still charging stuff like groceries. It's unplugging the house phone because of the calls, but it's ringing in the garage. It's lying in bed unable to sleep because you're afraid you'll lose your home.

It's also not telling anyone what's going on because you're just too damn embarrassed. I recently told one of my dearest friends about this chapter, and she was very surprised. I never said anything at the time, because frankly I was mortified. I did confide in a couple close friends and they were a lifesaver. Their support and caring were priceless.

What doesn't kill you makes you stronger....so true. It's very humbling and makes you grateful when you come out the other side.

I first started giving out food and clothes to homeless people in Los Angeles around 1993. At the time, I didn't think why I was doing it. I just did it. Going broke was sheer misery, but it really changed my thinking. Now, when I see a homeless person, I think, "That could be me."

So...how does a married couple endure this hell and come out stronger, let alone still married?

Here's some advice from our success couples who went through money struggles.

- Don't blame one another. Even when you're miserable, find a way to stick together.

- Get out of the house and take walks.

- If your phone is ringing nonstop from bill collectors, mute it or turn it off before you get too stressed. Protect yourself in this way.

- Find fun activities that don't cost any money

We will talk more about denial later in this book. Denial can be invaluable in this situation; here's how. You have to get through the workday, so pretending your finances aren't a disaster can actually be quite beneficial.

I got us into our mortgage nightmare in 2008; no doubt about it. Robert complained many times about the situation, but he never pushed the blame onto me. He knew I felt awful enough about it already.

The next thing is to control what you can. If you're broke because you're spending too much, get some help. There are numerous resources that specifically help with debt and spending, and many of these can be accessed for free.

## Be As Nice To Your Spouse As You Are to Your Co-Workers

Later in this book, under the "C" section, we shall read the woeful tale of John and Loretta in its gruesome entirety. But now: a few juicy details about their home life. John passes gas whenever he feels like it, in any old room of their house. Loretta borrows his beautiful new truck and spills Starbucks, makeup and nail polish on the seat. He rolls his eyes and sighs heavily when she talks. She gossips about him daily to their two young daughters. He neglects to tell her when he's coming home late from the office, so she cooks dinner and he "no-shows." Both yell and scream at one another from different rooms of the house. In recent years, their mutual lack of respect has escalated into open hostility, and continues to worsen.

Now, we're not describing five-year-olds on the playground here. John and Loretta are both in their early 40s. If they tried any of this nonsense at their respective offices, HR would intervene in a flash. No one would put up with their nonsense. Instead, they treat each other this way at home... why? Perhaps because they know they can get away with it. If their daughters were able, they would probably take a leave of absence from their parents, citing a "hostile living environment."

Now, let's take a quick peek at how John and Loretta interact with their co-workers. Interestingly enough, they treat them just wonderfully. At work, John and Loretta are both known to be very polite; they say "good morning," "thank you," and "please." John wouldn't dream of passing gas at his office like he does so gleefully at home. If Loretta needs to borrow something from a co-worker, she's careful with it because she knows otherwise there will be consequences. Both are known at their respective companies to be considerate and polite individuals.

Therefore, when Loretta complains to her co-workers about what a jerk she's married to, she receives a plethora of sympathy. Everyone at her office knows how wonderful she is. They feel so terrible she has to put up with creepy John. They'd never in a million years recognize the nasty little pillbug Loretta is when she's at home.

It's the same with John. He doesn't complain as much as Loretta does, but Judy, his female friend at the office, who's now begun flirting with him in earnest as she sees his marriage falling apart, would never dream how badly he treats his wife.

Perhaps if married folks just treated one another as politely as they do their co-workers, there would be far fewer divorces.

## Blow It Out The Top of Your Head

Gentlemen, if you were perhaps dozing off after the last mini-section, but now have jolted wide awake, one hates to disappoint, but this section has nothing whatsoever to do with blow jobs. For that, you'll need to flip forward to our "sex" chapter. Nonetheless, now that I have your complete attention, please stay tuned, because this is still quite captivating stuff.

The gift of this amazing technique was actually given to me by a wonderful lady named Kit. At the time, I was going through a very stressful situation with a conniving "frenemy," and Kit gave me this fantastic advice.

"Just blow it out the top of your head," she stated. As she was saying this, Kit made a fist on top of her head, then a dramatic flinging motion toward the sky, whilst she simultaneously made a huge noise like a bomb going off.

Special note: if you need inspiration for the bomb sound effect, just watch Mel Gibson in the movie "The Road Warrior," when he says the gas tanks in his car are booby trapped. For convenience, this scene may be accessed on YouTube.

So, by the noise and physical action, you are actually blowing that stressful thought or concern right out of your head. Try it! It's eccentric, no doubt, but it actually works!

# Brag

We're all taught that it's bad manners to brag; it makes you look puffy and conceited and it generally annoys others. However, a moderate amount of showing off about your spouse will quite likely make them feel "fantastico."

What's critical is who you brag to, and how you go about it.

Boasting about your wife to your kids, for example, not only wins you brownie points with the wife, but also encourages your kids to treat her with respect and appreciation. Let's say your wife is a defense attorney and helped a client avoid an unfair sentence. How great if you compliment her to your kids. Or it could be her cooking, or how pretty she looks in her new dress.

Some applause to your kids about their dad is always nice as well. Maybe he got a promotion at work, or did a great job painting the spare bedroom. Or, how about saying something complimentary about your husband to his mother? Of course, mama already knows her boy is simply perfect, but a little bit more gravy on those garlic mashed potatoes never hurt nuthin'.

It doesn't have to be anything spectacular, by the way. Our daughter now lives on her own, so when Robert builds or repairs something around the house, I often send her a Snapchat detailing what he's done. I send him a copy as well.

Positive adjectives like "wonderful," "smart," and "amazing" are fantastic, by the way.

An acquaintance of mine is married to a veterinarian who spends a great deal of time in Mexico doing volunteer rescue work with stray dogs.

She acknowledges that this frequently takes him away from home, but she is proud of what he's doing. He, in turn, compliments her for picking up the slack with their children because he's gone so frequently.

So, choose your audience carefully, and don't overdo it, but a little well-timed bragging can earn you major brownie points with your spouse. It's going to make them feel appreciated and recognized, and who doesn't love that?

# C

## Change

Here's another tired old adage, "Women get married hoping to change their husbands, and men get married hoping their wives will never change." To some extent, this definitely seems to be true. Therefore, it's ultimately unavoidable that both sides will be gravely disappointed.

Both men and women will inevitably change, due to aging and maturity. Many men interviewed for this book reminisced fondly about the first time they saw their wife, usually when she was quite young. They used phrases like "thunderbolt," "blown away," "smitten," and "head over heels." Let's be honest, the word "lust" also came up with startling frequency. Fortunately, most happily married men do seem realistic about the fact that their wife is no longer in her 20s, with the same unlined, cherubic little face and girlish figure. They continue to describe their wives as "beautiful," "cute," "pretty," and "still takes my breath away after all these years."

But some men do have a more difficult time when their wives undergo change.

Also, here's an intriguing dynamic: men can transform *on their own* due to maturity, but most men resist and resent a woman's efforts to change them. The issue of a woman trying to change a man ties into the tricky subject we shall address later of control.

Happily married women interviewed for this book did mention they appreciated when their husbands stayed in good shape, exercised and took care of their appearance. Many of them used adjectives such as "still handsome," "still looks good to me," and "still takes my breath away."

Ben and Cindy lived in Charleston, South Carolina, and had been married for nine years. He was a very successful attorney, and she stayed home with their kids. They'd had three children in less than five years: a four-year old daughter and 18-month-old twin boys. Prior to becoming a mom, Cindy had always been extremely fit and slim. She'd taken a lot of trouble with her appearance, worn cute clothes, and always had her hair, nails, and makeup done. Ben was inordinately proud of Cindy and loved to brag about his "beautiful wife." Okay, let's be honest: sometimes he referred to her as his "hot wife."

Ben had been a self-described nerd in high school. Back then, girls had ignored him, so as an adult, he relished having a wife he could brag about.

But having three small children in such a short time had played havoc with Cindy's appearance. When their daughter Hayley was born, Cindy had not gone back to work, but had bounced back very quickly. She'd lost the baby weight within six months and absolutely loved motherhood. Cindy continued to see lots of her friends, as tiny Hayley was so well-behaved she could be brought to any restaurant, as well as Cindy's favorite place, the shopping mall. Cindy constantly received compliments about her beautiful, sweet little daughter. The two often wore matching sweaters and dresses. It was a heavenly time.

But all this changed when Jayden and Jackson, aka the "little hellions" arrived on the scene. Both were colicky and napped at different times. Taking the twins anywhere was exhausting and embarrassing for Cindy, as both were loud screamers. After several disastrous attempts, she stopped making plans with her girlfriends. Some days she barely had time to use the restroom, let alone bother with her hair or makeup. Instead of eating healthy meals, she grabbed stuff off the kids' plates. Jayden and Jackson took turns waking up all night and screaming for attention, so Cindy never got enough sleep.

As Ben pointed out, they could afford to hire help, but Cindy feared loss of privacy with a stranger in the house. Also, several of her friends had had nightmare experiences with nannies.

When Ben returned home in the evenings, cheerfully asked about her day and offered to watch the kids so she could hit the gym, Cindy felt insulted. She knew he was dropping hints about her weight. Sometimes Ben glanced at their wedding photo on the wall and mentioned how beautiful she'd looked that day. This made Cindy extremely resentful. All his compliments were about how she used to look.

Instead of inspiring her to work out, his comments really – pardon the expression –pissed her off. She was already self-conscious about the 45 pounds she hadn't taken off since the twins were born. She couldn't fit into any of her old outfits, and she hated her new clothes. She felt frumpy and old before her time.

Had Ben been smarter, perhaps he would have lavished her with (well, okay… fake) compliments. Cindy confided in her girlfriends that she felt unappreciated by Ben, and that his main focus was on her appearance. Her saucy friend Marla told her she was wrong to hold it all in and to just "let him have it!"

This couple then had some ugly arguments where Cindy yelled at Ben and refused to speak with him for several days. Maybe this wasn't great communication, but she finally got her point across. Of course, it would have been far preferable had she not yelled and had spoken calmly. Hey, in a perfect world! And, better this than being a martyr (we will learn much more about martyrs later on).

So, here was the crux of the situation. Cindy was angry and resentful. She felt that Ben did not accept and love her as she was.

Fortunately, Ben was no dummy, and he realized that Cindy was more hurt than angry.

He then proceeded to do two things right. One, he humbly apologized to her. Two, he followed this up with action. He asked what he could do to help.

Once the lines of communication opened up, Cindy made Ben understand just how exhausted she was. Ben was also frank in saying it was silly not to hire help when they had the money to do so.

Cindy saw the wisdom of this and hired a cleaning lady and a part-time nanny to help with the kids. Ben added that he missed going out to nice dinners and date nights, and she compromised by hiring a babysitter on a regular basis.

To Cindy's surprise, the cleaning lady did an excellent job. Hiring a part-time nanny meant that three days a week Cindy could go to lunch with friends, or run errands by herself. She even began seeing matinee movies on her own.

Ben also resumed his habit of bringing Cindy flowers and candy for no reason.

He also announced that he was taking over the cooking three nights a week. This actually ended up being takeout, or food delivered from a restaurant, but gave Cindy a break from cooking every night. He also began watching the kids after dinner, so that she could hit the gym.

This meant Cindy had to give up control to return from the gym and see the twins still awake, or Hayley wearing strange outfits. Ben, like many dads, did things far, far differently than his wife. But by getting a break from the kids, Cindy could relax and admit that she'd been a control freak with parenting and the house in general.

It took over a year, but Cindy was able to lose almost all the baby weight and get back in shape, not like when they were first married, but really fit for having had three kids. Ben's compliments and obvious pride in her during the process helped keep this positive momentum going.

Cindy and Ben also got some alone time by going out Friday and Saturday nights. Without the constant distraction of their kids, they again began to feel more romantic toward one another.

This issue could easily have torn Cindy and Ben apart, but they were smart and worked through it.

The most important part of their story is this: Ben apologized, vowed to make changes and carried out his promises, and this in turn inspired Cindy to make positive changes as well. They were both willing to compromise and to be more flexible.

What are some ways a couple can remain close as their lives transition over the course of many years?

Here are just a few:

First, let's look at the situation of a husband or wife pursuing a new hobby. Perhaps this is something they've always loved, but had to keep on the back burner for years. What are some ways their spouse can support them? Here are a few:

1.  They respect the fact that their partner will evolve over time and may develop new interests.

2.  Tangible actions on their part demonstrate that they truly support their spouse's new endeavour.

3.  They defend their spouse if naysayers attempt to minimize the new hobby, activity or "passion."

Dan and Michelle had been married for nearly 25 years when she "suddenly" became interested in the theatre, enrolling in acting classes twice a week at a junior college.

Dan joked to friends that this was her midlife crisis because their youngest daughter had just left for college. Michelle had always loved acting and the theatre, but her parents had discouraged her from pursuing this as a career, so she'd become a therapist instead.

Signing up for the acting class made Michelle feel her childhood dream was not dead.

Although Dan's entertainment choices generally ran to Vin Diesel movies and riding his motorcycle, he totally supported and encouraged his wife in this new interest. He insisted on driving her to and from her evening classes because the junior college was in a somewhat shady part of town.

When Michelle's mother, who had never supported her in anything, predictably made fun of this new hobby, Dan staunchly defended his wife. He told his mother-in-law he was very proud of Michelle for what she was doing.

Several years elapsed, during which time Michelle displayed real talent for the stage. She received roles in local productions and some as far away as Chicago (this couple lived in Southern Illinois). Dan told Michelle he loved that she was pursuing her dream. Most importantly, he took concrete steps to display this support. He drove her to rehearsals, attended all her performances, and rehearsed her lines with her, even for plays like "Hamlet" and "Macbeth."

Another way to keep a strong connection throughout life's changes is to keep the relationship romantic. This can be with little notes, candy, flowers, you name it. Victoria, one of our success story wives, fixes special lunches for her husband Joe when he goes to work. I buy Snickers bars and peanut M&M's for Robert because they are his favorites, and he buys me flowers. One of our success husbands Bill brings his wife Mary coffee each morning. Susan, one of our success story wives, could easily receive three Michelin stars for her cooking. Susan's husband John is unfailingly appreciative of her efforts. Little notes to your spouse are a nice touch as well.

Another way to stay united throughout change is through compliments; perhaps how nice he looks in his tropical shirt, how pretty she looks in her dress, how great a job he's doing on the rose bushes, how fantastic her pasta dinner was.

If you've fallen into the habit of rarely complimenting your spouse and don't display much appreciation for them, when you first begin doing this, they may be quite stunned. They may actually look at you in utter shock. They probably think you are an alien. But keep the nice comments going, and it will pay off.

## Communication

I must warn you... this section is simply scandalous! It goes against the grain of so much popular marital advice.

Let's begin by saying: if someone is great at communicating *their* feelings and *their* needs and even is an excellent listener, but still treats their partner like crap (pardon the expression), the relationship will still suck.

I recall a college pal Sharon. Sharon was exceptionally bright; so far ahead of her time. Quite unusual for that era, she'd already spent several years in therapy by the time we graduated college. Sharon was incredibly articulate and an absolutely remarkable listener. She gave you her full attention and made you feel so understood; it was wonderful talking with her.

If communication were a cruise ship, Sharon would have been the Captain, sitting securely at the helm.

However, Sharon was also that friend who would ditch plans with you absolutely last minute in favor of a date with some creepy guy. She would conveniently forget about your birthday celebration if anything else (usually a date with some *other* crummy guy) came up, even last-minute.

Sharon always had elaborate excuses for why she didn't buy a birthday gift for her own sister, or couldn't pay back the money she'd borrowed from you *last year*. She frequently complained how broke she was, so that you'd treat her to lunch, but then she'd never reciprocate. Sharon always ordered expensive wine when eating out, but then lacked cash for a decent tip for the waitress.

Everyone raves about communication being so important to a relationship. It's great, no doubt about it. But if other good qualities are absent, communication will not compensate. If someone communicates beautifully but is selfish, rather like our poster child Sharon, the relationship will still be poor as a church mouse.

Now, if you're basically a good person, treat your spouse well, and wish to better your relationship, certainly, there's nothing wrong with improving your communication skills.

It's helpful to break habits such as hogging the conversation or interrupting.

Due to structural differences, communication between the sexes can often be challenging.

Let's give a few examples, based upon complaints heard from both men and women. One challenge is that women like to relay information and they love to vent. Typically, when a woman is really upset over a situation, she tends to repeat herself, perhaps over and over. For many women, it's very helpful to rehash... it actually eases the stress of the situation. Quite like a pressure cooker, it lets off steam.

When upset, many women just want to vent. They *need* to vent. They may also wish to discuss different angles, and various possibilities why the upsetting situation occurred. This actually is very therapeutic for them.

Frequently, given the same set of circumstances, men complain once or possibly twice, and then it's a wrap; they're done. At that point, further discussion annoys them or makes the situation more stressful. They're done discussing it; now they want to drop it.

I recall a stressful experience some years ago. My devious little co-worker at US Airways — let's just call her Jill — promised to cover my shift Thanksgiving Day.

Employees were required to sign a book if they covered someone's shift. Jill pocketed the cash incentive I gave her, and we signed the book.

Three days before Thanksgiving, HR contacted me. Apparently, little rascal Jill had signed up to work for me after promising someone else first and had likely pocketed their cash as well. HR said Jill was in scorching water, but nonetheless, I was still "on the hook" to work Thanksgiving Day.

HR added that my manager might override this, but wouldn't be in the office until the following day. So, it was a stressful limbo situation. That night, as you can imagine, I was extremely upset, furious with Jill, stressed out – after all, we were expected at my in-laws' in Los Angeles Thanksgiving Day.

My two best friends at this job were Stuart and Belinda. I called Stuart first, and he was very upset on my behalf. He agreed it was crummy and offered some possible solutions. Stuart was very helpful and sympathetic, but the conversation lasted perhaps ten minutes, tops.

Then I phoned Belinda. We spoke for a deeply satisfying hour and fifteen minutes.

At the time, Andrea was small; Robert gave her a bath and got her ready for bed. He left me alone because he knew I was "in therapy." Also,

Robert wisely realized that dealing with a lively toddler was far easier than listening to me re-hash the story over and over and over and over.

But Belinda didn't see it that way. She and I talked about every possible motivation Jill had, every potential solution, including if I just refused to show up for work. It was an immensely satisfying conversation.

It wasn't that Stuart was unsympathetic... he was actually very helpful. But like most males, he didn't see a reason to go on and on about it.

Most men generally have little interest in hearing their wives tell them repeatedly about an upsetting scenario. Instead, men are programmed to fix things. They want to help, so perhaps they offer advice or a solution. They truly believe they're being helpful, so then are genuinely surprised when their wife becomes annoyed. This can result in much frustration for a married couple.

Now, of course, we're generalizing. Not all men and women are like this, but many, many are.

Rebecca and Phil had been married for 12 years. Rebecca liked to vent and didn't want advice or solutions. Phil loved offering recommendations and adored fixing things.

Frequently, Rebecca complained about her boss, Angela. Angela was disorganized and forgot deadlines; this drove the orderly Rebecca chock full o'nuts. Consequently, Rebecca had to contend with frequent last-minute emergencies. She sometimes arrived home angry and frustrated, and needing to vent.

But in many ways, Angela was a wonderful boss, extremely generous with raises and in approving vacation time. Rebecca never used sick or vacation time when attending school events with her children. Rebecca loved her job and liked working for Angela ... most of the time.

But, on those occasions when Angela drove her "bananas foster," perhaps twice a month, Rebecca just wanted to vent.

When she grumbled to her best friend Marie, Rebecca came away deeply satisfied. Marie sympathized, agreed that Angela could be a nightmare, but didn't offer solutions. She mainly just listened, which was all

Rebecca really wanted. Rebecca knew nothing would change her work situation and she definitely didn't want to quit her job. She was well aware another boss might be better organized, but also a "tight-ass" with raises or vacation time. So Rebecca just needed to complain and to be heard. She didn't want advice or a solution.

When Rebecca complained to Phil he always had suggestions for how she could fix the problem. He frequently offered advice, usually that she go over Angela's head to the company owner.

Rebecca ended up annoyed and disappointed. Phil was also frustrated, as he saw his helpful advice ignored by his wife. He took it personally when his suggestions were disregarded. These two ended up exasperated with one another, and often argued, each feeling frustrated and misunderstood.

One solution could be for Rebecca to limit the amount of information she shared with her husband. Many wives choose to do this. There's less friction this way, but also perhaps less closeness as a couple.

So, how could they resolve this? Rebecca can be upfront with Phil by stating clearly she just needs to vent about something. "I just want to unload and don't need a solution," she can say. One of our success story wives, Lynn, does this with her husband Larry. Sometimes she tells him simply, "I just need you to listen."

If Phil can learn to just listen, and not give suggestions unless asked, then Rebecca will open up to him more. If he persists in the same behavior of giving heavy-handed advice, she may then just vent to her girlfriends instead.

With same-sex couples, there are still often major differences in the way each partner communicates. But same-sex couples who were interviewed said the differences are less pronounced, due to the fact that both partners inherently communicate in a somewhat more similar manner.

So, now we get to the point of this section, which, as we've stated before, flies brazenly in the face of most standard marital wisdom.

Here it is: drumroll please... for many couples, even those who get along quite well, verbal communication may never actually be all that great.

Therefore, let's ask one question. Truthfully, is good communication the reason couples fall in love and get married in the first place?

In most cases, the answer is a resounding *no*! The number one reason most individuals claim they got married was because they were so in love. They wanted to spend the rest of their lives with this one incredible human being. They found them *irresistible* and *could not live without them*. This wasn't necessarily due to any fantastic communication skills... just adoration, usually combined with a fair amount of lust.

Sadly, though, as the years pass, these same folks frequently become irritated, bored, disillusioned or just plain sick and tired of their marriage partner. A thousand little disappointments, annoyances, hurt feelings, and misunderstandings pile up over time.

That glorious feeling of being "in love" went down the tubes long ago. At this point, maybe six or seven years into the marriage, they don't even like each other anymore.

They realize their marriage is in trouble. Maybe there's already been talk of divorce. Perhaps they've already separated. But, they want to save their marriage, so what do they do?

These same folks are then led by media and popular opinion to believe that most of all, they must forge better communication and then presto! This will save their ailing marriage.

Folks, we're being fed a line of BS here! If communication was the main tool to solve this problem, if it was the secret, would the divorce rate continue to be as incredibly sky-high as it is today?

Here's how it often works. When couples who are not "jiving" go see a marriage therapist, the stated goal frequently is to improve communication skills. Often, this is a major focus. And no one questions this! It's like the Holy Grail.

"Couples need to communicate, *just communicate*, bla bla bla"— we've all heard it a million times.

By the way, I'm not knocking couples therapy. It's worked very well for many folks, and I give numerous examples in this book. There are many aspects to therapy, besides improved communication skills. For many couples, seeing a knowledgeable, caring professional can be a lifesaver.

But unfortunately, many couples spend a tremendous amount of time and money on marriage therapy, but still end up divorced.

Let's picture a scenario where a couple wishing to keep their marriage intact works diligently to boost their communication skills. After a while, there's definite improvement. Perhaps they've both become better listeners. Rather than yelling or interrupting, they've learned to speak calmly and to express themselves more clearly and respectfully. But nonetheless, to their dismay, they still feel crappy about each other. Maybe one partner still wants to divorce.

Why is this? Let's recap. This couple spent time and effort on therapy. They learned how to communicate well, but nonetheless, they still don't like one another. They don't enjoy each other's company. There is no pizzazz in their marriage.

After all that work, and all that money spent, so many couples split up anyways. The divorce rate is about 50 percent, as of this writing for first marriages, and 60-70 percent for second marriages.

Ok... now let's present an unconventional strategy. Get ready... this goes against everything you've been told.

Here it is: drumroll and cymbals: rather than focusing on communication, do one thing instead. Here's what it is: work very, very hard to create a way for you and your partner to once again find each other irresistible.

I will repeat this: create a way for you and your partner to once again find each other irresistible.

If it's been months, years or even decades since you experienced that wonderful feeling, this won't change overnight. Patience, by the way, is a topic coming up later.

If two people haven't felt "in love" or even "in like" with one another for years, it will take some time to achieve this.

But, it *absolutely* can be done.

Animosity, dislike, disdain and resentment can eventually give way to tolerance, then harmony, affection, friendship and then ideally, back to love.

Let's take another look at John and Loretta. These two were briefly discussed in the section about being as nice to your spouse as the folks in your office.

Currently, John and Loretta are sick of each other, tired of being married, and frankly, can't stand the sight of one another.

But if you went back not so many years, these two were very much in love. They adored spending time together, they laughed together, found one another to be wonderful, charming and most of all, irresistible.

But the years have not been kind to John and Loretta. Many little grievances, disappointments and misunderstandings have built up over the years just like muck. So now, not only do they not care about pleasing one another, they actually both take an almost sadistic delight in angering and disgusting one another.

John and Loretta are parents to two lovely young daughters, Ashley and Jordan, ages seven and nine. They're all in good health, they live in a beautiful house, and both John and Loretta have excellent jobs. To all outward appearances, these folks have everything.

But, it's no exaggeration to say John and Loretta find one another repulsive. They're very likely headed toward divorce. When couples see a marriage therapist at this stage, sometimes it's just too late. Or, if they don't actually divorce, due to religion, inertia or family pressure, they then spend the rest of their lives being miserable.

As of this telling, John and Loretta have been married for 11 years. Both have separately confided in friends that the only thing still keeping them together is Ashley and Jordan. John recently told his co-worker Judy that he wanted to stick it out until Ashley went off to college, but now doesn't think he can bear to live with Loretta until then.

John and Loretta fight constantly. Their relationship was still decent about six years ago, much worse four years ago, and the last two years they've descended into outright animosity. They barely speak unless it's to argue, and are like two angry strangers living in the same house.

Surprisingly, there was no one huge event, like financial disaster or infidelity which drew this couple apart. Instead, it was just the cumulative effect of many little offenses and disappointments over the years.

Who even knows what the initial event was? At this point, does it even matter? John and Loretta simply gave up on being nice to one another.

Here are just a few examples of how they interact, and please pardon any crudeness:

John passes gas frequently in front of Loretta, not just in the bedroom or bathroom, but all over the house. She tells him it's disgusting and he just shrugs.

Every night, Loretta wears ratty old nightgowns to bed. John has complained about this, but she responds that since they almost never have sex anymore, who cares what she wears to bed?

Loretta spills makeup on the bathroom counter and floor and leaves it there, even though she's aware that John hates this.

John used to buy Loretta flowers or candy "just because," but hasn't done so in at least three years.

Six weeks ago, John bought a beautiful new Ford F-450 truck. He's meticulous about his vehicles, keeping them in pristine condition. Loretta used to respect this: no more. Last month, she spilled pink glitter nail polish on the grey cloth seat, then a week later, a Starbucks upside-down caramel macchiato on the other seat. She mopped it up, but the upholstery was still stained. She eats potato chips in his truck and the crumbs get stuck on the seats. She doesn't fill up on gas even when she nearly empties the tank. John always parks in an end spot to avoid door "dings." Loretta parks any old place, and now there are already several "dings" on the side doors.

When John drives, he usually gets lost and won't ask for directions. He doesn't pay attention, so he gallivants right past his freeway exits. When

Loretta is with him, she yells and they then argue the rest of the way. On family road trips, Ashley and Jordan keep their ear-buds on to drown out the noise of their parents' arguing.

Loretta hangs around when John talks on the phone with his brother. She interjects comments in the background, although he's told her repeatedly not to.

John absolutely detests cigarettes. Loretta had quit smoking before they were married, but began smoking again last year. She sneaks cigarettes, but John knows their daughters have caught on. He feels deceived because she'd promised him before they married that she'd never smoke again.

John frequently works late; he's always done this. But he no longer calls or texts Loretta to say he'll be late. When she texts to ask when he'll be home, John takes his sweet old time replying. Loretta knows he always has his phone on him, so she realizes it's deliberate.

Rather than confiding in a girlfriend when she's upset with John, Loretta vents to Ashley and Jordan. Like many young girls, the two are very protective of their mom. Therefore, their relationship with John, formerly always excellent, has become increasingly strained. Both girls had always gone with him on special outings to the movies or the arcade, but for two years now, have refused his invitations.

Ashley and Jordan have become world-class experts at manipulating both parents. Since John and Loretta are not in alliance, are in fact barely speaking, if one parent says "no," the girls can usually get the other one to say "yes."

John frequently rolls his eyes when Loretta talks. He sighs heavily when she's speaking, as though terribly bored, often doing this in front of their daughters.

So, what's the main problem with this couple? There are so many, where does one even begin? But it's clear what's largely missing on both sides is respect. Each partner deliberately strives to disgust and irritate the other. Both have abandoned all attempts to be attractive or accommodating.

Sadly, in the process of trying to outdo and one-up each other, John and Loretta have created what can only be described as a hostile living environment for their two young daughters.

I've interjected comedy throughout this book, but it's hard to find humor in this situation. If Ashley and Jordan were able, they would run straight to HR to tattle on their folks. John and Loretta would receive verbal warnings, then written warnings, and perhaps after 60 days, if no improvement, get fired as parents. The sad part is that both of these folks love their daughters and aren't deliberately trying to hurt them.

John and Loretta are an extreme example, no denying it. But let's not forget, all the tales in this book illustrate actual stories heard from co-workers, friends or acquaintances. The tale of John and Loretta is a mingling of two actual couples; one couple is now divorced, but the other couple turned their relationship around and stayed together.

John and Loretta are both immensely popular at their respective jobs. Each has sympathetic co-workers who only hear their side of the story.

When a married couple has reached a "John and Loretta" level of malfunction, the standard path is to split up. One rationalization is that kids shouldn't live in that toxic environment. When children are little they'll often beg their folks to stay together, but as they grow older, they may tell their parents, "Just get a divorce."

One of our success story couples, Juliette and Daniel, married when she was just a little cupcake age 16, and he was only 18. As she recalls, they began married life with poor communication skills. In their early years when they disagreed, their interactions were not positive. However, at just 16, Juliette totally transformed her way of interacting with her husband. She trained herself to be considerate, kind, a good listener and capable of compromise. When upset, she taught herself to wait before she spoke, and to choose her words carefully.

So, if a 16-year-old can do this, we older folks who come across poorly when upset, and believe you me, I'm included in this group – can definitely, absolutely, positively improve. Frankly, it takes a whole lot of humility.

Another success story couple, Brad and Karen, always find a way to meet in the middle. If annoyed with one another, both still treat the other kindly and with patience. This couple raised four children and still are very happy together. When asked her secret, Karen said to always be considerate and always respect what is important to your partner.

For example, John's vehicle is very important to him. Even if Loretta doesn't care about her own car, she needs to have respect for his. John, in turn, needs to respect her when she's speaking and not roll his eyes and act annoyed, whether or not their daughters are around.

Rather than focusing on communication, John and Loretta must get that "irresistible" part back. There's a long, dusty, gravelly road ahead. It's full of potholes ... maybe even sinkholes at this point.

So, where do they start? Well, for lack of a better term, let's just say they both need to stop acting like such total assholes. Pardon my French! Pardon a moi! For starters, stop thumbing their noses at one another. Lots of couples do this and it's an evil habit.

Here's the incredibly sad fact: deep down, John and Loretta still love one another very much. The love is still there; it's just buried under layers and layers of ugly muck.

Specifically, what are some things they can do?

First off, John is not a five-year-old boy. Barring any horrendous intestinal issues, he can "hold it in" like the rest of us, and pass that wind in the privacy of his bathroom. In this way, not only Loretta, but also his young daughters won't be "treated" to his gnarly gas attacks.

Loretta can visit Victoria's Secret for a few cute nighties. If cost is an issue, there are always adorable things at Target or Kohl's. Loretta can clean up any makeup she spills on the bathroom counter and floor. This will also set a nice example for Ashley and Jordan, so their college roommates won't detest them someday.

John can stop on his way home from work just once a week to buy a nice bouquet of flowers for Loretta. If she's like 99 percent of women, she will be very pleased. It will also be nice for Ashley and Jordan to see their mom getting spoiled for a change.

For those who say flowers are crazy expensive, just compare the average cost of a modest bouquet, about $10 -$15 these days, to $330 *per hour*, the standard fee for a divorce attorney in our golden state of California.

Now, it ain't much cheaper in the middle: Illinois divorce lawyers charge at least $260 per hour.

Loretta has been treating John's truck like *garbage,* and this isn't exactly enriching their relationship. Next time she borrows his truck, since she does tend to make crumbs, maybe she should leave the sour cream and chive Pringles at home. If she usually spills her coffee, she can restrict herself to a bottle of water. This won't kill her: Starbucks is expensive and they'll soon be paying for two college tuitions.

When Loretta drives his truck, she should stop at the gas station, fill the tank and wash the windshields. She could also have his truck washed and detailed. If there's still that nail polish stain on the seat, maybe she can get it cleaned or the upholstery replaced. While she's at it, perhaps she can get rid of those dings on the side doors. Otherwise, every time John drives his truck, he'll be reminded of Loretta, and not in a good way.

John's truck exemplifies how the standard advice of communication would bring little success. Let's just say Loretta tried to communicate with words to John that she felt badly for trashing his truck. Chances are excellent this would just result in a shouting match.

In situations like this, actions have more success than words, no matter how eloquently those words are delivered.

Next, how about John pays better attention when he drives? But since he's told Loretta he hates when she's a "Back Seat Betsy," she might just let him miss his freeway exits. Perhaps then he'll begin to pay more attention where he's going.

Hey ladies, I know this one is super tough. It's excruciating to just sit there and not helpfully interject as your husband blissfully scampers past your freeway exit. We never said any of this was easy! And I must practice what I preach. I've gotten better, but hey, Robert didn't make up that term "Back Seat Betsy" for nothin'!

When John's on the phone with his brother or anyone else, Loretta should go into another room of their house and "bug off," for lack of a better term.

John made it very clear before they married he wouldn't live with a smoker. His mom had suffered from emphysema, so for Loretta to pick up smoking now is pretty crass. Ashley and Jordan are no "stupnacles," and getting too old for Loretta to fool. Loretta might ask herself: does she really enjoy the cigarettes, or are they just a spectacular way to say "Screw you, you bastard" to John?

John usually knows by early afternoon if he'll need to work late that same evening. Therefore, by texting Loretta to say he'll be home late for dinner, this prevents inconvenience for her. Perhaps if he were more considerate this way, she'd again make some of his favorite dinners, just like she used to.

So, esteemed reader, does any of what you're reading sounds hideously familiar? Has your marriage descended to a murky depth similar to John and Loretta's? What if it's sunk so low, it's lurking in the corner of the Freddy Krueger boiler room? What if you can just barely see a fashionably striped red and green sweater out of the corner of your eye?

If so, what, for the love of God, do you do now?

First off, please don't wait for your spouse to change. You could be sitting around until you're old and prune-faced.

Okay, here goes: immediately start being 100 percent nicer and don't keep score. Live in hope that if your partner sees *you* making positive changes, they'll also begin doing the same.

Depending upon the level of dysfunction in your marriage, when you first begin playing nice, your spouse may be shocked and suspicious. They may even look at you like you're an alien. Ha! It wasn't so long ago we first read about aliens!

Do not, I repeat, do not let this discourage you! It can take awhile for things to get better. But, in the meantime, even miniscule improvements are one move in the right direction, and one step away from expensive and emotionally draining divorce court.

Listed below are some suggestions to give an angry, blah or luke-warm relationship a caffeinated jolt of invigorating and hopefully romantic adrenaline.

1.  Really *really* listen to your spouse when they're speaking. By the way, it likely won't be about anything "deep." He could be chatting about a car show on TV, or she might be dishing about her friend Margie's latest lipo disaster.

2.  Ask questions. Be interested in what your partner's talking about. You probably will have to fake it sometimes... hey, we get it. But give it the old college try! Act like you're fascinated, even if he's warbling for the 9th time how Mitch down the street got a new Toyota truck, the V8, the tires, the rims, etc. Pretend you're riveted, even as she's droning on for the 7th time about that bossy mom with big blonde helmet hair at your toddler's day-care.

3.  When we say "7th time," this brings up a painful truth: we *all* repeat ourselves. We *all* do. None of us is above this. *Queen Elizabeth* was probably guilty from time to time. Maybe Prince Phillip didn't even care two figs what the royal corgis did that day. But for those two to last for so many years, you know for certain Prince Phillip faked it. So, even if you're secretly bored out of your everlasting gourd, it's not gonna kill you to listen.

4.  When you're out with your spouse for dinner and a movie, even if you've been together forever, pretend you're on a date. Dress nice, wear makeup, perfume, cologne for the guys...put on a little ritz. Bring out the pizzazz! Refrain from looking at your cell phone when your partner is talking, even if they're driving

and you're a passenger in the car. We know... this is the hardest part. "I have to see if my boss got that report I emailed him!" you protest. Well, okay, of course there are exceptions like your boss or your kids' day-care. Facebook, Instagram, Twitter, Tik Tok, texting friends are not, we repeat, not exceptions.

5.  Fix your partner's favorite meal, or take him or her to a nice restaurant that *he or she* likes best. Bonus points if the meal is complicated and takes extra time to prepare. Similarly, if the restaurant is far from home, which entails driving out of your way, your partner will notice the extra effort.

6.  Every day, say "thank you" and "please." Compliment your spouse's cooking, or the nice job they did weeding the flower beds. Thank them for stopping off at the market after work. Super important: don't make them "fish" for compliments. For example, if your spouse makes a nice dinner, say it's delicious before they ask you how you like it.

7.  Answer your spouse positively, politely, and don't brush them off when they're speaking. Pretend your spouse is the most important co-worker you've ever had. If folks were only as charming to their spouses as their office colleagues, fewer divorce attorneys could gallivant around town in those Mercedes Benzes with the windshield wipers on the headlights.

8.  Buy your spouse flowers, gifts and candy. Even the slimmest, most disciplined women love receiving candy. They might eat just one-half piece per month, but they will still adore it.

9.  Men love flowers, incidentally! This has been proven scientifically. They adore sunflowers and daisies. Even real "macho" guys do. They're especially pleased and surprised, because they rarely, if ever, receive them. They may act all nonchalant, but they love this nonetheless. Please trust me on this one.

10. Surprise your spouse with tickets to a play, movie, car race, or concert...something you know *they* will really love. Bonus points if your spouse knows it's an event which, left to your own devices, you definitely would have skipped.

Then, make it a point to have a *glorious* time, no matter what!

On the outing, the number one rule: don't complain ab*out any-thing*. This may take an absolutely herculean effort, plus nerves of tensile steel. Ladies, stay cool, even if the weather's 95 degrees with 99 percent humidity at the car races. Smile graciously and say "no problemo" when Bubba in the bleachers above you spills half his Bud Light smack dab into your hair. Men, find a way to thoroughly enjoy that "chick flick." Search for something about the movie to compliment, even if it's just the previews. Ignore Susie in the row behind you as she sobs loudly during the barely sad parts, kicking your chair in her desperate grief.

11. Make more of an effort with your clothes, hair and appearance, like you did when you were dating, or newly married.

12. Find new ways to connect with your spouse. Perhaps discover a new hiking trail, a new favorite restaurant, a Netflix show that you both love, or a new hobby. If your kids are grown, you can nimbly fill that empty nest. These days it won't take you nine months! In one brief Saturday afternoon, you can adopt a dog, cat, horse, bunny, or llama together.

13. If you don't enjoy the same hobbies as your spouse, don't force it. Many happily married couples have *zero* hobbies or inter-ests in common. But here's the key: they support one another's activities even if they don't love those things themselves. Go camping occasionally, even if you don't enjoy it too much, but don't feel like you must drag yourself there constantly.

14. Book a trip someplace your spouse has always wanted to go. If you do this as a surprise, it will be even better, unless your spouse dislikes surprises.

15. Be extra nice to your spouse's friend, the annoying one, the one you kinda can't stand, because unfortunately, that friend is sacred to your spouse.

Most of these tips involve taking action as opposed to communication. Try some and see what results you get. You may be pleasantly surprised when your spouse begins making more of an effort as well. If they seem oblivious, well, soldier on! At some point they may come out of their trance.

Let's view a challenging situation: being nice to your spouse's obnoxious friend. No doubt about it, this is even tougher than that beef jerky you bought at the gas station on the 5 freeway out in the middle of nowhere at 2 a.m. in Coalinga, California.

Victoria and Brandon have been married for nine years and like each others' friends, with one glaring exception.

Brandon's best buddy Ken is loud and tells crass jokes. He frequently makes offensive comments about women. Ken himself is out of shape, but still wonders aloud why every woman doesn't drop a little weight or somehow improve her looks. He once pointed at Victoria's stomach two months after she'd given birth, and asked if she'd been skipping the gym. When Ken met Victoria's friend Alice, who regrettably does have a rather long face, he later observed that Alice was spit and image to Ciao Bella, his prize Thoroughbred racehorse.

Victoria detests Ken, but some folks find him funny and charming. Additionally, Brandon and Ken have been best friends since 8th grade. Not just good friends... best friends. Brandon knows Ken can be offensive, but he loves him nonetheless. When the two get together, Brandon can relive his teenage years. The two ditched high school together, roomed together in college, then backpacked for six months throughout Europe.

Fortunately, Victoria sees Ken only infrequently, as she and Brandon live in Cleveland and Ken resides in Florida. Brandon flies to Florida for fishing trips twice a year and Ken visits Cleveland a few times a year. Ken owns a very successful business, so he makes his own schedule.

So, let's just say Victoria is encouraged to honestly communicate with her husband. What good would it do for her to convey her utter distaste and disdain for Ken? Brandon loves his friend... Ken is his brother. In the past, Victoria and Brandon have had huge arguments over Ken.

A better alternative, though deeply challenging, would be for Victoria to find something positive to say.

As it so happens, Ken does possess some excellent qualities. He's very well-off financially and (we all know this isn't a frequent combination) extremely generous. He sends fabulous birthday and Christmas checks to Brandon and Victoria's two daughters every year, and has treated Brandon and Victoria to several vacations. When Brandon's parents moved to Florida, Ken helped with many of the arrangements, financial and otherwise.

So, next time Brandon begins packing for a fishing trip with Ken, instead of making a snarky comment, how about Victoria gives Brandon a nice gift for Ken, and keeps her opinions to herself. Brandon will be pleasantly surprised... and no unnecessary communication will have been made. (By "unnecessary communication," I mean that it accomplishes *nada*.)

If she needs to, Victoria can always vent to a girlfriend.

When Ken visits, he stays at a hotel or occasionally stays at their house. Victoria can make the best of it, as it's just for a few days, but she doesn't have to tolerate rude comments. She's an adult and entitled to speak up. The next time Ken makes a tactless comment, perhaps about one of her girlfriends, Victoria should speak up.

Speaking up in the moment isn't easy, but it's a skill that makes you feel like a real grown-up. As one gets older, it's wonderful to become more thick-skinned and learn to speak up to someone disrespectful or rude. By the way, you can always add just a dash of Tabasco, aka humor.

If it's too stressful for Susie when Ken visits, she can always stay at a friend's or her sister's house. Again, it's just a few days, twice a year. Her two daughters adore Ken, who never had children of his own, and he has always been unfailingly kind and respectful to them both.

So, the moral of this story is: some thoughts don't need to be relayed. You may think you're expressing yourself, but it just sounds like criticism to your partner. If your spouse is a mediocre cook, terrible dancer, misses the subtler points of conversation, or has an annoying hyena laugh, chances are good, it's always been this way, and ain't gonna change, no matter what you say.

Or, if your partner has a friend or family member you can't stand, but whom they adore, find a way to see this individual as infrequently as possible, and refrain from commenting. Your spouse will be pathetically grateful.

To wrap this up, sometimes communication just makes your spouse feel lousy and not in alignment with you, which leads us to our next sub-category ... competition.

## Competition

Competition, ah yes. Men are by their very nature extremely competitive. Women certainly can be as well, but with men, it's literally programmed into their hard drives.

Competitiveness can be a great thing in business, sports, or car racing, but not so hot in a marriage.

When a husband and wife compete, it's kind of like a contest. One's a winner and the other loses.

Although in kids' sports this isn't really true anymore, is it? Nowadays doesn't every kid get some kind of little trophy, even when they totally suck?

When a couple competes, rather than supporting one another, they try to outdo each other. This is often seen with "power couples," where both are very successful in their careers. Each is accustomed to being on top; while this is great in business, it spells doom for a marriage.

Kate and Mickey were both extremely successful in their respective careers. He was a property manager and she was a realtor. Robert and I double-dated with them in Los Angeles while they were still married (they eventually divorced). At the time, they were three years into their marriage. Both were extremely outgoing, charismatic and successful type A's. All these are fantastic qualities.

Side note: I'm sure many of you reading this can relate: one of the casualties of being married a long time is losing couple friends to divorce. It's a real drag, no doubt about it.

Kate and Mickey's issue was this: both always wanted to be center stage. They always tried to "one-up" each other. If she told an entertaining story, he interrupted to tell an even better one. When he told a joke, she usually disparaged the joke.

Kate and Mickey succeeded in every other area of their lives, but could not make their marriage work. They were not in tandem or in cooperation, but in competition, and split up after six years of marriage.

Savannah couple Marguerite and Roger, married five years, had a similar problem, but a happy outcome. She was an attorney and he was a manager at a large corporation. Roger had a very good job, but worked a standard nine to five schedule. Marguerite, on the other hand, put in a minimum of 80 hours per week to meet the requirement for billable hours at her law firm.

Roger became resentful of her long hours. When Marguerite was promoted to junior partner, a huge accomplishment, he didn't seem that happy for her. When friends commented on her success, Roger either didn't answer, or joked that she was never at home.

They began to have many arguments where she told him she was tired of his lack of support. Their relationship began to go on the "skids."

However, fortunately, when Roger complained to his secretary Shirley, she didn't respond with sympathy, as his friends had.

Shirley candidly informed Roger that he seemed resentful of his wife's success, rather than being happy for her. She helpfully added that he was behaving badly and appeared envious of his own wife. To top it off, Shirley even suggested he get therapy to see why he was so insecure. Kudos to Shirley! Tellin' it like it is, sister!

At first, Roger was livid. He couldn't believe Shirley had actually told him he needed therapy. How insulting! The damn nerve of her!

But then he remembered that he and Shirley had worked together for many years, and she was 15 years his senior. Roger knew Shirley genuinely cared about him, and unlike most of the ass-kissers working under him, always "told it like it was." Five years earlier, Shirley had called him on the carpet for his alcohol consumption, and this had led him to quit drinking before it became a huge problem.

To his credit, though it was painful, Roger then did an honest self-assessment. He realized to his mortification that Shirley was correct. He wasn't happy for his wife; he was instead envious and resentful.

Roger then did a courageous thing: he went for individual counseling.

There he realized that he'd always been an overachiever in a vain attempt to impress his alcoholic mother and his disinterested father. Not only had it never worked, but both his parents had passed away before he'd resolved issues with them.

Roger had another epiphany: he was afraid of losing Marguerite if she became too successful. Once he truly comprehended this, he began to show her in numerous ways that he was proud of her hard work. He began cooking weeknights and doing nearly all of the housework. He frequently brought dinner by her office when she had to work straight through. He bragged about Marguerite to others and told her frequently that he was proud of her.

The dynamic between these two changed completely. They became a much more loving and unified couple. Rather than living in competition, they began to truly support one another. They also joined a weekend softball league where they could compete in a fun and healthy way.

Marguerite and Roger are still very happily married and are parents to two golden retrievers, Bella and Gracie.

So, what if you and your spouse frequently try to "one-up" each other? Perhaps this has gone on for years, or even decades? How do you change this toxic dynamic?

Sitting down with your spouse and talking about it might be helpful. On the other hand, it could also cause a big argument. Go easy on the delivery, because if you're both competitive by nature, chances are better than average you also argue readily.

Try coming right out and saying, "I think we compete with one another."

If your partner is not receptive, or denies this is a problem, maybe drop it for awhile and work on yourself first. Make it a point to encourage and support your partner. Celebrate their wins. Be truly happy for them. "Fake it 'til you make it," if you must. After awhile, your new habits should come naturally. Hopefully your partner will notice the difference, and their attitude will improve as well.

## Compromise

The subject of compromise deserves a very large section; one could write an entire book about this crucial topic. Compromise is the glue that holds everything together. Without at least some level of compromise, a relationship will have difficulty surviving, let alone flourishing.

We all know people who can't accommodate anyone else. Everything must be their way. Sadly, they're incapable of compromise. The last time we checked, there are two partners in a marriage. If only one always gets their way, the other may eventually want out, and who could really blame them?

An inability to compromise also manifests itself in the "know it all" syndrome; this person insists they're correct every time. They're never, ever wrong. No surprise then that this attitude is extremely wearing on their partner.

We've all heard the famous saying "Do you want to be right, or do you want to be happy?" An alternative version might be, "Do you want to be right, or do you want to stay married?"

A good exercise for couples is what Robert and I call the "happy compromise." Let's use the example of eating out. I love Asian food best, and Robert likes steak places best. He's come to love sushi over the years; we have a couple favorite places.

Here is how "happy compromise" works. Let's just say I'm in the mood for Thai food (Robert can take it or leave it). He wants a big steak, something like Black Angus or Outback Steakhouse. He's okay with Asian food to accommodate me, or I'm fine with a steak place to accommodate him.

But, there's another satisfying alternative. We both love Italian and Mexican food, so either of these is what we call our "happy compromise." Neither of us gets our first choice, but we both get something we're happy with.

The point of course being this: neither one gets their way every time. If one partner always insists on having their way, at some point they may find themselves single again and trolling online for dates.

Folks whose attitude is "my way or the highway" may one day find themselves sprawled out solo on the blacktop.

One character trait often seen with long-time singles (folks in their 40s who've never married) is they dislike compromise. This also may apply to those individuals who once were married, but have been single for many years. They're accustomed to thinking of their own preferences most of the time. If we notice this in a friend, how does this look to a boyfriend, girlfriend or prospective marriage partner?

Harrison only liked action, scary or horror films. His former girlfriend Beatrice was super easygoing. Very rarely, maybe only once every few months, she'd suggest to Harrison they go see a comedy. Each time his response was, "I am not interested in that movie." Notice that his sentence began with the word "I." Talk to Harrison a little longer and you'll also frequently hear, "Me, me, me."

Apparently, it never occurred to Harrison that someone else might have an actual preference. Beatrice, the most laid-back of girls, finally threw in the dish towel and Harrison reverted to being single. He'd had many girlfriends before Beatrice, but no lasting relationships. Harrison was very handsome and saw himself as quite a "catch." Therefore, he was perplexed his relationships were always so darn short-lived. It wasn't just the movies, by the way. Unfortunately, his selfishness extended to things such as restaurant choices. As Beatrice said later, the choice of movie or restaurant wasn't even that important to her. But when she truly realized the extent of his self-absorption and failure to compromise, this eventually turned her off, despite Harrison's six-pack, baby blue eyes and dazzling smile.

"I won't eat at that place, or about 20 others as well." Patricia had a kind heart and some very fine qualities, but was super set in her ways. She'd been divorced for about 15 years. She frequently mentioned she'd love to remarry, and couldn't understand why, after just a few dates, guys stopped asking her out. Patricia was a great conversationalist, very intelligent and well-read. But she had difficulty compromising, and enjoyed complaining... a lot. Patricia made a big fuss about things that most of us jokingly refer to as "first-world problems."

For example, Patricia disliked dark meat chicken, so if a restaurant served this instead of white meat chicken, she would never, ever return to that restaurant. Never mind that her dining companion might really want to go there. Or here's a novel idea: how about Patricia go anyway, since it's not all about her, and order seafood instead? Her friends suggested this once when she was refusing to visit a particular Asian restaurant, but she wasn't interested. That particular establishment sat on a long, long list of places she wouldn't return to ever, so long as she herself should live.

It's not an issue about "Pollo Loco," or a particular genre of movie. It's the impression this person gives off that the world revolves around *them*. They've had their own way for so long they've forgotten how to compromise.

By the way, restaurant or movie choices are minor issues. But as any divorce attorney will attest, those teeny little matters build up year after year until "suddenly" one partner revolts and blows that pop stand. It's rarely ever sudden, by the way. It just takes a long time for some folks to finally get to the end of their tether. They then realize they're so fed up that even if change did occur at that point, it's too late. They're done.

If a couple is already married and realizes they can't agree on big issues, this may become almost insurmountable. The adoption issue, for example, is a crucial one to discuss before marriage; often there's no way to know in advance if there will be fertility issues.

Gena and Charles had been married for nine years. They were going through a very rough time because they didn't agree about adoption. They'd never discussed this before marriage. But in nine years, Gena had not been able to become pregnant. Fertility specialists could find no reason. Four very costly in-vitro fertilization procedures had failed. This had strained both their finances and their marriage. Charles was very disappointed, but made it clear he was not receptive to adoption.

Gena was in her late 30s and felt that her biological clock was running away fast. She wholeheartedly wanted to adopt, but Charles absolutely refused. There was no way for them to compromise on this gigantor issue.

To bring a little levity to this grim discussion, is anyone here old enough to remember the "Gigantor" cartoon from the 60s? "Gigantor the space aged robot, bigger than big, taller than tall, Gigantor the space aged robot!"

On the TV show "Grey's Anatomy" one of the characters said, "You can't exactly have half a kid." Therapy can sometimes be helpful with this type of dilemma.

A large issue can be deciding where to set down roots. One California couple, Frances and Vince, used a type of bartering system. Vince begged Frances to move to Mississippi to be near his family. Frances was reluctant, as she detested the weather. The deal this couple made was quite unique. Mississippi is closer to Europe, and cheaper than California. So, in an odd but creative bartering system, in exchange for putting up with the bugs and humidity, Frances visits Europe each and every year. Last year this couple visited Austria and Norway... not too shabby!

It must be said that the importance of compromise was mentioned repeatedly by nearly all of our success story couples at the end of this book.

## Compliments

Let's now revisit Cindy and Ben, previously mentioned in the "Change" section. As you may recall, Cindy was out of shape after having given birth to three children. Her self-esteem was low and she was embarrassed. When she began working out and eating healthy, Ben's obvious pride in her and his compliments made all the difference in their relationship. Cindy appreciated that he didn't wait until she'd reached her fitness goals before making positive comments.

It's a frequent complaint of both genders that their partners rarely say anything flattering to them. They'd done so in the past, but as the years elapsed, no more.

Most folks, even those who pretend not to, do enjoy hearing positive statements about their appearance, cooking, how they dealt with a nosy neighbor, the hard work they do at their job, and so forth.

Let's take Valerie. She's an exceptional cook... really amazing! Grateful tears gush down your face when you enjoy her wonderful meals. It's no exaggeration to say that Valerie could be a five-star chef. Yet her husband Bob never compliments her cooking. He used to, but he no longer bothers.

Apparently, Bob feels that scarfing down her gourmet meals is quite recognition enough for Valerie. At dinner parties, while guests rave over her fantastic dishes, he never contributes to the conversation. Valerie has begun to resent this. She used to enjoy cooking for Bob, but no longer. Over the years, she's stopped making much effort unless they have guests over, since those same guests make her feel appreciated.

A further note about compliments: if your partner has to go "fishing" for them, they ain't worth so very much, now are they? Valerie can manage to squeeze a half-assed compliment out of Bob if she asks, "How's the Beef Wellington, Bob?" Between mouthfuls, he finally grunts out just one word, "Great."

Bob, why so stingy with the compliments? Never forget that, left to your own devices, you'd be lucky to choke down Arby's, takeout, or TV dinners each and every night.

Why, why are so many of us miserly with compliments to our partners? Are we afraid they will become conceited and dump us? This is unlikely to happen; in fact, quite the opposite is true. Everyone can use a little build-up of their ego. We are referring to genuinely nice and positive comments about looks, intelligence, skills, or personality. We're definitely not talking about the fake, gushing, "Hollywood-style" compliments here. "You look so wonderful dahling!"

If life in general is going great, everybody's health is good, nobody's unemployed, there are no money worries, well, then it's easy to say nice things. It's *effortless.*

But when you're going through a rough patch individually or as a couple, positive statements might be difficult to rustle up. Maybe it's tough to think of "pats on the back" at this time, but it's especially imperative when things aren't going so swell. Maybe your wife got passed over for that big promotion at work, for the third time. This might be great timing for you to say some nice things to her that are completely unrelated to her career. Or, maybe your husband was suddenly laid off from his job of over 20 years. To add to the fun, you found out the same dang day your preteen Brandon needs braces and your nine-year-old Hannah needs a math tutor. The roof in your family room suddenly developed a small leak. This all happened yesterday, by the way.

Your husband had planned to stay at his job until retirement, but now must search for a new one in a depressed economy. Although he has lots of job skills and education, he's competing with younger candidates willing to work for less pay. He's feeling low and discouraged. Looking for a job when you've been laid off is the pits. Lord knows I've been there myself... three times.

Dear reader, if you've never been laid off from a job, I deeply envy you!

Anyways, let's say two weeks later your husband is dressed in his best suit and is getting ready to leave for a job interview. An admiring comment about how nice he looks will not only boost his confidence, but will make him feel supported. It doesn't have to be anything elaborate. It could just be something like he looks handsome and professional in his suit, and if you were the one interviewing him, you would hire him for sure. Or it could be acknowledging that he has a lot of skills and experience, and will "ace" the interview.

In addition, your spouse doesn't have to be going to a special occasion like a job interview for you to say something nice and positive.

Here are a few examples of complimentary statements you can make to your spouse. If you're seriously out of practice, these may help. Someday, when it becomes more comfortable, you can insert things you've thought of yourself. But this can be a start.

If it's been awhile, your partner may look at you with total bewilderment. However, once they get over their initial shock, they will likely be quite pleased.

Here are some examples of a little pat on the back:

"You look beautiful in that dress."

"You look so handsome in that suit."

"Thanks for fixing the kitchen sink. You're so smart."

"Honey, this dinner was fantastic. You're such a great cook.

"I'm so happy for you about your promotion at work! I am so dang proud of you."

Notice that you're taking the initiative in offering the compliment so that your spouse doesn't have to go "fishing" for it.

Here's one of the most powerful statements you can make: "I am so proud of you." It doesn't have to be about anything huge, by the way.

This brings us to a painful topic: many of us grew up with critical parents. We baby boomers were especially pressured to be that perfect son or daughter. It wasn't enough to be an A student: you had to be cute, popular and thin to boot. So, praise was usually connected to performance in school, and particularly for girls, performance in school and appearance.

I resolved this many years ago when I realized my parents had sometimes seemed critical because they loved me so much. They wanted me to be the best Linda I could be. But when your parents have such high expectations for you, it's a lot of pressure and can result in being hard on yourself as an adult.

Therefore, it feeds your soul when someone you love tells you they are proud of your kind heart, or how you give to homeless people, or that you help animals, that type of thing...not just your achievements.

Here are a few complimentary phrases. Notice they are about relatively minor things.

"This smoothie is fantastic, just delicious. Is there a banana in there?"

"Thanks for taking such good care of our dogs."

"That was so kind of you to help my uncle with that painting project."

"You look beautiful/pretty/lovely/handsome."

And an all-purpose favorite: "Great job honey!"

"I am so proud of you."

If some of these statements sound cheesy, that's okay. Create your own and use them frequently.

The point is this: when you give your spouse positive feedback, they will likely feel better about themselves. When people feel good about themselves, they are generally easier to live with. So, in a way you're really doing this for yourself...to make your own life run more smoothly.

Let's now address "third-party compliments." These can be a big boon to a relationship. Here's how they work: you compliment your partner to someone else whilst your partner is well within earshot. Bonus points if you act like you don't know your spouse is listening in.

Kids are perfect to enlist for this. For example: "Your daddy is so smart, he fixed the VCR (insert something like: he fixed the kitchen sink, he got an award at work, whatever)."

The point is to say something complimentary about your partner and have them overhear it, or hear about it later, second-hand.

One common theme amongst unhappily married men and women is they feel taken for granted. They don't feel appreciated. Stella works her butt off to get promoted at work and Mario barely comments; there are no celebratory flowers, gifts or dinner out for Stella. Jim spends all weekend weed-whacking their three acres and Stephanie says something like, "It's about time." When Jim finishes the job and comes into the house, dehydrated and weary, Stephanie is drinking a lovely iced tea, but doesn't think to offer him one.

So, when you receive little or no appreciation from your spouse, it stands to reason that you will begin to care less and less about pleasing them.

Something to avoid: the dreaded back-handed compliment. We all know folks who are geniuses at dishing these out. Their expertise is such that the compliments blended with insults fly out of their mouths so fast and smoothly you didn't even know what hit you. I kept my first horse, Terra, at a stables; my "frenemy" there could have won blue ribbons at the back-handed compliment. Let's just call her "Denise." Denise was witty and funny, and I didn't mind riding horses with her, because out on the trail, conversation is limited. But when we began to socialize outside of the stables I realized just how toxic she was. Her statements sounded positive at first, but were in actuality dreadful insults.

Even Denise's boyfriend Phillip could not escape her "back-handed" compliments. Robert and I met them for dinner one evening, and Phillip was wearing an attractive blue shirt. When I complimented the shirt, Denise found it necessary to add, "Phillip has terrible taste in clothes, so I picked it out for him."

When Robert and I bought our first house, Denise's observation was, "Oh, this is nice for such a small place." When she met my father, she said, "Wow, he's incredibly good-looking for an old guy." Needless to say, this friendship did not last long.

Why do folks like Denise fling out these creepy backhanded compliments, which in actuality are thinly veiled insults? The psychological explanation, no surprise, is that they feel badly about themselves. By throwing others off-kilter with toxic remarks, they gain a glorious sensation of power. It amuses them and fills them with momentary joy when they see the dismayed reactions generated by their comments. By putting others down, they receive an emotional payoff. Their cerebral cortex goes, "ding ding ding ding ding!"

What this really stems from, of course, is their low self-esteem. By putting others down, they're attempting to build themselves up. They may feel better temporarily, but in the long run, this won't improve their poor self-image.

Best advice: stay far, far away from people who give back-handed compliments. Avoid them like the plague, Covid and herpes all rolled into one Zig-Zag.

The mere mention of herpes brings to mind a radio interview from the early 80s with the glorious Billy Idol. The interviewer asked, "Billy, why did you choose the name 'Idol?'" Billy casually replied, "Well, you know, all these punk bands were picking names like VD and herpes, so I thought, 'oh I'd just go with Idol.'"

Now, if you should realize that you yourself engage in this toxic behavior of back-handed compliments, slap yourself silly and don't do it anymore. Otherwise, you'll continue to drive others away. And, if it's your spouse who's doing this, call him or her on it. Don't just put up with it, because it generally will worsen as the sorry years elapse.

So, to wrap up our original topic, because perhaps we've gotten a bit off course, do compliment your spouse frequently. In fact, go "hog wild," and make an approving statement to them three times a day for the next month. You'll be amazed at how beneficial this can be.

## Cooking

This subject deserves at least a brief mention, as it can become an issue for more than a few couples. Generally, one partner likes to cook more than the other, and perhaps is better at it as well. One possible solution could be for one partner to cook and then the other to clean up afterwards... this is how Robert and I do it. Eating out is a great solution, although of course it's more expensive.

Hey, you ladies out there: if you really hate to cook, don't "fake it" when dating. You may get stuck with it "from now to eternity!"

There is always the option of ordering take-out. Even if one partner does all the cooking, they ought to get a night off at least once or twice a week. We have this marvelous invention here in San Diego called "Taco Tuesday," which is inexpensive and massively popular. You can get great fish tacos for only about $4.00 each.

## Criticism

Well, now, this *is* a biggie. No matter how wonderful your spouse, there will be times you're just plain sick of them and can't help but view them in a critical manner. A long-time married pal Gwen phrased it so eloquently; please pardon the language. When you live with someone day in and day out, month after month, year after motherfucking year, many of their habits, speech patterns, even the way they clear their throat, can get on your nerves beyond any and all human comprehension.

The annoyance–o–meter can range from mildly irritating to completely and overwhelmingly obnoxious.

Sometimes the most random items can become a nightmare. One lovely autumn morning, New York City architect Diane was suddenly gripped by a terrifying realization. She discovered to her absolute horror, she could no longer tolerate for even one more day her husband Fred's ritual of standing and holding a bowl of ice cream whilst stuffing spoonfuls into his jaws as fast as humanly possible.

How had she gone all these years without noticing that Fred chewed his ice cream so quickly she could actually hear his mandibles grinding?

Thereafter, she prayed to God in heaven that for once, just once, Fred would actually sit down with that Goddamn bowl? But no, he *had to stand*.

"I wish he'd just go away," she'd mutter to herself whenever he stood in the middle of their den, cramming in the Ben & Jerry's. Oddly enough, for the entire first 12 years of their marriage, this habit didn't bother Diane in the least. But then, on a glorious October day, as the gold and maroon maple leaves wafted gently to the ground, precisely at the 12-year mark, presto! Fred's standing ice cream pose began to drive Diane slowly, inexorably, completely berserk.

Now, Fred is a prominent Manhattan criminal defense attorney who works at least 70 hours a week, so it's highly unlikely that leisurely ice cream eating is in the cards for him. Additionally, Fred does most things with great panache. And Diane is truly fond of this man. But we get it!

Anyone who's been married a long time totally gets it. It's entirely possible as well that Diane initially loved and even admired Fred's rapid-fire ice cream eating mode.

But, now, after 12 years of marriage, this is driving her right over the edge. Diane can't take it anymore. When she sees Fred clutching a bowl of Baskin-Robbins, her blood pressure shoots through the roof; she must excuse herself and quickly exit the room.

In all seriousness, it's so easy to fall into this trap of criticizing your spouse. This can be done verbally, directly, behind their back, or perhaps silently seething at everything they do. Incidentally, there's a special bonus section on "seethers" coming up soon. Yes, seethers!

They sound like this: seeeshhhss.

Of course you're going to criticize your spouse from time to time, as there's no denying they'll get on your nerves to the point of insanity, but do find a way to kind of limit it.

Unloading to a trusted friend can be an absolute lifesaver, but care must be exercised as to whom you select for this most coveted role. Ideally, they should be a sounding board, to listen and provide encouragement, and most of all, never go repeating to *anyone* the terrible things you tell them.

A good therapist is a captive audience, since after all you're paying them to be. Diane's therapist expertly helped her overcome her issues with Fred's ice cream-eating routine. Tragically, the therapist was so traumatized in the process that she is now unable to enjoy even one scoop of sorbet, let alone gelato.

My previous co-worker Kurt married his sweetheart Brenda a few years ago; both were children of divorce. Kurt worried that he and Brenda would one day split up as well. I told him when they returned from their honeymoon and the day-to-day grind set in, they would likely show some signs of incompatibility. I warned Kurt that this happens to 100 percent of couples, and to please complain to someone like me who's been married for a long time.

It's inevitable that your adored spouse will be super annoying at times. Let's repeat: *super* annoying. But if you find that criticizing them has become your only hobby, it's time to take up pickleball, tennis or golf.

You don't want the exact opposite of that saying, "No one is perfect... until you fall in love with them."

To watch a really critical spouse in action can be excruciating, as our next example shall demonstrate.

Several years ago, my good friend Gayle was on an airplane flight; seated across the aisle in first class was Spencer, a popular local TV weatherman from Gayle's hometown. Spencer is a cheerful, personable guy. He was accompanied by Joanne, his extremely thin, brittle, and nervous wife.

Now, Spencer is a gentleman who's not only beloved by his TV audience, but also by the citizens of his hometown for his inexhaustible charity work. He pulls down at least a million dollars a year between his job and various endorsements, plus he invests endless time and energy toward humanitarian projects.

Throughout the flight, Gayle and other passengers simply couldn't help but observe how horribly Spencer's wife was treating him.

She berated him the entire flight; takeoff, beverage cart, dinner, snack time, and landing included. Joanne didn't nap a wink during the long voyage; oh, no, this woman had real stamina. Instead, she hissed at Spencer in a loud stage whisper the whole time. Nearby passengers were treated to comments such as, "What are you eating that roll for... aren't you even trying to get rid of that belly? Did you ever get around to signing those papers Ed sent you? Why not? I told you three times....I have to remind you of positively everything. I'm so sick of you forgetting to do things," and so forth.

Astoundingly, Spencer appeared to be not the least bit perturbed by Joanne's charming comments. Quite possibly, he was wearing teeny-tiny earplugs on the flight? Hopefully he's learned to tune her out. Or possibly he has a girlfriend who treats him way better, and he's fantasizing about her. Maybe the happy-go-lucky image is all an act; inwardly he's seething and plotting to either murder Joanne or eventually escape her.

One side note: The disdain which fellow passengers felt for the mean and bossy little Joanne was tempered with grudging admiration for just how agile and quick she was.

Throughout the entire flight, Joanne continually retrieved items from her suitcase in the overhead bin. This procedure took place once every 15 minutes like clockwork, baby.

Anyone remember that incomparable movie, "To Live and Die in L.A.," where William Petersen says, "Like clockwork, baby, like fucking clockwork?"

Anyhew, every 15 minutes, Chanel dress and Manolo Blahniks notwithstanding, Joanne would self-launch from her window seat, clamber with the greatest of ease on all fours over Spencer's prone figure, then land nimbly in the aisle. She'd pull down her train case from the overhead bin in one fluid motion, and balancing it on her miniature knee, rapidly unzip it. With deft precision, Joanne would grab an item, always just one. She'd then zip the case, return it to the overhead, and crab-crawl back to her seat before anyone could say, "agile little spider monkey." One brave flight attendant who ventured forth with an offer of assistance was cowed immediately and retreated to the other end of the plane.

So, you never know what goes on with some couples. Perhaps Spencer was secretly a real crum. But as my friend recalled, everyone within earshot was just cringing for him. Amazingly, this couple may never divorce. Spencer may be willing to endure Joanne for a lifetime. Then again, one day she might just deliver the final straw, insult or criticism, and he will be out of there like a hot flash in January, as the saying goes.

Meantime, unless Joanne is a whole heckuva lot nicer in private, it appears she is that individual most commonly known as a "miserables," extracting the maximum out of Spencer while robbing much of the joy from his life.

## Compatibility

Sometimes, no matter how deeply two people care about one another, the relationship still fails because they are incompatible. This has happened to most of us at least once.

At first you think, "Oh joy!" You've found the "love of your life." Initially you're crazy about them, but then you realize you're just not well-matched. It's possible their personal habits and lifestyle are too foreign for you, or perhaps you fight constantly over dumb stuff.

This is why it's helpful to date your beloved for awhile before getting married...two years minimum if possible. By then you'll know if his mother controls his every move, or if her five incontinent indoor cats simply *must* sleep on your bed each and every night.

All joking aside, it's most crucial to see how your intended behaves under difficult circumstances. If you're planning to attach your fortunes and future to another, it's good to know ahead of time if you can count on them when the going gets tough. Do they rise to challenges or do they sink like the Titanic? Do they behave like an adult or a crying, whimpering little baby? Are they someone you can count on to be strong and positive when the going gets tough?

You don't have to live together to discover these things, by the way. Instead, just go camping, preferably in hot and muggy mosquito season. Borrow someone's infant or toddler for the camping trip. A colicky infant would be simply divine. I promise you that you will find out everything you need to know about your intended during that one camping trip.

## Control

Let's now do a "flashback" to 1978. Some of you weren't even born yet, you adorable little spring chickens! Well, this here "seasoned hen" was in high school at the time, and I was miserable over the loss of a friend. Brenda and I had been extremely close in junior high, and at the beginning of high school. At this time of my life, girlfriends were uppermost in importance. But in 11th grade, Brenda became very involved with the school's theatre department and her new friends there. I felt completely left out.

I trudged home alone after school one day and cried on my mom's shoulder, so to speak. My mom, Carmel, was a very smart, very wise woman. She had an extremely high level of emotional intelligence, although back then that term did not yet exist. I tearfully relayed my hurt feelings over this friendship that I felt was slipping away from me.

My mom then asked me: "What happens to a handful of sand if you grip it too tightly? Doesn't it run out of your fingers?"

Now, if you've never done this before, next time you're at the beach, try to hold onto a handful of sand while squeezing tightly. Be sure to pick up dry sand, by the way. This doesn't work well with damp sand.

My mom told me to next picture cupping the sand carefully in my hand so that it would not run out. Again, you can do this yourself with a handful of sand (dirt works too if you're landlocked).

This illustrated beautifully one of the most crucial and painful lessons I've ever had to learn. The more you try to control, cling to and hang on tightly to friends or loved ones, the more they'll disappear like sand running right out of your hand.

Side note from the 80s: this concept is nicely summed up in the 38-Special song "Hold on Loosely."

Many of us have been the victim of a control freak in a relationship. My experience was with a college boyfriend... let's just call him Dominic. We really enjoyed each other's company and had much in common. We fell in love very quickly- too fast for me to realize that I didn't really like him as a person. That knowledge came later.

The downfall of our short-lived relationship was that Dominic was very jealous and controlling. It's now clear that this stemmed from his own insecurities. But in my early 20s, I initially took this as a token of how much he cared. At first, I was flattered that he was so crazy about me; he was jealous of time I spent with others, even just my girlfriends and college roommates. Boy, was I ever naive! This kind of jealousy has nothing to do with how much someone loves you.

Dominic was very resentful of my guy friends. Truth be told, he didn't even like it when I went places with my girlfriends. He always asked questions such as, "Who's going to be there; will guys be there?" Eventually this led to his breaking up with me. He demanded I end a friendship with a platonic guy friend, and I refused. Had I been more mature, I would have seen these warning signs and would have wisely extricated myself.

If you're the insecure one in your relationship, whether you are dating, engaged, living together or married, please get some counseling. Otherwise, eventually this will damage or even end your relationship.

And it will make you crazy trying to control someone else, which is an exhausting and ultimately futile task.

## Cultural Differences

It's challenging enough to build a successful marriage when two people come from similar backgrounds.

To top that, when you and your spouse are products of very different cultures, like our next couple, many issues can arise.

Dallas couple Tiffany and Paul were in their mid-30s, had been married just two years and came from vastly different backgrounds. Her family was white, middle-class from the Middle (or shall we say Midwest). Her father frequently told people they were one of those "American as apple pie" families. Although Tiffany was close to her parents and saw them frequently, she was also quite independent of them.

Her parents knew approximately how much Tiffany earned; however, they had no precise knowledge of her finances, nor did they expect to, since she was an adult. Although they now lived only 15 minutes away from Tiffany, they never dropped in on her at home, nor did she drop in on them.

On the other hand, although Paul had grown up in the States, both his parents had been born in Korea and were very close to their Korean roots. Their own marriage had been arranged. It had been their express wish for Paul to choose a Korean bride, preferably one whose parents were their friends.

Paul had defied his parents by marrying a Caucasian girl. Although they'd expressed their disappointment, his parents did like Tiffany. In particular, Paul's father and Tiffany had hit it off quite well.

However, unfortunately, variances between their families were already causing problems. Tiffany had never dreamed her in-laws could exert so much influence over her young husband.

Before the wedding, Paul had lived in his own apartment, but had eaten dinner at his parents' house every night unless out with Tiffany or his buddies. His mom had visited him at least a few times a week to do his laundry and bring him food. His father had complete knowledge of Paul's finances and was constantly putting in his advice, or "two cents," as Tiffany saw it.

After they'd married, Tiffany resented the time Paul spent with his parents; not just in person, but also on the phone. Paul's parents also frequently dropped in on Tiffany and Paul. Paul was accustomed to this, but Tiffany found it intrusive. Unfortunately, Paul's parents especially liked dropping by Sunday mornings after church, which was generally when Tiffany and Paul slept in and had a little weekend "romance time."

Paul and Tiffany argued frequently over what she viewed as constant intrusions by his parents, and this began to cause a real rift in their relationship.

However, Paul and Tiffany truly loved one another and wanted to stay married, so fortunately they did two smart things: they saw a marriage therapist, and they compromised.

For starters, Tiffany became more accepting of the frequent phone calls Paul received from his parents. She began a new strategy. When one of Paul's parents called him in the evenings, rather than lurking around eavesdropping and acting annoyed, Tiffany immediately went to the other end of the house to take a very long, hot bubble bath.

When Paul realized Tiffany was making this effort, he met her halfway by firmly telling his parents they must no longer drop in unannounced. Paul's mother was extremely upset, but Paul's dad firmly backed Tiffany on this.

Tiffany then took the step of inviting Paul's parents over for dinner at least once a week. She told Paul's mom to put her feet up and not do anything but enjoy hanging out visiting her son. Paul's mom was accustomed to doing all the cooking; this was initially an adjustment, but then she began to really enjoy these relaxing visits.

Their marriage therapist encouraged Paul and Tiffany to take a tolerant and long-term view of their situation. She advised them to be patient with the fact that they came from vastly different backgrounds and she emphasized that they'd often encounter differences between their families as the years went by.

The therapist also suggested that Paul and Tiffany begin mixing both sets of their parents together socially. They had completely avoided doing this up until now. Both sets of parents had only met twice, once before the wedding and once on the wedding day. There had been no attempts to combine them, as both Paul and Tiffany had assumed this would be disastrous.

Surprisingly, nothing could be further from the truth. Against the dire predictions of both Paul and Tiffany, their parents got along incredibly well. The two couples relaxed in each others' presence and laughed a lot. Paul's mom began teaching Tiffany's mom some authentic Korean recipes, and Tiffany's mom invited Paul's mom out for lunch and shopping.

Paul and Tiffany could now combine holidays with both set of parents, which made everything easier and also helped solidify their marriage. Paul and Tiffany have been happily married now for seven years with a little daughter named Tabitha.

## Courtesy

If you're rude to your partner, clearly, this isn't beneficial for your relationship. Sounds obvious, doesn't it? But, as in the previous story of the hapless Spencer whose wife Joanne tortured him throughout an entire plane trip, not everyone realizes how their behavior comes across.

Two themes mentioned repeatedly by happily married couples were respect and courtesy. The overriding message was to treat your spouse how you yourself would like to be treated. Some of these are basics our moms taught us: saying "thank you" and "please" and speaking in a polite voice.

Nearly all of our success story couples cited courtesy toward one's partner as a foundation of their marital happiness.

There are also non-verbal displays of courtesy. Some of these are things like looking interested when your spouse is talking, or opening doors for them. Robert opens my car door for me, even when we're at a gas station out in the middle of the sweltering desert, I've got sand in my hair and I'm wearing sweats. It just takes a moment, but it means so much.

A lack of courtesy can be a big contributor to a failed relationship.

Kim and James divorced about 13 years into their marriage. She was polite, considerate, and patient to her co-workers; just a lovely person to work with. Kim would actually recall that your dog Fido had surgery and then later ask how Fido was doing. Not surprisingly, she moved up quickly at her company and was a favorite of bosses and subordinates as well. Everyone adored Kim.

When Kim's husband James left her suddenly, everyone was shocked. She tearfully told co-workers he'd moved out without any warning whatsoever. I recall thinking, what a complete jerk! Everyone at our office was flabbergasted that lousy James would leave such a spectacular individual as Kim.

However, a year later, Kim had moved on to a different company and a new co-worker named Becky arrived at our office. Apparently, Becky and her boyfriend Will had socialized quite frequently with Kim and James before they'd broken up. Becky said it was straight outta "Jekyll and Hyde."

Kim was so obnoxious to James it was unbelievable that this was the same person we knew. She constantly interrupted him when he spoke, rolled her eyes whenever he was talking, and insulted him. She contradicted pretty much everything he said. When he tried to tell a story about his brother encountering a bear while camping, she kept saying, "What are you even talking about; that's not how it happened," and would interject her own details.

Becky said she and Will kept socializing with them even though it was "cringy," because James was such a sweet guy. She added that just once, it would have been nice to see him tell Kim off, but he never did. Becky later assumed he'd reserved all his sassyfrass for divorce court.

No doubt about it, Kim had two personalities. One was her "company manners" at work, which were impeccable, and the other was the way she treated her husband.

As mentioned earlier, you can't really get away with being rude to co-workers. Not to mention, if someone you've treated shabbily becomes your boss one day, your life can then become sheer living hell. Muahahaha!

Perhaps because there isn't always an instant negative outcome, some folks feel they can get away with being rude and crummy to their marriage partner.

We're not just talking about words. Nonverbal signals like rolled eyes, heavy sighs, and disgusted expressions erode a relationship.

It can also frequently be reciprocal; each one trying to outdo the other in being nasty. We've all been on a double date like this. How do you spell awkward?

If you and your partner have fallen into the habit of, for lack of a better term, being "snotty" to one another, take it upon yourself to change this. Don't wait for them to change first.

Don't even discuss it... just try to turn this around as quickly as possible. Your good example might just bring your spouse up to a higher standard of behavior as well.

## Courage

Simply staying married in a world where divorce seems to be the norm can take colossal guts. It takes courage to say you're in it for the long haul, and that you refuse to be another divorce statistic.

Now, let's also speak about courage in your relationship. If your partner is truly inconsiderate, possibly they won't know if you never tell them. If you've been a martyr in your marriage for many years, perhaps it's finally time to show your spouse you deserve better treatment...you owe it to yourself.

If you don't assert yourself, well, then you could be stuck in the same rut, year after year, possibly decade after decade.

Also, although this book is about staying married, it must be said that it takes the greatest courage to escape a truly toxic or abusive relationship.

But, barring that type of situation, if your marriage is in trouble but still salvageable, it definitely takes guts to announce that you wish to improve things.

Now, how about if you are in the wrong? It also takes bravery to apologize first, to change your behavior and to admit that you are at fault. So, courage and humility can go hand in hand. Remember Paul and Tiffany from the "Cultural Differences" section? She stopped resenting the time he spent on the phone with his parents, and started taking long hot bubble baths instead. This then caused a positive chain reaction where, in turn, he supported her by telling his parents to stop dropping in on them.

One of the greatest books and movies of all time is "True Grit." For those of you who don't know the story, a little girl rides the range on horseback, with an older cowboy as her only companion, to avenge her father's murder. She's just a young girl, but she does it. She has "true grit." So in your life and your marriage, be bold, and be strong.

It takes true grit to admit to yourself that you have responsibility for how mediocre, strained, or bad your marriage is, and to make necessary changes to improve it. Be courageous, my friends! You know what they say...no guts, no glory!!!

# Child-free

Alexa, my pal at Curves gym, was a bright, fun and bubbly lady, but one day when I saw her there, she seemed completely down and out. She and her husband Bruce had been trying for several years to have a baby, and a fertility specialist had just informed them they'd never be able to have biological children. Neither Bruce nor Alexa wanted to adopt.

I told Alexa about my dear friends Louise and Dan, who never had children and have had a wonderful life, full of fun, travel, and freedom. Louise and Dan traveled constantly, taking two big trips a year. The year before, for example, they'd visited both China and New Zealand.

Alexa and I ended up having a great conversation about all the perks of being "child-free."

Just a note: many individuals with kids envy child-free folks because they're free from the worry that all parents have. This worry is a burden carried by all parents, whether their children are five years old or thirty.

The next time I saw Alexa, she said that our conversation had come at a perfect time. Over the next few months, it was apparent that she was beginning to truly embrace the concept of a child-free lifestyle.

Shortly thereafter, Alexa moved out of state and I didn't see her for almost 11 years. When I finally saw her again, it was wonderful to see what a rich and happy life she and her husband had created, and how they were truly comfortable with the choices they'd made. During the interim, she'd worked hard at a challenging career, and she and Bruce had traveled a great deal. She'd also forged very close relationships with her niece and nephew.

It's unfortunate that our society places so much pressure on individuals, women in particular, to become parents.

For those who stress you need children to look after you in old age, there are no such guarantees. Your kids could ditch you at any given moment! We've all seen friends who stick their elderly folks in nursing homes; of course that part is often unavoidable. The ugly part is when you see them rarely, if ever, visit.

Here are just a few of the fun and glorious advantages to being child-free:

1. No obligation to pretend you like animated movies.

2. Travel when and wherever you like.

3. Much, much more money in the bank. Oodles more! Get this: the average cost of raising just one child is over $200,000.00!!

4. Live free from the worry that all parents have about their child's safety.

5. Sleep in late on the weekends.

6. No need to fake it that you like soccer or Barney. And you don't even have to pretend you've seen the movie "Frozen."

7. Free to focus more energy on your career.

8. Whilst driving, listen to whatever music you want...no Disney tunes unless *you* actually like them.

9. No juggling day-care with a job.

10. No feeling guilty that you aren't a perfect parent.

11. Enjoy being a fantastic aunt, uncle or godparent... on your own terms. When you're sick of the kids, just toss them, sugared-up and hyper, right back to their parents.

Mae and Shane, one of our success story couples, had both been married and divorced before they met. Neither wanted children, but have enjoyed being aunt and uncle to their nieces and nephews.

Without "rugrats" tying them down, Mae and Shane can partake in fun activities and travel whenever they want. The financial advantages of not having children, as we've mentioned before, are staggering.

They enjoy double dates with other couples; some of their friends have kids, others do not. Most of their friends' kids are grown now so it's a non-issue. Many of their friends were child-free as well.

Both Mae and Shane are content with their decision to not have children. People have asked them in the past, "Who's going to take care of you when you get old?" Mae is emphatic about the fact that there are no such guarantees.

So, let's now view a difficult situation... as sticky as taffy: you don't want kids, but your significant other does.

Christina and Owen on "Grey's Anatomy" immediately come to mind. It's very true that you can't have half a kid. If this was agreed upon before marriage, but one partner changes their mind, this is a real dilemma. Many couples begin arguing over this after the wedding bells have stopped jangling. There are no easy answers.

Sue and Dave had been married for four years when they hit an impasse. Dave desperately wanted children, and they'd "agreed" before marriage to have kids, but when the time came, Sue was terrified of pregnancy and childbirth. She'd been a gymnast, and as a teen had broken her back in a balance beam accident.

Sue's gynecologist had also expressed concern that her back wouldn't endure a full-term pregnancy and could even re-break during childbirth. Dave then suggested they enlist the help of a surrogate mom. Sue and Dave now have two beautiful, healthy daughters, ages seven and three. The cost and struggle to make this happen were exorbitant, but they both feel that it was well worth it.

## Carpe Diem

Most of us know this is Latin for "seize the day."

"Seize the day" can have several meanings. These can range from frivolous, such as "eat, drink and be merry," to more earnest interpretations such as "live your life in a productive and meaningful manner, because it's fleeting."

How does this translate to marriage? Let's say you and your spouse are in a rut. You get along okay, but nothing's really that special. You go to work, you come home, you're tired, barely talk, perhaps eat in front of the TV, and don't make time for fun anymore. You're trapped in the day-to-day grind of just getting by.

Next thing you know, 20 years have elapsed, and you never took that trip to see Mount Rushmore. You still haven't visited the Grand Canyon. You never went up in the Eiffel Tower or experienced Mardi Gras. The two of you planned to take a pottery class together, but somehow two decades elapsed, and even that didn't happen.

Remorse, disappointment, and feeling that life has passed you by are not great emotions. We've all been there... regretting things we wanted to do, but never made time for.

So, here's one possible strategy. Sit down with your spouse, each of you armed with a piece of paper and a pencil.

Does anyone even use pencils anymore? Not to date myself, but I actually still own quite a few. My true challenge is that I don't have a pencil sharpener anymore, so what possible good can these pencils do me anyways?

Okay, back to our exercise. You and your spouse each make a list of the top ten things you want to do within the next five years. This doesn't have to be a trip to Paris. It doesn't have to be Europe or Asia. Maybe smaller trips are more feasible, depending upon your age and your bank account. But if you still can get around, dang it, just get on that airplane!

Maybe it's taking that cooking or painting class together. Perhaps it's going to the beach, seeing a drive-in movie, anything to get out of the day-to-day rut.

Next, think of a plan so you two can make these things happen.

Maybe now you're in your late 40s or 50s, and the simple act of reading this is bumming you out. Let's say you always wanted to take speedboats down the Nile, but you still don't have the cash, or maybe now it's too dangerous to travel there. Perhaps another goal on your list like Mount Rushmore or the Grand Canyon would be more doable.

If you've always dreamed of white water rafting, but you're not in shape for that anymore, it doesn't have to be a total loss. Maybe there's a substitute just as fun... how about a nice riverboat trip on the Mississippi? Furthermore, it's a great excuse to drop in on that American city that's more like Europe than perhaps any other, the Big Easy, the incredible, the one-of-a-kind, NOLA, New Orleans!

Oh NOLA, my love, where do we begin? The architecture, the history, the oyster po' boys, the chicory coffee, the haunted tours, the Mississippi, the pralines, the swamp tours, Antoine's, the boat cruises! Oh, Nola, just where have you beignet all my life?

Anyways, we all will leave this earth someday without having done everything we'd hoped. But we can still manage to do some wonderful things we've always dreamed of doing.

"Carpe diem, baby!"

## Chivalry

Years ago, some "horsey" friends gifted me a magnet in the shape of a cute black horse that looked exactly like Terra, the Thoroughbred mare I owned at the time.

Terra is now galloping fast somewhere over that rainbow bridge.

The inscription on the magnet read: "Treat a woman like a Thoroughbred, and she'll never become an old nag!"

Maybe the phrase "old nag" isn't PC, but we're going with it anyways!

So, be chivalrous to your wife. After all, you don't want her turning into an *old nag*, do you? Open those doors, particularly her car door. Buy her flowers for no special reason. Spoil her on her birthday, Mother's Day, Christmas and Valentine's Day. Help her bring in the grocery bags from the car. If she's had a long day, give her a nice shoulder rub.

Let's add a quick word about Mother's Day. Some men feel they don't need to do anything for their wife, because, as they put it, "She's not my mother." Yes, Siree Bob, but she's the mother of your children and you wouldn't have them if not for her. Um-hmmm that's right!

Here's a great idea: if you live in a cold climate, get up a few minutes early and scrape the ice off her windshield. If you live in a tropical climate, there's still a way to impress her with your boundless gallantry. Mayhap a few stray palm fronds have dropped onto her windshield and you can go brush those off whilst reciting one of Shakespeare's beautiful and romantic sonnets.

These are all small items, but can add up to a woman who feels pampered. And if she feels spoiled, she's far less likely to turn into that cranky, crabby little old nag!

# D

---

## Debt

Possibly more than anything else, financial struggles can place an enormous strain on a couple. We previously addressed this miserable, drab topic in the "Broke" section.

Some of this is unavoidable (job loss, medical bills, prolonged unemployment), but some is self-inflicted (buying too much, maybe showing off a bit, keeping up with the Joneses and the Smiths).

One of the greatest stresses is living beyond one's means. I should know... I've done it before and I'm certainly not proud of it! I'm sure some of you reading this have made the same blunder.

Adam and Suzanne had been married for over 20 years, and for most of this time, had lived far, far beyond their means.

Suzanne has impeccable taste and loves designer clothes, shoes, and purses, and sadly, Adam cannot tell her "no." Plus, he's no saint with the spending himself... he gets a new car every couple of years and spends a fortune on maintaining his boat.

Suzanne and Adam both have excellent jobs; they should have some savings by now, and be preparing for eventual retirement. But now, in their late 40s, they have zero savings and a mountain of debt. At this point, they need a complete reworking of their spending habits. A good financial counselor could help them come up with a firm plan.

With many couples, one is a spender and one is a saver – this can create conflicts, but also perhaps a balance. However, if both are spenders, such as Adam and Suzanne, this can cause financial precariousness.

Now, if both are savers, there's no other way to put this, they may become chintzy over the years. They then miss out on fun things like vacations. Either way, when the two members of a couple have different ideas about how to spend and how to save, this can cause issues.

Jared and Anna struggled over money in their early years of marriage. Jared was a saver and Anna just loved to spend. They had countless arguments, but then came up with a clear solution. They agreed to save a certain amount of money every month, which made Jared (the saver) happy.

They decided to allocate a certain amount per month which each partner could spend on things like entertainment, and in the case of Anna, clothes, shoes, books, makeup, and so forth. Anna struggled with this for awhile, but eventually found it easier to curtail her spending when she knew in advance exactly how much she could spend. She also found it helpful to only carry one debit card and to leave her credits cards hidden away at home.

One of Anna's friends advised her to freeze her credit cards into a block of ice. You've never seen such excitement as when Nordstrom's did their annual sale and Anna hastily defrosted a card in the microwave. For future notice, it's best to refrain from doing this with metal credit cards. The sparks that came out of Anna's microwave didn't start a kitchen fire, but you can be sure there was drama in the house. Anna also discovered that credit cards can melt if overly-defrosted.

Side note: Let's refrain from using the term "budget," shall we? It's wonderful to feel sexy in your marriage, and nothing detracts from that more than the word "budget," with the possible exceptions of "chore" or, God help us, "portion control."

So, luckily Jared and Anna were able to compromise (there's that word again!). He will always be more careful with money than her, but fortunately they both agree about saving to buy a house in the next three years.

Let's now observe one disaster for couples; the sneaky little devil that goes by the name of "financial infidelity." Here are some examples: one spouse hides extra earnings, they keep secret bank accounts, hide excessive spending, or, worst of all, keep their partner in the dark about the fact that their mutual financial ship is sinking faster than the Titanic.

Let's look at the "sinking ship" scenario. One partner is blissfully unaware; believing all is well. Meanwhile, the partner in charge of finances knows they're behind on bills, rent or mortgage, and chooses to keep this information from their spouse.

Gambling is at the root of much financial infidelity, and caused the divorce of Will and Laura. Before splitting up, this couple had been happily married for nine years.

Will was unaware of Laura's gambling problem. He knew that she liked to go with her girlfriends to the local casino and play a few slot machines. In Will's mind, Laura played the slots with whatever cash she had in her wallet at the time. He had absolutely no inkling that in less than one year, her gambling had gone completely out of control.

It had started out innocently enough. Laura lost several hundred dollars on the slot machines, so withdrew a little money from their checking account to cover it. It wasn't a large enough sum to mention to Will, and she had every intention of winning back what she'd lost.

Next, Laura won over a thousand dollars on a slot machine.

This was one of the best experiences of her life. Everyone cheered for her, and the casino gave her a special winner's card, gift cards for free drinks at the casino bar, and other prizes. Laura treated the two girlfriends with her to lunch, and then took Will out that night for a fancy steak dinner.

She and Will had been badly in need of a new washing machine, so the money she won enabled them to pay cash for a new one.

Her win gave Laura so much joy and exhilaration that over the next few weeks she visited the casino more frequently, even up to several times a week. Her two girlfriends couldn't always join her, so she began going alone and made friends with other regulars.

Unfortunately, Laura's winning streak ended with that first big win. Over the next few weeks, she lost nearly four thousand dollars, funds she withdrew from their joint savings account.

Most of all, Laura wanted another win to re-experience that intoxicating fun and excitement. She was sure she'd have another big payoff soon, so began to use her credit cards to withdraw money to gamble.

Over the next two months, Laura won and lost, always losing more than she won, charging over five thousand dollars on one credit card alone. Will knew nothing; she'd always taken care of paying their bills. She did consider telling Will at this point, but knew he'd be angry and still believed she could win back the money.

When all their credit cards had been maxed out, Laura kept their boat afloat by withdrawing $20,000 from Will's 401k retirement account. She lost that money as well.

Two years elapsed, during which time Laura lost over $300,000.00, nearly all of Will's retirement. He had no idea, as she intercepted and hid the statements before he could see them.

One day, quite by accident, Will's 401k statement was mailed to his office instead of their home. Several co-workers were there when he opened the envelope and found that all his retirement money was gone. At first he thought it was some weird accounting error, but when he called Laura, she confessed the truth.

Their marriage ultimately fell apart. Laura was completely heartbroken and Will was as well, but as he told friends, "How could I ever trust her again?"

In this scenario (a true story, just names and some details have been changed) Laura gambled exclusively on slot machines at a regular casino. If you find it inconceivable that someone could lose over a quarter of a million dollars on slot machines, visit a casino and spend two solid hours on the dollar slots. Unless you are randomly lucky, you will be out at least a few hundred dollars, probably much more. There's also sports betting, online poker, other types of online betting... a multitude of ways gamblers can get into serious money trouble.

If you're lying about how much you gamble, or gambling to recover your losses, or if someone has expressed worry about your gambling, please get some help. Psychotherapy and support groups are two of the most successful methods to help with gambling addiction.

## Divorce

This seems like an easy one...don't get one! Of course, there will always be divorces. But starting off a marriage with that kind of thinking is not so great. Right after jetting back from her Bora Bora honeymoon, Tabitha was overheard saying, "Well, if it doesn't work out, hey, we can always get a divorce."

Big mistake, Tabitha! Big! Huge! (Please picture Julia Roberts in "Pretty Woman" telling off the snooty saleslady). Of course, in many cases, divorce is (and should be) the only option, such as in a case of physical or emotional abuse. No one should feel obligated or pressured to stay in an unsafe, abusive relationship.

This, of course, isn't what we're referring to here. We're talking instead about the assumption that if things don't work out, divorce is the automatic result. This mindset makes it easy to give up when things begin to skid downhill.

Kari was a self-described "neat freak" who loved everything perfectly in order and couldn't tolerate the slightest amount of clutter. When she first married Sebastian, she knew he was a little messy, but thought she could change this.

By the way, Sebastian wasn't really that messy. But if he ate a bowl of pasta, he left the empty bowl on the counter. Yes, it would have been glorious if he'd placed the bowl in the sink, or washed it, but most people wouldn't think this was exactly earth-shattering. He would always return later to wash out the bowl, but this process was never immediate.

Unfortunately, however, this drove Kari absolutely nuts. Once they'd married and began living together, this caused a daily argument, as Sebastian adored his pasta at the kitchen counter when he returned home from work.

Sebastian also liked to cook on the weekends, and sometimes left dirty dishes in the sink until late in the evening. Kari always wondered aloud why he couldn't clean up right after dinner, like she did. She then did the dishes herself in a big huff, and she and Sebastian would have an argument.

We shall address this dynamic in our "petty" section. Rather than thinking, "Well, Sebastian fixed dinner so it's no big deal, I can clean up," Kari instead made a big stink. Eventually, these dirty dishes became the focal point of every weekend, when this couple could have been enjoying their leisure time.

Rather than accepting that Sebastian was no neat freak, Kari turned the pasta bowl and dirty dishes into a huge issue (inability to compromise rears its ugly head again).

Kari complained bitterly to her friends, and began talking about kicking Sebastian out.

It's noteworthy that when Kari and Sebastian married, they didn't get a new place together. He moved into *her* house. So, there was a bit of a territorial issue there as well. When things became strained, Kari's first line of reasoning was not to work things out, but instead to kick Sebastian out of *her* house.

Incidentally, it seems sheer lunacy that divorce should occur over a mere pasta bowl. But perhaps that's why divorce attorneys can sashay over to Rome whenever they wish, for "real-deal pasta al dente," plus maybe some du con glace gelato, all because of things like pasta bowls and toothpaste tubes.

Number one, Kari had known Sebastian wasn't a perfectionist when they married. Number two, she had initially loved his relaxed nature and sense of humor. Prior to their living together, his easy-going personality, so different than her own, had been a huge plus. Kari had grown up with a very critical and exacting mother. Nothing she'd ever done had been good enough for mommy dearest, who always found a way to criticize.

So, it's ironic and sad that Kari was replicating this exact same behavior with her husband, whom she incidentally loved very much.

Luckily, although it's not always wise to complain to a divorced friend at a time like this, in Kari's case, it actually turned out to be a blessing. Kari vented to her smart divorced friend Valerie, who strongly discouraged her from splitting up and who also recommended an excellent marriage counselor. Fortunately, Sebastian was receptive to seeing a therapist as well.

Kari and Sebastian both really liked their therapist, who was professional, kind and nurturing. Kari also saw this therapist individually for a few years. This was a lifesaver, not just for their relationship, but for her as well. The therapist helped Kari realize that her nitpicking at Sebastian over small things stemmed from her critical mom and indifferent dad.

Kari realized that what she'd viewed as Sebastian's problems were in actuality her own. Sebastian will never be as neat as Kari, but she now takes this in stride. She realizes how lucky she is to have a husband with so many great qualities.

If you tend to become annoyed over little things your spouse does, or vice versa, there's a great exercise you can do together as a couple. It works so well, I mention it several times in this book.

Each of you writes down 15 of your partner's good qualities for every one negative trait. Use an actual piece of paper and a pen to write on; not your phone. This way you can keep the notes and look back on them many years later.

Don't get fancy: whatever comes to mind. Don't put a lot of thought into it. Just do it quickly.

If you and your spouse are talking divorce, this simple exercise might turn your thinking around. It may help you realize how unimportant small annoyances are, compared to your spouse's excellent qualities.

## Divorce Part Two

Now, let's display the other side of the coin. Fortunately, we live in a time when it's possible, at least in the United States, for someone to escape a bad marriage if they really want to. There was a time here in the U.S., and in some countries this still holds true, when you would be stuck with your marriage partner, no matter what, until one of you was "#coffin-ready."

Needless to say, if there's any kind of physical violence, get the heck out immediately. This should not be debatable at all.

By the way, there's nothing more infuriating than when religion is used to help excuse and perpetuate physical abuse. Ellen was in her late 30s; her husband was severely abusive, beating her and intimidating her. She appealed to the pastor of her church, begging for help, and what was the pastor's response? He advised her to be more cooperative, so then her husband would not *need* to beat her. This was not a century ago; this took place in the 1990s. Ellen finally escaped this horrible marriage, but only after several more years of physical and emotional abuse. The lousy advice given to her by someone in a position of authority, and someone whom she trusted, kept her in a terrible and dangerous marriage for several more years.

Happily, Ellen is gloriously remarried to a kind, gentle and wonderful man.

## Don't Sweat the Small Stuff

This phrase and philosophy are often credited to the amazing Dr. Richard Carlson. He was my former classmate at Pepperdine University in the 80s, and he authored several books on the subject. He and his lovely wife Kristine co-authored a book as well, and Kristine wrote a great book on the same subject for women. Their insightful publications illustrate this concept beautifully. Richard was a wonderful person, family man and philanthropist who sadly passed away some years ago and is missed by so many.

The basic concept is simple: don't sweat or stress over small things in your life. This also definitely applies to marriage. We've all heard wacky stories about couples and their toothpaste tubes. One's a neat freak who squeezes out the Colgate perfectly, while the other scrunches the tube from the middle, thereby driving the neat one bonkers on a daily basis.

Okay here goes: a great solution! Two tubes! Maybe even go hog-wild with separate bathroom drawers! So that way, it's a non-issue.

One of the greatest questions to ask oneself is: "Will this matter one year from now?"

## Dignity

When I hear the word "dignity," I always recall the wonderful book, "The Cheerleader," by Ruth Doan MacDougall. It's the story of Puddles and Snowy, cheerleaders in the 1950s. The two girls had auditioned for cheerleading and are stampeding over to the gym office, where the names of those who made the squad are posted on the door. Puddles instructs Snowy, "We must do this with dignity," and so they slowly walk over to the office (well, they are 15-year-olds, so they begin running as they get near).

When married folks conduct themselves with dignity, it's a great thing to see. When the opposite occurs, it's definitely entertaining for those who witness it. Anyone who says they've behaved with 100 percent dignity their whole life...hmmm I just don't believe it! Putting all embarrassment aside, I'll share here one of my own stories. Of course, there are a plethora, a virtual multitude to choose from, mostly from my teens and 20s.

When we were first dating, Robert and I got into a huge argument on his parents' front lawn. Who knows what it was even about? Probably it was nothing significant. His street was very quiet, so surely a few neighbors could hear *me* yelling.

In a rage, I jumped into my beloved 1969 Camaro "Max," tore off down the street, driving way too fast, and drifting before it was even a "thing" onto nearby Manchester Blvd.

I then lost total control of Max, did a dramatic 180-degree turn, so that I was actually facing oncoming traffic. Cars were coming at me at about 50 miles per hour.

Luckily, all the drivers just barely managed to stop in time and sat there staring at me out of their windshields. In humiliation, I turned my car around, drove back 10 miles per hour and apologized to Robert.

Now, I should mention that at the time of this story, I was 22. My maturity level was so low it never actually occurred to me I could have killed myself or someone else, only that I might have dented my precious car.

I've matured tremendously since then and don't go driving crazy when I'm mad. I've learned to slow down, count to three, all those things you're supposed to do.

But, what about couples who are well into their middle years, but still act like dramatic little toddlers?

Recently I met a friend for lunch at Rubio's, that San Diego favorite for casual Mexican food, which proudly features our much-adored local staple, the glorious and scrumptious fish taco.

As I motored into the parking lot, even over my car stereo I could hear the shrill screaming of a woman standing at the passenger door of a Ford Explorer. A man, presumably her husband, was in the driver's seat with both front windows rolled down and he, too, was shouting at the top of his lungs. Let's just dub them Fred and Betsy.

Working in tandem, these two created a truly spectacular decibel level, which was even more impressive given the poor acoustics of the Rubio's parking lot.

The Explorer's back windows were rolled up and tinted, so who knows if there were children in the back seat. The combined yelling of Fred and Betsy was deafening. She then began banging on the door frame of the Explorer with her fist, and, not to be outdone, he repeatedly honked the car horn.

By this time, diners inside the restaurant were peering out of their windows for a better look. San Diego is an attractive town, to be sure, but can't compete with the excitement level of say, Los Angeles or New

York, so the Fred and Betsy revue constituted solid entertainment for a Saturday afternoon.

This duo continued screaming a few minutes longer, and then Fred started the engine of the Explorer and began to slowly roll out of the parking spot. It appeared he was leaving Betsy in a lurch, but then she nimbly jumped in and they drove off.

Okay we get it... couples will argue from time to time. They will of course yell on occasion. But when you're screeching in the *Rubio's parking lot,* for God's sake, loudly enough for everyone inside to hear you... well, maybe there's not a whole lot of dignity there.

When your partner's annoying as hell, it's tough to keep your cool. It's difficult to conduct yourself with composure when things are going badly in your life.

By the way, before I appear to be on some judgy high horse here, never forget I was the one facing oncoming traffic in my bright yellow 1969 Camaro back in the day.

A most original technique to show your spouse you're mad as hell while still maintaining absolute dignity is the "bent spoon technique" invented by the late great Helen Gurley Brown, former editor of Cosmo magazine. If Helen and her husband David were seated at an elegant dinner or event and she was angry with him, she had a creative way of letting him know. Helen would remove a silver spoon from the table, place it into her lap, and would sit there bending it. Once the handle was bent in half, she would place the now-decrepit spoon into David's hand.

This was a subtle, yet lively and creative way of letting him know she was absolutely pissed off without causing a scene. If she was really riled up, tiny Helen could manage to deform three spoons over the course of an evening.

However, sometimes behaving in a dignified manner means you are a wimp. That's right!

One day Rebecca, my favorite clerk at our local market, was being berated by a man who stood in line behind me. This giant was easily 6'7" tall, and wearing a sleeveless T-shirt. He very much resembled "Mr. Clean" from the old TV ads.

"Mr. Clean" was loudly ranting to everyone in line, rudely criticizing Rebecca, how slow she was, what a terrible job she was doing, how long the wait was, and that he should have gone to Walmart instead.

Rebecca's father had recently passed and she was going through a very rough time. I winked at her conspiratorially, thinking that she was amused, but then I realized she was nearly in tears.

Well, you know, we all have those times we don't plan what we are saying, but our mouth opens up and whatever comes out... well, this was one such time for me.

"Why don't you just shut up?" I yelled at Mr. Clean. The man in line directly behind me was reaching for a bag of Dorito's in the display case; when I yelled, his hand froze right there in mid-air. He didn't say a word and neither did the man behind Mr. Clean.

I'm sorry... but what a couple of namby-pambys.

However, giant kudos to the 4'11" lady in her 80s near the end of the line. She piped in and spryly yelled at Mr. Clean, "Yeah, mister, be quiet, we're all tired of listening to you."

So, not surprisingly, Mr. Clean then backed down faster than you could say, "Big Old Bully." He then began whimpering how everyone was picking on him and he was just in a hurry because he such had important places to be, bla bla bla, so on and so on.

You'd better believe I was not dignified that day, not in the least. But when Rebecca winked at me, it made it all worthwhile.

So, we're not referring to every situation here... just how you conduct yourself most of the time and in your marriage. There's a big difference between defending a friend against a bully and airing your dirty drawers out in public.

## Don't Go to Bed Angry

Here we shall quote Lynn; she and Larry are one of our success story couples. They're two of the best people on earth and have been married for 60 years. They're supportive, kind and loving to one another.... in a nut-shell, an amazing duo. As Lynn describes it, if you go to bed mad at each other, this will spell doom for the relationship. It's so important not to go to bed angry. Even if you spend just five minutes discussing what went wrong and trying to rectify it, giving each partner a chance to hopefully apologize, this can make the difference between staying together and splitting up.

Now, let's just add here: this tip *may not work* for every couple. If you're weary from arguing, sometimes it's better to get some rest, take a break, and then hash things out in the morning, or sometime the next day.

This especially applies to couples with small children. These folks are already sleep-deprived. Maybe going to bed angry is better than getting no sleep and transforming into "Walking Dead" zombies the next morning.

*Special note: If the strategy of "Don't go to bed angry" doesn't work for you, please see the chapter entitled "Go to Bed Angry."*

## Don't Take It Personally

First off, this is far, far easier said than done. But not taking things personally is an invaluable skill and was also listed by many of our success story couples.

Time, therapy and experience can all help one overcome the habit of taking things personally, but this can still be challenging.

Let's imagine your husband has a difficult, critical mom. His dad passed a few years ago and his elderly mom lives alone, about a half hour away. It's not easy spending time with her, given her temperament. But your husband is a good son and visits her a couple nights a week and on the weekends to keep her company and do odd jobs around her house. His siblings live out of state, so for the most part, it's all on him. His mom is rarely appreciative and criticizes how he does *everything*. She's always got something to say and it's rarely nice. She's only gotten worse with age.

Little surprise then, when your husband returns home after spending time with his mom, he's cranky, easily annoyed and down-spirited.

Your husband is normally a happy, funny, and kind fellow, but after his mom gets done with him, he snaps at you and the kids and acts like a bratty little boy, which he's completely devolved into by this point.

Knowing how difficult your mother-in-law is, and how stressful it is for your husband to be around her, you can't take it personally.

Easier said than done, we know.

Perhaps create a strategy which enables you to support your husband without being the brunt of his bad mood. First, determine whether or not you can distract him or joke him out of his crankiness, or if you're better off leaving him alone. Second, keep in mind that this is about him and his mom, and it's not about you. Third, if you need to discuss anything with him, don't do it when he's just returned from visiting "Crabby Patty."

Now, let's imagine your wife has a rather toxic sister. It's difficult for you to understand their weird dynamic, because you and *your* sister have a fantastic, uncomplicated relationship.

But not everyone has siblings who make them feel great. Therefore, when your wife returns from a Palm Springs weekend with her sister, she's not in a good mood. The two are competitive and have lots of shared baggage, so although they do love one another, it's an unhealthy dynamic. Your wife's sister has a habit of "poking" her. They'll enjoy a great visit, but then at the very end, her sister will bring up something from the past, or insult her. It's rather the equivalent of a nasty playground punk running up and poking another kid, then gleefully dashing off.

This doesn't mean your wife will necessarily want to talk about it, however. Or, on the other hand, she might vent about it incessantly. When this happens, she gripes so much, going on and on, the boredom of it makes you suspect you've fallen into an actual coma.

Chances are excellent your wife is saying horrendous and horridious things about her sister, but if you dare contribute the tiniest morsel, she'll hotly defend her. This happens even if every word you utter is true, and virtually identical to what your wife's been saying for the past two hours and forty-seven minutes.

Perhaps your husband finally got that big job promotion last month. He was incredibly happy, just over the moon. He's making lots more money, and the new job is far more prestigious than the old one.

Unfortunately, the grass on the other side ain't so very green now that hubby's gone and hopped the fence. It's wilted and dried out, with giant foxtails. Travis, the new boss, to quote Niklaus in "The Originals," is a ghoulish atrocity. Travis has zero personal life, so he calls endless last-minute meetings at the very tail end of the day. Travis also loves to micro-manage. In essence, he's the complete opposite of the old boss.

Therefore, when your husband comes home grouchy and grumpy, it's got nothing to do with you. So just take it in stride and don't take it personally. Easier said than done, of course, but bear in mind now you can finally afford that trip to the Bahamas you've always dreamed of.

## Double Dates

It never hurts to find new ways to make your marriage fun. Married life should be as interesting and joyful as possible, so we hereby announce the revival of the double date. If you and your spouse have been together a long time, it can be really fun to "shake it up" by going out with another couple.

We're not talking about husband or wife-swapping here, by the way. But that's an option for sure, and we'll address it in our "sex" segment, scout's honor. But right now we're just talking about wholesome fun double-dating, like the 1950s in a top-down convertible at the drive-in movies.

Interacting with another couple can bring fresh energy to your twosome.

Unfortunately, it's not always easy to find two couples where everyone "clicks." Your husband and his buddy may be "bromance central," but you're sitting there with the wife, struggling to make conversation. You two you have nothing in common...zero. Or, the opposite – you and your girlfriend are having an incredible time, but the two guys are sitting there with fake zombie smiles, just completely bored out of their gourds.

But when the double date does "jive," it's a truly glorious experience.

Double dates are also a way for you and your spouse to try new adventures. For example, if the other couple enjoys unusual travel destinations or unique restaurants, you may experience things you'd otherwise have missed.

One caveat: double dates can be super awkward if the other couple has lots more money. We've encountered this several times. The worst was with one couple years ago, Scott and Candace. They always chose expensive places. He had a thriving business, she had a huge job, but we, on the other hand, were sad sacks. We'd just bought our first house and were totally broke.

So, what do you do in this instance? Perhaps just go along with their restaurant choice if it's an occasional dinner. Ask for separate checks and order something less costly. If you go out with this couple frequently, you can also sometimes suggest less expensive places.

One evening we were driving to meet Scott and Candace at a swanky restaurant they wanted to try. On the way there, I warned Robert, "Don't order anything expensive, we can't afford it." Once we'd opened our menus, Robert immediately proclaimed he was ordering the giant prime rib. Horrified, I kicked him under the table: no response. Later in the meal, Robert made a somewhat crude joke. The other couple laughed and didn't seem offended, but I kicked him anyways, a second time. Once again, there was no response.

When we got into the car at the end of the evening, I was ticked off. "Why'd you order such an expensive dinner? We're broke!" He said he'd forgotten. I then mentioned that I'd kicked him under the table. "No, you didn't," he said. I added that I'd also kicked him a second time, after his offensive joke. "No, you didn't," he insisted.

Okay, now I was mystified. By the way, these weren't huge kicks, just tiny little taps with my foot.

Two days later, on Monday, my office phone rang. It was Scott, the husband from our Saturday double date. He asked how I was. "Fine," I replied. Scott then asked what I was wearing. "My blue silk dress," I responded. Before I could think about what a unique turn this conversation had taken, Scott asked if I wanted to get a drink that evening. "Sure," I said, "let me just check with Robert."

"I thought we'd go just the two of us," Scott replied.

Only then did I realize that it had been Scott I'd kicked so carefully under the table.

Ah well, that was a great double-date foursome while it lasted!

If you're planning a vacation with a couple who has more money than you, fight embarrassment and let them know beforehand roughly what you can afford. You might consider first going on a short, local trip. This way you can see how well you all travel together before undertaking something as extensive as Europe.

The short trip will disclose how well the four of you "jive" and how well your travel styles work together. Perhaps the other couple gets up at the crack of dawn to madly rush around and see everything there is, while you prefer to sleep in a bit, then sightsee at a more leisurely pace.

Another issue is if you and your spouse don't drink, and the other couple usually spends $70 on cocktails and wine at dinner. The best solution here: separate checks. If you all enjoy drinking, there is wine-tasting at a vineyard or going on pub crawls. And of course, if cost is no object, Tuscany awaits the four of you, dahling!

## Drive You Nuts

So, in this little book, I'm addressing the good, the bad, and what my father used to call the "double-ugly." No doubt about it...this is one of those "double-ugly" topics. Okay, here goes: when you're married to someone for a long time, it is absolutely *unavoidable* that at some point, he or she *will* DRIVE YOU NUTS.

It makes no difference whatsoever if your spouse has a 190 IQ, won the Nobel Peace Prize, looks like a combination of Chris Hemsworth and Brad Pitt or Sofia Vergara and Jennifer Connelly, earns six figures, speaks five languages and whips up gourmet vegan meals.

At some point, even if they verge on sheer human perfection, rest assured, they will still bug the living bejeezus out of you!

It might be how they watch television. Perhaps they talk throughout the show, so you miss the dialogue, or they crack jokes at the wrong time. Maybe they like to flip channels (not such an issue anymore with Netflix) or they hog the remote.

It might be his or her driving. Maybe they tailgate, or at age 45 still have not *quite* mastered parallel parking or the challenges of the three-point turn.

It might be him insisting that you cook keto every night, but then you discover he's been eating pizza and drinking beer out bowling with his buddies, plus buys Twizzlers and Cheetos on the daily from his office vending machine.

It may be her buying yet another pair of red pumps when she has 13 already and you know your credit cards are all approaching the dreaded "max."

If you've been married for more than one year, I predict with absolute certainty that your husband or wife has already driven you nuts in one way or another. Of course they have! How could they not?

At times, you'll gaze upon your beloved, and know in your heart of hearts they're part extra-terrestrial. You'll begin to wonder where they've been hiding their spaceship all this time (if needed, please do re-read the patented ALIEN section).

Going into the marriage, you thought you knew them inside and out, but trust me when I tell you — ghastly and strange-o surprises lurk around every corner.

But let's repeat this painful truth: your spouse may really be working your last nerve, but if you divorce them and remarry, rest assured, the new spouse will also drive you up the wall. It will just be in *new* and *state-of-the-art* ways!

Let's just imagine you toss out your first spouse and get a new and improved edition. At first, you're so happy with your current husband or wife. They're just wonderful. In fact, they're perfect. They don't have those same God-awful traits your first spouse did; you made absolutely certain of that.

But then you realize you've merely done an "alien switch-aroo."

In place of the first husband's horrific driving and procrastination, it's the second husband's bossy mother and annoying friends. Husband number one relentlessly flirted with your girlfriends and never, ever mowed the lawn, but husband number two is argumentative and keeps getting fired from jobs.

Instead of the first wife's overspending and talking too much in the mornings, you're now facing the second wife's God-awful cooking and sociopathic sister. The first wife was bossy and controlling, but the new wife accidentally divulged she detests your golden retriever Molly, and she just crashed your beautiful Audi...for the second time.

And, you're discovering all of this after spending a fortune on divorce, alimony, and child support.

By the way, none of this is meant to discourage remarriage. But if you're on your first marriage, contemplating divorce because your spouse is tremendously annoying, this chapter is meant to give you pause... by illustrating that *they all are annoying.*

Now, let's get to the crux of this. What makes a successful marriage different than one which fails? Well, it's largely how you handle these differences. Foremost: the humility to never forget that you, too, are only human and so believe you me, at times you're absolutely bugging the bejeezus out of your partner as well.

Respect, patience, understanding, compromise, and possibly most of all, a sense of humor, all contribute toward keeping you happily married.

Humility, kindness, gratitude and tolerance help you forge a strong and enduring relationship throughout the years, even with an alien.

These qualities ideally will enable you to stick together through thick and thin, richer or poorer, bad jokes, toothpaste tube, and wacko in-laws.

## Distractions

Imagine you're telling your spouse about a frustrating day at the office. Your co-workers are challenging, to put it mildly. Clyde screwed up a customer's order, then managed to pin the blame squarely onto you. Annabelle heated up some leftover fish in the break room, nuking it repeatedly because, as she joked, it was a little elderly. One bite and she realized it was no good. The break room is adjacent to your office, so all day long, you were treated to the scent of vintage tilapia. You're pouring your heart out to your spouse, relaying every detail, because this is really important to you....but guess what?

Your sneaky suspicion is that your spouse isn't paying attention... and you're right... they're not! They're focused on text messages, social media, emails, you name it. The distractions we face nowadays were unheard of even 20 years ago, and literally boggle the mind.

Some of these include: cell phones, texting, Instagram, TV, computer, Facebook, Twitter, Tik Tok, kids, online gambling, and Instagram. Whoops, did I say Instagram twice?

How many times have you caught yourself looking at your phone as your partner is trying to tell you about their day? You may say out loud, "I'm listening," but you're not really paying attention.

I've been guilty of this a trillion times... haven't we all?

So, the challenge is: know when to eliminate distractions and focus on your partner. But this is no piece of "boondt" cake.

Ryan and Heather had been dating for one year; at Valentine's Day dinner he announced he wanted to see other people. Heather looked up from her cell phone, aghast. She couldn't believe it. How could Ryan want to break up? They got along perfectly, with such great chemistry. They never, ever even argued.

When Heather tearfully asked why he wanted to break up, Ryan said he was always tempted to grab her cell phone and plunk it smack dab into her water glass. He sensed he was getting perilously close to that kind of dramatic gesture, so felt it was time to say "sayonara."

Heather protested that they never even argued! Ryan's response was they never argued because they rarely, if ever, carried on a full conversation.

So, a few ideas to minimize or eliminate distractions:

1. Turn off the TV.

2. Mute your phone and turn it over so you can't see even that alluring little blinking light. Many people leave their phone on vibrate, but unless you're expecting an important call, it may be preferable to just mute the little sucker.

3. Turn your computer off entirely in the evenings and back away very slowly. Pretend it's a wild and vicious grizzly bear you've encountered in the woods, maybe even that cocaine bear. Don't turn your back on it until you're out of sight.

4. If you're a relic like me and still actually own a house phone, unplug it most of the time, especially in the evenings.

Let's address the overuse of cell phones a bit further, because this was the #1 complaint of married folks who were interviewed for this book. #1 – wow!

Cell phones are so addictive that some people spend every waking moment looking at them.

So... what if this is your spouse? For starters, make sure that you, too, are not an offender.

When you're at a meal, movie, or social gathering, put away your phone. When at home, perhaps devote a set time of day to look at your Facebook, Instagram, or Twitter. The rest of the time, keep your phone turned off and in the other room.

If this advice seems extreme, you may be a bit of an *addict*.

If setting an example for your spouse isn't making a difference, it's time for more direct action. Sit your partner down (no cell phones in hand) for a serious talk. Calmly and clearly explain that you're beginning to feel like their phone, and not you, is their true, beloved significant other.

You likely won't get quick results. In the meantime, set an example by staying off your own phone as much as possible. New habits take about 21 days to form, by the way.

Thousands of relationships are being ruined due to "phubbing," snubbing someone in favor of a phone. "Phubbing" entails more than just looking at your Facebook or emails. It's denying your partner attention in favor of that mini screen.

Now let's address the distraction of children. Even if your kids are the cutest dumplings on the block, perfect little cupcakes, they nonetheless make it challenging for you to connect as a couple. Time and energy for sex, adult conversation, time to relax – these all sail right out the window when kids arrive. You're sleep-deprived, you're stressed, and maybe your child also has colic or is otherwise high-maintenance. Whatever it is, your relationship is sitting on the back burner. The main advice is to go out on date nights at least once weekly and continue this until the munchkins leave your nest and sashay off to college.

You may feel guilty leaving three-year-old Henry with a sitter, but please consider the fact that adorable Henry will be home with you until about *college age*. When he hits his teen years, Holy Moses, Henry will likely rebel and become a hellion. If you and your spouse have a good con-nection going, this will help you in the event you must deal with a teenage mutant nightmare. After college, Henry may likely move on abruptly and start his own independent life, so it will help to have something in com-mon with your spouse to fall back on.

I understand the guilt...I really do. But regardless what you do as a parent, you will always feel guilty, so you might as well put your marriage first from the very beginning.

Remember this: the best gift you and your spouse can give your kids is a good marriage.

Let's repeat this: the best gift you and your spouse can give your kids is a good marriage.

Sharon and Vince's kids were in day-care all week, so they were hesitant to stick them with a babysitter on Saturday nights. Their toddler Bonnie also slept in their bed most nights. Vince didn't like this a bit, but Sharon insisted it was just for a little longer.

So, this couple got no "alone time." None whatsoever.

How long before they look at each other with bleary, sleep-deprived eyes and forget why they fell in love in the first place?

Fortunately, there appeared a knight in shining armor for Sharon and Vince; 14-year-old Ashley. Tiny, bubbly Ashley, their neighbor's daughter, needed to be home by 11 p.m. on weekends, but this meant that Vince and Sharon had time for an early dinner and movie. They could share popcorn and hold hands. They could actually engage in...drumroll please... adult conversation. These date nights kept them from going certifiably crazy.

## Date Night

Many of our success couples mentioned how much they love their regular date nights. Saturday nights are the favorite; Fridays a close second.

If you haven't been out for awhile without your kids, it may seem surreal just the two of you at first. That's okay... the weird feeling will pass.

Babysitters are expensive, no doubt about it. If you absolutely can't afford to hire one, perhaps do a "babysitter swap" with a friend.

If money is tight, here are some fun, relatively inexpensive ideas for date nights:

1.  Casual dinner out and bowling

2.  Sonic or other fast food and a drive-in movie

3. Make out in the car in a parking lot. Careful ... more places have cameras now. Especially keep this in mind if you're parked in the lot of your husband's office.

4. Walk around and shop at a large mall (if the husband actually likes malls).

5. Go to the beach or park.

One happily married fellow said his top advice for a happy marriage is to never stop dating. That same evening, he was getting ready to take his wife to go see a reggae concert at a local bar.

Couples interviewed said their favorite dates included movies, dinners, concerts and long walks in the evenings. Some top spots included the park, the beach, the lake or the waterfront.

# Difficult
## (also see Easygoing)

We all know a few difficult folks. They're never really happy, are they? They *love* to complain. They never can just go with the flow. One of their top trademarks: they're virtually never happy at restaurants.

To see the true nature of someone, observe how they treat servers in a restaurant.

It's no fun eating out with this person. For one thing, it's embarrassing as hell. You just want to enjoy your spaghetti carbonara, and they're moaning their lasagna needs more sauce and there's better wine at home.

This is symbolic of a deeper issue: this individual lacks gratitude. They're too busy griping to appreciate the simple fact that they're in good enough health and have the money to eat out.

The difficult person may be a complainer, or argumentative, or, for extra fun and games, both. They like being in control and can't just "go with the flow." Nothing is ever easy with them.

This individual often has fixed and rigid ideals and is critical of others. No great surprise then; this is not an easy person to be married to.

Olivia is married to a difficult man. Steve is a successful accountant who owns his own CPA firm. He's intelligent, hardworking and basically a decent guy. He's financially generous toward his family and is a hard worker. But Steve *never* can just go along with whatever others want. In a group setting, it embarrasses Olivia that he must always be in charge, whether it's at movies, concerts, or restaurants.

For example, when everyone else is craving Chinese food, Steve just doesn't feel like it. It's not that he dislikes Chinese food, by the way. It's just that he wants to make the decision. If there's a new movie Olivia wants to see and he's heard it's no good, he "won't waste time" watching it.

Last year, he and Olivia visited London with another couple. Steve insisted on renting a car, although everyone said this was a waste of money. They drove the car just one day to see the countryside, and had to pay nearly 800 pounds to park it during their two-week trip.

Olivia is frequently frustrated with Steve over things like this, and it's caused much friction in their marriage. She believes he doesn't intend to be a pain in the arse, but is so used to running the show at work, he must do the same in his personal life.

Are you yourself perhaps that difficult person? Do you recognize yourself here, even somewhat? If you suspect that you are, it's a good idea to talk with your partner. Darn them, they'll likely confirm it.

Please then skip to the "easygoing" section below for some practical solutions. Individual therapy can be helpful also.

If you're married to that challenging individual, it's probably frustrating and sometimes rather embarrassing as well. Olivia makes her marriage work, but she does do a lot of socializing without Steve...it's just easier that way.

## Dumb and Dumber

For lack of a better term, "dumb" is that goofy thing your spouse does which makes you scratch your head and say, "What in the actual heck?"

You may be mildly perplexed and annoyed the *first time*. Fast forward 15 years of marriage, and guess what? Your spouse is still making the same mistake, or a very similar one. Something that was a bit exasperating, maybe even somewhat cute, the first 301 times, now grates across your nerves like Freddy Krueger nails on a chalkboard.

You cannot believe they did it *yet again*.

What a wonderful dream come true if your spouse miraculously no longer made the same dumb-ass mistake. But alas, this section does not include a wonderful Disney ending. This section deals with harsh realism. So buckle your seatbelt, and strap yourself in to hear some stories of spouses who do the same foolish things *over and over and over.*

William and Joanne have been married for over nine years. As a general rule, William is not absent-minded, but for reasons unknown, consistently forgets to lock his car. This wouldn't be too terrible, but William also leaves things in his vehicle that thieves want and love, like his wallet, filled to the brim with credit cards and cash.

Quick aside: has anyone seen the beautiful film, "Spirited Away?" One character proclaims: "Dad's got credit cards and cash."

Now, back to William. Six years ago, he stopped on his way home from work to visit his college buddy Doug. The two were considering opening a Subway franchise together and wanted to discuss the business plan. William parked his car on the street, unlocked as usual, leaving his briefcase on the back seat. Later, he could have sworn he'd put the briefcase into the trunk. Now, did we happen to mention that William's briefcase also held his wallet? Inside were a couple checks and every last one of his credit cards.

By the time William left Doug's house an hour later, the thieves had duplicated his driver's license and bought themselves some wonderful things at Home Depot and Best Buy. In less than two hours, more than $11,000 dollars was charged to William's credit cards.

By the way, this story took place before online shopping; nowadays, that $11,000 would easily have been $25,000.

Joanne was annoyed and frustrated. But she consoled herself by thinking that this could happen to anyone, right?

Fast forward six more years. William has had *three* more wallets stolen. Including the first wallet in his briefcase, this totals a whopping *four* wallets. So... this is where dumb goes to...dumb and dumber! It can drive a spouse completely out of their mind.

What are some ways to cope if your partner does the same dang dumb mindless thing over and over? How do you keep from just completely losing your marbles? Joanne admits this has been unutterably frustrating. She was furious with William when he lost his wallet a second and then a third time. When he lost the fourth wallet, she'd already come to the sorry conclusion that he was an alien. This was rather advantageous, as she'd now become somewhat resigned.

William was always very apologetic, by the way. He would feel terrible, but then would go and make the same mistake *yet again.*

Yet again!

For a brief time, Joanne grew rather despondent, thinking she'd been foolish to pick William for a husband. But then she decided it was pointless to blame herself for his sorry mess-ups.

Joanne also handled things very differently with the second, third and fourth wallets.

The first time, she had undertaken all the hard work of calling the bank, the credit card companies and so forth. The second, third and fourth times, she refused to do a single thing. She told William it was all on him.

Nowadays, William's wallet holds just one credit card, a minimal amount of cash and no checks. Joanne feels this at least mitigates damage, because unfortunately, although he's responsible about pretty much everything else, William seems destined to keep falling into the "stolen wallet vortex."

In all other respects, William is a great husband; generous, considerate, fun to be around, and a great dad to their kids. Therefore, Joanne lives with the wallet situation, painful though it may be. William and Joanne remain together and overall are still happy.

Now, onto another saga...Graham and Anne of Los Altos, California have been married for 14 years. Anne has many wonderful characteristics ... but she's a talker and cannot keep a secret. She never, *ever* intends to "spill the beans," but often confides in the wrong person or says too much. This has angered Graham many times in the past.

Graham is a manager at a large software firm. Last fall, he'd been up for a major promotion to West Coast Division Manager. This would have entailed a substantial pay increase and, best of all, a share in the company's profits.

At the same time he'd been striving for the promotion, Graham had been considering moving to his friend Adam's company. When the promotion at his current company was announced, Graham was bitterly disappointed ... the job went to his co-worker Nick. Nick hadn't worked there as long as Graham, nor had he produced equivalent results.

Graham's disappointment turned to anger when he spoke with his boss, Ted. Ted explained, "Well, since you're out there exploring other options, we chose someone else."

Graham had not told anyone at his company he'd been considering a move. As it turned out, his wife Anne was the culprit. Graham's company had put on a lavish Christmas party one month earlier. While thoroughly enjoying top-notch champagne, Anne had chatted up Ted's wife Lila. Somehow, unintentionally of course, Anne had giddily "spilled the beans" that Graham might relocate to another company.

Graham was furious; he told Anne he was sorry he'd trusted her. Her blabbermouth had cost him a huge promotion. Anne was sincerely contrite, but as Graham reminded her, this type of thing had happened before.

Several years earlier, Graham's brother Henry had stopped speaking to him for nearly three years. Anne had let it slip that their father had lent Graham money for a down payment on their house. Henry had requested the same help from their father and had been turned down.

Henry was irresponsible and never paid back a dime, and this was why their father had not helped him. But when Anne "spilled the frijoles," Henry had been furious.

This caused a three-year rift between the two brothers, which could easily have been avoided if not for "Chatty Anne."

So, what does Graham do? Like most people, he's going to feel betrayed when someone breaks his confidence. When that someone is his wife, the feeling is magnified 1,000 times. Anne is always sincerely contrite, but like "Wallet William," she seems destined to repeat the same mistake.

So, as the years go by, Graham confides in Anne less and less. He feels he cannot trust her... and unfortunately, he's right. Although this couple remains married, they've lost a great deal of closeness as a result.

So, how do you cope with this? For starters, humility can be a blessing, and one way to maintain your perspective. Think carefully... can you think of a mistake that you yourself are in the habit of repeating?

Chances are excellent you can. Hopefully this will make you more understanding of your spouse's shortcomings. And of course, something like Shelly forgetting to pay the gas bill over and over is not quite as serious as Fred forgetting that he shouldn't be hooking up with his secretary Courtney at the downtown Hilton over and over!

## Drop It

Let's envision a scenario where your spouse does something rather annoying or careless. Maybe they forgot to let your fox terrier Mindy out last night, and so this morning, your beautiful off-white carpet is less than pristine. Perhaps they posted an offensive comment on social media. Or maybe they forgot to make a bank deposit, and now five checks have bounced from your home in Chicago all the way to Waikiki beach.

You're really perturbed, but it's not quite the end of the world.

You've said your piece; you've expressed your irritation. Your spouse possibly apologized, or promised not to do it again. Maybe they removed the tactless comment on social media; at the very least, they acknowledged your feelings.

This is a "fantabuloso" time to ... drumroll please... drop it.

Knowing when to "drop it" with finesse is a priceless marriage skill.

At this point, for you to still carry on would be akin to beating a dead politician. Depending upon which politician we're referring to, continuing to beat them would be immensely satisfying, but in a marriage, not so good.

You're gonna gain pretty much nothing.

Of course, it's tempting to keep harping on, but knowing when to let it go can actually be an art form in itself.

Enough said... let's "drop it" now!

## Don't Make Your Problems My Problems

This was a favorite saying of one the smartest people who ever walked this earth, my husband's late, great Uncle Bob.

"Don't make your problems my problems." In the context of a marriage, what exactly does this mean? If someone in your life is draining your wallet, energy, or resources, not surprisingly, this can create an enormous strain on your marriage.

Lydia and Ted lived in London, were in their late 40s and had been married just three years; it was a second marriage for them both. Their kids were grown, they both had solid careers, were in good health and both loved to travel. This was supposed to be their carefree stage.

Unfortunately, Lydia's older sister Evelyn had been draining her time and finances since the two girls had been in their 20s. Evelyn drank heavily and never could hold down a job for more than two months at a time. Not only had she borrowed vast sums of money from Lydia and had never paid back a dime, Evelyn had a most unfortunate habit of ringing Lydia late at night to cry and complain.

Although Lydia and Ted had dated for three years before marrying, Ted had not realized the extent to which her sister leaned on her and drained her energy. After they had been married for a few months, Lydia mentioned in passing that she'd lent Evelyn more than 19,000 pounds in the past three years alone.

Ted grew increasingly frustrated seeing his bright, hardworking wife being used and abused by her sister.

It also was very disruptive when Evelyn rang their flat late at night, drunk and crying on the phone.

These situations are rarely as simple as they appear, particularly when involving family. Lydia had deep guilt over her sister's situation. Their alcoholic mother, long deceased, had put gin in Evelyn's baby bottle when she'd cried too much. Lydia firmly believed this would have been her fate as well, had she been a colicky baby like her older sister.

But Ted told Lydia there was a difference between helping family out of love and loyalty, and being used and manipulated. The two argued over this, but gradually Lydia realized that by constantly bailing out her sister, she was enabling her to continue drinking and was not doing her any favors in the long term.

Lydia began refusing to lend Evelyn more money. She worried her sister would end up homeless, so she paid the rent on her flat. Any cash given to Evelyn would be spent at a pub, so Lydia bought her groceries instead.

Lydia also discontinued her habit of dropping everything when Evelyn called, drunk and crying on the phone.

A few months later, Evelyn found a recovery program which she believed would be more helpful to her than AA. This support group proposed reduced drinking over a period of time versus cold turkey. Evelyn eventually quit drinking altogether and also found and held onto a decent job.

Best of all, and to everyone's surprise, Evelyn began mailing checks to Lydia once a month. They were tiny amounts to be sure, but still, this was an attempt to pay her sister back.

Evelyn began to call Lydia just to talk and to actually ask how she was.

Once Evelyn had been sober for two years, Ted surprised both sisters by gifting Evelyn the down payment on a beautiful flat of her own.

So, moral of the story, if someone is draining your time, energy, or finances, you needn't feel guilty about thinking, "Don't make your problems my problems."

## Dr. Linda Comedy Marriage Boot Camp

Welcome, welcome to the Dr. Linda Comedy Marriage Boot Camp. Enter if you dare... muahahahaha!

This simple, one-month program was specifically created to revive the most struggling marriages, those perilous unions that are quite literally at death's morbid doorstep.

Please forgive in advance if ghoulish humor is interjected throughout this section... a difficult topic is easier if we can make fun of it!

The Dr. Linda Comedy Marriage Boot Camp is basic training for a withering marriage. It's designed for a couple so totally out of sync, their marriage train has run so far off its rails, even Ozzy or Liam Neeson couldn't save the day. This marriage is like a teal blue 1969 Cadillac careening, swerving and skidding down Mulholland Drive, racing to divorce court.

This boot camp may be slightly challenging, but it's totally doable.

And the best part?

It has the potential to turn your marriage around *very* quickly. Just follow all eight steps for one month. Special bonus: you don't even have to eat low carb or keto!

You may or may not choose to discuss this process with your spouse before getting started. That's entirely up to you. But take heart in its proven track record. Over the years, I've recommended a similar program to friends and co-workers, and its success rate has been just about 60 percent. Those odds aren't bad. Better than the Dodgers versus the Padres!

So, how to determine if you're a good candidate for enlistment? Well, if you're literally ready to throw in the towel, or smother your partner with a pillow, or even hit 'em over the head with a non-stick frying pan, please do consider enlisting.

For sheer comic relief, speaking of non-stick frying pans, let's enjoy a brief time-out. Grab a gourmet snack and watch the "Hell's Kitchen" episode where Chef Gordon Ramsay becomes enraged when a contestant neglects to use a non-stick pan! How dare she? Chef Ramsay's fury is glorious... it's a wonder to behold!

Okay, YouTube break's over; back to business.

If you're basically done with your marriage, if you're truly contemplating divorce, would you consider delaying action for just one month?

By the way, we were almost totally joking about the frying pan and pillow.

For starters, let's make this whole process a tad more entertaining. Begin by visualizing yourself at an actual boot camp, but one that's just a little ...well, swankier. It's beach-adjacent, it's got palm trees, a swimming pool, a waterslide, chaise lounges, balmy weather and why not, since we were discussing talented chefs...the finest gourmet cuisine imaginable.

Next, create your "marriage boot camp" alter ego ... possibly one straight out of a film. You might select the funny and adorable Goldie Hawn from "Private Benjamin," or the handsome, charming Richard Gere from "An Officer and a Gentleman." The world is your apple, so feel free... use your imagination. Younger boot camp attendees might envision themselves as the hunky and fearless Chris Hemsworth from "The Extraction," or the dazzling and brave Jessica Chastain from "Zero Dark Thirty."

The process is quite straightforward. You simply complete the following steps for 30 days. If you begin in February, you only get 28 days, so what can I say? Make 'em count.

If you truly can't stand your partner for even one more week, let alone a month, please keep in mind that modified versions of this actual marriage boot camp have helped many struggling couples over the years. You've got a lot going for you when you decide to take on this challenge. You have unofficial research, time-tested methods, and me, Dr. Linda, like a close personal friend, encouraging you, cheering you on, and supporting you throughout this entire process.

Picture me, Dr. Linda, rooting you on like your own personal drill sergeant, but I'm wearing a flowered dress and sneakers. Back in the day it would have been three-inch high heels, but folks, honesty forces me to admit... "them days are over."

Now, if at the end of the month, you see *any* improvement in your marriage, and I mean *any*, repeat the entire process for another month. After the second month, if you see more progress, once again repeat the steps.

At this point, three entire months will have elapsed. Your relationship will be on an upward trajectory and your main task will be to continue the positive momentum.

Although these steps were a bit annoying to you at first, by this time, ideally, they will have become second nature.

At any moment, you can elect to divulge the details of this process to your spouse, but don't feel as if you have to. Instead, confide in a trusted pal.

So, to begin:

Let's say literally every single thing your spouse does bothers you, so much so in fact that you've already programmed the digits of your friend Mel's divorce attorney into your mobile. However, you haven't yet called, and after all, you've taken the time to buy this book, so please, please, consider giving this a try.

Without further ado, here it is in all its glory: "The Dr. Linda Comedy Marriage Boot Camp."

The eight steps are: 1) Adjust your thinking, 2) Do something very special *every three days* to pamper your spouse 3) Write down ten of your partner's good qualities on a piece of paper every day 4) Make an appointment with a good marriage counselor and attend once weekly 5) Go out on a date every Friday or Saturday night, preferably both 6) Sex twice a week, minimum, 7) King and Queen, and lastly, 8) Get more space.

The only step which you may be unable to commence immediately is the hiring of a marriage therapist. Don't wait until you locate one to begin; please kick off with the rest of the steps in the meantime.

We have now checked into our private rooms at the Dr. Linda Boot Camp. We're obliged to make our own beds, but otherwise, it's most luxurious. There's even a jacuzzi in each room! Out the window, you can see palm trees and the ocean. A cool breeze is blowing off the Pacific. Change into a comfortable outfit and sneakers, or ladies, even your cutest high heels!

And now, we are ready for Step 1.

Step 1: The first step, "Adjusting your thinking," might just be the most challenging of all. If you've spent months or even years feeling that you no longer love or even like your partner, take a moment to contemplate just how you got to this point. Was it one big event, such as infidelity or financial disaster which drove the two of you apart? Was it something that you can forgive? Or, was it just the everyday "wear and tear" your relationship went through and a gradual lack of attention, respect, affection or compromise?

The very next time your partner does or says something that upsets you, take a moment to determine if your reaction is in direct response to what just happened, or is instead a result of your mutual negative history.

When a marriage significantly deteriorates, it sinks below sea level, and then it doesn't take much for one partner to completely aggravate the other. The relationship becomes rather like New Orleans, slowly sinking all the time. And there are no beignets, no jambalaya, and no crawfish étouffée to lighten the mood. So, no matter what your partner says or does is pretty much gonna bug the bejeez right outta ya.

When this happens, you usually respond to your partner in a negative manner. Break this habit *today*. Instead, respond to your partner as you would your favorite co-worker or your best and most cherished friend.

Next, begin at once to pretend that you really like your spouse. If you dislike or even hate them right now, we realize this will require a herculean effort.

If it helps, close your eyes and imagine that you are your favorite actor or actress.

Immediately, one visualizes legends such as Robert De Niro, Al Pacino, Meryl Streep or Helen Mirren. Depending upon your age, you may prefer to go with Jake Gyllenhal, Channing Tatum, Anne Hathaway or Emma Stone. This is what's commonly referred to as "fake it 'til you make it!"

Pretend you're going for that Oscar, or at the very least, a daytime Emmy. Be really nice; it's okay if you are faking it. But don't act fake, if you catch my drift. Initially, your spouse may not even notice an improvement. Maybe they've been tuning you out for years. Or, alternatively, they may detect the change and are skeptical. They may even regard you with dread, as though you've been taken over by body snatchers.

Don't let this any of this deter you in the least. Remember... it's only for one month.

You can do *anything* for one month.

Soldier on, no pun intended, as this will become easier every day. But results won't be immediate. Not to throw out a stale cliché, but Los Angeles wasn't built in a month.

Now, here's the divine part, and I should know, because I've recommended this exact process to quite a few friends over the years. To your shock and surprise, within about 9.5 days, you will very likely be getting better vibes from your spouse.

Your niceness, even though it's a totally fake act at this point, has set off a positive chain reaction. You really didn't think your marriage could improve, and yet your partner is starting to be a bit nicer back.

Also, at this point, please pause for a little self-assessment.

Take a moment to ask yourself a few questions. You can be totally honest here, because you're not going to share this with anyone. No writing down answers in this book; there are no cute little workshop pages. The reason is this: yours truly has read virtually trillions of self-help books. Not one single time, not once, did I ever complete those cunning little workshop pages, and over the years this has saddled me with residual and impotent guilt.

Okay, here are the questions:

- Have you gotten into the habit of feeling sorry for yourself or of being a martyr in the relationship?

- Do you fail to speak up for yourself and then become upset when you don't get what you want?

- Alternatively, do you speak up over every single miniscule issue so that your spouse no longer pays you any attention...you're the boy or girl who cried "coyote ugly?"

- Do you expect your spouse to be a mind-reader?

- Do you hold everything in, but then explode, or do you hold resentment in indefinitely, but then employ nasty little passive-aggressive techniques?

Okay, we've unpacked our boot camp duffle bags; we now are ready for step 2.

Step 2: "Do something lavish to pamper your spouse *every three days.*" Do this religiously for an entire month.

Why every three days? Well, it's one of my luckiest numbers, coming from my mom Carmel. She was born on March 3rd of 1930, and she had three siblings and three daughters. So the number three is very lucky... and we're gonna go with it.

There's also a psychological component here. If you do something wonderful for your spouse every three days, these sublime events shall then continuously fall on different days of the week. Your partner will be consistently surprised and unable to find a pattern, which is perfect. The intention is to catch them off guard, and to surprise them, but in a good way.

You may be rolling your eyes and groaning right now. I get it. If you feel like you're just "done" with your partner, the very idea of doing something nice for them could make you feel just a trifle nauseous.

But really, when it comes down to it, you're doing this for yourself. Think back to that time when your marriage was happy. Wasn't life easier then? Don't you want that part back, or maybe even better?

Think of ways to improve your marriage, even if your spouse doesn't change. For example, you and your partner are angry, you're tired of one another and you both know it. Neither of you do wonderful things for each other anymore. Perhaps you haven't in years.

That went by the wayside when she got drunk at your company party and told off your boss's wife, then ran all your credits cards to the hilt vacationing in Rome with her spoiled-ass girlfriends.

Or, you threw in that towel when he lost half your savings at the casino, then to top it off, backed your new Camaro into the neighbor's wall, shamelessly blamed the wall, and refused to apologize afterwards.

So, whatever the grievances, set them aside during boot camp. Leave them at home; they do not go into your basic training duffle bag. Next, visualize yourself as your favorite actor or actress... hair, makeup and lighting are perfect...ready, set, go! Action!

Here's some inspiration for how to pamper your spouse every three days.

Wives, let's imagine your husband worships and adores your homemade German chocolate cake. It's your Aunt Jill's treasured and guarded creation; there's nothing like it on the entire planet. You had to beg Aunt Jill for the secret recipe and she only caved one night after three glasses of prosecco. This cake is the most glorious melding of chocolate, caramel and coconut imaginable.

When you and hubster were so deeply in love, you baked him this fantastic treat at least twice a month. He'd gobble down three pieces immediately, then two pieces the next morning for breakfast, then bring the leftovers to his office. His co-workers fought over that cake and raved about how lucky he was. He always joked that he was a celebrity at his office when he brought in your scrumptious cake.

But that was before he gambled away your savings and crashed your car. He's gotten control over the gambling, but you're still resentful. You're hanging onto the anger, and why shouldn't you? He probably whines to everyone at the gambling support group how it was your fault he lost all that money, which took five years to save and two months to lose, incidentally.

It's been over six months, and you have no intention of pulling those baking pans out of the cupboard. Why should you? You can't even stand the sight of him, so why would you spend three hours making that f'n cake?

Okay, husbands, recall how your wife absolutely adored when you washed, waxed and detailed her sports car. You did such a beautiful job, her car looked brand-new. You even used Q-tips to reach every surface. Vacuuming the interior took half an hour alone. She'd brag to her girl-friends, who joked that none of them had such an amazing husband. But then she had to go and embarrass the hell out of you at the company party by getting drunk and snotty to your boss's wife. Plus, who can forget her trip to Rome? It will take you three years to pay off all the credit cards she "maxed out" shopping with those snootsy women.

When it comes down to it, you've been sick of that "witch with a b" since 2018, so no way in heck will you spend half a Saturday laboring over her damn car. She can just take it to the car wash herself.

Okay, you guessed it! Step two will be to do something really special for your spouse, such as the German chocolate cake or detailing the car.

Your mission, should you decide to accept it, is to do something comparable *every three days*. Boot camp is now well and truly underway!

Given the current state of your relationship, it's understandable that you don't feel like doing anything nice for your spouse, let alone something elaborate that will take hours of your time.

That's okay – please do it anyways. Keep it up for one month. *Every three days.*

Boot camp means *business!*

Here are some possible ideas:

- Bake his or her favorite cake.

- Wash, wax and detail his or her car.

- Clean out the garage on Saturday.

- Paint the spare bedroom, the one you promised to do back in 2017.

- Get concert tickets for her favorite band, the one you can't stand.

- Every three days walk her dog, the dog that hates you, even if it's raining.

- Fix a gourmet dinner, one that involves lots of ingredients and effort.

- Find the negatives for his 1993 fishing trip, have them developed and put them in a nice photo album.

- Bring her to see her favorite classic film on the big screen. Bonus points if it's in black and white. Double bonus points if you remain fully awake 'til the credits roll.

- If you live in a cold climate, rise early to warm up her car and scrape ice off the windshield.

- Substitute ideas of your own, things you know your partner will like and best of all, be very surprised by.

Now, let's march toward the ocean on our way to step 3. Along the way, let's sing in unison, "Who's gonna stay happily married, we are, we are!"

Step 3: "Write down on a piece of paper ten of your partner's good qualities every single day for four weeks." List ten items per day minimum. It's likely you write things on your phone nowadays, but an actual paper and pen are best for this.

Items listed needn't be grandiose. If you find it difficult to envision any positive traits, there's nothing wrong with miniature listings such as "remembered to take out the trash."

If your relationship has descended to open hostility, this here step may seem ridiculous, if not downright impossible.

Please, please do it anyways. I promise: it will get easier.

If your partner has done "crummy stuff," it's far more comfortable to continue resenting or disliking them. The physical action of writing down their good qualities begins to change your thinking. Ideally, you'll again view your spouse as a well-rounded person, one with positive attributes as well as negative.

This exercise is kissing cousin to the gratitude journal. By thinking of ten items each day, you're seeking the positives, rather than only shortcomings.

Now, on the double, let's all do one and one-half push-ups. I'm only going to force you to do as many push-ups as I myself can!

Next, let's march over to step 4! If you dislike marching, no one's going to force you: in fact, several attractive golf carts with full beverage service are "at the ready."

Step 4: "Hire a marriage therapist." Invite your partner to accompany you, but if they refuse, go on your own.

Here comes the challenge: you only get to tell your therapist the truth. I know, I know! Lying or omitting details is the fun part of therapy! I should know, I've certainly done it. But a boot camp rule: don't sugar-coat your own screw-ups. Even if your therapist is super cool like mine, and you want to impress him or her, don't waste your money. You're paying a lot of cold, hard cash, so be willing to relay the good, bad, and ugly, not just about your spouse, but darn it anyways, about yourself.

Many folks lie to their therapists to make their partner look like the culprit. I mean, who can blame them? I get that this is very tempting.

Now, if your spouse does agree to couples' therapy, make an honest effort to listen to what they say. You may hear things you don't like or possibly things you've never heard before.

In any event, nonetheless stay cool like a cucumber that's been sprinkled with fresh dill.

On our way to Step 5, let's run an obstacle course around the entire boot camp. Feel free to stroll if you prefer, especially if you're wearing heels.

And no one, but no one, expects you to climb over that wall thing. That's only in the movies!

Step 5: Go out on a date with your spouse at least once a week, twice minimum. For starters, recommend *their* favorite restaurant or movie choice. You needn't go with only their choices forever; this is just initially to lure them out of the house. Ladies, dress nice, wear jewelry, some makeup if you like. Men, use cologne and wear a tropical shirt or something comparable.

Pay attention to your spouse's conversation. This might be awkward at first, but not nearly as unpleasant as shelling out $330 per hour to a divorce attorney.

Don't discuss anything serious, and don't argue. Pretend you're a new couple out on a nice date, and stay on your very best and most charming behavior.

It's all going to seem tremendously fake and phony. But as time goes by, your pretended affection will ideally give way to the real thing.

After all, you had the real thing at one time.

As these dates continue, remember that the Boot Camp motto is to find ways to make your relationship more romantic. Hold hands again. Maybe pull the car over on the way home for a little "roadside romance." Hey, if a cop cites you for indecent exposure, this tale could be a lively way to embarrass younger generations once you hit your golden years.

"Man, great-grandma was a firecracker back in the day! Holy cow! Some of her stories!"

We've now done enough marching and singing to last a lifetime. Enough of that!

Let's now hit the pool. There are chaise lounges and drinks with little umbrellas and fruit wedges. Dr. Linda's Comedy Marriage Boot Camp is also about fun, as our next section shall illustrate.

Step 6: "Have sex twice a week minimum." If you're rolling your eyes whilst reading this, maybe your sex life is in the dumps. Maybe you're so angry with one another you aren't sleeping together at *all* anymore.

If so, you may at first feel like a Victorian girl who was advised to close her eyes, carry on and think of Mother England.

Not to sound bossy, but just do it! If your spouse totally rejects your advances, maybe do all the other steps, then try hanky-panky again in a week or so. Start small by just holding hands if sex is really out of the question. But this is a good way to forge closeness. Any progress in this area will be helpful.

Now that we've lounged by the pool for awhile, it's time for the barbecue. We've got it all, even vegetarian and vegan options. Fill your plate a couple times; the food's included in the price of camp admission.

Step 7: "King and Queen." Okay, this will be the shortest section. Basically, if you are a woman, try to make your husband feel like a King. Make him feel like he's an important guy. Buy him those candy bars he likes. Brag about him to the kids. In short, make him feel like royalty. Men, go through this same process with your wife. Treat her like a Queen. Pamper her and buy her little surprises. Tell her she looks beautiful. Get her flowers or candy; whatever is her favorite.

Last step: Step 8: "Get some space." Many relationships did not survive Covid; a "lack of space" was cited in many breakups.

How do Robert and I maintain space? Even though gas is so expensive, we often drive places separately. He listens to heavy metal in his truck and I play 80s tunes in my sports car. Tonight we're having dinner with another couple; I'm leaving early to walk at the mall and then we'll meet at the restaurant. Our house isn't large, but if he's in the den watching TV and I'm in the living room reading, this gives us some breathing room.

It's smart to maintain some healthy distance. Couples have a chance to miss one another when they aren't crammed in together like two cranky little sardines 24-7. If you and your spouse are frequently annoyed with each other, ask yourself if you get enough space.

Some couples blissfully maintain, "We are best friends and we do *everything* together. Absolutely everything." Oh, brother. Good for you!

Let's just see you in about ten years. Wait, did that sound kind of mean? I'm probably just envious when I hear that kind of glorious statement.

For the vast majority of couples, doing everything together just might result in one partner shoving the other off a sheer cliff. Just joking, of course! However, it is noteworthy that a recent "Forensic Files" episode re-enacted almost precisely this same scenario.

Okay, so there you have it...those are the boot camp steps.

If you decide to enlist, I heartily congratulate you. This semi-patented boot camp has been successfully executed by couples who lived to tell the tale. They said it was weird, it was fun, and that initially, they doubted it would help.

Approximately 60 percent of them said it improved their marriage tremendously.

You can do this! Si se puedo!

At the end of the month, congratulate yourself! Give yourself a big pat on the back. You survived boot camp!

At this time, please take a moment to re-assess your relationship. You likely will have noticed some improvement after just one month. Your spouse may have also commented positively, and hopefully initiated some changes as well.

At this point, it's recommend that you repeat the boot camp at least once more, and make adjustments where you see fit. After that time, you can continue utilizing the steps indefinitely.

Side note: if time is a factor, after a couple months, you can cut a few corners. For example, if you sometimes buy a cake from a bakery, or take your spouse's car to the car wash, nobody — and I mean nobody — will judge you!

# E

## Easygoing
### (see Difficult)

When you're involved in a relationship with someone easygoing, your life is probably a whole lot less stressful.

I was lucky to marry a man who is easygoing and he's been a good influence on me over the years in becoming more that way myself.

This is definitely a personality trait that you can build upon. Sometimes it takes a combination of hard work, therapy and determination to evolve from a person who stresses over little things to someone who takes the difficulties of life in stride.

Perhaps you're thinking, "Easier said than done." For example, you have a high-pressure job, a demanding boss, a rebellious teenager who appropriated your car last week then promptly crashed it, and your house needs new plumbing.

Here are some steps you can take:

Number one: consider therapy, which can help strengthen your coping skills. In therapy, you can deal with current stressors as well as past issues which continue to hamper you today.

Number two: becoming more "chill" is a learned trait. You can work on nurturing and honing this skill. When things get on your nerves, such as the job, the boss, finances, traffic, the weather, or your spouse, there are exercises you can employ.

Here are just a few: take a few deep breaths, count to ten, and think of all those things you are grateful for. Humor also works wonders. If you can laugh at misfortunes or annoyances, they will have less power over you.

"How am I supposed to giggle about losing my job, my huge stack of bills, or my ill parent?" you might ask. While none of these situations are the least bit funny, if you're resilient, you can more efficiently deal with them. And, as it so happens, humor is a fantastic aid in developing resiliency.

"Laughter is the best medicine," we've all heard it a trillion times. During Covid, one thing that helped was watching great comedians on TV... Kevin Hart, Kevin James, John Mulaney, Jerry Seinfeld, and Ali Wong, among others.

It's also seeing humor in everyday situations. Being able to laugh is freeing, especially if you tend to be hard on yourself when you make mistakes.

Exercise classes, dancing, even dancing to music on your own for 15 minutes in the evenings can help. Walking is a great stress reliever. Some folks love yoga or meditation.

If you've read thus far, surely by now you're used to the strange-o but well-intended suggestions of Dr. Linda.

So, here's an odd exercise. For each letter of the alphabet, state aloud one positive adjective. For example: Amazing, Beautiful, Courageous, Determined, Energetic, Fighter, etc. Go all the way to Z. Repeat aloud several times a day, and again at night if you have insomnia. It's rather like brainwashing or a positive mantra. You can even do this in the shower, as loud as you like.

## Empty Nest

If your eldest child is less than 13 years of age, skip this section and revisit it when they turn 15. The main "take-away" now is to spend "alone time" with your spouse, such as date nights and short vacations. This will help keep your "couple vibe" alive for when you'll most need it... the empty nest years.

If your children are in middle school, the concept of an empty nest still seems oceans away. But then it's amazing how fast it sneaks up on you. One day you're watching your daughter play high-school basketball and the next you're helping her move into her college dorm; her roommate has green hair, owns Prince posters, and is named Lindsay.

Many of our success story couples love their empty nest because they'd already been in the habit of spending time together without their kids. Bo and Geoff and Brad and Karen take frequent vacations together. Pamela and Craig enjoy date nights and take long walks on the weekends.

But for some couples, the empty nest is lonely and heartbreaking. Many parents experience loss and sadness when their youngest – or only – child moves away.

For us, it was more gradual. Andrea lived on campus during college, but her dorm was less than an hour away, so we saw her frequently. When she studied abroad in Europe, it was for six months, but we visited her, so the time flew by. By the time she moved out, we had already adjusted to her being on her own.

If you're struggling with empty nest syndrome, here are some practical steps to hopefully ease this transition:

#1: Stay busy. You'll have less time to wallow in grief and self-pity. This sounds like our parents' generation, but staying busy helps you "suck it up." If you're working this helps; if not, charity organizations are desperate for volunteers.

#2: Rekindle romance and fun with your partner. See a drive-in movie during the week because hey, you can! Have sex in every room of the house. Take fun trips you two always wanted to take; ideally, someplace impractical.

Detroit couple Janey and Ron had a rough transition when their only son Joshua moved to California. Janey wished to follow Joshua to California, but Ron's elderly parents lived in Detroit, so this wasn't feasible. Plus, Ron had heard of parents who followed their kids to another state, only to have the kids up and move on them again.

Ron's entire family had originally been from Ireland, but he'd never had a chance to visit. Janey surprised him with a trip to Dublin and they had an incredible time. This began a marvelous new phase of their marriage.

Up 'til now, Janey and Ron had always been so practical. They'd typically taken road trips to California, where Janey's younger sister lived. Now, an entire new world opened up to them, as they began to travel overseas. Once each year they visited Italy, France, Germany, the Netherlands, and then again, Ireland.

#3: Develop a new interest...perhaps something you always wanted to do, but never had the time. Keep in mind: no law demands that you and your spouse both develop the same hobby.

Alan and Jean had both poured everything into raising their four children. Now that their youngest was out of the house and Alan had retired, he bought a boat. He began sailing nearly every day with two buddies. Jean joined him occasionally, but wasn't a big fan of the water. She was also still working. But she'd always loved to play golf, and she now resumed this hobby. Alan and Jean frequently met for dinner after she'd finished her golf game and he'd docked his boat for the day.

#4: Put the energy into your spouse you'd always poured into your children.

Teresa and Mike had one daughter, Alice. For many years, Teresa had fixed elaborate vegetarian meals for Alice. They'd never admitted it at the time, but neither Teresa nor Mike particularly enjoyed vegetarian meals. When Alice moved out on her own, Teresa at first heated frozen dinners, and she and Mike ate them on trays in front of the TV. In no time at all, this grew as stale as the TV dinners.

Mike then suggested they take a cooking class with their next-door neighbors, Bill and Emily. Teresa and Mike loved the cooking class, and began experimenting with new recipes several nights a week.

They started watching foodie cooking shows and competitions and invited Bill and Emily over for gourmet meals. In turn, Bill and Emily treated them to gastronomic adventures next door.

Now, for the first time, Teresa and Mike shared a hobby. Along with Bill and Emily, they began planning a French culinary cruise. The boat will travel through Burgundy and Provence and will explore food adventures from fromage to fondue and crepes to croissants!

## Empathy

Empathy is placing oneself in another's shoes and understanding what that person is going through. This is not the same thing as sympathy, where one feels sorry for another.

Empathy for one's partner is crucial to a successful marriage. Happily married folks often describe their partner as being "in their corner" and "rooting for them."

Face it, everyday life is tougher than a lamb chop baked on a cookie sheet for three and a half hours. It's demanding, stressful, and often discouraging. Job losses, money worries, family issues, health problems, just to name a few.

If you don't feel your partner empathizes with you, or has compassion for you, you'll probably feel quite lonely. Lonely married people tend to be unhappy. They may look elsewhere for someone they can relate to. This is where marital infidelity often begins.

"She always used the word 'silly' when I was upset. She never wanted to hear anything negative," was the complaint I heard from a buddy years ago. He eventually left his wife for another woman.

"He always sees the other person's point of view, and tells me it's my fault," was a comment from an unhappily married girlfriend.

What these two people are saying, in essence, is they didn't feel their spouse was on their side. That's pretty awful, from someone you've vowed to spend the rest of your life with.

We human beings have an enormous need to be heard and feel understood. This is wonderful to receive from our partner, although friends can help fill this emotional requirement.

When you've been around as long as I have, you've seen many marriages flounder and ultimately fail. It isn't an overnight process.

But...here's some good news! Relationships can turn around; they can get better and stronger. Marriages can nearly always improve, through effort and caring.

If you're reading this book and feel you're stuck in an unhappy marriage, there are steps you can take to improve it.

It's never, *ever* all the fault of just one partner.

For example, if your partner isn't paying attention when you talk, where are you both located? Are you standing in the kitchen, and calling across the room as he's in the den watching TV?

I've been guilty of this exact practice thousands of times. I'll be in the kitchen cooking, calling out to Robert, who's in the den watching car races. Later I'll ask him, "Remember I told you xyz?" And he'll reply, "No, you didn't."

How about when your spouse is talking to you? Do you sneak glances at your cell phone? If he's venting about Josh, his ass-kissing rival, who just beat him out of a big promotion, and you're peeking at your phone, this sends a very clear message.

A side note: Although I effortlessly pump out these tacky scenarios, I myself have been endlessly guilty!

Mute your phone and turn it over, or for brownie points, put the little sucker in another room. Truly pay attention to your partner. Otherwise, it becomes harder to keep that connection, until one day it's completely gone, and you don't even know what happened.

Apparently, there's even a name for this: "phubbing," or snubbing someone with your phone. There's an indirect link between "phubbing" and depression, because if your partner ignores you in favor of their mobile, this may negatively affect your self-esteem.

# Envy
## (see also tailgating)

Ahh...envy... that monstrously delicious, horribly guilty feeling which we've all experienced.

When Robert and I had been married for about four years, we became close with Lou and Diana. About five years older than us, they were a ridiculously beautiful couple. Not just beautiful... indescribably gorgeous, rich, fun, successful and actually very, very nice to boot. Darn it, there was nothing unlikeable about *either* of them. I never realized it then, but they might have been too good to be true. Looking back, I wonder if they were some kind of "Stepford couple!"

Fortune smiled daily upon Lou and Diana. They had a darling little boy, a beautiful house, gorgeous cars, and took frequent jaunts to Jamaica and Europe. Lou was a successful chiropractor and Diana stayed home with their small son. They were both sociable and fun, radiating youth, prosperity and good looks. In other words, Lou and Diana seemed to have it all (I say "seemed" because now in my late 50s as I write this, I realize no one has it all. But back then, I was 29 and had little perspective).

We had a great time socializing with Lou and Diana, but sometimes it was difficult. We'd just bought our first house and were enormously strapped for cash. Only today can I finally admit that it was sheer envy I experienced watching Lou and Diana gallivant around town in their new "his and hers" BMW's, remodel their house and frequently travel, when we were struggling to pay both our mortgage and utility bills in the same actual month.

It didn't help matters that we were living in Los Angeles at the time. By the way, quick insert: if you haven't seen the "Megan and Harry" Netflix series, it's just glorious how Harry pronounces "Los Angeles" in the show.

Los Angeles is a town that was built upon envy and eats it for breakfast, lunch, dinner, boba tea and snacks. I don't recall feeling this way growing up in Westchester, a small suburb of L.A. near the beach. It was the best time and place, kind of like living in a small town inside a huge city.

But as an adult, there's something about living in Los Angeles where no matter what, one never feels quite enough, not a real part of things, not rich enough, not famous enough, and certainly never thin enough. Even celebrities frequently admit to this.

Dear reader, you will *always* have friends with more than you. It will kind of make you sick sometimes... I do get it. In addition, you will have friends with *less*. The most important thing to remember is: don't envy and don't tailgate.

Easier said than done, I know. We all know what envy feels like, and it sure ain't pretty.

Envy is often confused with jealousy. You envy someone's gorgeous figure, beautiful house or bank account. Jealousy is when you find out your ex moved in with his new girlfriend. Envy is an ugly emotion to be sure, but jealousy can cause folks to commit murder.

Tailgating is another term for trying to keep up with the Joneses. If you allow it to, tailgating wears you out and it saddles you with massive debt as you vainly try to keep pace with your richy-rich friends. Focus away from their huge bank accounts, perfect figures, amazing jobs and trust funds. Again, easier said than done!

You quite possibly have some friends who are envious of *you*. That kind of competition isn't healthy for a friendship. You can't do a whole lot to change their attitude, but of course it goes without saying that if you avoid bragging to your friends, you're much better off. Of course, no one here has ever been guilty of bragging, myself included, ha!

What is the antidote to envy? It is gratitude.

The gratitude section will be "coming round the mountain" soon. But, we shall address it just a wee bit here.

First, think of everything good in your life. There's simply no way to be happy, whether on your own or in the context of a marriage, without gratitude. If you observe individuals who are consistently miserable, you can "bet your bippie" they lack appreciation.

I've kept a gratitude journal for the past 10 years; each night at bedtime I jot down three things I'm grateful for. I highly suggest an actual physical diary where you write things down on paper.

No one else will see what you write. So if it's late and you're exhausted, you can even just think of something and then draw a little representative squiggle. You'll still reap the same psychological benefits.

I once discontinued my gratitude journal for about six months. When I resumed, I found it difficult to think of three things to list. Perhaps during the hiatus, I'd become less conscious what I should be thankful for.

When I once again began this practice consistently, I rarely listed only three items per day. Typically, I come up with at least five or six. These can be as simple as baby bunnies munching carrots on our front lawn, or drinking a great Starbucks.

## Exercise

Poor health and serious illness are issues which even young couples may face. Sometimes, even if they do everything right, folks can become seriously ill. We've all known or heard of individuals who never smoked or drank, ate healthy, weren't overweight, exercised, and still died tragically young.

This gets sickening when you picture Charles Manson in his jail cell (he was still alive when I began writing this book, but has since passed away) draining taxpayer money year after mother frickin' year.

Couples can exercise together to maintain or improve health, and it can be fun. Some superstar couples run 10K's, hike for miles, and climb mountains. These are all fantastic ventures, but don't feel like a lame-o if walking is your primary exercise.

Some couples ride bicycles together, or visit the park or beach with their dogs.

You can build a playlist on Spotify and dance around like an absolute nerd. Of course, *I've* never done this: a "friend" provided this tip.

One of our success story couples, Pamela and Craig, walk together almost every evening and take extra long walks on the weekends. It's one of their favorite ways to spend uninterrupted time talking.

## Everything They Do

When researching this book, I encountered several married individuals who stated they were "done" with their partner. Done, done, done. They were still wed, for reasons of finances, religion, or inertia, but very, very unhappily.

Sadly, some had reached the point where they believed their spouse had no redeeming qualities whatsoever.

So...what if this is *your* current situation? What if you are completely "done" with your marriage partner?

Perhaps you've already taken steps toward divorce. Or maybe you're unwilling to split up, but you're facing the rest of your precious life stuck in an unhappy marriage.

If this is you, and you've taken the time to buy this book, please do just one thing.

Try the special "Dr. Linda Comedy Marriage Boot Camp," patent pending.

It's listed in precise detail, just a little back in the "D" section of this book.

## Exciting

Tragically, everyday married life can become routine, rather "ho-hum," if you will.

"Blah" is one adjective which appallingly springs to mind.

So, if your union is dreary and boring, how do you keep it interesting?

One common attribute of our success couples (their stories are at the end of this book) is they love to do things just for fun. Kathy and Kevin do wind tunnel and they travel. Bo and Geoff travel frequently, visit fun restaurants and sightsee in their beloved New York City. Claire and Sam once traveled to Europe for two entire months! Bill and Mary travel to her original home of England and all over the U.S. Lynn and Larry see their large circle of friends constantly for dinners and card games.

Joe and Victoria frequently visit new restaurants and pubs, and love sailing their boat. Susan and John entertain and socialize with friends. Isn't "entertain" a glorious word? We're tossing it in here just to keep it in circulation! Sebastian Maniscalco, if you're reading this, please do include the concept of "entertaining with real silverware" in a future skit. Susan is a fantastic chef and she and John indulge their friends with wonderful dinners. Candace and Tom go on tropical cruises. Juliette and Daniel love Disneyland, where they dress up in gorgeous retro costumes and ride the train. Gary and Julie have six kids, including two sets of twins, but still visit Las Vegas and Palm Springs.

Travel is a great way to make married life more exciting. Unfortunately, you can't travel constantly! Luckily, even one night away at a close location can do wonders for the morale.

Double dates are fun; when your kids are younger, so is socializing with their friends' parents. We loved dinners, barbecues and swim parties with the parents of Andrea's friends.

One success story husband offered this advice: as the years pass, do not allow yourself to become lazy about sex. It doesn't have to be a marathon, maybe just a "quickie" sometimes. "Hey honey, Sons of Anarchy starts at 9 p.m.; we've got 17 and a-half minutes!"

"A proposito," a glorious multitude of steamy advice awaits you in our upcoming "sex" chapter.

So, in closing, any departure from the normal routine can make married life more exciting. If you typically visit good old reliable Gino's Italian restaurant near home, "shake it up, baby now" and drive to Guido's Ristorante at the beach.

Guido's may actually "suck arancinis" compared to Gino's, but hey, you tried something new!

You know what they say: Variety is the cardamom of life!

# Egg You On aka Huevos Galore

So, who exactly is that clever, conniving individual we hereby dub the "egg you on?" Let's give them the super-sassy nickname of "huevos galore."

"Huevos galore" is that trusted friend or co-worker whom you confided in about the sad, sorry-ass state of your crumbling marriage, and who now energetically campaigns for your divorce.

It's far preferable to divulge in a happily married friend, rather than one who is single or divorced. The happily married friend likely has endured rough patches and emerged victorious. Therefore, they are apt to suggest you stick it out, for lack of a better term.

Now, beware! An *unhappily* married friend might urge you to throw in the towel. Although miserable with their *own* spouse, it's possible that for reasons of fear or finances, they're stuck. Ergo, they adore living vicariously through you and witnessing your exciting flight of freedom.

Psychology plays an enormous role in this process; the majority of human behavior stems from the subconscious mind.

Therefore, avoid well-meaning friends like Claudia at all costs.

Claudia simply detests her boring, controlling husband Ed, but would never dream of divorcing him, for then she'd be obliged to work. Poor Claudia! She's not even aware of what she's doing as several times a day she snap-chats you divorce attorney billboards whilst cruising the 405 freeway in her new powder-blue Jetta, Starbucks carmel frappe in hand.

Put away your damn phone Claudia! You're gonna rear-end somebody!

Now, the part which really sucks "huevo rancheros," for lack of a better term, is this: a helpful pal like Claudia may actually disappear into thin air once the dust from your break-up clears.

In the beginning, Claudia commiserated whenever you needed to vent. She checked in with you constantly and was so understanding and supportive. Regretfully, she did encourage you to dump your spouse.

Claudia helpfully recommended a luxury divorce attorney, one whose offices held panoramic views of the waterfront and whose high-heeled assistant Heidi offered you mineral water with cucumber essence in a chilled glass, including a paper-thin slice of real cucumber *and* a lovely, fresh sprig of mint.

Claudia was a dream come true, the most supportive friend imaginable, so who could have ever predicted she'd "Criss Angel" you by vanishing into thin air soon after your divorce finalized.

Natalie and Alan lived in New York City and had been married for six years. Alan intensely disliked Natalie's best friend Suellen because she borrowed money from Natalie repeatedly and never paid back one thin dime. Alan viewed Suellen as a user and abuser. But the gals had been best friends since high school, so there was no raining on that estrogen parade. Suellen detested Alan as well; she was certain he'd influenced Natalie to finally stop lending her money.

Natalie and Alan began to have infertility issues, which eventually placed an enormous strain on their previously happy relationship. Natalie was heartbroken when she failed to become pregnant, and wanted Alan to be as distressed as she was.

Alan was just as sad, but trying to be strong for Natalie's sake. Unfortunately, she believed he was unfeeling and cold. This happens frequently: the man tries to be stoic, so the woman mistakenly believes he doesn't care.

Natalie and Alan, once so close, drifted further and further apart. Less than one year later, this previously happy couple was barely speaking to one another.

Natalie increasingly looked to her best friend for support; Suellen was there for her 100 percent. Natalie told her Alan didn't even want children. Nothing could have been further from the truth, and Suellen actually knew this. But with selfish "eggster motives," she jumped on this opportunity and encouraged Natalie to leave Alan and to move in with her.

Suellen's disgruntled roommate had just moved out in a huff; Suellen was desperate for a replacement to split her rent. Suellen also believed that once Alan was out of the picture, Natalie would again bail her out financially, just like the good ol' days.

Alan begged Natalie to reconsider. He suggested they see a counselor and said he'd do anything to keep from losing her. He also suggested they adopt a child, which they'd previously discussed as a viable alternative.

When Natalie repeated this, Suellen recounted every story of bungled adoptions she'd ever heard, and reminded Natalie that Alan didn't even want kids.

There's no denying that Suellen was a textbook "huevos instigator." At last, she'd found something at which she could truly excel. She had the advantage of history, and could recall with crystal-clear clarity each mistake Alan had ever made, many of which Natalie had long forgotten. Natalie was emotionally fragile, so she was putty in Suellen's capable hands.

Of course, Suellen can't be blamed absolutely. We could phrase it this way: Natalie *allowed* Suellen to "huevo her on."

Who knows? This couple might have split up anyways, but there's no denying Suellen had a major influence as she continually reminded Natalie of all the fun they'd have as single girls.

Natalie moved in with Suellen two weeks later, and then filed for divorce.

Once she'd moved in with Suellen, Natalie's life was just as entertaining as promised. The two girls went out constantly. They enjoyed spa treatments, fun restaurants, dancing, drinking, clubs, the movies, and even a Las Vegas girls' weekend. Natalie footed the bill for most everything, but as she told herself, this was the least she could do for such a good friend. Hadn't Suellen been there for her 110 percent during the roughest time of her life? Also, Suellen had a crummy job, while she, Natalie, had a fantastic career, so why not be generous?

Over the next six months, Natalie and Suellen met guys on singles websites and went on many double dates. None of the guys were as nice as Alan, to be honest, but it was fun going out.

Suellen, for her part, was thrilled to have someone to go out with, and most of all, to pay half of the rent. There's no waiting period in the state of New York, so Natalie and Alan's divorce became final in just six months.

Natalie and Suellen then visited sunny Cabo San Lucas to celebrate. At the Cabo resort, Suellen met Paul, a handsome, charming guy from Los Angeles. The two quickly fell madly in love and within three months, Suellen had relocated to the palm trees and Pacific. After she'd hit the west coast, Suellen rarely picked up the phone when Natalie called. She kept promising to invite her for a visit, but was so darn busy decorating the apartment she and Paul had rented together, there just never seemed to be a good time.

One can't totally blame Suellen for the turn of events. Natalie was a big girl, but admittedly was swayed by her friend who "egged her on" for a divorce, then ditched her like an overcooked cheese, jalapeno and avocado omelette for a new life in the City of the Angels.

Now folks, this may seem like an extreme example, but this really happened; just names and details have been revised.

# F

## Facebook
### (see Instagram)

No one loves Facebook more than I do! This is mortifying, but in a flash of nerdy generosity, I've even sent two grateful messages to Mark Zuckerburg, thanking him for creating Facebook.

However, as we've mentioned here before, Facebook, Instagram, Twitter and other social media are all genuinely addicting! If you're constantly on social media, this can erode your marriage due to lack of time and attention.

It's always amazing to see (and this has been too many times to count) married folks posting unflattering comments about their spouses on social media. Maybe it's better to say positive things or nothing, because once it's up there, buster, it's there for good.

You may be an extremely private person who doesn't appreciate your partner spouting off about politics or personal issues. Or, it could be the other way around. Have an honest conversation and let your spouse know that there are things you're not comfortable with them sharing, and see what feedback you receive in return.

## Faith

The greatest quote ever heard was from a college-age kid who talked to me and Robert at a hotel jacuzzi. He said, "Religion is what happens when God leaves the room." Another great saying is: "Sitting in church doesn't make you a Christian any more than sitting in a garage makes you a car."

Having mutual faith in God, Budda, a higher power, is something that many of our success story couples believe is helpful. Faith in God is something to hold onto in difficult times. When the going is tough, it is so important to have faith that things will get better.

Here are some of the statements happily married folks made about this subject:

"Faith is what keeps you going when nothing else does."

"I feel God is counting on me to make my marriage a success."

"God planned for me to be alive in challenging times like these so I can make positive changes however I can."

"Going to church as a family keeps us more united."

"Praying together makes us more of a team."

"God put you and your spouse together for a reason."

"We've made close friends through church and they share our commitment to staying married."

"Don't just look to God for hope – look inside yourself."

Now, I'm not bragging, but Robert and I are what you might call "Cafeteria Catholics," definitely attending at Easter, Christmas and weddings.

However, we do pray throughout every day. We pray before meals, at bedtime, and for friends and family who are ill or going through struggles. Our faith definitely keeps us close as a couple and as a family.

Faith and religion are two separate things. Faith is what gets you through the tough times: not just faith in God, but faith in one another and faith in your relationship.

Sharing the same religion is not a necessity unless one partner insists. Also, for example, there's not as much difference between a Baptist and a Protestant, compared to the difference between a Muslim and a Buddhist.

These are definitely issues to be worked out before putting on the tux and wedding dress!

Folks interviewed for this book stated it's usually not helpful trying to convert your partner to your religion. Some of the best marriages are two individuals who don't share a religion but who respect one another's beliefs.

Also, before marriage if possible, a crucial issue to resolve is what religion you want your kids to be raised. If you never discussed religion prior to marriage, but now disagree whether your child should go to religious school, see if you can find a way to compromise.

## Fatigue

The greatest "Kings and Queens of Fatigue" are couples with small children. The only folks on the planet more exhausted are those whose partner always talks politics! All joking aside, the weariness of couples with small children is compounded to the "nth" degree when both work full-time.

Such was the draining scenario of Austin duo Jane and Ron, married eight years, both full-time workers and parents to two small boys. Jane and Ron's relationship had become increasingly frayed, largely due to exhaustion. On weekdays, Jane worked later than Ron, so he picked up the boys from day-care. By the time she got home and they'd all eaten dinner, helped the boys with their homework (whose bright idea was it to give little kids homework *anyways*?) gave them their baths, story-time and bedtime, it was often nine p.m. or later.

By this time, Jane and Ron had been awake since five-thirty a.m., and now strongly resembled two soulless corpses of the Walking Dead. They were too drained for conversation, let alone anything resembling sex or romance. They'd watch Netflix in the den until after midnight, because they were just too tired to get up. To add to the fun, both zombies frequently fell asleep in their matching barca loungers. Jane would usually "come to" at about 2 a.m., shake Ron awake, and then they'd crawl blearily into bed.

Jane always fell back asleep promptly, but typically awoke again at about 4 a.m., and she rarely got back to sleep. The whole merry-go-round would then commence the next day at the crackola of dawn. Yawning and ghoulish-faced, Jane chugged coffee and fought desperately to keep her eyes open. She frequently dozed throughout work meetings, but so far, no one had even noticed. There is a God and she goes by the name of Zoom!

Side note of advice: purchase a good hypnosis tape. Thus, should you awaken at 3 a.m. or any such ungodly hour, give this a whirl. Insert your ear-buds so you don't wake your spouse, and then listen to a hypnosis or meditation tape. Ideally, you will fall asleep until you awaken the next morning, refreshed and invigorated.

Let's now revisit our young zombie duo, Jane and Ron. On weekends their boys had constant activities and parties, plus soccer and swimming, so Jane and Ron, ghoulish with fatigue, dutifully carted them to and fro. Therefore, instead of beginning their week well-rested, they were even more tired on Mondays, because of relentlessly over-scheduled weekends.

In the past two years, Jane had become increasingly impatient and rude toward Ron when she was tired. Since she wasn't merely tired, but frankly exhausted most of the time, this rudeness had become habitual. As a result, their relationship had plunged sharply downhill, because most evenings nowadays, weary and cranky Jane snapped at Ron.

Ron was a quiet kind of guy and rarely replied, but he deeply resented this treatment. Also, their sons were getting to the age where nothing got past them, so their older boy had begun imitating Jane by being "sassy-frass" toward Ron as well.

This all combined to make Ron feel far, far less romantic toward Jane. He rarely held her hand anymore, he almost never initiated sex, and when she suggested it, he often turned her down. This had never happened before they'd had kids.

So, here's an interesting issue we need to address. Common wisdom holds that men are sex machines and can "do it" no matter what. In reality, many men, like Ron, would rather "have their own party" than be intimate with their wife if seriously annoyed with her.

It should be noted that Ron isn't doing anybody a favor by being a martyr. He doesn't stick up for himself, so, since she's unchecked, Jane is becoming more and more of a shrew. She isn't really a tyrant, but since no one's calling her out, all her bullying instincts are floating to the surface like the Pennywise balloon. Ron is increasingly becoming a verbal punching bag. Jane does feel momentarily better taking out her frustrations on her husband, but it's at the cost of her previously happy marriage.

Ironically, Jane takes enormous pride in being very patient with their two young sons. She's completed several parenting classes and has read a multitude of books on the subject. There's a lot of social pressure on parents these days to treat children with respect and patience. Of course, that's a good thing.

But, what's not so positive is the dynamic when a parent meticulously watches every word said to their children to preserve their self-esteem, but who snaps at and talks down to their spouse. What message does it send if they treat their kid like a prince but their kid's parent like garbage?

So, by Jane acting like a (pardon the expression) "witch with a b," Ron was turned off by her emotionally, which after awhile translated into less desire for her physically. Their sex life, which had always been excellent, took a sharp downward turn. Jane felt rejected by Ron, thinking mistakenly it was the extra ten pounds she hadn't been able to lose after their younger son was born. But in actuality, this had nothing to do with the ten pounds.

Ron resented that she expected him to forget how badly she was treating him when she was "in the mood." Interestingly enough, this is the exact opposite of the scenario we've been conditioned to believe only happens with the woman not being interested in sex.

So, lacking an emotional connection or the intimacy of sex, Jane and Ron began to resemble two ghoulish roommates and not in the least a romantic couple. After awhile, Jane couldn't even remember why she'd married Ron in the first place.

Pleased to report, however, there's a "rainbows and glitter" happy ending for this young zombie couple. Fortunately, what started out as a negative exchange one evening turned things completely around. Jane made a romantic overture toward Ron, and when he refused, she burst into tears.

These two ended up having their first solid conversation in over two years. Ron said he was fed up with her snapping at him. She had really "frosted his gourd," as the saying goes. He was sick and tired of her lack of respect. Jane was flabbergasted. She hadn't even realized how much of a habit this had become. She apologized sincerely, and this one acknowledgement was the beginning of their new marriage.

Ron and Jane were able to connect emotionally again. Ron expressed how angry and hurt he was over how she'd been speaking to him, and Jane conveyed that his continually turning her down for sex made her feel rejected and unloved. She mentioned the extra pounds and Ron assured her that she was still just as beautiful to him as always. He also apologized for not being up-front with her sooner.

Note: both Ron and Jane were willing to apologize and to show humility. Only by being frank and upfront with one another were they able to get past their anger and resentment to realize that: a) they still loved one another very much, and b) both wanted to stay married, and c) their overly busy schedule was wearing them both out physically and emotionally.

The ultimate solution for this couple was for Jane to quit her job. Although she'd earned a solid pay-check, day-care costs for the two boys had eaten up a huge percentage of her take-home pay. Rather than eating out or picking up takeout almost every night, Jane began cooking almost all their meals at home. This saved an enormous amount of money. Friday and Saturday nights Ron cooked, or he took them all out for dinner. Jane picked up the boys up right after school at 2:45 p.m., and had them complete their homework before dinner. Thus, the boys got to bed much earlier, which gave Ron and Jane some quality time together in the evenings.

They also decided to quit the boys' soccer league and just participate in the minimum soccer games their schools required. This freed up their weekends to relax more and enjoy downtime. To their surprise, their sons were not at all upset by this change. They, too, had been tired of running all over creation every weekend.

Jane and Ron also created a strategy whereby Ron used the code word "grapefruit," a food they both hated, when Jane fell back into her old habit of snapping at him. This worked perfectly, as their two boys had no idea whatsoever what this code word meant.

As time went by, Ron rarely said "grapefruit," as Jane had transformed her communication. Both also made it a point to say complimentary things to one another in front of their sons. Ron felt more respected by Jane, and in turn, this made him much more affectionate toward her. He began to initiate sex much more frequently, as he'd done when they'd been dating and as newlyweds. He began to bring her frequent gifts such as tulips and chocolate almonds, her favorite.

If you have small children and your situation is similar to that of Jane and Ron, to save your peace of mind, sanity, and possibly your marriage, it may be a good idea for one spouse to take some time off from work. If that's not financially feasible, cutting down on sports or other activities may be helpful so that you get more "down" time.

Some young moms fear their careers will never recover. A gap in employment due to raising small kids is generally viewed more favorably than other employment gaps. It doesn't have to be the wife who gives up her job, incidentally. It can be the husband; some couples base this decision upon who earns more; this spouse generally keeps working.

Another option is to find a part-time nanny or babysitter who can pick up the kids, help with housework, make dinners and so forth. It may be well worth the expense, although it's often difficult to find someone reliable.

Jane and Ron also realized they needed time without their sons. They found a good babysitter and went out every Saturday night, sometimes Fridays as well. They were able to have actual conversations where they could finish an entire train of thought without interruptions from their two small boys.

Babysitters can be one of the biggest joys in life. So, take the plunge, find one, pay them a dollar an hour over the going rate, tip them well and get the heck away from Dodge for awhile. Do it on a regular basis... once a week minimum.

One important caveat: make it crystal clear to your sitter they cannot invite even one guest whilst babysitting your kids. In this way, you greatly minimize the risk of coming home and discovering 15-year-olds Tabitha and Tristan doing the "wango-jango" in your four-poster.

If you and your spouse haven't gone out alone in ages, you may feel very weird without kids underfoot. What are you going to talk about? Don't be surprised if all your first conversations are about the kids. Someday you will transition and again begin talking about lots of fun things.

No lie, it will be super strange at first without the kids in tow. But you'll soon lose that bizarre feeling, and after only a few dates, will look at your spouse with new eyes.

Most importantly, you will remember what made you fall in love in the first place.

## Fatal Flaw

Although we've strived for a tone of utmost levity throughout this book, tragically, only sick and sad humor may be found in this segment. How could it possibly be otherwise, when we're discussing the horror, the Nightmare on Elm Street, of fatal flaws!

Okay, here goes. Tragically, at some point in your marriage, you'll realize, to your utmost dismay and chagrin, that your spouse has at least one of what we shall christen a "fatal flaw."

If you're shaking your head because you haven't yet seen one, rest assured, you haven't been married long enough.

Let's observe a few charming couples.

Tracy and Warren have been married for nine years. Warren just loves to gossip and chat, and absolutely can't keep a secret. He "spills the frijoles" about details Tracy would much prefer remain confidential. She could ask him 'til she's blue in the face not to, but it doesn't matter. Warren means well, but he just loves to blabber, there's no other word for it.

Last year, Tracy was unexpectedly laid off from a job that she adored, and was then unemployed for nearly 11 months. She was quite upbeat at first, "pizzazzing" her resume and applying for hundreds of jobs online.

But she had very few interviews and they didn't pan out. As the months progressed and she couldn't land second interviews, let alone a job offer, Tracy began to slop around the house watching TV, munching junk food and swilling it down with diet soda. She sporadically and masochistically tried on her lucky interview suit, which became ever tighter and tighter as the sorry months elapsed.

If you've never been in this exact predicament, dear reader, ah, I envy you.

Toward the end of Tracy's long and gruesome unemployment stint, she and Warren attended his company's annual Christmas party. Over rum eggnog, Warren's boss Larry kidded Tracy about eating Pringles and binge-watching TV. Tracy laughed bravely, but was angry and humiliated. On the drive home, she confronted Warren, who didn't even recall having said anything to his boss. This was always his excuse, by the way. So, it might be said that Warren's fatal flaw is that he's a "blabbermouth."

Paula and Steve have been married for 12 years; it's a second marriage for them both. Her elderly parents are devout Catholics and very fixed in their views. Steve is quite liberal and Paula's father often offends him. No matter how many times Paula has asked him not to, Steve invariably mentions politics or religion, which instigates a heated quarrel. Steve feels her parents have obnoxious views. Paula insists that at their age, they are unlikely to change. This has caused countless arguments. So, Steve's fatal flaws might be tactlessness and stubbornness.

Abigail and Dan have been married for just six years, but during that time she's totalled two beautiful, brand-new cars. Abigail also dented Dan's jeep last week when she backed it into the garage. She swore there was plenty of room on the left, but somehow misjudged the distance to the wall.

Dan was not amused, although he joked that their monthly car insurance might end up actually costing more than their mortgage. Abigail's fatal flaw is her horrendous driving, and, as luck would have it, this couple lives in Los Angeles.

For those who haven't visited the City of the Angels, it's a place where public transportation is grotesque, for lack of a better term, and folks stare at you like you're a leper if you're seen trudging down the street.

To exemplify the deep stigma of walking in Los Angeles, let's now interject a true tale from Brentwood, California, circa 1987. The Big Cheeses at our real estate company frequented a luxury gym just down the street. Gymnasiums nationwide had recently surged in popularity, as executives had completely stopped eating lunch in response to Gordon Gekko's proclamation, "Lunch is for wimps." It was a mere five-minute stroll from our office to the gym, but run the risk of being spotted walking down San Vicente Boulevard like a peon? Anything but!

The valet downstairs fetched their BMW's and Benzes and the Big Cheeses motored glamorously down the street. Each Big Cheese drove solo so as to utilize their car phones, which at that time were prestigiously superglued to the interior of each vehicle. What would have been a five-minute stroll took thirty minutes due to lunchtime traffic. But no problemo; their state-of-the-art cell phones were imbedded in the center consoles of their cars, so they could chat the duration of the journey. Once at the gym, the valet parked their cars and an escalator swiftly whisked them upstairs. After their ultra-brief workout, the entire procedure was repeated, in reverse. Ah, Los Angeles! You've gotta love it. No place like it on earth!

So, have you discovered your spouse's fatal flaw? Perhaps they are a cheapskate, a slob, drive terribly, talk too much or say the wrong things — the potential list is endless.

The reason it's called "fatal flaw" is because it's something your partner cannot or will not *ever* change. You can have endless arguments, but they will still persist in their undesirable behavior until the proverbial cows come mooing home.

If someone who's been married a long time actually has the damn nerve to deny that their spouse has a fatal flaw, guess what, they are deceiving you. Ha! They're *lying through their teeth*. Everyone, but everyone has a fatal flaw. It just depends if it's something you can live with which determines whether you'll stay married.

If your spouse talks too much and is a complete slob around the house, but is kind, generous, and great in bed, you may conclude that you can tolerate his fatal flaw. If you're bossy and always late, but you're a great cook and his family and friends adore you, he may be able to endure *your* fatal flaws.

It's crucial to introduce this most excruciating topic. Wide-eyed youngsters have stars in their eyes at the beginning of their marriage, but then, it's inevitable: the fatal flaw calamity hits them just like a two-ton rhino.

They feel utterly betrayed when it doesn't improve; they mistakenly believe if their spouse loved them enough, they would simply eliminate the flaw.

The years go by and their partner's defect remains; it almost undoubtedly gets worse with age. This makes them want to turn in their spouse for a recall; they may even phone the local car dealer to ask if they can just drop them off. Later, after the divorce, they swear they were blindsided by their ex's hideous defect.

However, unless this couple had eloped after just two months of dating, they *absolutely knew* about the fatal flaw, but naively believed they could eliminate it.

By all means, give it your best shot — try to change your partner's shortcoming. You never know...some fatal flaws can be fixed... but most, sad but true, are for life.

You just have to figure out if you can live with them.

# Flowers

This may appear to be a trivial topic, but can be quite important. Robert's buying me flowers has helped hold us together as a couple. When we were dating he lived at home with his folks, so he had money for grand gestures, such as the 100 long-stemmed roses he presented me with one Valentine's Day. When we were saving for our first house and watching every penny, he brought me one single red rose every Friday from the local 7-Eleven. That sad little 7-Eleven rose in its wee plastic cylinder was a tad droopy... to be honest, it was usually missing some petals.... but it didn't matter. It was the thought that counted.

Men – buy your wives flowers! Women – I beg you, unless you hate flowers, please don't mention the cost! Abigail did this with her husband Ron; not just with flowers, but with other gifts. She always questioned how much he spent. And after awhile —- surprise, surprise! Ron gave up and stopped buying her *anything*.

Over the years, I've been the recipient of flowers more often than the giver, but on some occasions I've given Robert flowers and he likes them a lot. Most men happen to love sunflowers, incidentally.

# Forgiveness

Forgiveness is tricky; it's not the same thing as forgetting. If you're the wronged party and your spouse f'd up something major, first decide whether or not you even want to stay in the relationship.

But if you do, you need to find a way to truly forgive your partner.

If you appear to forgive them, but then bring up their transgression during every argument, this will take a sorry toll.

Far and above one of the best books ever written about forgiveness is "The Gift," by Dr. Edith Eger. Dr. Eger was imprisoned at Auschwitz in 1944 and just barely survived. She eloquently describes her transformation from a bitter, terrified victim to a strong and resilient survivor. She explains how forgiveness enabled her to become the person she would have become, had war and the Nazi camp not turned her life upside down.

Most importantly, Dr. Eger explains how the act of forgiving herself was so crucial to happiness and peace. This comes at the very end of the story; for those who haven't read this amazing book, no "spoilers" here!

Volumes have been written about the subject of forgiveness. It's also been proven that holding onto anger or blame towards someone damages you far more than it hurts them.

## Full Disclosure

There's a large distinction between a married person who continually deceives their spouse and one who doesn't need to share every little thing.

For example: "girl talk." If one of my girlfriends shares something with me, she doesn't need to tell me it's confidential. That trust is sacred in our friendship. I absolutely *do not* go blabbing and gabbing to my husband.

If I tell a girlfriend something important, I, in turn, expect she'll keep it between us. If I discover she's "let the cat out of the bag" to her husband, she immediately falls into the category of "acquaintance." I may enjoy her company immensely, but I'll never again confide in her.

Another example is spending. If you and hubster are in reasonably good financial shape, must he absolutely know that you dropped $200 on those glossy vegan leather cowgirl boots? Maybe you deserve them. Of course you do! By the same token, if he splurges $200 to see Iron Maiden with his buddies, hey, "carpe diem!" He deserves to see Iron Maiden, who quite possibly won't play in your hometown again for many years.

Does some law on the books state that you two need to discuss the cowgirl boots or the concert ticket beforehand?

Obviously, this is a personal decision for each couple to work out, but sometimes "TMI" just isn't helpful.

It shouldn't come as a surprise that money can be one of the touchiest subjects with couples.

Now for a footwear example: Sabrina was an absolute shoe fanatic. Friends lovingly christened her the blonde Imelda Marcos of Santa Barbara. Her husband Jeff once bravely attempted to count her footwear, but he gave up in sheer exhaustion. Once he'd tallied 92 pairs and realized dozens were yet uncounted, Jeff's heart rate skyrocketed and he collapsed, dizzy and breathless, onto his Barca Lounger. He wearily admitted his utter defeat.

Jeff sounds a trifle elderly, now doesn't he? In fact, at the time, he was only 36. But anxiety over Sabrina's shoe obsession was aging him well before his time. Jeff became particularly traumatized on those days Sabrina waltzed gaily through the front door, clutching shopping bags filled to the brim. It was never three or four pairs; that's for rank amateurs. Nope, a pro like Sabrina couldn't be troubled to buy less than five or six pairs at once, *minimum.* The moment Jeff glimpsed her, laden down with boxes and bags like a fashionable little pack mule, his blood pressure shot through the roof. Watching in terror her multiple trips to the car, he'd dish out a sassy comment, and invariably, the two would have an enormous argument.

Sabrina was careful about other spending, but shoes were her life's great indulgence, her joy, if you will. It should be noted that Sabrina had a fantastic income, and she and Jeff were financially very secure. The shoes were not denting their bank account in the least. But Jeff was a practical guy, and her habit of buying more shoes every couple weeks when she already had 132.5 pairs seemed insane to him. Unfortunately, Jeff worked out of the house, so he was always there, lurking around when she returned from the shopping mall.

Sabrina then cleverly invented a most ingenious strategy. Whenever she returned home with new shoes, if Jeff inconveniently happened to be around, she'd leave everything inside the trunk of her car. She'd then wait patiently, like a well-dressed little spider in heels, until Jeff got into the shower. Then, moving quickly, she'd smuggle the shoes into the house, minus boxes and bags.

Sabrina, aka Mrs. Bradshaw, wore high heels 99 percent of the time, even around the house. The one percent exception was during this shoe-smuggling process, because she could only run so fast in four-inch heels. Sabrina strategically placed a pair of Keds sneakers inside the front hall closet at all times specifically for this purpose. Their house didn't have a garage, so she was forced to park conspicuously on the street. Who knows what their suburban neighbors thought about her dashing madly to and fro?

Sabrina also stashed a chilled bottle of Evian water in the front hall closet so she could take swigs between shoe relays. She was quite conscious of her health and the need to stay well-hydrated throughout this entire bootleg process.

Once all the new shoes were safely ensconced in her closet, Sabrina removed her sneakers, once again put on her high heels, and relaxed. Her job was done.

The scheme was a total success. From that point on, Jeff never noticed more new shoes. They just kind of blended in with all the rest. In this way, he was spared the stress and alarm of seeing Sabrina dashing in and out with all the boxes and bags. He assumed with the deepest relief that she'd finally become weary of shoe-shopping, and he tactfully refrained from ever commenting.

When Sabrina first told me about all this, I was still in my 20s, had only been married for a few years, and it all seemed rather childish and dishonest. Now, I look back with more wisdom and I realize ... Sabrina was a genius! After all, shoes are not worth fighting over, are they?

Sabrina got her shoes, Jeff was spared needless stress and high blood pressure, and everyone was happy. And, after all, Sabrina's smuggling new shoes into her bedroom was a whole lot better than her sneaking in the cabana boy!

Who hasn't felt a tad envious of those couples who perfectly jive and are joined at the hip? They do everything together, kinda like little twins... but they do often split up ... maybe it's just too much time together.

Marcella and Tim lasted five years. Tim insisted on full disclosure about everything and wanted to spend every waking moment together. Tim worked evenings, and brought lunch to Marcella's office on the daily. They would sit there at the cafeteria every dang day. Marcella had lunch with co-workers just twice in five years when Tim miraculously came down with the bubonic flu.

Tim followed Marcella around the house. If she made lasagna, he simply had to grate the cheese. He stood outside the shower when she was shampooing her hair and he filled her in on all his latest news. Tim also wanted to know precisely how much Marcella spent on everything. He pored over receipts from her trips to the market and commented on the cost of *each item*. This was all quite fascinating for Tim.

Now, Marcella was one of those super-sweet, calm, very tolerant and kind personalities. But, you never know when there will come the day that a person will finally say, "basta!" which is Italian for "enough."

For Marcella, this was a beautiful Saturday in May. Tim insisted on joining her and her girlfriends for tea and antique shopping. Apparently, this was the proverbial straw on the llama's back. The following weekend, Marcella was out of there like a hot flash in January. Three years later, she remarried. Her new husband Adam is an avid fisherman and is gone nearly every weekend. It's a match made in heaven!

# Fun

Is anyone left on planet Earth who hasn't yet heard the Cyndi Lauper song, "Girls Just Wanna Have Fun?" When this song first came out, I was a junior at Pepperdine University in Malibu, California. My roommates and I decided to throw a "Girls Just Wanna Have Fun" party. We were on a shoestring student budget, which left zero money for decorations.

We therefore needed to be enterprising...so my girlfriend and I bought a widget from the local hardware store. We cruised up and down Hawthorne Boulevard, stalking attractive palm trees. Working quickly, hoping not to get caught, we relieved many unlucky trees of their palm fronds. We then tacked the fronds up on the walls of our college apartment and presto! Free decorations! It was one of the best, most fun parties ever.

No one wants you to deface public property, but the point is you don't have to spend a lot of money to have fun.

Robert and I both grew up near Los Angeles International Airport – both of our families had fun at the airport without spending much money. Robert's family would buy ice cream cones at the local Thrifty's and sit on a bench on the bluffs overlooking the airport runway. They'd eat their ice cream and watch the planes take off and land.

My family would hang out at the airport gate (back in the good old days when you could go all the way to the gate) and wait for our relatives to arrive from Canada. We'd arrive super early to people-watch travelers getting off planes.

It was so much fun! And it didn't cost a cent, unless you counted the gasoline to drive there. This brings me to tears as it was probably 50 cents a gallon back in the day.

My favorite airport memory was in 1976; I was seated watching people deplane. A beautiful Asian girl in her 20s walked off the ramp wearing a white tennis outfit, carrying a tennis racket and that was it! She wore a beautiful diamond tennis bracelet. No suitcase, no purse. This seemed like the ultimate pinnacle of glamor to 8th grade me.

Robert and I like to eat out, see movies, concerts, car shows, and travel; these things do cost. But we also sit in his truck and watch the planes take off and land at our little local airport. We drive to the mountains or the beach. We walk our dogs at the park. Luckily, we've always lived in climates (Los Angeles and now San Diego) with mild weather and lots to do outdoors, but there are fun and inexpensive activities in every town.

If you don't have much money, don't let this stop you from having fun. You just have to get creative.

You and your spouse, plus your kids if you have them, can find free or inexpensive activities that are enjoyable. We have a beautiful hotel here in San Diego called the Hotel del Coronado. It's very old (by U.S. standards, that is!) and just gorgeous. It's located on an island and situated right on the beach. We drive over Coronado Bridge onto the island, and then walk around the hotel pretending we're staying there. There are lovely shops, a candy store, the gorgeous beach to walk on and a very creative fellow who makes the most incredible sand sculptures every single day. Except for the gas it takes to get there and a few bucks to get a Starbucks (optional), it's a nearly free, beautiful, wonderful, relaxing way to spend the afternoon.

Now, let's peruse an awkward situation: a total homebody paired with someone who likes going out frequently.

Riverside, California couple Adam and Clarice had been married for 14 years and had one preteen daughter, Caroline. Adam loved to go out; he quickly became bored at home. He enjoyed double dates, ball games, the beach, movies, you name it. Clarice, on the other hand, joked about being a "total homebody." Adam was not at all happy about this. He said they could be "total homebodies" when they were 80. This caused an eventual rift in their relationship. As Adam pointed out, Clarice hadn't been this way when they'd married. She'd enjoyed going places and trying new things.

As time went by, Clarice became more and more adept at turning down invitations. She always had excuses for not going places. She may have been depressed... who knows? When their daughter began high school, Adam left Clarice for another woman. Adam's new wife loved going places; she was almost the complete opposite of Clarice in this regard.

Having fun together does seem to be something that happy couples make ample time for.

If a couple gets into the routine, some might even say "rut," of simply going to work, slopping in front of the TV watching Netflix, then on the weekends just doing chores or running errands, well, then excitement, happiness and joy may just slowly seep out of their lives and their relationship.

Nothing against Netflix, by the way! It's fantastic, incomparable. But it's just when a couple never goes anywhere that life can become stale, kind of like dry melba toast.

Do they even make melba toast anymore? Haven't thought about it in years!

By the way, what seems boring or odd to one couple may actually be quite entertaining for another – as our next tale shall illustrate.

San Diego couple Tina and Alan had been wed for 12 years and spent every weekend engaged in a most unusual hobby: "coupon shopping." This dynamic duo energetically clipped coupons from the newspaper all week, and then on weekends they drove from store to store redeeming them. They'd begin at Von's, purchasing 18 cans of tomatoes for five dollars, redeeming their coupon. They, then raced to Albertson's for three pounds of peaches for two bucks, and then dashed to Smart and Final for frozen chicken at 99 cents a pound. Some folks might equate this with all the fun of a root canal, but for Tina and Alan, it was like a giant scavenger hunt and they just loved it. It was something they enjoyed doing together, and for them it was FUN.

Here's a great motto: Life is short, so you've got to have fun!

If you and your partner find yourselves in a slump, maybe your schedule has become too routine, too predictable and blah. Broach the subject to your partner... and come up with some new and fun activities you'd like to do together.

## Flaws

We must differentiate this section from "fatal flaws."

Your author here is personally as full of flaws as Swiss cheese is of holes. And those are just the flaws I notice... doubtless, there are many more I'm blissfully unaware of.

One of my best friends said, "There's your ideal self, and there's your actual self." He explains we see ourselves through rose-tinted glasses, and to some extent, that's not such a bad thing. Denial can be an invaluable tool, such as when you're falling apart financially. You ignore impending doom throughout your workday just so that you can get through it (yes, you betcha, been there, done that too).

So, do you acknowledge your own flaws? Or, do you deny or ignore them? Your flaws are so inherently part of your overall package; it's easy to be sentimental about them. Shortcomings are difficult to change, even when you want to.

Your partner will of course have flaws as well. A very true saying is "Nobody is perfect until you fall in love with them." So, this is why it's a good idea to date awhile before getting engaged, then to be engaged for awhile until you get married. If you can do it in this order: date, then get engaged, and then marry, you are way ahead of the game. This is because you will have time to see your partner's flaws, and vice versa, before making that gigantic step.

Here are just a few flaws you or your partner can have, individually or shared:

- tardiness

- spends too much money

- stingy

- disorganized

- forgetful

- sloppy

- compulsively neat

- bad driver

- procrastinator

- snores

- hogs the covers in bed

- talks too much/doesn't listen

- complains a lot

- whines

- bad temper

- passive-aggressive

- anger issues

- selfish

- self-centered

Ask yourself: which of my own flaws can I change? Not just for the sake of my relationship, but to improve my life overall?

And, in the case of your partner: what flaws can I accept from them, and which do I absolutely need them to change?

Couples who stay happily married for many years learn to live with one another's flaws and accept their partner's "overall package."

As for the success story couples, it's readily apparent that they accept their partners' flaws and appreciate their favorable characteristics. They're also humble about the fact that they themselves are not perfect. Gratitude, patience and humility are characteristics we shall discuss in depth later.

## Few Words As Possible

My wise friend Ruth illustrated this concept just beautifully, using an example from a New York restaurant. Ruth and her husband David were eating dinner at Scalini's, their favorite Italian eatery. Scalini's is not a casual joint; it is fine dining. There are white linen tablecloths, waiters in tuxes, and unfortunately, the couple at the table behind Ruth and David. These folks opted out of Chuck E. Cheese to instead bring their little "nasty-cakes" four-year-old Gregory in for a bite. Please don't judge me for calling Gregory "nasty-cakes;" I am only paraphrasing Ruth.

Now, how did Ruth know this tiny tater tot's name? Well, because his parents used it over and over again. They indulged in long, rambling sentences as they impotently begged their adorable little tyke to calm down, stop squalling and cease and desist banging on his plate with his knife and spoon.

"Gregory, all the big grown-ups in this restaurant want to eat their yummy Italian food, so let's use our indoor voice, please."

"Please don't bang on your plate because it's so noisy and the plate could even break and we don't want that to happen, do we Gregory?"

"Gregory, mommy says please be a good little boy and eat this macaroni and let's stop crying please. Look at this yummy pasta, oh it's so delicious. I'm going to eat a bite just so you can see how much I love it."

"Gregory, daddy's going to have to take you out for a time out pretty darn soon because you're just not being a good sport and having nice restaurant manners."

I have just one question to ask: did adorable wee Gregory actually deserve the word "please?"

So, of course Ruth was extremely vexed and David finally complained to the restaurant manager, begging him to end the torture. The manager then spoke with Gregory's minions, whereupon the merry trio left the restaurant in a huff. One can only hope they paid for their food, though of course the marinara-splattered white tablecloth could not likely be salvaged.

What Ruth was just itching to tell Gregory perfectly describes the point we're making. "Why didn't the parents just tell him firmly to "shut up?" she wondered. Or, to make it more "Scalini's appropriate" they could have said firmly, "Quiet, Gregory, please."

So, let's now apply the "Gregory principle" to your own relationship. If your spouse doesn't fully listen when you're upset, if you reckon they actually tune you out almost entirely, let's try something new.

When attempting to get a point across to your spouse, imagine you're speaking to a very young child. Utilize as few words as possible. Single syllables actually have much greater impact.

Conversely, the more you babble, the higher your word count, the more you dilute your message. Sometimes it's even helpful to write down in advance exactly what you want to say.

Therefore, I highly recommend the amazing, diminutive post-it note.

Post-it notes are wee, loyal friends who've never let me down. At my previous job in education, the majority of my co-workers were in their 20s, or at most, early 30s. I was rather like a seasoned hen surrounded by little tiny spring chickens. I didn't need to exactly fit in, but I sure as heck didn't want to really stand out. So my clucks had to coincide, at least to some degree, with those stylish millennials who surrounded me.

Don't judge, but for example, I would consult beforehand with the ever-patient Andrea to ascertain if a certain slang phrase was still in style. If it got the go-ahead, then I'd meticulously jot it down on a post-it note, which I'd then cleverly conceal in my purse, pocket or even brassiere.

Then I was "#ready" to utter some trendy slang at the office and fit in effortlessly with my thousands of youthful co-workers. This worked out just splendidly until Andrea had to go and leave for six months' study abroad in France, January of 2016. Nooo!!

During that challenging time, I recall with trauma being the only one in my entire office who persisted in using the outdated phrase "I know, right?" One of my previous co-workers swears that during that horrific era, she overheard me proclaim, "Peace, love and Bobby Sherman," and "Groovy, man," but I'm sure she was just "joshing and jiving" me.

All joking aside, next time you wish to convey something important to your spouse, write it down (a post-it note works great) and condense it into as few words as possible. Next, relay *only those words*.

Here's the crucial part: once you've made your point, *stop talking entirely*. You may be pleasantly surprised by the favorable response you receive.

Also, just because your spouse doesn't immediately agree, apologize, or give you the reply you think you're entitled to, doesn't mean that continuing to talk will help your case.

This is so powerful, I'm going to repeat it.

Just because your spouse doesn't immediately agree, apologize, or give you the reply you think you're entitled to, doesn't mean that continuing to talk will help your case, or your relationship either, I might add.

As Keshia discovered, she received more respect from her husband Ben when she learned to say just a little, then stop talking and then let it marinate, so to speak.

"I used to follow him around the house, talking and talking," she recollects, "but I didn't get a good response. Especially when I'd start following him around, he'd become really annoyed." Now, as she's learned, "I say a little bit, and then I give it a rest. To my surprise, a day or two later, he'll apologize and say I was right and so forth. But it takes him a little time."

This all ties in with patience, an all-important but challenging skill we shall address later.

# G

## Gambling

My father, Nick Nimchuk, was a very successful blackjack player. He also loved keno, and over the years won a fair amount of money at both. Our family took fun trips to Reno, Lake Tahoe and Las Vegas. We actually came out ahead financially as a result of my dad's gambling.

It's actually quite uncommon for a family to get ahead financially through gambling. I didn't know how to spot it at the time, but my dad was not a compulsive gambler in the least. He treated it almost like a business; if he started losing, he got in his car and drove back to L.A., or caught an earlier flight home.

Unfortunately, this is rarely the case with folks who love to gamble. Frequently, gambling is a destructive influence for married couples and families. Now, more than ever, due to modern technology, gambling is incredibly accessible. It's no longer even necessary to physically enter a casino. Gambling can be done online, using one's computer or phone.

You may recall the sad story of Laura and Will, where she gambled away his entire retirement account, and this ended their marriage.

My dear friend Natasha worked some years ago as a dealer at one of our local casinos here in San Diego. She relayed sobering stories of people bringing in the pink slips to their cars, deeds to their houses, and spouses calling the casino begging them to send their husband or wife home before they gambled away every penny. Casinos have multitudes of ATM machines...and no clocks.

One day Natasha was on her break buying an iced coffee from the cart outside the casino. It was a blazing hot summer day; over 100 degrees. Natasha noticed a little girl, perhaps four years old, with no parent in sight, standing outside in the heat, holding onto the bars of a stroller. A toddler was inside the stroller.

Natasha hurried up to the child and asked her where her mommy was. The child pointed to the casino. Long story short – the mom was inside gambling and had left her children outside, since they weren't allowed in the casino. The casino manager was summoned and they located the mom, who was then asked to leave.

If you're dating someone who exhibits signs of a serious gambling problem, try to imagine being married to this person. Think about the absolute havoc this can wreak on your finances, peace of mind and possibly your safety. Loan sharks lend money to compulsive gamblers in every large city, not just Atlantic City or Las Vegas.

Gambling can affect folks of any age. Steve's mother has a gambling problem and she is in her *80s*. Many times over the years Steve has bailed his mom out when she's fallen behind on her credit line at the casino.

If you're involved with someone with a gambling addiction and they're willing to seek help, there are excellent support groups, such as Gamblers Anonymous. If they won't stop, think seriously about breaking off the relationship. And most importantly, do not link your finances to this person... you will live to regret it.

## Grace

Simply put, the concept of extending grace is this: you show forgiveness, kindness and mercy to someone when they least expect it. To put it simply, you cut them some slack, and you're gracious about it.

And what better recipient of this largesse than your spouse, the person with whom you've chosen to share your life?

One thing to always keep in mind when extending grace to your spouse: this ideally sets an example for them to someday reciprocate when you "flub up."

# Go to bed angry

The title of this section flies in the face of that popular marital advice: "Don't go to bed angry."

Haven't we all heard this three million times? This advice is as All-American as baseball, hot dogs and apple pie à la mode.

Married folks are always told, "Never, *ever* go to bed angry." If I had just one dollar for each time I've heard this platitude, I could buy 650,000 acres of land and fill it with wild horses (my life's biggest dream).

So, let's now turn this sage advice on its head. Sometimes, it's actually far, far better to *go to bed angry* and just sleep on it for a night. Oh wow, I said it! Will a lightning bolt strike me down?

Going to bed angry actually works best for lots of folks. When they get tired, perhaps if an argument is creeping past midnight, their fuse gets shorter, they become cranky, or they say hurtful things. This is not a good scenario *at all* for working out a disagreement.

Granted, going to bed with things unresolved is not ideal. But it may just be preferable to staying up until 2 a.m. trying to hash out an agreement, with both partners growing wearier and more annoyed every minute.

If you're exhausted and angry with your partner, perhaps little gets resolved anyways. It might just be better to instead "agree to disagree," give it a rest, and get some sleep.

This technique works for Denise and Jonathan. Denise doesn't like to be rushed when she's annoyed or angry. She prefers to take her time and give the relationship a "rest" until she's less annoyed. This took some adjustment for Jonathan, but now he's used to this and he knows they will discuss the matter in good time.

This strategy won't work well if one partner feels insecure with the status of the relationship. They may fear that if they don't resolve the argument or issue right then, their partner might break up with them. It might be helpful if their partner assures them they are not going anywhere, but that they just want to wait and deal with the issue the next day or at a later time.

# Goblet of Honor

When Andrea was a toddler, Robert and I attended a parenting class. We took just one thing away from that evening – the ritual of the Goblet of Honor. This has become a cherished and integral part of our family life. By the way, couples without kids can do this as well.

We'd never heard of the Goblet of Honor, but our class instructor explained it perfectly.

When a family member accomplishes something special, such as a promotion at work, good grades in school, painting the garage, or any such thing, the family then conducts a short ceremony and the recipient proudly drinks out of the Goblet of Honor.

The goblet need not be anything fancy like an heirloom from Germany or England. Ours is a pretty stone goblet with a long stem. I keep it in a special place where Andrea and Robert know to find it also. We simply fill it with water; the choice of beverage is up to you. You can go authentic and buy something that looks like "Game of Thrones" and fill it with mead. You can choose an elegant crystal decanter and white wine (or grape juice for the kiddos).

Here's how we do it: whoever decides to honor someone calls a family meeting in the living room. They then announce, "Hear ye, hear ye, we are gathered together to honor (insert name here) tonight." Then they hand the goblet to the recipient. They proclaim something along the lines of, "I'm proud to announce the recipient of tonight's Goblet of Honor is none other than our own Robert George Watson for working so hard to build a gorgeous hay villa for our horses! Robert, drink from the Goblet of Honor!" Then everyone cheers.

Does this sound cheesy to you? Well, yeah, it is. But this corny tradition has been an integral part of our family for over 20 years and it's brought us closer.

For a couple without kids, one possibility is to sit down to a nice dinner at home and have the Goblet of Honor in place of a water glass for the recipient. This is more low-key, but still special.

# Grudge

This isn't some cringy Japanese horror flick. Actually, what I'm referring to is the toxic effect that holding a grudge has upon a relationship.

A grudge is when you hold onto anger or resentment. You may act all nonchalant, pretend everything is rosy, but you're actually fuming, bottling up your feelings. Inside, you're like a shaken Dr. Pepper bottle that could erupt at any given moment.

One of my favorite bosses of all time had this saying: "There are no silent sufferers on our team." What she meant by this was that she wanted her employees to speak up when upset or angry. No surprise, I loved working for this person because I could be honest with her.

If you keep your feelings suppressed, you may think your spouse doesn't know. However, chances are excellent that he or she is well aware that your hostility is seething right below the surface. Maybe you grind your teeth at night or roll your eyes without even realizing it. Or, possibly you have a "resting witch face" 24/7 but don't know it, because when you pass a mirror, you smile. Or, perhaps because you're angry about something major, you tend to be super cranky about little things... all the time.

We shall discuss the dubious joys of living with a passive-aggressive spouse later in this book. But suffice to say, this dynamic is poison poured down the throat of a marriage.

Anger always comes out somehow.

Let's say your spouse is the passive-aggressive one; they may often blast you with a nasty zinger. What's a zinger, you ask? Well, a zinger was a delicious little snack cake back in the day. At my elementary school, Cowan Avenue, if a lucky kid had a zinger in their lunchbox, well, their social status was assured. But in this context, a zinger is when your spouse says or does something malicious, yet all the while pretends everything is just fine. Even when you call them on it, they act innocent, they have an excuse, or they pretend their nasty action was just meant to be "helpful."

Eloise and Adam lived in Chicago and had been married for 15 years. Eloise deeply resented the amount of traveling that was a requirement of

Adam's job. Currently, she was furious because his latest business trip to Brussels meant he'd miss their nine-year-old daughter Hayley's school play, "The Princess and the Pea." Hayley didn't have a speaking role, she was just a lady-in-waiting, and Adam had promised to attend next year, but Eloise was nonetheless enraged.

Instead of talking to Adam, Eloise vented to his mother, Jean. Eloise complained how Adam would miss Hayley's play, and was never there for his family. Eloise bypassed entirely the fact that Adam worked incredibly long hours at a stressful job to pay for their lavish lifestyle, which included Eloise not working and Hayley's ballet lessons, riding lessons, French tutor and private school.

Eloise vented frequently to her mother-in-law, and bless her little heart, Jean never failed to disappoint. She invariably sided with Eloise and energetically scolded Adam for neglecting his family. This infuriated Adam, but if he confronted Eloise, in the time-worn tradition of our own beloved U.S. politicians, she expertly denied any and all culpability. Eloise was brilliant at acting confused and innocently claiming, "Oh, I don't remember saying that?" If one day Eloise re-enters the work force, she should seriously consider going into public office.

Eloise would, at most, claim to have mentioned something *quite* by accident. She also vented to her girlfriends, and in recent years had begun complaining to Hayley. In short, Eloise griped to everyone except the one person who could change things: her husband.

So here's another scenario of the "holding a grudge" dynamic. Last night at dinner with friends, your husband made fun of your mother's driving. It's true she's just about the worst driver on the planet. Last week she backed her new silver-blue Buick Regal out of her driveway and kept going backwards all the way across the street until she'd overturned three of her neighbor's trash cans. Your mom's street is so wide there's a center divider, so she actually reversed half the length of Gillette Stadium. Only the trash cans stopped her from plowing the neighbor's lawn for free.

Nonetheless, you weren't too amused when your husband compared her driving to Tony Soprano's mother. After all, the three trash cans made a complete recovery... it's not as though she landed someone in the hospital.

So your husband apologized, and the two of you resolved things, but you're still kind of irritated. The next morning, your husband mentions your upcoming camping trip; this outing is supposed to take place next weekend.

You reply that you're not sure you still want to go.

So, this is what we call holding a grudge. He apologized, but you don't want to "drop it." You want to hang on and ride that train 'til the very end of the line.

Josh and Naomi hailed from San Antonio, Texas, and were wed just two short years before they divorced. They had terrible, endless arguments; incredibly, they once went *three entire weeks* without speaking one single word to each other. Not one word in three weeks. Incredibly, they were living together in the same house that entire time.

Bo and Geoff, one of our success story couples, discuss this dynamic. Neither of them tends to hold a grudge, but they can also sulk from time to time if their argument was a bad one. However, they both make a point to not be overly stubborn. Neither feels it's worth it to hold a grudge because their relationship is too precious. As Bo adds, she also likes to talk, so she never cares to keep up the silent treatment for long.

Now, let's get back to Josh and Naomi. After their divorce finalized, Naomi's sympathetic co-workers agreed that Josh was just so stubborn. No wonder she couldn't stay married to him! Well, sure he was... but what about her? It took two to dance that last tango in San Antonio, that's for certain.

For two full-grown adults to last *three entire weeks,* that's three-quarters of a month, without even speaking once, their stamina just boggles the mind. Obviously, both were holding a grudge. You can't point the finger at just one. But fortitude of that kind would serve both Josh and Naomi very well on a reality show such as "Naked and Afraid."

Now, let's look at what successful couples do. Over and over again, when interviewed for this book, happily married couples emphasized that although they'd had tough times, they made it a point to stick together. They did not hold onto grudges. They forgave their partner for mistakes, they compromised, tried not to be too stubborn, worked to meet each other halfway, and endeavored to be flexible.

Gratitude, humility, forgiveness – these terms came up repeatedly with our success story couples.

Here's an inescapable truth: there will come a time during your marriage – frankly, many times over the years, that you believe your partner is a total idiot or jerk.

We are not gonna sugar coat this here ginger snap.

Let's face it: he or she is driving you absolutely nuts, you can't stand them right now, and you'd just really prefer to stay angry. You just want to hold a grudge.

However, you cannot hold a grudge and maintain a happy, long-term relationship.

This is so compelling, let's repeat it. *You cannot hold a grudge and maintain a happy, long-term relationship.*

Hanging onto a grudge like Cary Grant clinging onto the side of that cliff in "North by Northwest" serves only to exhaust you and erode your partnership.

## Gratitude Journal

What differentiates a happy individual from a miserable one is not necessarily their circumstances, but instead their attitude. Happy people look for the silver lining, the glass to be half full. They realize they have blessings in life and are grateful, even if they have struggles to overcome.

Some of the happiest people out there have endured severe misfortune in their lives. How do they still manage to be content? What is their secret? Well, for starters, they always find a way to be grateful for the blessings they have.

Miserable people, on the other hand, habitually complain and focus on the negative. Okay, right now, picture the most miserable person you know. Dang it, we all can think of someone. When they visit a restaurant, invariably something's wrong with the food, service, or atmosphere. They never think how lucky they are to be able to afford to eat out, or to be in good enough health to actually visit a restaurant.

Fred lives in Colorado Springs; he is now middle-aged, but still blames everything on his crummy dad Charles. Charles was no picnic in the park, that's for dang sure. He was a neglectful, angry alcoholic who was verbally abusive to Fred and his wife Marilyn and was chronically unemployed. Marilyn worked three jobs just to put food on the table. Charles would disappear for weeks at a time; they never knew whether he was alive or dead. When Fred was twelve, he discovered that Charles had fathered two other children with another woman. Charles then pressured Fred to keep this secret from Marilyn.

No doubt about it, all of this is horrendous. But, let's pose this question: at what point does Fred choose to move on from his victim mentality? When will Fred stop blaming Charles, who incidentally has been dead for nearly 15 years now, for his own misery?

Also, it's noteworthy to mention that Fred's mother Marilyn was absolutely wonderful. But since Fred only focuses upon the negative, everyone only hears about his lousy dad. Fred rarely mentions his mom since she doesn't fit into his bleak agenda.

We're all acquainted with, and, at the risk of sounding somewhat unkind, generally bored stiff by gloomy folks like Fred. Miserable people believe life handed them a raw deal; they dwell on things they don't have. In actuality, they might have plenty to be thankful for, but you'd never know it by listening to them. They're either focused on a painful past, or what's currently going badly, rather than viewing and appreciating any positives.

Unfortunately, there's a payoff, a psychological reward for the complainer. Their venting commands attention, which in turn perpetuates their behavior. It's usually negative, weary attention, but it's still a form of recognition.

We Americans are famed worldwide for being the tiniest bit whiny; how dare they say this about us? Ugh, I'd die rather than admit this to a European, but perhaps there's just a kernel of truth to this. Most of us Yanks just aren't accustomed to putting up with much inconvenience. We are kind of – oh, can I say it? - spoiled. There's an incredible array of choices at the supermarket. Few of us have ever lived without electricity or running water. Particularly on the west coast, most of us own our own cars, so although we often sit in traffic, we rarely must deal with the grubby inconvenience of public transportation.

Gratitude is unparalleled for its ability to transform one's happiness. Creating a gratitude journal is very simple: buy a notebook or calendar and each day write down three or four things for which you're appreciative.

A mindset of gratitude also improves how you view your spouse. It is basic human nature to take loved ones for granted; we've all done it.

How many times has someone whose marriage ended said that they wished they'd appreciated what they had before they lost it?

It's easy to lack gratitude for your spouse, focus on their shortcomings, and view them in a negative way.

As the years elapse, you may begin noticing your friends' spouses and comparing them to your own. Particularly if your own marriage is going through a slump, Joanne's husband Brent just seems smarter, better-looking, more interesting, dare we say it, sexier than your good ol' reliable hubby.

Well, that's because you don't live with Brent. If you did, you'd know that he hogs the covers in bed, throws recycling in with the trash, and nearly worst of all, forgot their wedding anniversary four years ago because he was so busy shagging his devastatingly attractive life coach Annabelle.

It's easy to peer over that fence and see only peaches and cream on that emerald green lawn. To avoid this type of thinking, start thanking your partner for everyday things they do, even simple things like walking the dog. Try to do this every day. Your partner may be surprised at first, but if they're like most folks, they'll be pleased as well. One of our greatest human needs is to feel appreciated and acknowledged.

You can also list items in your gratitude journal which specifically mention thankfulness for your spouse. Don't hesitate to show them what you've written down.

## Good People

There's something all of our success story spouses shared when interviewed. Every single one described their spouse as "a good person." They all phrased it differently, but this was the prevalent message which came across.

They mentioned things like their partner treats others well, is honest, has integrity, has a generous spirit, and is kind and giving to others.

Particularly if you're not yet married, but considering that next step, take a good, long, impartial look at your partner. Try to be objective, even if your relationship is in the early throes of passion and adoration.

Is your partner what one would call "good people?" Are they honest and trustworthy; do they treat others well? How do they interact with waiters and waitresses? Are they rude, condescending, or impatient? If they think you won't notice, do they leave a paltry little tip?

Believe it or not, this indicates with bulls-eye accuracy how they'll treat *you* in the long run.

Beware of folks who use religion in an attempt to make themselves look "just grand." If someone constantly describes themselves as being "Christian," please fire up your "BS radar." Precisely why do they find it necessary to brag so much? If most of their social media posts say they are "#blessed," you needn't be a rocket scientist for little warning bells to start jingling.

You may be uttering the words "Christian Shmistian" after you've dated them for awhile and witnessed the full extent of their hypocrisy.

Be very observant, because this can be subtle. Watch closely to see if they're arrogant and seem to believe others are lesser than them. Particularly if they're nasty to pets and children, this is a big red flag.

Beware though, as this can be deceptive. If your nephew Jamison, that truly ghastly toddler, screams repeatedly in their ear and they act like it's really cute, their nice act is likely fake and phony. It's also a potential clue that they're ingesting vast quantities of Prozac, and that there is gonna crack open a whole 'nother can of sardines.

So, watch carefully to determine if they're a quality person before you "hook up for life."

We aren't talking about a practical offense like throwing out a jury duty summons, by the way. This is a forgivable offense, as is stealing washcloths from hotel rooms.

Speaking of hotel rooms, carry on, dear reader! This topic is coming up soon.

## God Give me Strength aka God Give me Patience

God probably hears this plea from married folks all over the planet at least 50 million times a day.

If you're going through a trying time with your spouse, don't be surprised if all of a sudden you sound much more devout.

"God, give me patience" is a plea which virtually *all* married folks cry out periodically. "God, give me strength," is its close second.

If your arms are raised heavenwards at the same time, you've got this down pat.

I've included this topic so in case you say this frequently, just know that you're not alone!

# H

## Hotels

If your marriage is in a rut, kind of stale like overdone avocado toast, with or without black sesame seeds and balsamic drizzle, perhaps steal away for a night or two. Better yet, a few days, or even, dare we say it, a whole week?

Not everybody likes staying in hotels, but most people do enjoy it. A change of scenery can really stave off boredom. No matter how beautiful and well-appointed your home might be, it's still tedious if you never leave it.

Some fun aspects of hotel getaways are as follows:

- No housework.

- Sex is often better and more exciting.

- You don't even have to make the bed afterwards.

- Room service is a "rolling cart and mini-condiments" dream come true.

- Swimming pool and jacuzzi (extra-special if you don't have these at home).

- Leave behind the kids, housework, yard work, dogs, horses and nosy neighbors.

- You can always stay at a hotel in town ... aka "staycation," or perhaps one just an hour or two from your home.

- If you can stay a couple weekdays, it's much more affordable than weekends. Las Vegas and Palm Springs have fantastic weekday deals.

- Hotels.com is a good resource and they give you one free night after you've booked ten.

Hotel stays are one way to change the scenery and get away from the same old, same old.

Here's a novel thought: you adore your partner, but need some space, so there's always the concept of getting away yourself for some precious alone time.

My horse trainer friend has a fantastic partner, but loves solo hotel stays on occasion. She adores the jacuzzi, swimming pool and alone time, all of which recharge her batteries.

You can also substitute camping for the hotel, but only if you both truly enjoy this. If you know for certain your wife gets cranky with bugs and dirt in her hair and she absolutely requires air conditioning and a fluffy mattress, don't drag her out to the desert for tent camping and expect some kind of "Valentino romance."

## Hostility

Hostility is an emotion often deeply rooted in childhood. There's a basic psychological connection between past experiences and the emergence of an antagonistic personality. Hostility isn't the same as anger. Anger is a common feeling everyone experiences on occasion, in response to something specific.

For example, a careless driver slams into your brand-new Audi; it's understandable this makes you angry. Within the context of a relationship, your spouse doesn't consult you before inviting his chain-smoking college buddy to crash on your couch for two weeks. It's normal and natural to feel irate in situations such as these.

Hostility, on the other hand, is emotionally charged aggressive behavior. It isn't necessarily in relation to an event, such as someone hitting your car. In addition, it's spiteful behavior out of proportion. This can manifest itself in very aggressive speech or actions. It can be difficult, not to mention embarrassing as heck, to be married to a hostile person.

Jill and Ralph live in Ohio and have been married for four years. During this time, Ralph has had screaming confrontations with many of their neighbors. It's gotten so bad that Jill now hesitates to even walk her tiny beagle Bellissima down the block.

Ralph quickly becomes enraged over minor events, such as a neighborhood dog running on his prize lawn. He screams at the dog's owner and uses foul language. Ralph's reactions are always blown completely out of proportion to the event.

Since this couple lives on a cul-de-sac, kind of a Cincinnati Wisteria Lane, with barbecues and block parties, socializing has become increasingly awkward for Jill and Ralph.

Their next-door neighbor Larry was recently the recipient of a verbal assault from Ralph.

Ripley's believe it or not, this drama started over trash cans. Larry usually removed his cans from the curb around 6 pm on Tuesdays. Ralph preferred to put his own cans out about 5:45 pm, and he became hostile if Larry's trash cans had the damn nerve to still be sitting there.

Ralph had warned Larry jokingly that he would push his cans onto the street if they ever got in his way. Last week when Jill drove home from work, she observed regretfully that one of Larry's trash cans had been shoved out onto the street, had been smashed by a car and was sadly now flat as a plastic pancake with no butter or syrup. When Larry had asked Ralph about the can, Ralph had completely lost his temper and screamed obscenities to the point that Larry had threatened to call the police.

So now, Larry and his wife Heidi no longer spoke to Ralph and Jill. Jill told Ralph she wants to sell their house and move to Youngstown, but she has a sneaky suspicion the same disaster will occur all over again in a new neighborhood.

Hostility takes many forms. Renee and Marlon lived in Savannah and had been married for nine years. Marlon was a laid-back guy until he got behind the wheel of a car. Then, it was like stepping into a horror movie....Marlon became possessed by that little demon kid from the

Gregory Peck/Lee Remick original version of "The Omen." If someone cut "Road Rage" Marlon off in traffic, it was truly frightening to witness. He'd had several screaming confrontations with other drivers in the past year alone. Last month, he and another driver pulled off the road to scream at one another and the other driver had brandished a pistol in Marlon's face.

Renee avoided getting into a car with Marlon whenever possible. It didn't improve matters if she drove, because as a passenger, Marlon became equally "cray-cray."

No one is born with a bad temper! It's something we learn, and something we can unlearn.

This is where premarital counseling comes in very handy. If you or your intended has a truly bad temper, hostility or rage problem, get some help before you tie the knot.

## Housework

When both partners work and get home late every night, the last thing anyone wants to do is cook dinner, let alone do housework. Then, on the weekends, time is spent running errands, shopping for groceries, seeing friends, watching sports! Who has time for housework anyway?

If a couple can afford it, a good cleaning lady twice a month is a real lifesaver. If cost is prohibitive, perhaps something else can be sacrificed (eating out less frequently, for example). Even if you can only afford to hire someone once a month, this is still a big help.

If hiring someone just isn't possible, there needs to be give and take on the issue of housework, particularly if both spouses work.

Wives, if you've somehow gotten yourself into the predicament of working full-time, plus doing all the cooking and cleaning, oh heck yes, time to turn that Princess cruise ship around.

It's up to each couple to create an equitable arrangement. Perhaps he likes vacuuming and she hates it, but she's fine with dusting. If you both hate all housework, perhaps make a list and switch off every few weeks.

Ladies, don't make the mistake of insisting he can't do laundry as well as you, or that he flubs up everything in the kitchen. Accept that your husband will do things differently. If you insist that everything is done your way, *you may just get stuck doing it all*, and that's no good for anyone! No good for you because you will be resentful. No good for your husband either, because resentful women are generally *cranky* to live with.

## Hygiene

This may seem like a rather odd topic, but as previously stated, many married friends and co-workers contributed to this book. Some are happy with their spouses, some not.

Therefore, one surprisingly frequent complaint by both husbands and wives, but one rarely stated as a reason for breaking up, is irritation over one's spouse being lazy or sloppy about hygiene.

In a relationship, this works rather like a small pebble in your shoe. It's a low-level irritant which gets on your nerves more and more as time goes by.

The most frequent grievance from both men and women is their spouse had been gloriously clean and fresh prior to marriage, but over the years had become increasingly lazy about hygiene.

A surprising number of individuals actually employed the adjective "gross."

It's surprising and notable that more gripes actually came from men. They mentioned their wives neglected to shave their legs and shampoo their hair. Legs and hair were the top two items mentioned.

One fellow complained that his wife now shampooed her hair only once or twice weekly; her stated reason was it would all fall out if she washed it more frequently. But he wasn't buying that excuse because as he put it, she'd washed her hair every single day when they'd been dating and lived together prior to marriage, and she still had a full head of hair to this day.

I'm going to break my own rule right here about TMI by saying I shower every morning, and then take a long hot bath every night. I shower extra times when I go to the gym or if I'm out with my horses. I've shampooed my hair every day of my life, with few exceptions, and I'm quite certain I'm not bald yet. My friends know that I'm fanatical about my teeth. Robert wouldn't have gotten a 2nd date with me if he hadn't been super clean and had nice nails.

Lest you think I'm sitting here bragging, I shall reveal my wardrobe is in terrible need of help and it's not likely to get much better. God bless them, my friends love me *despite* my limited fashion sense. My motto is: if you hang onto your clothes long enough, someday they will *surely* come back in style.

Both men and women described grungy teeth as a huge turn-off, by the way.

Thomas and Jennifer had been married for three years and co-parented two beautiful Labrador retrievers. Thomas loved Jennifer very much, but since they'd wed, she'd increasingly become "kinda nasty," as he described it. Jennifer rarely showered or washed her hair and didn't actually bother to change her underwear each day. It should be noted that Thomas did interject the adjective "revolting" at this point. Their dogs lovingly slobbered all over Jennifer from morning 'til night, which wouldn't bother Thomas, as he loved their dogs also, if Jennifer had taken just ten minutes out of her day to shower.

Not wishing to hurt her feelings, Thomas had never complained to Jennifer directly. He had, however, dropped quite a few hints, which proved to be unfruitful. But once Thomas started venting, it was apparent this was a huge turn-off. In related news, he also reported that Jennifer spent a fortune on shoes, but her last pedicure had been three months ago.

So, there's no subtle way to put this: a surprisingly high number of men mentioned poor hygiene as being a real turn-off in bed.

Women, as well, mentioned their annoyance when their husbands were lazy about showering, particularly on the weekends.

LaVerne and Will had been married for five years. She observed that he'd been great about taking showers, shaving, and using nice aftershave during their courtship and early marriage. However, he'd become progressively lazier, as she put it, over the past few years. Will watched ball games all weekend and sometimes never showered until Sunday night. When LaVerne nagged him, he laughed and ignored her. This really got on her nerves because, as she put it, Will smelled like beer and tacos all weekend but nonetheless expected her to be some kind of "love machine."

If this all sounds judgy, well, these are actual complaints from real couples. Don't expect your partner to tell you this stuff, by the way. Surprisingly few folks who were interviewed were comfortable bringing this up to their spouse; those who had done so complained that improvement was generally only temporary.

At first we hesitated to even add this section, 'cause it's kind of embarrassing. However, if a lack of hygiene negatively affects someone's sex life, they may not even realize it. Dang it, life's unfair!

As one man reminisced about his ex, "She really took time with her appearance before the wedding. Her hair was so beautiful and clean, I loved running my hands through it. She smelled fantastic... she was just a goddess. I felt like the luckiest guy on earth. But, less than a year after our wedding, she hardly ever washed her hair or shaved her legs. She wanted me to have sex with her but couldn't even wash her hair or shave her damn legs."

Hmm...this is *most* intriguing. It does appear her little "brillo pad" legs were by far his biggest gripe. Unlike many of the complainants, this fellow did directly protest to her on many occasions about her lax hygiene, but she alternately joked around or ignored him. These two are no longer a couple.

Apparently there were other issues such as her "cray-cray" family, but his main complaint was he felt deceived because she was gloriously maintained before the wedding bells and then kind of "sloppy" afterwards, as he phrased it.

So, this is all a bit of a revelation. It absolutely dispels the notion we've been fed by popular media, which says men are just mindless sex machines and can do "it" no matter what. Apparently, men get turned off by things like poor hygiene far more often than one might ever suspect.

To sum it up, according to both genders, gross lack of personal hygiene is definitely a romance buster. Fortunately, it's not a difficult or expensive problem to fix.

## Humility

Most of us can be arrogant from time to time. But what we're specifically referring to here is those individuals who have a superior attitude toward their spouse.

Their cocky point of view can manifest itself in several ways.

The arrogant spouse frequently interrupts their partner or talks over them. Their body language shows they feel superior to their partner. Maybe they believe their spouse's hobbies or interests are frivolous compared to their own.

At a recent fundraising dinner, four other couples were seated at our table. Janet and Arthur, the couple next to us, had been married for 15 years. Janet was simply delightful, on those very rare occasions she got one word in edgewise. Good ol' Arthur interrupted her constantly, talking over her with unbridled enthusiasm. He placed his elbows on the table and angled his torso so we could barely see Janet. His body language utterly excluded her.

It became apparent during the dinner that Arthur knew it all. When someone at our table disagreed with him over a minor point, he became visibly offended.

Arthur is a real big shot in the world of finance; Janet's been staying home for years raising their kids. When someone at the table complimented her for successfully raising three children, Arthur laughed dismissively, waved his hand and changed the subject.

Janet is obviously putting up with Arthur for now, but no telling if one day she'll have her fill of his superior attitude and tell him to go take a hike to the Rockies.

Humility is an important component in marriage. Here's an example of how the opposite works (this is actually an amalgam of two individual scenarios).

New Jersey couple Steve and Angela were wed 22 years before divorcing. They'd started out with nothing and had struggled for years, living frugally and making countless sacrifices to succeed. Early in their marriage, Angela had often worked three jobs at once to support Steve as he completed his education.

Steve built his own company, which became hugely successful over the years. He and Angela had agreed that he'd focus on the business and she'd stay home raising their two kids, Pamela and Jason.

For many years, Steve and Angela seemed like one of the happiest couples out there. All their years of mutual hard labor were finally paying off. When Pamela and Jason entered middle school, Steve and Angela began traveling and sailing on their boat, like they'd always dreamed of doing. Steve told friends he was the luckiest man on earth. He always gave Angela credit for the countless sacrifices she'd made for him and their kids.

Their daughter Pamela had just begun high school when a woman named Vicky was hired at Steve's company. Teensy side note: Vicky had been married and divorced three times and was slightly younger than Steve; okay, who's counting...she was 22 years younger. None of these potential rouge flags deterred Steve in the least, who became completely enraptured with Vicky in about five months.

Steve proclaimed he couldn't possibly live without Vicky. She was the "love of his life." In a surprise move, he announced to everyone that he'd been "miserable" for years with Angela, whom he divorced as quickly as possible. This stunned everyone, who'd seen that Steve had seemed quite content. He'd appeared to be very happy, in fact, until adorable Vicky had suddenly entered the picture with her buttercup-colored curls, torn jeans and teeny tiny little high heels.

Steve and Vicky then began planning their fairy-tale wedding. It was Vicky's fondest dream to have a wedding so magnificent that even Kim Kardashian would be gripped by envy. Steve was so enchanted with Vicky, so mesmerized in fact, he even succumbed to the pressure she put on him to *not sign* a prenuptial agreement.

Okay, can we repeat this? After his divorce, Stevie was still worth about *six million dollars*, six million smackaroos. This very smart businessman allowed the gorgeous Vicky to convince him to not sign a prenuptial agreement.

His friends were disappointed how Steve had treated Angela, but were still sufficiently loyal to beg him to protect himself. Many of these friends, remembering how Angela had stuck with him through thick and thin, smelled a rat with this new romance, and quite a few told him so.

However, Steve wouldn't listen to anyone, not even his son Jason. He wondered aloud if maybe his friends were just jealous of his hot new girlfriend. He was bound and determined to marry Vicky, and marry her he did, as quickly as possible. He lavished her with an enormous 12-carat diamond wedding ring, a huge, opulent wedding (Kim Kardashian, to Vicky's surprise, did not even R.S.V.P.) and a lavish honeymoon in Jamaica. Most of Steve's friends did attend the wedding although they were unhappy about the union.

Angela, to her everlasting credit, rose sharply above the occasion by never saying anything negative about either her ex-husband or his new wife. She wisely saved it for her therapist, who undoubtedly heard it all.

Their son Jason refused to attend the wedding. He believed his father had not only betrayed his mother, but had lied in claiming he'd been unhappy all those years.

However, their rebellious daughter Pamela was one of 17 bridesmaids and she wholeheartedly supported the union. She and Angela had been having typical "mom and teenage daughter" arguments for some time. Pamela admired her new stepmom tremendously because Vicky took her shopping, bought her expensive clothes and makeup, and let her do whatever she wanted when she visited.

Vicky even convinced Steve to give Pamela her very own American Express card with no limit, and a brand-new, bright red BMW for her first car. Vicky was a polar opposite to her mom, who always worried about her, wanted her home by 11p.m. and who'd recommended her first car be a sensible used model.

At first, things were glorious, simply divine. Steve told friends he was the happiest he'd been in his entire life. He and Vicky got along flawlessly. She quit working at his company and thereafter occupied herself with shopping, going to the gym and lunching with girlfriends. Vicky spent a small fortune each month on clothes, jewelry, purses and shoes. Steve told himself he could well afford it, and that all this shopping was so she'd look good for him.

It did greatly trouble Steve that Jason avoided him and absolutely refused to spend time with Vicky, to whom he'd given a series of accurately cruel nicknames. Still, the next four years were a giddy time for Steve, filled with travel, romance, and plenty of sex.

Steve then sold a portion of his company and made several million dollars in the process. As this was money he'd earned after their marriage, it was considered to be community property.

Perhaps then it won't come as a total surprise that Vicky and her electric hips left Steve seven months later for a dashing weightlifter she met at the gym. Emilio competed in Ironman competitions and was much closer to Vicky's age. Steve confided in friends that their marriage had disintegrated quite rapidly after he'd refused to revise his will, giving Vicky a larger share than either of his two kids.

Much lighter in wallet by this time, Steve then bravely attempted to reconcile with his ex-wife. He actually believed there was a strong possibility a joyful reunion might occur. However, he found to his astonishment that Angela now had a thriving career and was very seriously dating a handsome professor she'd met online.

Go Angela! Um hmm that's right!

Steve did learn a hard lesson, but at the expense of his marriage and considerable pain to his wife and kids. If only he'd had the humility to listen to his friends, at least about the prenuptial, he might have realized the adorable Vicky was just a wee bit too interested in his bank account. His first wife, who'd helped him build a life, raise his kids and had been loyal to him when they were poor, had been devastated by his actions, but had moved on and was able to start a new life – without him.

## Holidays

A burdensome issue for many couples is where they'll spend holidays. This can be a hot topic when both sets of parents expect to celebrate with "the kids."

Alternating visits is one possible idea. Seeing both sets of parents is a frequent solution, but it can be exhausting trying to race to both places.

Celebrating holidays can be more challenging if a couple has two different religions. Some compromise by doing a little of each; a little Hanukkah and a little Christmas. Or a lot of both!

The key word here, of course, is *compromise*. If one or both partners have that sticky attitude of "my way or the highway," holidays will then be just one more opportunity for conflict.

This is definitely an issue to discuss before the wedding, but even when details are agreed upon beforehand, this generally will require some fine-tuning.

Holidays can be emotionally and physically exhausting. Buying presents, decorating the house, attending holiday parties with friends and at work...there's just not enough time to do it all. If this sounds familiar, perhaps downsize the decorations and gifts one year and see if this works better.

Maybe one year you'll decide to take a break from the regular holiday schedule by taking a trip. What a lovely idea to skip decorating the house and go someplace completely different. If you live in a sunny climate, what about going someplace with snow? Friends of ours did this and loved it! They said it was such a wonderful break. The trip was in lieu of gifts... they just bought each other one small $20 souvenir; both said the trip was the best present ever. Our little family of three took a two-week trip last Christmas to Charleston and Savannah and it was glorious to get away and be in a completely different environment.

If your kids are greedy, demanding little suckers when it comes to Christmas gifts, perhaps buy them only a few small presents, and let them pick a charity as their main gift. For many years, Andrea's largest Christmas gift was a donation made in her honor to "Smile Train," an organization that fixes children's cleft palates. When she was small we told her Christmas isn't about a little girl who already has so much getting even more, but is about giving.

Bringing food to the homeless on Christmas is a nice thing to do and let's be frank: this also prevents you from "scarfing up" all the leftovers.

If you're short on cash, music, cookies, homemade fudge, modest presents, all of these can create a wonderful holiday. Claire and Sam, one of our success story couples, mentioned that when they were broke one newlywed Christmas Claire hand-made cute festive ornaments and this made it one of their best celebrations ever.

## Humor

When you laugh frequently, you actually reduce your risk of heart attack or stroke by 40 percent. Watching comedy is three times more effective at reducing stress than meditation or calm music.

This doesn't have to be bona fide jokes, by the way. Just seeing the humor in everyday situations gives your brain a shot of dopamine, a neurotransmitter linked with reward, which signals pleasure.

How does this benefit a married couple? Laughing together definitely contributes to happier, longer relationships.

But what do you do if you are married to someone who seldom laughs, who has a rather somber outlook? What if you've gone and gotten hitched to someone who looks as though they spend their spare time staring down into open caskets?

Carly and Ben have been married for 12 years; initially they might seem somewhat mismatched in that she is very outgoing, bubbly, is often silly and loves to laugh, and he is very somber and serious. They don't like the same type of movies or television. Ben prefers scary movies, like "Silence of the Lambs." Carly dislikes those types of movies; she loves sitcoms, which she finds hilarious and which Ben does not care for.

Carly will always be much more jovial than Ben. But Ben does see humor in everyday situations. These two work by balancing one another. Carly is able to help Ben "lighten up." In turn, Ben has helped Carly become a more resourceful and mature individual.

## Honeymoon Sandwich

Let's add a little levity here... a honeymoon sandwich is...drumroll please...lettuce alone.

## Hero

Psychology plays an enormous role when it comes to understanding your partner. Once you realize what motivates them, this takes the struggle out of– for lack of a better way to put it – getting them to do what you want.

Ladies, listen closely: men have a very strong hero instinct. They love to save the day. They thrive when their partner appreciates them. This is one reason why superhero movies are so overwhelmingly popular.

Now, a crucial secret: men can also be rather sensitive, far more so than many women may realize.

Bill and Laurie had been married for four years; she was upset because he no longer was attentive. In her opinion, he didn't make much of an effort anymore. Laurie felt that Bill wasn't the same person she'd married. He no longer washed her car on the weekends. He rarely spoiled her with flowers and little gifts, like he used to. He seldom helped her carry in bags of groceries when she returned home from the market. In short, Laurie believed that Bill had become lazy in their relationship, after just four short years.

The two visited a marriage therapist, and this proved to be helpful, although it took some time. Bill clammed up in early sessions, but opened up eventually. What he finally had to say came as a complete shocker to Laurie.

Bill complained bitterly that no matter how hard he tried, Laurie always found something to criticize. She also made jokes at his expense. Initially, Bill had enjoyed Laurie's dry sense of humor, and had viewed her as a witty individual. But in the past few years, she'd become increasingly sarcastic. Bill no longer found her comments amusing; he saw them as rude and insulting. He told their therapist he was living with a real bitch.

Ooh...sorry for the language: I am just quoting Bill.

This rather stunned Laurie, who believed that sarcasm was one of her finest personality traits.

But sarcasm is rather like crushed red pepper on pasta, or wasabi in soy sauce. It can spice things up very nicely, but a little bit goes a very, very long way.

In researching this book, I talked with many men and came to realize that some of my preconceived notions about men were way off base. Men can be incredibly sensitive, oftentimes more so than women. But here's a crucial fact: they are far, far likelier to hide it when their feelings are hurt.

The pressure society puts on men their entire lives works its magic; contemporary men still often stuff down their hurt feelings.

This goes back to childhood. When you observe kids on the playground, little boys and girls are still treated very differently. When tiny Heather falls on the playground and scrapes her miniature knee, she receives a plethora of sympathy and attention. "Oh my gosh! Poor little Heather, are you okay, ohhhh!"

When little Brandon falls and scrapes his arm, there's pressure on him to suck it up and to not cry. If his parents don't place this demand on him, the other kids surely do. "Get up Brandon, and quit your snivelling, you're fine."

When they become adults, men are praised for being sensitive... but only up to a certain point. Too sensitive and they get labeled a wimp or soppy.

So wives, if your husband is not as affectionate as you would like, if he doesn't go out of his way to treat you the amazing way he used to, is it possible you are too critical? Do you make him feel appreciated, or do you put him down a lot? Do you make sarcastic comments or jokes at his expense? In short, does he feel like he's your hero?

This is just some food for thought.

Always remember that men love, love, love to be heroes. It's crucial to their makeup... this makes them feel loved and appreciated. They adore feeling that they are important. If he feels that you value and respect him and he's your hero, he's going to want to move mountains for you. Or, at the very least, he's going to help you carry in groceries from your car and bring your flowers.

## Helpless

Here's an intriguing little tidbit: when interviewed for this book, quite a few men complained their wives acted helpless. These same guys added that they didn't think this was cute, but instead, rather annoying.

Hmmm! Being a woman myself, I'm of course protective of my fellow sisters and so this stung just a little bit.

But as stated before, this book shall include the good, the bad and the ugly, so we're tossing it in like bacon bits and croutons! Or, for a more modern twist, pepitas and craisins!

We do all know a couple women who act real helpless. No driving on the freeway for Valerie unless hubby Stanley is at the helm of that Prius. The gardener wants a small raise; Sally can't possibly handle it without first consulting Ted. Wanda makes excuses for not going someplace if Earl can't either come along or drive her there.

Ladies! If you recognize yourself here, may we remind you that we women have been able to vote in this country since 1920! It's been over one hundred years! So please stop acting like you can't do it without a man to help! Yes, you can! Si se puedo!

Here's the rub: dependent women who lean on their men to drive them places, or to help them make minor decisions, may believe this makes their husbands feel important. Yes, it does, in the case of some guys, but apparently, not most. When this topic arose, most men stated emphatically that they don't really like this. To them, it feels more like a burden.

Most of all, they admit it lessens the respect they feel for their wives; they'd have higher regard for a more equal partner. Now, we're not talking here about an elderly couple, by the way. That's another thing entirely. We're talking about a young or middle-aged woman acting helpless. One man added that when his wife did this, she seemed old before her time.

Apparently, Stanley would far prefer that Valerie drive herself to the bookstore and not lean on him for a ride. Ted would have more respect for Sally if she informed him, "The gardener asked for a raise and I handled it," rather than always asking him. If Wanda pushed herself and ran errands on her own without Earl, he'd have a chance to actually miss her.

Now, ladies, don't just think we're only picking on you here. When interviewed, a high percentage of women complained that their husbands are often super helpless with housework and cooking. Guys, if you truly hate housework, consider springing for a cleaning lady twice a month. When it's your turn to cook dinner, there's no need for a Gordon Ramsay competition. Many wives adore takeout, or that good old standby, a pre-cooked chicken and salad in the bag. Your menu will surely be a hit if you include King's Hawaiian rolls with slightly melted butter...let's face it... those rolls make every meal a veritable feast.

## He's Already Got a Mama

Helicopter parents are found worldwide, and most commonly located at private religious schools. Unlike our beautiful bald eagles, they'll never go extinct. Visit any elementary or middle school campus, and with binoculars you can just barely discern them, circling up in the blue skies. Even if it's stormy, you can still spot them. Their devotion is "rain or shine." They are carefully whirly-birding right over their sheltered little darlings, watching their every move.

"Lord, no! Jason is talking with a girl! She'll be pregnant by next month!" "Oh my heavens, Ashley is smoking something... it'd better not be marijuana!"

Helicopter wives... well, they're kind of similar. Let's take a peek at this unique dynamic... we are dubbing it the "mama syndrome."

He's already got a mama. Hmm ... for some reason, this statement sounds much more charming with a Southern accent.

Why, he's already got a mama. Her name is Loretta Sue, and she lives two states away in South Carolina. You, young married lady, on the other hand, have a very important role in his life, but it sure ain't mama.

So, when you're babying that grown man, reminding him about every little thing, making sure he takes his vitamins, scolding him for not getting enough sleep, well, you're kinda treating him just like a little tiny toddler.

And, Miss Savannah Claire, what do you suppose happens next?

Well, he will truly appreciate all that pampering...at first.

However, in a country minute, he'll rebel on you like a 12-year-old boy whose mama took away his skateboard 'cuz he went too darn fast and skinned his knee.

Ladies, listen up. When you make those thoughtful, caring gestures, reminding him to take his vitamins, warning him about that upcoming freeway exit, scolding him if he doesn't get enough sleep, treating him so lovingly, just like a little boy, what exactly are you doing?

Well, you're putting yourself right smack dab in the role of mama, and gals, we are just gonna put it to you bluntly - no man wants to get romantic with mama! So this right here is where it will backfire on you worse than a Silverado truck going down that bumpy twilight Mississippi road.

You're giving him love, all right, but not an amorous, passionate kind of love. Instead, it's gonna make him feel downright suffocated. It's guaranteed to give him claustrophobia and cause mutiny quicker than you can say "fried green tomatoes."

Many wives make this mistake because they love their husbands so, so much. And, being women, and of course we are so wonderful, it's instinctive for us steel magnolias to care for, pamper and nurture those whom we cherish and adore.

But again, we warn you ladies, if you do this with your feller, you're putting yourself right there dead center in the role of...you guessed it... mama!

Women go out of their way to show their love, but then wonder how on earth it went so wrong. All that pampering just brought out the mutinous little boy in him before you can even say, "You're grounded and no Georgia peach pie for you!"

How on earth can it backfire when you're being so wonderful, so loving, so caring?

Again ladies, it's the perilous "mama syndrome" hard at work.

How do you tell if you're babying your man too much? Hmm, let's see. He treats you like a nag and ignores what you say, or maybe loses interest in sex, or possibly the cad even goes elsewhere for romance. Now, we're not making any excuses for philaderin' here! Not for one Alabama minute!

But we do maintain if you smother that boy like too much gravy on chicken fried steak, or too much pimento cheese dip on Ritz crackers, well, this will not bring about that romantic union you've always dreamed of.

Okay, enough of that!

Just for fun, let's toss in a joke from my favorite brother-in-law. Marcella had just gotten married, and being a traditional Italian good girl, was still a virgin. On her wedding night, staying at her mama's house, she was understandably quite nervous. But her mother reassured her. "Don't worry, Marcella. Alessandro's a good man. Go upstairs and he'll take care of you." So up she went. When Marcella got upstairs, Alessandro took off his shirt and exposed his hairy chest. Marcella raced downstairs and cried, "Mama, Mama, Alessandro's got a big hairy chest." "Don't worry, Marcella," said her mother, "all good men have hairy chests. Go upstairs. He'll take good care of you." So, up she went again. When Marcella reached the bedroom, Alessandro took off his pants, exposing his hairy legs. Again, Marcella raced screeching downstairs. "Mama, Mama, Alessandro took off his pants and he's got hairy legs!" "Don't worry. All good men have hairy legs. Alessandro's a good man. Go upstairs and he'll take good care of you." So, up she trudged again. Next, Alessandro took off his socks and on his left foot he was missing part of one toe. When Marcella saw this, she ran downstairs screaming. "Mama, Mama, Alessandro's got a foot and a half!" "Stay here and stir the pasta," said the mother, shoving her aside. "This is a job for Mama."

# I

## Irritation

Tragically, in order to remain happily married long-term, one must somehow tolerate an almost endless amount of irritation.

Those of you who've been married for at least four years, I see you out there nodding your heads knowingly.

Here's a bitter truth: when you live with another human being, no matter how much you adore them, or how close you two become, nonetheless, they'll always be an entirely separate person than you. This shall often drive you bananas foster.

In the early, passionate stages of a relationship, even the first few years of marriage, it's so easy to forget this unsexy fact. Then, when it hits you right in the teeth like a june bug as you drive your convertible T-bird through the desert en route to Vegas, it's catastrophic and sad. It's similar to that sinking feeling when you first realize you're living with an alien.

You may have noticed your spouse gets on your nerves more than your kids do. This is not at all uncommon. After all, you raised your children and imprinted on them your habits and mores, so even during their insane teenage years, their wildest shenanigans sometimes made more sense than your spouse.

This is utterly normal. Dating someone for a couple years gives you ample time to spot their flaws, see if you can live with them, and if not, to cut and run fast for the hills.

Some folks really can't deal with irritation. Eloise told friends she'd love to remarry, but the guys she dated were simply too difficult. She never realized that she herself shared this same trait; Eloise had to have things done *her* way.

Eloise was funny, intelligent and entertaining, but even being friends with her was challenging. Simply picking a restaurant was troublesome as there were countless places Eloise refused to eat. Sadly, this bright, well-educated woman never realized how demanding she was. She complained that others were difficult, never her. She always pushed to get her way, and generally succeeded. But the price she paid was loneliness. Eloise had few close friends and could not sustain a long-term romantic relationship.

By the way, please don't think I automatically toss other singles into the "Eloise rowboat." Most single folks are very considerate, accommodating and can compromise on large and small issues.

So, now let's return to the subject of irritation. Sharing space can lead to massive exasperation. This holds true whether you share a studio apartment or a 10,000 square-foot "Selling Sunset" mega-house. Obviously, getting space is easier in a jumbo dwelling, but either way, you're sharing territory with someone we've already established is an extra-terrestrial.

Here are just a few of the four trillion ways your spouse can really bug you. These all were supplied by married folks, by the way:

- Talks too loudly or too much.

- Mumbles, or calls out to you from another room.

- Talks or sings to no one in particular. Sings "Sweet Home Alabama" over and over, and has done so on a near-daily basis for the past 17 years.

- Croons baby talk to the pets.

- Barely speaks to you in the morning, but then is overheard joyfully yodeling to your dog.

- Makes a mess in the kitchen and doesn't clean it up right away, or ever.

- Sneaks cigarettes while bragging that they quit.

- Plays loud music that you can't stand.

- Leaves one, just one, dirty dish, cup, or spoon in the sink.

- Cooks or eats food that you find well, kind of gross.

- Gabs for hours and hours to her sister on the phone, when the two of you share a one-bedroom apartment.

- Forgets to remind you they're working late (substitute gym or errands).

- Uses up the very last butter, milk, eggs or cheese and leaves the empty container sitting in the fridge. This counts double if it's ice cream. Triple if it's Ben and Jerry's.

- Insists their poodle Chloe sleeps on your bed. Chloe barks, farts and claws at the bedspread, waking you constantly throughout the night, while your spouse snores on blissfully.

- Chats when you're trying to read or watch TV, so you constantly have to stop to listen.

- Laughs at unfunny parts of movies at the theatre, so people around you get annoyed.

- Drives too fast and tailgates, or so slowly in the fast lane that people pass you, screaming and flipping you "the bird."

We could go on and on and on. If you're married, you can doubtless supply dozens of additional items to this list.

Now, here's something important to NEVER, ever forget... guess what...?

*You* are annoying as well! Yes, *you*! Everybody is!

That person who thinks they aren't... THEY ARE DEAD WRONG! They think their Dixie cup don't stink! Ha! Who are they fooling?

In order to stay happily married, you cannot let your spouse's irritating habits bug you...that is, bug you too much.

Constantly remind yourself of one thing: EVERYONE, *including you*, is annoying at times!

Let's view this from a purely practical standpoint. If you karate-kick Niklaus to the curb and find a new partner, undoubtedly, your "newbie' won't irritate you in the same ways as the "Original." You made absolutely certain of this. You were wisely on the lookout for those exasperating traits so you wouldn't get stuck with them a second time.

However, drumroll please....once the honeymoon phase of your second marriage takes its last gasping breath, as it inevitably will, you may then find yourself living in a B-rated horror movie. You're now realizing in sheer terror that the replacement model is getting on your nerves just as much as the old one, perhaps even a tad more, just in *new and state-of-the-art ways.*

Then, to top it off, your divorce attorney Janet just mailed you the loveliest picture postcard from Bora Bora. Surely, this was dispatched to you in error. You and Janet aren't personal friends, although you did clock more hours talking with her than even your therapist last year. Perhaps your address was over-programmed into Janet's computer because she has mailed you so many invoices?

At any rate, that postcard is all you'll see of Bora Bora since your divorce, since now all you can afford is a quickie motel stay in El Centro, California!

So, if you *are* going through a stage in your marriage where your spouse is bugging you more than usual, and it is inevitable this will occur every so often, please re-read this chapter.

Sad but true, married couples still split up every single day of the year, Sundays and holidays included, over trivial items like the poodle on the bed, the Ben and Jerry's ice cream, or somebody's horrific driving.

## In-Laws

Our gruesome section about mothers-in-law; most specifically mothers of sons, is right around the bend. It's aptly entitled "Mothers-in-law straight outta hell."

When you marry your beloved, for better or worse, you're also taking on their parents, siblings, and grandparents, as well as other extended family. If it's a second marriage, there might be step-kids as well.

How often they visit, if they'll stay at your home or at a hotel, whether you help them out financially, if they'll someday move in with you, all of these are major variables. It's crucial to discuss everything before the wedding invites get printed.

Of course, I'm a complete hypocrite preaching this, since Robert and I never discussed any of this. None of this ever even crossed our minds. When you're young and planning a romantic wedding, who on earth talks about practicalities?

Often, however, in-laws can cause friction early in a marriage. Let's travel to Lafayette, Louisiana, and visit Laura Beth and Wyatt.

Laura Beth and Wyatt had been wed for just one year but already had a large source of conflict: Laura Beth's family. Her parents and younger sister Candace lived two hours away in New Iberia. They visited quite frequently, with Chesterfield, their adorable 90-pound sheepdog puppy, always in tow.

This merry foursome stayed a minimum of five nights, sometimes longer. Laura Beth's parents were extremely generous, bringing armfuls of gifts, including of course bottled hot sauce, and they took Laura Beth and Wyatt out to eat, to movies, shows and other fun outings.

Unfortunately, they were also loud, boisterous and messy houseguests. Laura Beth's father flipped pancakes each morning and stampeded from the chaotic kitchen afterwards. Candace left a trail of candy and snack wrappers behind her and spilled her makeup all over the bathroom counters. Laura Beth's mother was neater than the other two, but she'd grown up in Lafayette and to this day had at least one dozen best girlfriends still living there, so these ladies frequently dropped in at any time of day or night for sweet tea and gossip.

Laura Beth was accustomed to all this, so it didn't bother her a bit. In addition, her two older sisters, Ashley Sue and Magnolia, lived nearby. These gals visited frequently as well, sometimes on weeknights. They drank wine, played loud charades or games, or noisily watched TV. Frequently, Magnolia tossed off too many peach bellinis and ended up sleeping in the spare bedroom. Once the bellinis partially wore off, usually at about two a.m., her insomnia set in and Magnolia would wander around the house, waking Wyatt repeatedly. Laura Beth's family members also helped themselves to food and drinks directly from the fridge and cupboards, which Wyatt found rather odd, if not rude.

Laura Beth's office was remote, so she could begin work later when her family visited. Wyatt, on the other hand, left for work early each weekday morning, usually on little sleep when Laura Beth's sisters came to stay.

Wyatt had just one sibling, his brother Jackson who was eight years older, so for much of his adolescence, Wyatt had essentially been an only child. His parents' idea of Southern hospitality had been quite small-scale, with visits from guests generally limited to dinners with polite conversation. Wyatt wasn't crazy about the extended stays from his in-laws, and he especially disliked the visits from Ashley Sue and Magnolia.

Back when they'd been dating, Laura Beth had loved that Wyatt was responsible, serious and methodical. Now, after just one year of marriage, she saw him as uptight and old before his time. Wyatt had once greatly admired Laura Beth's fun, spontaneous nature, such a contrast from his own, but now he increasingly viewed her as inconsiderate, loud and rude.

In the past, Laura Beth had been embarrassed when Wyatt had made it plain that her family had outworn their welcome. Wyatt felt Laura Beth was inconsiderate of his need to sleep, and he felt his life was continually disrupted. It wasn't that Wyatt was unsociable; it was mostly that he and Laura Beth had grown up with such different family upbringings. In addition, Wyatt's job as a warehouse manager was noisy and stressful, and he loved coming home to a quiet house.

If you study psychology, by the way, Wyatt is that personality type who at first glance appears to be rather sociable, but it's on his own terms. I can relate, because I'm very much like this myself. I always get credit for being more sociable than I am. I appear to be very outgoing, but I definitely require space as well. If I spend too much time with others, after awhile I simply must crawl alone into a cave, clutching a turkey drumstick with mustard.

So, what's the solution for Laura Beth and Wyatt? Their relationship is on a real downer. They're definitely sick of one another. They don't feel "in love" or even "in like" anymore.

And folks, this is after just one short year of marriage.

Let's not forget, by the way, that not so long ago, this couple was madly in love.

But now, Laura Beth feels Wyatt is making her choose between him and her family. Wyatt believes he's not receiving respect or consideration from Laura Beth.

If these two continue along their current path, they may very likely end up divorced. After all, Laura Beth sees nothing wrong with their arrangement; she just thinks Wyatt is selfish and uptight. Wyatt feels like an outsider with Laura Beth's family and thinks Laura Beth is inconsiderate and selfish. Notice that both view the other as being selfish.

To turn things around, some compromise by both parties is crucial. Wyatt must realize that it's Laura Beth's house as well, but she must back him with her family. They don't respect Wyatt because she doesn't appear to support his wishes.

One possible solution might be for Laura Beth's parents and younger sister to stay at a hotel when they visit. Particularly for visits lasting more than a few days, this would ease the pressure on Laura Beth and Wyatt's marriage. Even Laura Beth has admitted that her parents and sister do stay too long sometimes.

Fortunately, Laura Beth's parents are well-off financially and can easily afford a hotel. They could get two hotel rooms so Laura Beth could sometimes stay with Candace in the second room and it could be like a fun party. Laura Beth might also go places with Ashley Sue and Magnolia, rather than always having them visit. Wyatt doesn't object to her spending time with her sisters, just to their staying so often at the house.

Laura Beth must realize that although her family is used to frequent, extended visits, this doesn't work for her husband. His feelings need to be taken into consideration, particularly when her noisy sisters keep him up and then he has to awaken at six the next morning for work.

Wyatt can compromise more as well. If her sisters visit on a weekend, he may wish to go out and spend time with buddies or, if he stays home, make more of an effort to enjoy their company. After all, it's Laura Beth's house too, and it's not fair to her if family or friends never visit.

This couple is somewhat mismatched in a social sense, but that doesn't mean they have to throw in the towel on their relationship. They must find some common middle ground; again, here is that all-important word —- dadadada! COMPROMISE.

## Irresistible

We've all been told endlessly that in order to remain happily married, a couple needs to communicate. We're won't dispute this here, but perhaps communication is somewhat overrated.

Think of it this way: couples generally don't fall in love and get married because they communicate well.

Men, have you ever once in your life rushed up to one of your buddies, so excited, madly in love, on cloud nine, delirious with happiness, and say all in a rush, "I'm so in love with Jessica! She's such a great communicator!"

Au contraire, when you fall passionately in love, you're crazy about the way she looks at you, the color of her eyes, how it feels when she kisses you... in short, you find her irresistible. It's really about *you*... how she makes *you* feel. Note: please substitute gender when appropriate. Well, there's an annoying word for you: *appropriate*.

This is, of course, because being in love is simply one of the most narcissistic adventures a human being can undertake. When you become smitten with someone, it's such an incredible sensation, you can't think of anything or anyone else. You're glowing brilliantly with happiness, utterly joyful to have found your beloved soul-mate. You worship and adore this most marvelous being. You're in such ecstasy, you feel like you're glowing all the time. You can barely even sleep at night, you're so in love. You've transcended everyday life and are floating like an angel atop clouds of delight and adoration.

To paraphrase Harriet in the film "Wild Child," how sublime.

Overnight, you can relate deeply to every romantic song you've ever heard, even the most twangy country ones.

In short, your partner is irresistible to you.

It's kind of like that saying, "No one's perfect until you fall in love with them."

During this blissful stage, even if your beloved does something strange or annoying, you most likely will be in utter denial. After all, you're in the "honeymoon phase" of your relationship. Instead, you hasten to make excuses for them. You simply can't bear to tarnish the flawless image you're carrying around in your mind.

The two of you then get married; everything is marvelous and blissful, simply divine, as my dad would put it...well, at least for awhile.

Then, sadly, inevitably, over time, usually about two to three years, unless you're long-distance, you do lose that infatuation, that glorious feeling of being crazy about your partner.

Tragically, your marriage then begins to lose its bright glow, and that euphoric feeling that your partner is *irresistible* begins eroding just like Pacific Coast Highway in Malibu after a severe rainstorm.

Maybe there are unpaid bills, screaming kids, leaky roofs, demanding in-laws, quarrels that go unresolved. Whatever it is, that idealized, beautiful, adored and worshipped creature you couldn't live without has now displayed numerous flaws. The end result is that as of now, that perfect angel is just really working your last nerve.

Disillusioned spouses frequently describe this sorry comedown by stating they no longer feel like they are "in love."

So, now let's uncover the meatloaf and potatoes of this whole chapter. This is the stage of a relationship where listening to conventional wisdom is failing us in droves, kind of like our government.

Let's travel to Miami Beach, Florida and drop in on Jill and Ed. This couple dated for three years before marriage and believed they knew everything about one another. Both loved eating out and seeing movies, they adored walking their beagle Maisy at the beach, and pretty much agreed about everything. They laughed at the same jokes, they had plenty to talk about, both had solid careers, sensational chemistry, ah, life was grand!

No doubt about it, Jill and Ed got along spectacularly.

Now, here's the rub: this couple *thought* they knew everything about one another. However, they had never yet as a twosome encountered any type of difficulty or adversity during the course of their three-year courtship.

Side note: if you jump ahead to our success story couples, every single one of them has dealt with misfortune of some kind.

Only nine months into their marriage, Ed suddenly lost his job as manager of a paper company when the entire operation moved overseas. He was shell-shocked and devastated. He'd grown up at this company, had been there for nine years, and loved his bosses and co-workers. He couldn't wrap his mind around what had happened and didn't even have a resume. For three days, he spent most of his time on the phone with former colleagues as they all commiserated over the crummy hand they'd been dealt.

One month elapsed, and Ed hadn't yet typed up a resume or created a LinkedIn profile.

He was already driving Jill nuts.

Jill was that person who could galvanize herself into productive activity within seconds. You'd want Jill around in the event of a zombie apocalypse, just to witness the sheer entertainment value of her immediate spring to action. Jill would have had her resume updated within one hour and interviews lined up straight away. Therefore, four weeks later, she was flabbergasted and dismayed to see Ed's stationary figure on their den couch, wearing sweats, eating peanuts and glumly watching college basketball. When he wasn't watching sports, Ed was on the phone with his previous co-workers, grimly hashing and re-hashing the unfairness of it all.

Ed and Jill had more arguments in the next six months than in the past four years.

Ed finally found a job, not a great one, which made Jill bitter with disappointment. As she saw it, Ed had let them both down. She believed if he'd made an immediate concerted effort, he would have been able to pick and choose offers. As it was, it had taken Ed eight months to land a job. Since his unemployment had run out two months earlier, he'd grabbed the first job offer he'd received, taking a nearly $12,000 pay cut. Ed was tired and discouraged and sick of Jill's nagging. He told his brother that nothing he did was good enough, since she just "bitched and griped."

They no longer could afford their planned Christmas trip to New York. At Christmas dinner, Jill's father cracked a joke at Ed's expense and Jill laughed along with her dad. Although she later apologized, Ed felt that Jill was no longer in his corner.

Over the next year, Jill and Ed's connection declined rapidly. Jill told her best friend Tracy perhaps she'd made a mistake in marrying Ed. He wasn't the person she'd thought he was. Tracy recommended a great book about communication and a reputable marriage counselor.

When an unforeseen event which a couple is not equipped to deal with occurs, feelings can change quickly. Jill was disappointed with Ed's passivity, and she responded by nagging and pushing, which only increased his level of apathy.

Even without an event such as a sudden job loss, the feeling of being "in love" fades somewhat over time for nearly all couples. Notable exception: if one partner travels frequently, this whole process can be delayed, often for years.

As the grubbiness and everyday-ness of living together wear couples down, many of them seek answers. Perhaps they read books on how to improve their relationship. Maybe they ask others for advice. Typically, the sage wisdom they receive is to improve their — you guessed it — communication.

If their marriage is in trouble, many couples also see marriage counselors. Jill and Ed both read some marriage advice books and also saw a reputable therapist together.

And, with the assistance of the books and the marriage counselor, Jill and Ed did greatly improve their mutual communication. They became skilled at the art of expressing their needs, wants and emotions. They evolved into a couple who communicated beautifully. Jill stopped interrupting Ed when he was speaking and let him complete his thoughts. Ed became better at not taking things personally and realized that Jill's attempts at humor were just to lighten the mood and didn't mean that she was minimizing him.

But here's where the rip-off so often occurs.

Jill and Ed did everything that they were supposed to do. They both liked their marriage therapist, incidentally. They no longer yelled during arguments and allowed one another to finish complete sentences. They practiced active listening and respectful communication.

It all sounds great, doesn't it? But, here's the surprising part.

Like an astoundingly high number of similar cases, Jill and Ed still couldn't (pardon the expression) fucking stand one another.

This is no good, folks!

After all that work, and all that money spent, for Jill to look at Ed glumly and think to herself, "Damn, I'm just sick of the sight of him." All that effort, all those therapy appointments, for Ed to still peer at Jill in dismay and go, "Geez, I'm just so tired of her."

And, this is after less than four years of marriage.

Now, for some good news: just because we've been told to do it one way doesn't mean there aren't alternatives.

If that gravy train of communication ain't rolling for you, fear not, there is another method!

If I told you that you can restore that wonderful feeling of being in love, of looking at your partner in a fantastic, glowing way, regardless of how long you've been married, folks, what would you say to that?

To be married for a substantial length of time and still feel that wonderful way about your partner means you're a winner in your relationship.

You are succeeding in something at which countless others have failed.

I'm not just talking about staying married for a long time. I am talking about staying *happily* married for a long time.

Some folks succeed at anything they turn their hand to. They run multi-million-dollar corporations, they come in first place in marathons, they fly helicopters, perform open-heart surgeries, heck, they don't even need to eat gluten-free pasta!

Geez! They're pretty much perfect!

But to their frustration, they cannot maintain long-term relationships. They're victorious in every single thing they do, except relationships.

To be successful in marriage often entails the use of unusual skills. And we've been fed such a line of total "baloney" about what it takes to make a marriage great, and what will fix it if it's in the "dumps."

Now, for the plan: a way for you and your partner to see one another as attractive, enticing, fetching, appealing, and captivating!

Let's call this: The Irresistible Factor.

Firstly, how do you pull this off? How do you possibly manage to see your partner as irresistible when you've lived with them day in and day out for many years, possibly even decades?

To truly grasp this, let's first look at the flip side of the coin.

I shall now list here some attributes which work to *detract from* the irresistible factor. These habits or behaviors tend to make your partner view you as less attractive.

By the way, these items were supplied by three groups of individuals: those who've been married a short time, those who've been married a long time, and lastly, those who are now divorced.

Here they are, in no particular order.

- Gross personal habits and poor hygiene.

- Bossiness.

- Argumentativeness.

- Moodiness.

- Irritating habits such as spilling food on the kitchen counter and doing a half-assed job cleaning it up (these are direct quotes, by the way).

- Interrupting you when you speak.

- Stinginess, particularly more stingy after the wedding and as the years go by.

- Takes others' sides in arguments.

- Doesn't listen to you.

- Looks at their phone when you're speaking.

- Never gets dressed up or looks nice anymore for special evenings out or dates.

- Doesn't want to go fun places anymore.

- Complains all the time.

- Doesn't do their share of the housework.

- Doesn't pull in their fair share of the income.

- Leaves your waiter or waitress a stingy tip, thinking you won't notice.

- Never wants to have sex or always makes excuses why they can't.

- When you do have sex, they're not that into it.

- Never wants spur-of-the-moment sex anymore.

- Insists on always watching *their* shows on TV.

- Makes fun of or makes insulting comments about your best friend or close relative.

- Careless with your possessions.

- Inconsiderate such as always showing up late when you meet someplace.

- Never calls you by the cute pet names you had while dating.

Now, these are just a few. If your own marriage is in a bit of a slump, I'm certain you can supply numerous items of your own.

So...those were some items which detract from the "irresistible factor." Now, for the fun stuff: what are some things which contribute to it? Here are a few; these were all supplied by happily married folks:

- Hold hands.

- Surprise your spouse with gifts or flowers.

- Compliment your spouse when they do things well. Do this frequently.

- Thank your spouse simply for being a wonderful person. They don't have to accomplish something: just make them feel appreciated for the person they are.

- Be nice to your spouse even after you had a rough day at work.

- If someone bullies you and you don't speak up for yourself, don't take it out on your spouse later.

- Spend fun time as a couple, including date nights WITHOUT your small children (note that the term WITHOUT is capitalized ten thousand times).

- Make time for sex (even if it's just a quickie).

- Really take time to enjoy sex and don't act like it's a chore.

- If your partner is generally the one to initiate sex, turn the tables sometimes.

- Don't be stingy about oral sex.

- Cook your partner's favorite foods and treats.

- Be nice to your partner's friends and co-workers.

- Support your spouse's hobbies and leisure activities.

- Listen to your partner when they talk and give them your full attention. Don't look at your phone when you're out together at a restaurant or on a date.

- Don't behave like a jackass when your partner makes a mistake or screws up something.

- Be giving and generous. Remember that selfish people frequently end up alone.

- If you can't say anything nice about your spouse's friend or close relative, refrain from commenting if at all possible.

- Men: open the car door for your wife. She will love it. Tell her she's beautiful and that you are a lucky man to have her. You almost cannot overdo this one.

**ABSOLUTE TOP OF THE LIST:** Capitalized and highlighted a million times: never, ever put your partner down in front of others. This most especially includes your children.

Instead, say positive, complimentary things. If you're not crazy about something your spouse did, wait until the two of you are alone before bringing it up.

We could go on and on with this list, but you get the general idea. Be nice. Don't be lazy with compliments. Say and do things to make your partner feel appreciated, respected and loved. Remember, it's a romantic relationship, so make time for sex, holding hands and romance in general.

Incidentally, respect is huge. When our success story couples shared their secrets, a frequently listed item was treating one's partner with respect.

Now, sometimes couples are so intensely annoyed with one another, it's like they're sinking deeper every day into the thick, gooey sludge of the La Brea Tar Pits in Los Angeles. Folks, that ain't a great place to be!

One of our success story husbands mentioned that it takes several positive experiences to outweigh a negative one. Therefore, think and pause before you say something negative, rude, hurtful or critical to your partner. Surprise him or her with flowers, their favorite candy, make them coffee in the morning, wash their car, walk their dog, or heat a heat pack and put it on their side of the bed in cold weather.

This is what's called positive momentum. You do something nice, they hopefully reciprocate, and so forth. Then, to your surprise, your relationship starts to turn around for the better.

Don't get discouraged if results aren't immediate. Just soldier on and give it the "old college try."

# Intimacy

When we refer to intimacy, we are not talking about sex. Sure, sex is a form of intimacy, but for many folks, emotional intimacy is more difficult to achieve than physical.

Why is this? First, let's define intimacy. It's the state of being close to another human being, sharing and trusting, all built up into one. This is difficult, or downright impossible for many individuals due to issues in their past. Those issues could be absentee or abusive parents, parents who were emotionally unavailable, psychological traumas in the past and so forth. It's easier to keep walls up.

If your partner is truly incapable of emotional intimacy, it may be difficult or impossible to stay married to them. It's a lonely place trying to share your life with someone who is so closed off. Of course, not everyone expresses themselves in the same way.

Let's now observe Atlanta couple Gary and Sonya. To outward appearances, they looked like a beautiful, blessed twosome. Most people would have been amazed to know that Gary was miserable in his marriage of just four years. Sonya seemed to have it all; she was absolutely beautiful, smart and well-educated. She had a successful career as a top stockbroker. Her income was huge and she was very generous, surprising Gary with splurges like a new Corvette for his 40th birthday. Gary had a daughter, Hannah, from a previous relationship, and Sonya sent Hannah a regular allowance and paid her school tuition.

Although this all sounds wonderful on paper, in reality, Gary led a lonely existence. Sonya was constantly occupied with her career, her friends and other activities and made little time for him. But the largest issue was that any time Gary tried to talk about anything that was not "surface," Sonya would crack a joke and change the subject. If he attempted to pursue the conversation, she either changed the subject or walked out of the room.

When Gary's mother was diagnosed with cancer, he was heartbroken and worried, but when he tried to talk to Sonya about it, she would make a breezy comment such as, "Don't let it bother you," or "Don't worry about it, she'll be fine." After his mom died, Sonya helped with the arrangements but never asked how he was feeling and changed the subject whenever he brought it up.

They'd only dated for six months before marrying; in hindsight, Gary realized he'd known Sonya was rather distant, but he'd thought he could change this once they were married. Once or twice she had alluded to a very difficult past which she never wished to discuss.

It would have astounded their friends to know Sonya had come from a very poor background and had been homeless several times growing up. Gary was aware of this only because Sonya's younger sister Bella had told him. When Sonya found out that Bella had shared this information, she severed their relationship.

A few times during their four-year marriage, usually when she'd been drinking, Sonya opened up just a little to Gary. It was only then he'd learned that both of her parents had been alcoholics and her childhood had been pretty awful. Gary would feel that they had connected somewhat, but then Sonya would shut him out completely again.

Gary felt theirs was a surface relationship, and asked her to consider going with him to counseling. Sonya told him he was needy and it was a waste of their money. When he tried to tell her that he felt isolated in their marriage, she rolled her eyes and looked at her watch.

Gary finally realized after their fifth anniversary that Sonya would never be willing to invest time or effort in their marriage. She was financially generous, but material things were not important to Gary. Feeling that he was close to another human being was far more critical to his happiness.

These two began to argue frequently. Once during a disagreement, Sonya let it slip that she'd never really planned to get married, but since all her friends had been doing it at the time, she'd thought, "why not?"

This was the last straw and Gary asked for a divorce.

Today, nine years later, Gary is very happily remarried to a woman named Ellen. Ellen is not nearly as accomplished or spectacular in appearance as Sonya. She doesn't earn much money, so she can't buy fancy gifts for Gary. But he never cared about those things. Ellen makes time for Gary and she makes him feel understood. Perhaps most importantly, he feels that he is sharing his life with someone.

Even though this is a book about how to stay happily married, in the case of someone like Gary, it's fortunate we live in a time and place where someone can get a divorce if they so wish.

It's not that Sonya was a bad person by any means, but their relationship was not a priority for her. Clearly, there were things in her past which made intimacy very difficult, if not impossible. Had she been willing perhaps to consider counseling, she might have been able to deal with those issues.

None of us come from perfect backgrounds. We all have painful things in our past which make it difficult for us to have healthy relationships, but we can work to overcome these if we are willing to deal with them.

If you're currently single and you're reading this book, here's one takeaway. When you're dating someone, before you hitch your wagon to theirs, this is the time to see if they make you and your relationship a priority. If they are distant and uncomfortable opening up to you, if you feel lonely in the relationship, this won't magically change once you're married.

We've all heard the phrase "emotionally unavailable." In truth, this description should read, "emotionally available only in quick bursts, and then shuts you out again." They may open up to you in brief, tiny increments, but then close themselves off entirely. If you love this person, this is often more difficult than if they'd never let you in at all.

Before you tie the knot, make sure your partner puts you first, because this won't magically change once that ring's on your finger. If you see a gigantic red flag, the way Gary did before marrying Sonya, believe what you see, and think twice before linking your future to this person.

# Illness

"In sickness and in health" is included in most wedding ceremonies, but couples don't usually listen to this part. If they're young and healthy, this subject won't even touch their consciousness.

But sadly, good health can't be taken for granted. Too many of our friends have had cancer and other diseases for us to be blissfully unaware.

Robert's best friend Joe died from brain cancer in 1995, one month before our daughter was born. He was the funniest, smartest, kindest person in the world and everyone adored him. Joe gave the best advice of anyone. When you talked to him, he gave you his entire attention. Joe brightened the lives of everyone around him.

My college friend Laurel passed away from cancer in 2011. She was like a sister to me. Laurel was unselfish and giving, with the purest soul. Right before we graduated from college, I had my heart broken and Laurel was there for me 100 percent. She was the most beautiful and kind person imaginable, and no one could ever take her place.

When one's marriage partner gets injured or becomes ill, this is a true test of a relationship. Many other struggles can then result. These might be job loss, loss of income, and the painful realization that family or friends who were expected to be supportive have suddenly disappeared without even a puff of smoke.

Here's some advice from those who've dealt with a sick or disabled spouse:

"When my husband was going through chemotherapy, outside support was a lifesaver. Friends tried to be there for me, but they didn't really understand. I joined a support group through my church and had much more in common with those people than lifelong friends. We were all going through the same crap: anger, money worries, exhaustion, and despair. My husband eventually recovered; I'm still close with friends I made in that group."

"For sure, get some help so you can get breaks. You can only do so much. After my husband's motorcycle accident, once he came home from the hospital, my neighbor helped more than my own family did. He came over and stayed with my husband almost every afternoon, so I could get out for a short time to the gym or the market, or go walk our dog at the park."

"Don't try to take on everything. You may need to rely on takeout or fast food and don't feel guilty. Nobody's expecting Martha Stewart. If you're exhausted, something's got to give."

"When my husband had his car accident, he was in intensive care for over two months. My so-called best friend said, "Tell me what I can do." Yeah, like I'm going to call you and say, "Here's what you can do for me." I never asked, and she never did a thing. I am no longer close with that person. A neighbor down the street didn't even ask, but God bless him, he took my trash cans out to the curb every week for months. Another neighbor filled my 5-gallon water bottles for me at the water shop. He left them on the side of my driveway so my teenage son could replace them. He never asked; he just did it. An acquaintance, who has since become a close friend, brought me a mac and cheese casserole or a tuna noodle casserole every week for two months. These may seem like little things, but I was fighting just to keep it all together. Having friends help with the trash cans and bring me water and casseroles without being asked...well, I'll never forget it."

"Keep your sense of humor... it's your lifeline. Comedy shows on TV gave me a break from the crappy reality I was dealing with. I always reminded myself my wife would have done the same thing for me if I'd gotten sick. Once I got over the self-pity, that feeling that I didn't sign up for this, I mean, who does... it was better and I was more able to deal."

"Eat healthy and take vitamins. Get enough sleep. Numero uno: don't turn into a martyr. You need your strength and energy. When my wife had her heart attack, she was only 47. We never dreamed this could be our life, but these are the cards we were dealt. I never slept more than three hours a night for what seemed like months. I was so drained and stressed out all the time ... I thought maybe I was going to get sick too. That's when I hired a lady to come in to clean and fix us some meals."

Alicia and Brian had only been married for six years and had a three-year old daughter, Hayley, when Brian suffered a massive stroke. The doctors were perplexed how this could have happened to a man who was only 33 and in seemingly excellent health. When Brian finally came home from the hospital, Alicia, who was only 31 at the time, quit her job with the intention of becoming his primary caregiver. The prognosis at the time for Brian's recovery was not favorable.

"I was overwhelmed," Alicia recalls now, 13 years later. "I was anxious, worried and cried myself to sleep every night. The doctors didn't think Brian would get much better, and warned me that he would likely have many smaller strokes in upcoming months. I couldn't believe that this was my life. It seemed like some monstrous joke. I was only 31 and I had a three-year-old daughter and an invalid husband."

Younger couples are far more likely to split up when a medical disaster of this magnitude occurs. Alicia's mom Stephanie called her several times a day, begging her to place Brian into an assisted-living facility. She assured her that she hadn't signed up for this, and that no one would blame her. Stephanie told her outright there was still time to find another husband while she was young. Alicia's best girlfriend Patricia said essentially the same thing.

Alicia's father Jim disagreed completely. He reminded Alicia she'd committed herself to Brian in sickness and in health. Jim then did a most incredible and selfless thing. He took an early retirement at age 53 and became Brian's primary caregiver. Jim also encouraged Alicia to go back to work, which she did.

It took three years, but amazingly, Brian made a complete recovery. He praises Jim for talking to him constantly and pushing him relentlessly with his speech and physical therapy. Brian also credits Alicia for sticking by him and not giving up on him or putting him into a facility, as so many people had advised her to do.

Today, Brian's right arm has less mobility than his left, but his only physical limitation is that he speaks somewhat slower, and can no longer drive a stick-shift car. This didn't hamper Brian from teaching Hayley, now 16, how to drive. No one meeting Brian today would ever guess that 13 years ago he'd suffered a major stroke.

## Interruptions

Uninterrupted time and conversation with your spouse are two of the most important gifts you can give your marriage.

I've already devoted space to this, so folks, I shall keep it brief. If your relationship is suffering, you and your spouse are not "jiving," this may be an issue to address.

Indianapolis couple Heather and Josh were both in their mid-30s and had been married for two years. Heather bitterly complained that Josh loved his phone a thousand times more than her. It was actually true that Josh was always on his phone. Nowadays, of course, this rarely meant that he was chatting with someone; Josh was typically on Facebook, Twitter, YouTube, or his favorite of all, playing online poker.

Heather often fantasized about tearing Josh's phone out of his hand and flinging it dramatically into the mermaid stone fountain on their front lawn. She was weary of repeating herself when she spoke to him. He always pretended to be listening, but in reality, 98 percent of his attention was on his phone.

The two had frequent conversations that Josh didn't later recall in the slightest. There was, for example, last year's awkward Las Vegas debacle. Josh had glibly agreed to fly with Heather to Las Vegas for Thanksgiving weekend. "Sure, honey, sounds great, let's do it," Josh had replied, as he was simultaneously dealt an online poker hand. Heather was thrilled and promptly booked their flights, their hotel, plus Criss Angel and Blue Man Group shows. But her "Vegas, baby" bubble burst two hours later when Josh reminded her he'd promised his mother they'd spend Thanksgiving with her in Cleveland. Josh professed to know "less than zero" about Sin City.

Heather vaguely remembered something about Cleveland. She did recall saying, "Oh, wonderful, absolutely," but she'd thought Josh was referencing a TV show with her very favorite actress, the adorable Valerie Bertinelli. In truth, Heather had been ordering new pink cowgirl boots online during the Cleveland conversation.

This seems extreme and comical, doesn't it? But this type of mix-up happens every day to couples. Maybe some details are different ... perhaps Cirque du Soleil show in Vegas and Allison Janney starring in the TV show.

All kidding aside: How can Heather and Josh fix this?

Well, for starters, Heather herself was no saint. She complained dolefully that Josh was always on his phone, but during lunch dates with girlfriends, Heather wholeheartedly enjoyed the conversation, but she shopped online simultaneously.

Heather bitterly vented to her girlfriends about the error of Josh's ways as she herself cleverly navigated her chopsticks, her bites of ramen and her iPhone with the practiced skill of a virtuoso. Not one drop of miso broth landed on her torn jeans, pink cowgirl boots, or the table. You had to admire her incredible technique.

Here's the rich part: Heather was secretly related to that woman we saw at the Omakase sushi house in Los Angeles; both had identical phone-and-chopsticks techniques down pat. These two ladies shall soon joyfully discover one another on Ancestry.

So… if your significant other is super-glued to their phone and this really bugs you, take an honest assessment of yourself.

I know, I know, I hate to honestly assess myself, too. I greatly prefer *denial*.

But, true confession time: are you always on your own little tiny gadget? Should your phone perhaps have a cute miniature pillow of its own because, every night, you actually take it to bed with you?

No judgements. We've all done it. During my blonde phase, I was once chatting merrily on my frosted pink flip-phone whilst bleach was being infused into my hair. It was all fun and games until the chemicals seeped in; both my phone and my phone charm had to be replaced at ridiculous expense. Embarrassing, yes! Sad but true. Quick aside: I'd completely forgotten about those phone charms until this very moment! At the time, I was "playing hooky" from work and answered the phone mid-peroxide… pretending to my then-boss that I was out and about, conscientiously doing sales calls.

If you can relate, do not despair! You can turn it around fast. We all know it ain't easy though, because cell phones are more addictive than premium-quality cocaine. The term "crack-berry" may be a little outdated now, but it still rings true.

Perhaps choose a specific time of day to feed that hulking beast, the internet. Some folks also disable their Facebook chat from their phones.

Ladies, if your girlfriends are "serial texters," let them know you're curtailing this from now on. They'll be stunned, but hopefully also impressed. One challenge is that friend who texts you expecting an immediate reply. Make sure they understand you won't be on your phone as much from now on. After all, isn't that supposed to be an advantage of texting or messaging, that you don't have to reply at once?

Try this: for the next two weeks, set not just a good, but a *sensational* example for your spouse, who may or may not even notice. We feel compelled to warn you that if their face is buried deeply in their phone, chances are excellent they will be unaware something has changed. Please do not let this deter you. Your spouse probably still notices you enough to call 911 if you go into actual cardiac arrest.

During the frenzy of March Madness, Julia's husband Ryan was on his phone every moment of every day. Julia became so irate she planned to fake a heart attack to see if he'd even notice. To be sure, there were other issues in their marriage, such as his mother, who hated her. Ryan and Julia had been married for five years, but Ryan's mom still persisted in calling her "Judy." Julia swore if he ignored the fake heart attack, she'd file for divorce post haste. Her best girlfriend Chloe stopped her in her tracks and foiled the plan. Chloe warned Julia it was terrible karma to fake heart trouble.

In reality, Chloe knew Ryan would have failed the test with flying colors, and this would have been disastrous. If Julia left Ryan right then, she couldn't possibly afford to join Chloe next spring for their long-awaited girls' trip to Positano, Italy.

Anyways, next step: after two weeks, it's time to address this issue directly with your spouse.

It's crucial that you've taken the two-week absence from your own phone first. Otherwise, you run the risk of looking like a complete hypocrite. Clearly and calmly, state your case that you two don't talk much anymore because of your phones. Your spouse will most likely protest. They will almost undoubtedly be in denial. Then again, they may not actually hear you, because they are sneaking a peek at football scores.

But don't give up! No guts, no glory!

Tracy and Greg had been married for nine years. One year ago, they realized they weren't verbally communicating much anymore. Between rushing around to their jobs, their kids' activities and so forth, they had little free time. Most of their spare time was spent sitting side-by-side, peering at their respective phones. It was as if they'd regressed to that stage where toddlers play side-by-side because they haven't yet learned to interact with one another.

As Tracy put it, "I knew we had a problem, because all our conversations began with some version of, "Did you see on Instagram?" Tracy and Greg then agreed to institute a "tech-free" time each weekday evening. When they first returned home from work, they both unwound, caught up on emails, texts, or whatever. But, starting with dinner and then for two hours afterwards, both muted their phones and put them completely out of sight.

This gave them uninterrupted time for each other and their two small children. Tracy immediately noticed that their seven-year-old daughter Lauren appreciated having her parents' full attention. Side note: let's just see Lauren in ten years! She'll be begging them to get back on their phones so she can sneak out of the house after curfew!

After the kids were in bed, Tracy and Greg began sitting on their living room love seat, holding hands and talking about nothing in particular. They'd always done this as newlyweds, but had forgotten to do so in recent years. Both noticed a fast improvement in their connection as a couple. Also, holding hands upped their romantic feelings for one another, and they began having sex much more frequently.

Elizabeth and Adam had been married for 15 years; recently, he'd begun complaining that she was on her phone too much. Adam said she was being rude when they watched TV together. As she put it, "I only look at my phone during commercials and slow scenes of the movie." Elizabeth's girlfriend Tracey agreed with Adam, because watching the movie was supposed to be a shared experience, and Elizabeth wasn't really giving him or the movie her full attention.

It's not an eternity, Liz... it's just a two-hour movie!

To be honest, I've gone through several bouts of lurking on my phone too much. Especially at bedtime, it's so easy to slide down that rabbit hole and waste an hour...or three. Next thing you know, you look at the time and sing, "Oops, I did it again!"

# Instigators

Okay, here we go! This topic was previously discussed in the "egg you on," aka "huevos galore" section. But because this individual is so dangerous, lethal if you will, let's elaborate just a little further.

Beware, beware the dreaded instigator! This life form at first appears to be quite harmless, but ultimately is horrific; a poisonous evil which has existed among us since the dawn of time ... muaahh!

The instigator sprang into action when your marriage began falling apart and has now become your staunchest supporter. Quite possibly, you two have become incredibly close in a short time, even if you're someone who doesn't generally rush into friendships.

But you're in crisis mode: your marriage is falling apart, you're emotionally vulnerable, and the instigator, for sicko reasons of her own, latches onto you like nothin'.

We shall use the pronoun "she," because men are sometimes guilty of this, but overall, this syndrome is far more prevalent with women.

Why does the instigator do this? What's in it for her? Well, perhaps her life is humdrum and she wishes to stave off boredom. Counseling you makes her feel needed, worthwhile and important. Perhaps, long ago, the instigator dreamed of becoming a therapist, but couldn't see the point in investing in all those long years of education and training. A lack of a degree won't deter her in the least from playing her favorite role, that of unofficial psychoanalyst. At any rate, she's become your cheerleader, confidante and psychologist, and is there for you 100 percent.

This is precisely why the instigator is so dangerous. She fills an emotional need you weren't even aware you had when you're the most susceptible. In addition, and this is the crucial part, she has no malicious intent. Her objectives, however misguided, are truly sincere. That's why a normally cautious person trusts the instigator, because their accurate gut impression is this person truly means to be helpful.

So, let's just imagine your marriage is falling apart, and an instigator has latched onto you. It's wonderful. Quite possibly, you've never before experienced such glorious support and encouragement. The instigator is there for you like mustard and relish on a hot dog, like ketchup and mayo on European fries. They're in your corner like Burgess Meredith was for Sylvester Stallone in the original 1977 "Rocky" film, now available on Blu Ray.

The instigator drops everything to listen to your latest drama. She chats with you any time of day or night, and invariably takes your side. Here, of course, is where we got that glorious term: "huevos galore," as she eggs you on nonstop.

After a long, heated conversation with the instigator, you're so riled up into a self-righteous frothing frenzy the idea of staying married to that "crum" is absolutely repugnant.

The instigator has entered your life at a time when your teenagers blame you for everything, your best friend sees your husband's point of view, and your boss doesn't care two figs about your personal life, so long as you get your work done. Maybe you aren't getting props from anyone right now besides the instigator, which then increases her power tenfold.

If there wasn't a gap or lack in your life, the instigator wouldn't be so successful at what she does; she fills that void in your life beautifully.

So that's why, shortly after your divorce, when the instigator drops you like a sizzling little hot potato with sour cream and chives, you're left feeling stunned, incredulous and betrayed.

What the heck just happened? Where on earth did the instigator go?

Well, now that you're divorced, you're not nearly so entertaining for her anymore. The instigator truly enjoyed helping you transition out of your marriage, and loved being your confidant. But now, she's clearly moved on – perhaps she found someone new to counsel.

Unfortunately, this sick cycle occurs with far greater frequency than you might ever guess.

As mentioned before, if your marriage is in trouble, try to confide in a happily married friend. Doubtless they've been through rough patches of their own, and emerged still breathing and still married, on the other side. Therefore, they'll likely suggest your ole' Model T is just traversing a bumpy, rocky road and blew out a tire, and you should get out, replace that giant old spare, and drive on.

By the way, all jokes aside, no one's pointing an accusing finger at divorce attorneys. They do the job they're hired to do, and it ain't convincing Dave to give Leila another chance.

## I Told You So

There's no quartet of words your partner might less appreciate hearing from you than "I told you so," unless it's something along the lines of, "My ex was hotter."

Ben and Teresa had been married for seven years, during which time he worked in outside sales, earning a massive income. In recent years, he'd cheated frequently on his expense account. Because he'd been a top producer, no one had ever questioned this.

That all changed overnight when his company was sold and every department was closely audited.

Ben had used his company credit card occasionally to eat out with friends or to take Teresa for expensive dinners. He'd been doing this for so long he didn't even think twice. On several occasions he'd taken Teresa to restaurants where, including wine and champagne, their bill had totalled over $400, and he'd joke that he'd better use his company credit card.

Once the audit was completed, Ben wasn't given any warning whatsoever; he and two other top sales reps were fired for misappropriation of company funds.

Ben was furious. He suspected that this had happened so the new owner could hire family members.

As we all know, job loss can be one of the biggest stressors for a married couple.

How does Teresa handle this? Well, she has two choices, really. One is to take the attitude of "I told you so." The other would be to wisely keep silent on the subject, and be there for Ben with support and encouragement.

Now that he's out of a job, if Teresa were to remind Ben that on several occasions she'd expressed concern when he'd used his company credit card, he would kind of hate her guts. Once they'd visited Las Vegas, and he'd used the card for dinner and a show. Teresa had protested that it was too expensive and that he might get into trouble. Ben had shrugged and replied offhandedly that he brought in so much money for the company they barely even glanced at his expense report.

So, if Teresa were to bring up something like this, particularly at a time when Ben has to brush off his interview suit and spruce up his resume, it's just going to cause resentment.

The last thing Ben needs to hear from anyone right now, in particular his wife, is "I told you so," even if she did actually tell him so.

Teresa would be wise to refrain from commenting at all, except perhaps to agree with Ben about what jerks and idiots they were to fire him. If she adds a second comment, it might possibly be to compliment him on how nice his interview suit looks.

At a time like this, to jump in with "I told you so," or "I knew this would happen," is equivalent to kicking your partner in the ribs with a pointy, metal-tip cowboy boot.

Loyalty, moral support and encouragement are qualities which our success story couples mention keep their bond strong. They strive to make their partner feel supported and cared for.

The phrase "I told you so," is best kept on the shelf and never taken out, rather like those blue-gray towels you got on sale at Kohl's. They were so cute in the store but look kinda drab hanging on your towel rack. Too bad you already took off the price tag, because there went your chance to "re-gift."

# J

---

## Jealousy

Jealousy is frequently mistaken for envy. As mentioned earlier, it's a common practice to confuse them, but they're actually two distinctly different emotions.

To refresh: you envy someone's gorgeous wardrobe or figure, their beach house, or bank account. Envy is a powerful emotion and can be destructive, but can also work in positive ways. For example, if you envy your friend's great figure, this might motivate you to join a gym and watch what you eat. Envying someone's happy marriage might inspire you to make positive changes in your own. So in this way, envy is not always a bad thing. It can motivate you to better yourself.

But envy pales in comparison to its drippingly evil cousin...jealousy.

Jealousy is that horrible sensation you feel when someone threatens to take away something that's yours; for example, your husband or wife. Jealousy is a far, far stronger emotion than mere envy. Jealousy can make sane folks go absolutely – pardon my Italian – bat-shit crazy. It can make people commit murder.

No one could blame you for becoming angry and jealous if you discover your spouse has been stepping out with a third party. Heck, anyone would feel the same way.

But, in order to stay sane and happy, married folks simply cannot allow jealousy to get the best of them when it is *unwarranted*. For example, all kinds of good-looking, interesting women very likely work at your husband's company. Husbands, same goes for your wife's office. There are attractive people at the bank, the market, the gym, Starbucks, even at church.

The point is: there are temptations *everywhere* for married folks to stray. If you let jealousy get the best of you, it can erode an otherwise solid relationship.

Janice and Troy lived on Key West, Florida, and had been very happily married for 14 years. One day, Troy, a police detective, was assigned a new partner at work. Janice had never been the jealous type, but when she saw Troy's gorgeous, younger new partner Katie, she admitted to her closest girlfriends she was "just the tiniest bit jealous." Janice tried not to think about the fact that Troy would be working with this beautiful new partner every single day.

Janice asked Troy if he thought Katie was pretty. He answered, "Sure," in a casual way. Janice also began speculating about their conversations. "What do you talk about?" she began asking him frequently. He claimed they just talked about their cases. Nothing Troy said or did indicated that he had the slightest interest in his partner.

Janice was frustrated because Troy didn't even know if Katie had a boyfriend. "I just started working with her; I'm not going to pry into her personal life," he said.

It only took a few weeks for Janice to become jealous and resentful. She vented to her girlfriends, who told her she was being paranoid. They suggested that if Janice met Katie, she'd realize she wasn't looking to steal away her husband.

So Janice told Troy to invite Katie to their next Sunday get-together for college football. Katie said she appreciated the invite and showed up… with her equally stunning girlfriend, Frances. As it turned out, Janice had nothing to worry about, and could have saved herself a whole boatload of misery. Ironically, Janice and Katie immediately hit it off and had much more to talk about than Katie and Troy ever had.

Janice later told her girlfriends that in retrospect, she felt silly. She realized her jealousy may have come from feeling she was getting older and less attractive. Hearing about her husband's young and beautiful partner had brought out her own insecurities.

Jealousy is one of the most powerful emotions on the planet. If taken to an extreme, it's a piranha that will devour you alive. I envy anyone who has never experienced this sharp, stabbing, sickening, excruciating gash in the gut. Although it was way back in 1985, I recall distinctly when I discovered my ex-boyfriend had moved in with another girl. It was one of the worst moments of my life. Fortunately, he was totally wrong for me; many times over the years I've been deeply thankful we didn't stay together. But at the time, though, it was absolute agony... one of the worst feelings imaginable.

So, if you're encountering that green-eyed ogre, ask yourself some questions. Number one: what's the state of your relationship? Is it precarious? Are you two getting along well? Number two: is there any foundation whatsoever to your jealousy? Sometimes, as in our example of Janice, jealousy is completely unwarranted and is instead a symbol of one's own self-doubt.

To dig a little deeper, if it's your own insecurity, how can you overcome this? Frankly, maybe you have too much time on your hands. Are your days full? Are you involved in a career that's satisfying to you? Is there a passion in your life that you have not yet pursued but can still consider?

If there's no basis for your jealousy, please find a way to ignore it.

## Joy

Besides your family, what brings joy to your life? Is it spending time with friends, going to the movies, volunteering at an animal shelter, working at a soup kitchen, spending time in nature, or maybe coaching a sports team?

Perhaps between your job and your kids, trying to make ends meet, going to the market, and running errands on the weekends, you're stretched out just as thin as one of those raspberry or apricot fruit roll-ups.

"I'm busy," you protest. "I've got a job, I've got to take the kids to daycare, to school and sports ... I've got no time for myself."

But if you can find a way to make time for things like friends, reading, movies, desert, beach, hiking, camping, whatever brings you joy, this can contribute to your life and your happiness in a big way.

As you go through the journey of life with your marriage partner, make time for activities which bring you satisfaction and feed your soul. And as much as possible, encourage your partner to do the same.

How does that saying go? Make time for the little things, because one day you'll realize they were the big things.

Los Angeles couple Adam and Betsy had been married for 19 years; they had no children. More than anything, Adam loved riding ATVs at the desert, but Betsy always complained and made a fuss. Whenever he and his friends planned a trip, she incessantly worried aloud that he might get injured or would get a flat tire out in the middle of the desert.

Betsy never understood why wives weren't invited. She was in complete despair wondering what she could do for an *entire weekend* while Adam was gone.

Not to sound judgy, but can't a grown-ass woman entertain herself for three measly days? Betsy didn't understand the concept of "guys' time." Whenever Adam's friends invited him, there was a huge argument. Betsy snubbed him for several days before the trip and for at least a week after.

Eventually, Adam grew weary. Like many folks saddled with a selfish spouse, he got tired of the hassle. There came a time when he found it easier to just tell his friends he was busy and couldn't join them.

Watching this dynamic play out with a friend is like slow torture; it's agonizing to witness.

So ultimately, Betsy got her way. Adam went to the desert less and less as the sorry years elapsed, until eventually, he stopped going at all. No wonder he told friends he was seriously depressed. Had his wife supported him in his *one and only* hobby, he would have been much happier, not just in himself, but in their marriage.

But, let's view this differently. Did Betsy stop Adam from doing the one activity he loved best, or did Adam *allow* this to happen? Here's where the "martyr" concept arises. By the way, we have a huge martyr section coming up shortly... stay tuned.

If you allow your spouse to rob you of something which brings you great joy, the onus is on you as well. Stick to your guns... this is your life!

Adriana and Josh lived in San Antonio, Texas, and had been married for six years. Her favorite hobby was pottery; she loved her weekly ceramics class. Adriana also attended exercise class on the weekends. She'd been doing these two activities since her college days.

However, two years ago, after their son Kyle was born, Josh insisted there was just no time for her pottery class. It should be noted, this was the only hobby she'd ever had, and she loved it. Adriana was also incredibly talented... her creations were just beautiful. But she allowed Josh to persuade her to quit the class.

She also stopped attending her exercise class on the weekends. Josh had bought her an exercise bike, which he said was a better investment. But inevitably, little Kyle needed her attention when she was riding the bicycle, so she rarely used it.

Adriana worked full-time and spent nearly all her so-called "free time" cooking, cleaning, and taking care of their son. Josh did virtually no housework or child care. Nothing got in the way of Josh's daily hobby, but no one called it a hobby because it was watching sports, and he did this every evening from home.

Adriana complained about this on a rare evening out with friends, who all said the same thing. Why couldn't Josh watch their son one night a week so she could go to her pottery class? We're talking one night a week here, folks! Sadly, she never did talk to Josh about it. Or perhaps she did, and nothing got resolved.

From that time on, if friends asked about the pottery class, Adriana just smiled in her quiet way and changed the subject. Gradually, as the years elapsed, on those rare occasions her friends saw her, there was an imperceptible change. It was like a balloon with the air very slowly let out... it seemed like much of the joy had steadily seeped out of her life.

As of this telling, Adam and Adriana are still married to Betsy and Josh. Betsy and Josh are what we at the Dr. Linda boot camp have dubbed "miserables."

A "miserables" is someone who extracts the maximum from their partner while sapping much of the joy from their life.

If your partner treats your hobbies or interests as silly or not worthwhile, well, you need to fight for these things. They are yours and no one has the right to take them away.

I should clarify that we're not talking about a hobby such as snorting lines of coke, leaping onto a Harley with no helmet and then accelerating to 120. As long as your hobbies don't endanger your life, don't give them up for your spouse, because eventually you'll resent them for it.

# K

---

## Keeping Up with the Joneses

This here is a dangerous, dicey and slippery slope. Years ago, Robert and I frequently socialized with another couple, Lou and Diana. You may recall this glam duo from the "envy" section. Lou and Diana were rich and beautiful. Their house was gorgeous. So were their matching BMWs. We all had a fantastic time together; we laughed and laughed.

But I guess we always felt kind of "lesser than" with Lou and Diana. They were a really nice couple, and it wasn't *their* fault we were acting like maniacs trying to keep up with them.

Luckily, we were completely unable to compete with them financially. At the time, we had limited income and almost no credit available. It was undoubtedly a blessing that we could not even pretend to keep pace with their spending. When Lou and Diana invited us to travel with them, such as to the South of France, we always found convenient excuses.

Speaking of limited credit, here's a story straight outta September 1988, just a few months after our wedding. Robert and I saw a commercial on Friday night TV for a gorgeous stereo on sale at "Radio Shack." They promised to extend credit *to all*.

Okay, great! We figured that meant *us*.

Saturday morning, we got dressed up for church, and paid a social call to Radio Shack. We had a fantastic time picking out a $2,500 stereo. Once we'd chosen the entire gargantuan setup, Brad, our expectant salesman, delightedly escorted us back to his office to "talk credit."

Brad cheerfully inquired whether we had good credit; he was clearly thrilled when we sincerely assured him that we absolutely did.

As soon as Brad sashayed out of the office, we started elbowing one another and trying not to laugh, because we had no idea whatsoever what good credit even meant. After all, I was only 25 and Robert was 23. Maybe kids weren't too sophisticated back then.

A few minutes later, Brad returned, wearing a pained expression. "Mr. and Mrs. Watson, you don't have bad credit, but it's actually even worse, you have absolutely *no* credit." So, that was the end of that particular shopping expedition, and as I recall, my college "boom box" was then obliged to last us for at least another five years.

Now, had we been able to obtain credit at that time, I can't imagine in my worst nightmares the hole we'd have dug for ourselves trying vainly to keep up with the captivating Lou and Diana.

Some couples do end up with massive debt from keeping pace with their richer friends. If you're on this trajectory, time to do a quick u-turn. Easier said than done! Chances are excellent that you really enjoy your outings and holidays with this other couple.

Sometimes prosperous couples realize who their real friends are when they lose all their money. Wendy and Ron had owned a very, very successful yacht sales business, but lost everything in the downturn of 2008. When they could no longer attend society dinners and charity events, their so-called friends dropped them just like proverbial sweet potatoes with no glazed marshmallows on top.

Janet and Steve lived in Coeur d'Alene, Idaho, and had been married for 12 years. They had two youngsters, Sam, age 8 and Hannah, age 11. Their closest friends Marla and Ed had one daughter, Olivia. Hannah and Olivia were only six months apart in age, had grown up together, and had been best friends their entire lives.

Ed was an investment broker with a very large income. Marla's parents were quite well-off and had given her and Ed an actual house for their wedding present. Steve earned a fraction what Ed did, plus, like most folks, he and Janet had a mortgage, plus they had a second child.

When Olivia began private school, so did Hannah. When Olivia began horseback-riding and ballet lessons, well, Hannah got riding boots and a tutu. This all would have been cozy perfection, except for one thing... Janet and Steve couldn't afford all this.

Janet and Steve sunk further and further into debt trying to keep up with the Joneses. This caused huge arguments between them. Steve wanted to tell Hannah she'd have to attend public school and choose between ballet or horseback-riding, but Janet became extremely upset over this.

Finally, it got to the point where they could no longer pay Hannah's tuition.

Janet's mother assured her that Hannah would not be warped for life if she heard "no" once in awhile. Janet and Steve moved Hannah to a free charter school which she actually loved from day one, then let her choose which activity she'd have to quit. To their surprise, she told them she heartily disliked ballet and was thrilled to ditch it.

## Keeping Score

This creepy little topic almost went under the letter P, because when couples consistently keep score, it's actually a form of pettiness.

Manhattan residents Lisa and Carlos owned two cats, Mike and Ike. Mike and Ike were, in actuality, Lisa's pets; Carlos didn't particularly care for them. The fur everywhere drove him nuts and the litter box disgusted him. Also, Ike had an unnerving habit of jumping onto the back of the living room couch whenever Carlos happened to be watching a scary movie, and Carlos found this frankly terrifying.

But Lisa had owned Mike and Ike "pre-Carlos," and would never part with them.

So Carlos knew that it was a package deal: Lisa and her cats.

But when Lisa left town on business, often for a week or longer, Carlos "forgot" to clean the litter box. He did give Mike and Ike their food and water, but never cleaned out the litter box.

After each trip, when Lisa returned home and discovered this, there was invariably a row, as the Brits would say. Therefore, it was no coincidence that for several days following, Lisa would then "forget" to close the cupboard door in their kitchen. Being much taller than Lisa, Carlos would then walk smack dab into the cupboard door with his face, each and every time.

This gave Lisa a grim sense of satisfaction as she thought about how he'd neglected her "little fluffsters" when she'd been out of town.

Carlos inwardly cursed Lisa for the cabinet hitting him in the head. He griped that he would lose an eye one of these days. This entire cycle played out every few months, year after Charmin-squeezing year. Come on, Lisa and Carlos! Are you for real?

Does this whole cycle sound rather juvenile? Rather like two little kids in a sandbox?

Lisa and Carlos are both in their 40s, with successful careers...these are adults. Given all that, it's amazing the childish way they "get back" at one another, but this goes on with lots of couples.

Far preferable for Lisa to sit Carlos down and resolve the litter box drama once and for all, rather than tagging him like a little kid on the playground with the "cupboard trick."

Or, she could hire a high school student to come over and clean the litter box. Problemo solved.

Joanne and Steve lived in Boulder, Colorado, and had been married for 14 years. Their two boys were ages seven and nine. Joanne only worked part-time, but in her pursuit of being a "perfect mom," she was perpetually exhausted and stressed-out.

One Saturday afternoon both boys were at a friend's house and Steve suggested a little spontaneous romance, since for once he and Joanne actually had the house to themselves. Joanne rebuffed his advances because as she put it, she had a million things to do, including baking homemade peanut butter squares for their older son's baseball game the next day.

Steve offered to pick up cookies at the market that evening, but Joanne said they wouldn't be good enough. Instead of indulging in a little spontaneous romance with her husband, Joanne spent an hour and a half making the cookies.

Will nine-year-old boys gobble down those store-bought cookies just as quickly as fancy homemade ones? You betcha. Will they even notice if Joanne spends some quality time with her husband and brings something from the Keebler elves? Not a chance.

Gabby and Brian live in San Diego, California, and have been married for 15 years. They never actually argue, but the air in their house fairly crackles with the electric current of their mutual animosity. So, where does this hostility come from?

Believe it or not, petty things like laundry.

Gabby's pet peeve is the laundry. She deeply resents when Brian places laundry into the washer, then forgets to move it to the dryer. Gabby then relocates the wet laundry to the dryer all in a huff, which takes less than one minute, but which "pisses her off" for the next several hours.

Gabby, girl, this ain't exactly hard labor, now is it? Laundry nowadays is a fluffy Tide pod dream. To look at the effort that used to go into washing clothes, read Tracy Chevalier's extraordinary book, "Girl With a Pearl Earring." There, you'll see a detailed accounting of the backbreaking work that went into doing 17th century laundry.

Nowadays, you chuck in the clothes, toss in a few Tide pods; heck, you can even stand backwards and fling them over your shoulder, a` la` Trevi Fountain, then press a couple buttons, and presto!

But for Gabby, laundry-gate rankles on a several-times-a-week basis.

Although she's seriously peeved, Gabby doesn't verbalize this. Nope, instead, she looks heavenward while sighing loudly throughout the day. This, in turn, makes Brian very uncomfortable. He's resentful because he knows she's annoyed about something, but he doesn't know what. He's asked her countless time, but Gabby always replies, "Nothing."

If you told Brian that he'd win one million dollars by explaining why his wife is always pissed off at him, he'd have to miss out on all those bucks, 'cause he's completely in the dark.

Sensing her almost continual hostility, Brian, too, has become rather snarky in recent years. He no longer brings Gabby flowers from their garden and he's not physically affectionate like he used to be. So, what is the result? Kindness, warmth and intimacy seesaw just a fraction lower every livelong day for this couple.

Individuals like Gabby are perpetually angry over small stuff. They keep score of everything they do in comparison to their spouse, and this makes them livid. Life is so short, it's sad that this is how someone spends their precious days, but Gabby is not alone in this behavior.

A happily married male friend presented this great idea: sing a song while you do some job around the house that your spouse should have completed. If the task can be finished before you're done singing the song, even up to a trio of songs actually, it's probably not worth getting upset over.

Try this next time. Let's say your husband leaves some dirty dishes in the sink. He frequently does this. It is super annoying, no doubt about it. But, if by the time you're done belting out two Eagles songs, the dishes are washed, well then maybe it just ain't worth stressing over! "Hotel California" and "Take It Easy" still hold up quite well, even after all these years.

# King

For balance and equality, we have an upcoming chapter entitled "Queen."

Hey, nothing wrong with "ladies first!" If you wish to skip ahead and read that section, then double back, please feel free.

If a man feels like a king, this is a wonderful thing for a marriage. He is going to be happier and he is going to be more positive.

So, how do you make your husband feel like a king?

Here are some ways; some were recommended by our success story wives, and some by female friends of the author:

- Pay attention to him when he talks. Don't look at your phone.

- Compliment how smart he is when he does something clever.

- Thank him for nice things he does; it can be something mundane like taking out the trash.

- Say nice things about him to your kids when he is within earshot.

- Initiate intimacy; he shouldn't always have to do this.

- If your kids are nasty to him, don't tolerate this. Make sure they respect their dad. They will also benefit from this by not growing up to be spoiled little punks.

- Frequently cook his favorite meals.

- Show him affection, such as holding his hand.

- Be nice to his buddies. They are sacred to him.

- Don't get in the way of his spending time with his guy friends.

- Encourage him in his hobbies.

These are just a few, but can make a big difference in your relationship. If you treat him like a king, he'll be more likely to treat you like the queen you know you are!!!!!!

# L

## Live for each other, not your kids

Jasmine was a baby of the 80s. Looking back, she still experiences guilt because her parents had no interests other than their three children. Once Jasmine and her siblings had grown and moved out of the house, her parents realized within a year they had no interest or energy for one another, and split up shortly thereafter.

"Live for each other, not your kids" is a platitude far easier said than done.

For many years, our main focus was on raising Andrea: bringing her to school, sporting events, horseback-riding lessons, gymnastics, and dance classes. Most weekends involved outings with her friends and their parents. It seemed that era would last forever.

Then, almost before we knew it, Andrea began high school, got her first car, started driving, got a part-time job, went off to college, and studied abroad. Now she's got her own condo and a busy career. The elementary school era took such a long time, but once high school started, time traveled at light speed.

Fortunately, when Andrea was little, Robert and I consistently went out on date nights. As much as possible, we kept that "couple connection" going and also made time for friendships. Nonetheless, it was a huge adjustment when she left for college.

We all know the harsh reality, which is that kids eventually (it actually seems very fast!) grow up, go away to college, move out, and begin their own lives.

Couples who never get a break from their kids go quietly crazy... rather insane, if you will. If both work full-time, they often experience guilt over leaving "junior mint" in day-care all week long. They may then be reluctant to hire a babysitter for a fun evening out. Of course, as parents we all experience endless guilt. It's inevitable; part of the territory. So, parents of young kids, you may as well get out and enjoy yourselves! If not, one day the kids move out and you're left staring at each other asking, "Who are you, and what do we do now?"

Some folks are "#blessed" to have a built-in babysitter, also known as grandma. Of course, bear in mind that when a family member babysits for free, they generally do things *their* way. This falls squarely under the polka dot umbrella of "There ain't no such thing as a free lunch."

But unless Grannie dispenses frothy iced bourbon cappuccinos to your toddler Ashleigh, or allows your seven-year-old son Jameson to sit on her lap 60s-style as her saloon car careens up and down the avenue, don't get involved, stay in your lane…just be grateful for freebie babysitting.

Now, those couples sadly lacking a babysitting grandma, or other relative, must then take a giant leap of faith in hiring a relative stranger.

This forces me to recall the cruelest practical joke Robert ever played on me. Andrea was age two and it was Saturday night; our neighbor's daughter Jessica was babysitting. We were seated top row at the movies. Right when I asked, "Can we even trust this girl to watch our baby?" a large, noisy pack of teenagers entered the theatre. Robert let out a huge fake gasp and said, "Oh, my God, there's Jessica! Do you think she left Andrea at home alone?"

Fortunately, I was only 34 at the time, so I fully recovered from my heart attack.

Now, if a couple is unwilling to trust anyone at all to watch their tiny little babushka, they risk ending up like our next couple, Maria and Tim.

Maria and Tim lived in Mobile, Alabama, and had been married for 11 years; both worked full-time. Their two boys, Brandon and Alex, were six and nine years old, respectively. The boys had both been in day-care since they were a few months old, and now attended an after-school program. Weekday evenings were all about dinner, homework, a little TV, bath-time, bedtime routine and so forth. Weekends were spent chauffeuring the two youngsters to their sporting events and get-togethers with classmates.

Tim loved his sons very much, but was wistful when he recalled the fun times he and Maria had enjoyed as a couple. He longed for the romantic connection they'd had, which now seemed firmly a thing of the past. Tim had loved going out in the evenings with Maria, just the two of them, to places like restaurants and movies, and he especially missed how they used to hold hands. He was tired of their sons barging in on their conversations. Tim had often suggested date nights and a sitter, but Maria absolutely wouldn't hear of it. She was "Paranoid Pauline" after hearing horror stories from the other moms at her boys' school.

The stories terrified her; admittedly, some were quite gruesome.

Carla and Joe had returned home early one fateful night and caught their 14-year-old babysitter Hayley in their bed with Brock, the skater kid with long bangs who lived next door.

Their other friend Denise's angelic 17-year old babysitter Olivia had the sheer gall to – as she put it – "borrow" Denise's brand-new Tesla. Olivia bundled her two young charges into the backseat, gallivanted to the local Starbucks, then promptly smashed into an adjacent BMW. Olivia professed confusion later, saying she was sure Denise had told her it was okay to take the kids "someplace fun." The damage to the Beamer and Tesla ran into the thousands, and Olivia's parents were quite uncooperative.

To add to the fun, a third friend, Annette, couldn't help but notice that after her babysitter Carly left, some of her sleeping pills were missing. However, Annette wasn't positive if it was the babysitter or the cleaning lady who'd pinched them, and she admitted that she herself sometimes lost count.

Of course, these are all hair-raising tales. There are some flaky-ass babysitters out there for certain. It's a narrow window of opportunity when young girls are even interested in babysitting. You've got to lasso 'em in at about age 13, then you've got them for a good two years, maybe three tops, before they find some gangly boyfriend and start working at the local Dairy Queen or McDonald's.

Locating a good babysitter is like excavating gold. If you're lucky enough to unearth a responsible, honest girl, treat her better than gold... actually, platinum. Bribe her remorselessly with little gifts like See's and Bath and Body Works, tip her lavishly, even if this means eating top ramen for a week. But most importantly, keep her an absolute secret.

*Tell no one about her.* Don't let down your guard, even for an instant. Trust me on this: that mom who professed to be your best friend will suffer no compunction whatsoever about stealing away your reliable little Gwendolyn in a country minute.

Competition over solid, dependable babysitters is fierce, quite similar to when New England fishermen drop their nets in Boston Harbor. In an unguarded moment, you happened to mention responsible little Gwen, and now you can just kiss your regular Friday and Saturday night gigs goodbye.

Tragedy strikes when suddenly, out of nowhere, you call or text Gwen to babysit and she's booked solid, three weekends in advance. How the heck did this happen? Gwen was so reliable, always available! Just imagine the feeling of sheer betrayal upon learning that Chelsea, one of the sweetest moms from your daughter's Girl Scout troop, cleverly swooped up little Gwendolyn, right behind your back.

How did Chelsea even get Gwendolyn's phone number, for God's sake?

Here's an appalling but true story from the mid-90s. Gayle's marvelous, reliable babysitter Bonnie was "spirited away" by none other than Gayle's so-called best friend Christina, since then known by the cruelly accurate nickname, "no face." One fine spring day, over frappucinos at Starbucks, Christina had casually pressed Gayle for details, including Bonnie's last name. At the time, it merely seemed like she was making polite conversation.

Gayle naively thought nothing of it; all the sordid details emerged later. Without one shred of guilt, Christina had located Bonnie's digits in the phone book. For you youngsters reading this, the phone book lives now only in our memory, kind of like the Road Warrior, but back then, we referenced it "on the daily." The treacherous Christina then phoned Bonnie and outright lied to her, claiming she got her telephone number from Gayle. Her sheer duplicity was beyond anything imaginable. Furthermore, Christina solidly booked Bonnie several weeks in advance, and paid her three extra dollars per hour.

Now, how do you compete with that?

Gayle had never felt so betrayed. Perhaps worst of all, Christina was quite unrepentant. She had stolen Bonnie outright, and now had her locked into a regular Friday and Saturday night gig. Gayle and Christina barely spoke for nearly two years afterwards as a direct result of "babysitter wars."

These are rather extreme measures, aren't they? In upcoming months, Gayle wearily admitted that although her little darlings were the most adorable kids in the entire galaxy, she nonetheless feared impending madness if she couldn't locate another sitter to replace Bonnie.

This brings us to ask a painful question: are anybody's kids really as cute and brilliant as their parents make them out to be?

Karen and Brad, one of our success story couples, raised four children together. They're now empty-nesters and greatly enjoying this stage of life together. They attribute this closeness to their date nights when their kids were little.

Now, let's drop in on Caroline Sue and Lance in Charleston, South Carolina. These two have been married for 12 years. Their adorable four-year-old son Ashton, nicknamed "little dumpling," went everywhere they did. He wasn't *quite* as fascinating as Caroline Sue believed, but hey, he *was* pretty cute as he sported his mini tuxedo and crew cut at every party, barbecue, picnic and wedding.

Lance desperately wished to resume date nights, but since Ashton was in day-care all week long, Caroline Sue couldn't bear to leave him with a sitter. As she told patient friends, "We just *love* taking Ashton with us everywhere – we just *adore* our little guy."

Mini dynamo Ashton was a fixture at every party, including one where he jumped on the jacuzzi cover repeatedly. Caroline Sue and Lance, chatting and sipping mint juleps in chaise lounges poolside, somehow missed out on all the excitement. After they'd left, their hostess Pamela Anne observed that had Ashton broken the jacuzzi cover, he'd have fallen in and drowned before anyone would have even noticed.

Charming, pint-sized Ashton also slept in Caroline Sue and Lance's bed each and every night. He'd sleep for a couple hours in his own room, and then wander into theirs. Lance greatly disliked this, but Ashton had been crashing the party since he was a baby and was in no way about to relinquish his position.

So, there's moonlight, crepe myrtle and magnolias out the window, but not much Southern romance for this couple. Let's recap: no dates... and the kid sharing their bed every night.

One day Caroline Sue walked into her office very upset; she and Lance had had an enormous argument. His boss had surprised him with tickets for the Red Hot Chili Peppers. They'd all have dinner first at Hyman's seafood restaurant, then go see the concert.

There was a stalemate. Ashton couldn't very well attend the concert, and Caroline Sue was not about to hire a sitter. Completely forgetting the jacuzzi debacle, she insisted no one, but no one could be trusted to watch her tiny sweet potato dumpling.

A co-worker volunteered that perhaps Caroline Sue was being a tad unreasonable. Caroline Sue admitted Lance was very disappointed, but she simply couldn't trust anyone to watch Ashton for even a few hours. Therefore, how could she possibly feel comfortable for the duration of dinner and a concert, though her heart was surely breaking at the prospect of missing out on Hyman's legendary hush puppies.

She told Lance he could certainly go without her. This really upset Lance, because he wanted her to join him, and this would also embarrass him in front of his boss.

Lance was one of those very easygoing guys who, 99 percent of the time, went along with whatever his wife wanted. Unfortunately, Caroline Sue had become so accustomed to getting her way she didn't realize the significance of this disappointment to Lance.

So, what did this couple end up doing? It would have been nice if Caroline Sue had seen the light and agreed to a sitter, but sadly, no. Both she and Lance missed out on the seafood dinner, hush puppies and the Red Hot Chili Peppers.

So, if one partner always gets what they want, this all too frequently leads to the D word... dumpling!

Nope, actually divorce.

Two years later, Caroline Sue and Lance did, in fact, divorce. The catalyst might have been her joyful announcement, "Time to start trying for another baby!"

Lance smiled and nodded his agreement. As Caroline Sue later told friends, he seemed really eager at the time, but two days later, his bags were packed, and off he went to live with his mother at her big old pink and white house with four columns on the Battery.

Ladies, if you think your husband doesn't miss your alone time as a couple, you are mistaken. Eventually, he can become so starved for attention and romance, he may seek it elsewhere. This can also work the other way. Sometimes a man becomes so wrapped up in his kids' sports or whatever that he forgets about his wife, and that's not such a good thing either.

## Loyalty

One way to display loyalty is to not complain about your spouse to others. Another is to not betray a confidence given to you by your spouse.

Now, of course, there will be many times over the years when you've just got to vent to *someone*! But, of course, there's a massive difference between confiding in a very close friend and venting to anyone who will listen.

We've all been bored stiff by that co-worker or acquaintance who gives daily updates to a long laundry-list of complaints about their spouse. They don't discern; they'll complain to anyone within earshot.

They want to ensure everyone pities them for having such a crummy husband or wife. And you do feel sympathy at first. But then, as the years pass, their story invariably never changes. They are *never* in the wrong. *Everything* is their spouse's fault. That's when you begin to smell a rat. After years of this, you finally think to yourself, "Just get a divorce then, why don't you... please?"

New Jersey couple Warren and Teresa had been married for nine years. Teresa had just been laid off from a job she'd had for 14 years and was having no success in finding another.

Teresa was in a real slump. She'd loved her job, and it was proving difficult to replace as she'd never completed her four-year degree. Warren had not one, but two master's degrees, and had nagged her for years to return to school.

Warren tended to chat and gossip, so although close family knew her situation, Teresa had made him promise not to tell anyone else, in particular his co-workers.

Teresa had sent out over one hundred resumes but had landed few interviews and no job offers. One prospective employer rudely complained that since she was lacking a degree, he didn't even know how she made it past HR into the interview. After three months of this, Teresa became more and more discouraged. She asked Warren again to please keep this all confidential, and he convincingly swore that he would.

Most of us have been here at one time or another. You're feeling crummy, down in the dumps, maybe your ego has taken a hit, or you just feel like a failure.

This is when you most need your partner to be in your corner and you need to see that they're rooting for you.

I've personally been laid off three times in my life. Please pardon the expression: it sucks the big one. Even if you hate your job, losing it still comes as a shock. You've done nothing wrong, but you're still out of work.

Six months later, Teresa was still unemployed. One evening, the two met Warren's co-worker Richard and his wife Peggy for dinner. Warren and Richard were rivals at work but did enjoy each others' company; Teresa had never cared for Peggy. During the meal, Peggy repeatedly inquired about Teresa's job search and helpfully reminded her that it was sure a tough job market, especially for those lacking a college degree. Teresa smiled and nodded but was angry and humiliated. She felt betrayed by Warren.

You may recall that we told an earlier story about another couple in a very similar situation.

On the drive home, not surprisingly, Warren and Teresa had a huge argument. He maintained he'd said nothing whatsoever to Richard. Finally, however, he admitted he'd possibly said a "little something" to another co-worker, which must have been repeated.

As Teresa pointed out, Richard had beaten Warren out of a promotion two years ago and she had been extremely supportive during that time.

As soon as they returned home, Teresa began packing a bag; she planned to spend the night at a girlfriend's.

What saved this situation, and possibly their marriage, was that Warren apologized profusely. In a dramatic and rather chivalrous gesture, given that this was November in New Jersey, he offered to sleep in the garage, rather than have Teresa leave the house late at night.

Teresa relented, and Warren spent the night on the couch.

He bought her flowers the next day and wrote her a card apologizing. He also swore to never make the same mistake again. Warren belatedly realized many of his co-workers gossiped even more than he did. He had been naive in thinking he could talk to one or two colleagues without others hearing the story.

One month later, Teresa was hired to work for a company that overlooked her lack of a degree in favor of her experience. She also enrolled in online college to finish her degree once and for all. This all happened eight years ago; Teresa and Warren are still happily married.

## Loneliness

When you're in sync with your spouse, ain't life grand? You've got a "partner in crime;" it's a great feeling of companionship.

However, if your spouse has let you down in one of a million possible ways, or you're just going through a "rough patch," marriage can be an awfully lonely place.

We're told that loneliness is an essential part of the human experience. The late, great Mrs. Gibbs, my high school English teacher, phrased it best. "We come into this world alone and we leave it alone. In between we make strong human connections and form very close bonds with others. But nonetheless, the essential human experience is one of loneliness."

Don't quote me precisely, because this was 1980, my senior year of high school... just a few years ago! But the basic message Mrs. Gibbs gave our class is one I've never forgotten.

I don't know about you, but this is alternately depressing and freeing.

This is also why it's smart to have friends, hobbies, and interests besides your spouse. That way, if no matter what you do, your marriage ends, all your proverbial pastel eggs have not been sitting pretty in that one little hemp basket.

We've all had times in our life when we felt especially lonely. My first year of college was tough. At the absolute last minute, after I'd already gotten a dorm reservation, I'd chickened out on UC Davis, so got stuck going to Santa Monica Junior College. It was actually quite a nice school, with great professors, but socially, for me at least, a big fat giant zero. Not like I'd been prom queen in high school, but I'd had lots of friends, so not having even one single friend at junior college was pretty hideous.

Kids raced out the door after classes ended, so it wasn't easy to meet anyone. Also, like many people who appear to be outgoing, I'm actually quite introverted, which probably didn't help much either.

At lunchtime, I'd walk into the cafeteria and pretend to sweep my hair out of my eyes as I surreptitiously scanned the room for even one familiar face. Never once did I recognize anyone, so I'd buy a Dannon coffee yogurt and slink out of there. I'd go eat lunch in Zorro, my trusty bright blue '66 Chevy Chevelle.

That year, hands down, Zorro was my best friend. If Santa Monica Junior College had been a closed campus, chances are excellent I'd have eaten my lunch in the ladies' room.

Los Angeles got a lot of rain in 1981, and Zorro had a slight roof leak. As I sat there eating my mournful coffee yogurt, I caught the drip with a washcloth. To add to the ambience, when parked on campus, the one station Zorro received was country music, the only kind of music I've never liked. Even now, when I look at a carton of that dang yogurt I get this dreary isolated feeling.

So, it was a hideously lonely time. Also, to add to the fun, my parents were disappointed in me for not going to UC Davis, so I wasn't getting along with either of them.

The only bright spots that year were spending time with my Aunt GG, whose Santa Monica home I stayed at a couple nights a week, and not too surprisingly, horses. Along with two other girls, Helena and Robin, I motored up the coast to Pepperdine University twice weekly for horse-back-riding lessons with the late, legendary Jim Wyllie.

There, I met and fell madly in love with Shiloh, a black bay gelding. I was so smitten with Shiloh, in fact, I impulsively decided to attend Pepperdine the following year, one of the best decisions of my life. Of course, it's easy to make friends when you live on campus, so within 48 hours there, I'd made some of my best friends to this day.

But maybe it's good I had that year of being friendless and isolated, because ever since then, I have kind of a sixth sense. I can usually tell if a person needs someone to reach to them when they're lonely.

So, last comment on this topic: it's smart to make yourself someone whose company you enjoy. This sentence may be confusing, so let's put it this way. The more emotionally healthy you become, due to a combination of therapy, hard work, and frank self-assessment, the better your marriage will be. Also, the more you will enjoy your alone time, which is not the same thing at all as being lonely.

# M

---

## Martyrs

Here's a great saying: "Nobody loves a martyr." We're not talking about religious martyrs here. Nope, it's those individuals who feel rather sorry for themselves, as they don't get any respect and they sacrifice so much, bla bla bla.

The martyr adores attention and pity, but ultimately frustrates others because he or she resists any attempt at real change.

I understand this entire dynamic only too well. I'm not too proud of it, but I was a world-class martyr for many years, in not one, but two distinct ways.

Although it's patently embarrassing, I shall soon relay both of these in mortifying detail.

Martyrs do appear to want advice. It often seems they'll take it, but in reality, this is a facade. Decades may elapse, centuries if they're an Original, but nothing varies. The martyr's sad tale of woe can be virtually unchanged for all eternity...muahah!

You offer help or advice, but eventually realize the martyr just wants to vent and elicit pity.

After years, or possibly even decades, your sympathy begins to fade. By then it's as worn out as that coin-sized dried-out little piece of dehydrated pita bread from last fall which one sunny day in July you discover in the back corner of the snack section of your fridge.

We've all had martyr co-workers, haven't we? It's a productive day and you're concentrating on your job, avoiding thinking about problems in your *own* life, which certainly ain't no picnic right now.

Then, in sashays your resident office martyr, Judy. Suddenly, everything becomes about Judy and her problems.

Believe me, I'm not judging here. As I'll soon relay, I was a martyr in a couple ways for many years. Undoubtedly, it was excruciatingly tedious for my friends. God bless them for their endless patience and for not dumping me out of sheer boredom!

Now, here are two martyr tales:

Gloria and Brady live in California's Bay Area and have been married for 22 years. Brady leaves his ice cream or cereal bowl on the den table when he's done with it. He'd never dream of carrying the bowl to the kitchen or going "hog wild" by washing it and putting it away. He does zero share of the housework, plus leaves his dirty clothes on the bathroom and bedroom floors, counting on the reliable Gloria to clean up the works.

Why does Brady have the nerve to think he can get away with this? Well, because Gloria lets him. She's super dependable. It's been this way their entire married life.

Gloria works full-time, plus has a second job teaching online, but Brady realized two decades ago she can't tolerate mess, and she faithfully cleans up after him.

To add to his charm, Brady chats up and compliments waitresses, the market checkout clerk, younger women in particular. In front of Gloria, he makes lewd sexual comments about his young, female co-workers. He's half-assed when it comes to Gloria's birthday, Christmas, Valentine's Day, you name it.

Brady has been treating Gloria this way for at least 20 years and counting.

Gloria has a tight group of girlfriends; there are six in all. These ladies became close when their kids were little, about 20 years ago.

Now, here's where the martyr part comes in. Rather than stand up for herself, Gloria complains to her faithful girlfriends. They've all heard a thousand versions of her story over the past 20 years and are comatose with boredom. They gave up offering Gloria any sincere advice about 18-1/2 years ago.

Why did her girlfriends give up? They eventually realized the sad truth: Gloria is miserable, but nothing will change. She's just going to remain a martyr. Why an educated, hard-working, smart lady like Gloria puts up with her crappy husband is a mystery to her family and friends. She is savvy in business and excels at her very demanding job. But when it comes to her husband, Gloria doesn't stick up for herself, and puts up with lousy treatment.

Jack and Adele have been married for 12 years. This couple doesn't have children, although the 16 pets in their home at any given time might certainly qualify. Where critters are concerned, Adele has an enormous heart. All her social media friends know she's the kindest person on the planet. Adele loves horses, dogs, rabbits, cats, you name it. She's rescued dozens of animals in the past few years alone.

Sounds awesome so far, right? What a wonderful, giving person Adele is. She's very active on social media and she posts constantly about her latest endeavours, garnering adulation, adoration, and admiration. It's a triple A of joy for Adele.

But here's the unfortunate reality. Once Adele brings an animal home, she loves it, talks about it and cares for it deeply, for about 2.5 weeks. Then, like a child with an outgrown toy, she loses all interest in that animal. She then shoves the responsibility for its care entirely onto the weary, allergic shoulders of her husband Jack.

From then on, Adele's primary interaction with that pet is taking numerous cute "selfies" with it, which she adorably posts on social media. She's addicted like crack to the attention and compliments she receives online.

After a short time, she's restless again and then she's off on her next adventure to rescue another animal in need.

Jack then ends up doing 99 percent of the work with Adele's rescues. He feeds and cleans up after all the pets. He must also deal with their carpet and furniture getting badly damaged on a regular basis.

What's most unfortunate, given the huge number of pets in their home, is that Jack is viciously allergic to both dogs and cats. It's most fortunate that Jack still has his real teeth; the sheer velocity of his sneezes would projectile false teeth right across the room.

There's also the space issue. Their house, although large, simply cannot contain the massive number of rescue animals Adele has brought home. In addition, Adele and Jack cannot afford the amount of money they shell out every month for food and vet bills. Her numerous "go fund me's" raise quite a bit of cash, but it's never enough.

But Adele just can't say no. Everyone sees what a giant heart she has and what a wonderful, kind and giving person she is from her online image. While Jack cleans the carpet and the litter boxes, Adele feverishly searches online to see what glorious compliments people are making about her at that very given moment.

Adele feeds on this attention just like a little animal-loving piranha.

So, where does the martyr part come in? Well, Jack complains to family, co-workers and friends on a nearly-constant basis. He's exhausted from doing all the work with the animals. He's weary of being broke. He's tired of sneezing and blowing his nose every waking moment of every day.

Jack loves animals, but realizes, as Adele does not, that they are in way over their heads.

Jack receives weary sympathy and attention, just like Gloria in our first example. But who doesn't hear Jack's complaints? You guessed it... Adele. Rather than speak up or try to change his situation, Jack remains a martyr.

The whole martyr dynamic is complicated. There's a lot in it for folks like Gloria and Jack. Numerous psychological payoffs ensue from being a martyr. One: lots of attention. Two: sympathy. Three: pity. Four: something to talk about.

The seasoned and truly accomplished martyr will tune out advice or suggestions, whilst simultaneously appearing to desire and actually consider all feedback.

If you identify a wee bit with either Gloria or Jack and suspect you might be a martyr, don't be too hard on yourself. Many of us, and I'm included in this elite group, have played the role of victim at one time or another.

The good news is this: if you want to change, there's a way.

Here are some practical steps:

1. Write on a piece of paper a list of the things you want to change in your life.

2. Make an honest assessment of how you can take control and change those factors which contribute to your unhappiness.

3. See a good therapist. Tell this professional everything and don't hold back, even if you're mortified.

4. Lastly, identify who is that someone (your spouse? your child? your parent?) whom you need to be honest with in stating your concerns or complaints. Begin to speak up and don't let yourself be intimidated.

One caveat: if that person has been "working you" for a number of years, they are very likely to resist change. Sure, why wouldn't they? They've had a good thing going for years.

So far, the examples we've given here are situations where someone was a martyr with their spouse.

There is a multitude of other ways in which one can be a martyr. I shall fight embarrassment now by giving two of my most awkward examples.

Mortifying but true: I was a weight loss martyr for many, many years. Anytime I vented about being unable to lose weight or keep it off, I had "martyr-like" excuses in sheer abundance.

One hallmark of the accomplished victim is they appear to believe circumstances are out of their control. So, in keeping with this time-honored tradition, when grumbling about my struggles with weight, I always made certain to include two crucial facts: I'm of Italian descent and I'm not very tall.

Therefore, it wasn't *my* fault for staying heavy, year after flapjack-flipping year. It was genes! I wasn't doing anything wrong. I made excuses 'til those little Italian gelato cows came home, never changed a thing, and elicited lots of sympathy.

In this way, I was quite the victim. My excuses and rationalizations continued for over *three decades*. I maintained the problem was out of my control, which of course was nonsense. I bored some kind people and got lots of sympathy, but you wanna know what? My weight never changed.

Now, here's the irony! I'm not even as Italian as I thought! Two years ago, I researched my ancestry and discovered I'm only 40% Italian! Not as if being Italian was ever a valid excuse anyways! Even as we speak, there are countless thin, short Italians seated in outdoor cafes, drinking espresso and eating small plates of pasta carbonara al dente!

But, by employing the convenient height and genealogy excuses, I got to feel sorry for myself, plus garner weary sympathy, rather than actually striving to change my situation.

Another way I martyred myself for many years was with my difficult mother-in-law, who is now deceased. It must be said that she was generous and had many wonderful qualities. If you were on her good side, she was a joy to be around, but she kept me on eggshells as she was unpredictably malicious. We have a whole upcoming section on mothers-in-law, particularly mothers of sons. It's often a most challenging relationship.

Whenever my mother-in-law was insulting or rude to me, rather than speak up for myself, I usually remained silent, but then would later vent to friends. I would also become angry at Robert, as though it was his fault that a) his mom was nasty to me, and b) I was too wimpy to speak up for myself.

Part of my reticence was because my mother-in-law was my elder and I was trained to respect my elders. But then when I hit 50 years of age,

I said to myself, "Hey, I'm an elder now too! I'm sick of this crap!" Not only did I begin speaking up if she was insulting or rude, but I no longer blamed Robert for her behavior.

What I'm about to say could fill another book entirely, but let's just toss this into the linguini alfredo, dear reader. If there's someone in your life who treats you as less than, who hits you out of nowhere with insults or demeaning comments, you have my permission to speak up *in the moment.* Feel free to use my name. Say, "Hey, Dr. Linda told me I don't have to take your crap anymore!"

Don't wait 'til it's three in the morning and you're lying in bed rehashing all the things you wish you'd said. It's called "spinning," by the way, endlessly obsessing over things in the middle of the night. You're going in circles just like a little hamster on that wheel, formulating all the responses you should have said...yesterday.

The rich part comes the next morning, when you have to drag your weary, sleep-deprived behind out of bed at 6:30 a.m. and go to work all day.

Learn from my mistakes. Don't wait decades to realize that you may be struggling to improve what my therapist calls a "doomed relationship."

Just what is a "doomed relationship?" It's one that, for whatever reason, history, competitiveness, personalities, will never be great...or even good.

Therefore, going overboard to please this person is an exercise in sheer futility. At times, they're as sweet to you as pecan pie with bourbon, which lulls you into a false sense of security. Then, when your guard is down, when you least expect it, they'll zap you with a dose of bitter acid. You will then kick yourself, because deep down, you knew this would happen... this person will never change.

Therefore, minimize your exposure to toxic people as much as possible. Would you open your mouth and spray in an entire can of Raid ant spray? Of course you wouldn't. But so many folks allow themselves to endure regular abuse from disrespectful, insulting people. Protect yourself, because just like poison, these folks can have a negative effect on your health... *if you allow them to.*

Quite like a slithering snake, the toxic person is chock-full of poison, but unlike a snake which strikes out of self-protection or fear, the venomous person attacks deliberately and with malicious intent.

So, always remember, you are number one... protect thyself.

This is your life and it is damn short, so don't let anybody rob your joy.

That person who seeks to undermine you gets a real psychological payoff from upsetting or flustering you. It makes them feel just a tiny bit less crummy about themselves, for a short time, at your expense. Knocking you down a peg gives them a momentary reprieve from their own self-dislike.

You don't need a dazzling comeback right at the time. Simple statements such as "I beg your pardon?" or "I don't appreciate that," will generally suffice. Invariably, the person who tosses off rude comments or insults is a mean little bully. After a few tries, when they realize to their astonishment you are no longer taking their garbage, they will generally back down.

Remember, this is your life and no one has the right to try and ruin it for you, so don't let anybody get away with this nonsense.

It was only after gaining confidence and learning techniques from my wonderful therapist that I trained myself to speak up in the moment. This is never an easy task, but it's definitely a skill which can be perfected.

Far better to speak up for yourself if someone is trying to minimize you or put you down than to blame someone else, act like a martyr, or wake up at four a.m. envisioning all the things you should have said ... but didn't.

## Money

Money is frequently a huge source of conflict for married folks, and it's not just about how much they save and how much they spend. It can be a real power struggle, particularly if one partner tries to control the others' spending.

If a couple has little money, arguments may run along these lines: Stella and Sam both have very modest incomes. Stella just coughed up the rent on their small Phoenix apartment and warned Sam they would barely, just barely make it until payday. Sam appeared to have heard her at the time, but in true alien mode, went to McCaffrey's pub with his buddies last night, picked up the tab, and promptly dropped $140 on drinks.

Now, if a couple is well-off, this doesn't automatically excuse them from money struggles either.

New York society couple Lily and William are financially quite comfortable, but did indeed take a thrashing in last year's stock market. Their financial planner has urged them to ease off on spending; for example, their habit of eating out every night. William agrees they should sometimes eat at home, but he's never learned to cook. As for Lily, she simply cannot survive without Bruno's, her very favorite restaurant. Entrees at Bruno's start at $45 a plate, and everything is à la carte, but as Lily maintains, "I do so love their Bolognese."

If a couple is truly rich, it's less about practicalities than it is a power struggle.

Perhaps Thorton wishes to invest in a second vacation home in Florida, but Ursula has her heart set on remodeling their entire house yet again and replacing their tennis court with a swimming pool. Their struggle is real and their arguments about money just as visceral as Stella and Sam struggling to pay the rent on their tiny Phoenix flat.

With many couples, there's a balance: one's a saver and one's a spender. This creates conflicts for sure, but at least there's equilibrium.

The potential for disaster is greater when both love to spend. This may continue without mishap for many years until there's a job loss or unforeseen medical bills, and then there's nothing to fall back upon.

If both partners are savers, at first this may seem ideal. However, if frugality is carried to excess, this couple can miss out on much fun in life. If they never take vacations, never do fun things, or they drive crummy cars when they could afford decent ones, folks, this ain't living the good life.

Plus, this often accelerates as the years elapse and this couple becomes somewhat miserly.

What did the bird in the tin cage say? Cheap-cheap!

A stingy couple may regret it someday when they're too old to go anywhere. If they're in their 50s and still maintain they're waiting for just the right time to visit New York, Hawaii, Jamaica, or Paris, sadly, that day may never come.

It's a balancing act for sure.

Your husband Brian buys his co-workers a few rounds at happy hour. "What a swell guy," everyone says, as each toss back three Patron shots. Brian's sensational, for sure, except you, his wife, planned to pay some bills with that money. Now, you've got the mortification of having to call the utility company and your cell phone provider for yet another extension.

But if you marry a tightwad, get ready to be embarrassed in a whole 'nother way. Years ago, my acquaintance Karla dated a fellow named Benjamin. We double-dated four times, then no more. Benjamin was so God-awful stingy it made your teeth ache. He actually left the table for the men's room the moment the bill arrived the *first three times,* and Robert got stuck paying the bill.

We only agreed to a fourth double-date because Karla was such great company. As we were being seated at the restaurant, I stage-whispered to Robert, "Let *him* pay this time!"

So, when the bill appeared, Benjamin predictably dashed off to the men's room. He was absent a full nine minutes; doubtless, he felt this gave Robert ample time to pay the check. When Benjamin returned and realized in horror the bill was still there, there was this very long and mortifying pause.

Finally, Benjamin picked up the check by one corner, like it was "doggie caca," and made a joke about going dutch.

Robert chivalrously made a move for the check, and I freely admit here and now, I promptly kicked him under the table. At the time, 1993, I was riding my first horse Terra just about every day. Terra was nearly 17 hands, weighed about 1,300 pounds, and was a bundle of equine dynamite.

So, trust me when I say that in those days, if I kicked you under the table, believe you me, you knew it.

Benjamin then slowly and with enormous reluctance paid the check, but first he took a *pocket calculator,* for Christ's sakes, from his jacket pocket, meticulously itemizing the bill for potential errors. This went on for all eternity. If you watch the show, "The Originals," about the vampires of New Orleans, and they talk about living for a thousand years, well, then you'll know exactly how we felt.

Benjamin then remarked with utter astonishment that the restaurant had charged one extra dollar for my onion rings, upgraded from fries. I mean, how do I even respond to this, Benjamin? The entire excruciating bill-perusing procedure took about 14 minutes. Our hopeful waitress circled the table five and a half times, and I memorized all the ingredients of the A-1 sauce bottle. Karla was clearly mortified, but made a valiant attempt at light conversation.

Benjamin had doubtless historically enjoyed great success with his patented "dodging technique," as it all seemed quite well-rehearsed. He was likely banking on the fact that most people would tire first and just grab the check away from him. But by this time, Robert had perhaps become fascinated watching him in action, so we just waited out the whole humiliating process.

Benjamin then (okay I admit I spied over his shoulder since I was on his right) left a two-dollar tip on a forty-dollar check. Oh my God, Benjamin! Are you for real?

Hey Benjamin, it's one thing to be careful with money, another thing altogether to be a complete "cheap-ass."

Karla dated Benjamin awhile longer, but then grew tired of being embarrassed in this way and left him for Jacob, an investment banker. The two have been happily married now for 18 years.

Benjamin then dated Leslie, another acquaintance of mine, several years later. By now, his stinginess had reached truly epic proportions. That relationship only lasted two months. While later reminiscing about Benjamin, Leslie compared him to the husband in "The Joy Luck Club" who charges his wife money for ice cream. Not totally surprisingly, Benjamin is still single.

Robert and I attended a premarital counseling group right before we wed, along with 40 other couples. At the time, I thought it was silly how extensively they discussed finances. Now, I look back and think they could have spent a week on that one topic alone.

I still remember what the speaker said: "Save three hundred dollars a month. Those of you who don't will end up working for those of you who do."

So, what if both your spending and debt are out of control? What if you owe so much on your credit cards, you can only make "the kiss of death," otherwise known as minimum payments? What if, just like John Malkovich in the film, "The Object of Beauty," you surreptitiously cross yourself like you're in church when you hand over your credit card to the waiter, as you're fervently praying it won't get declined?

When eating out, if you've ever snuck into the restroom to check if you have room on your credit card to pay the bill, I love and adore you, because we are now officially twins.

# Mary Jane
## (also see Alcohol)

Well, this is a potentially touchy subject and I'm certainly not trying to get you to do drugs. But, should marijuana actually be placed into the "drug" category? Fortunately, it's beginning to be legalized in more and more states. Here in California, we are at last having our day in the sun.

Unlike alcohol, which is a depressant but nonetheless makes people more aggressive, marijuana, also a depressant, generally makes folks mellower. Of course, this depends upon the strain. There are so many varieties one could write an entire book about this subject. Insomnia, anxiety, stress, and pain can be improved with this "Cheech and Chong" wonder formula.

Now, we're not advocating readers of this book become total stoners!!! But for some couples, a few puffs here and there in the evening can be relaxing and fun.

## Misfortune

When life goes swimmingly, it goes without saying it's easier to have a stellar marriage. Fortune is smiling upon you with fantastic careers, good health, the kids are a breeze, so maintaining that smooth connection might just seem "#effortless."

But, just how easy is it when things start going wrong?

What if life throws horrible curve balls at you? Illness, job loss, financial trouble... just to name a few.

If a couple is married long enough, it's unavoidable they will encounter some kind of misfortune.

Robert and I have been lucky with health, jobs and many other blessings.

But over the years, we've lost three parents (my mom had passed before we'd met) as well as dear friends, aunts, uncles, and beloved pets. Robert lost his younger brother Andrew at a very young age in 2011, which was incredibly difficult.

Couples who last are able to find ways to stick together through good times and crummy ones. Several of our success couples stated that you may think it's easier to take out your frustrations on your partner, but this only makes things worse.

It's like traveling. Some holidays, everything falls in place: flights are on time, luggage is a breeze, the weather's wonderful, your hotel and rental car are magically upgraded, and the itinerary goes without a hitch. It's so easy to get along great on trips like these: you're in paradise!

But when the luggage is stolen, the rental car goes kaput, the hotel loses your reservation, the weather's horrific, and you lose your passport, wallet, or credit cards.... ugh!

Then it's easy as apple pie to begin snarling at one another like rabid dogs. If you turn on each other like a little wolf pack of two, the trip goes from bad to worse, and what should have been a fun holiday becomes the proverbial trip from hell. Muaahahaha!

The consensus from successfully married couples is that at the worst times in your marriage, don't blame one another, and keep a stiff upper lip whilst at the same time maintaining a sense of humor.

No doubt about it, the sense of humor is indispensible. If you can laugh together, you're still a team. Then, when things do get better, you can "bet your bippie" that your spouse will recall that you behaved with grace instead of like a real creepo.

Self-control is crucial in these situations. Let's view lost luggage as an example.

Compared to a death in the family or financial disaster, a MIA suitcase may seem like a rather trivial topic.

However, to be candid, my personal fear of checking in luggage very nearly rivals my terror of that little girl with the long black hair who crawled up out of the well in "The Ring."

My strange paranoia stems from our honeymoon, circa June, '88.

Robert and I flew to Maui, but for reasons unknown, my luggage sailed directly to Guam. I got it back, but not for three days. Three days is a long time when you're on your honeymoon, but in retrospect, it wasn't exactly the end of the world.

Then, there was the San Francisco excursion of 1995; Suzy Q grabbed my lilac Samsonite suitcase off the conveyor belt, mistakenly thinking it was hers. We finally did a "switcharoo" the next day, but it was rather like a tense hostage exchange because we both arrogantly believed ours was the suitcase with superior contents.

Let's say you're forced to do the unthinkable...the airport personnel sadistically coerces you into checking in your bag. Quick aside... a little travel tip: at least try to carry your suitcase onto the jet. That way, if they do cruelly confiscate it last-minute, it's going into the belly of the plane. If you trustingly check in your suitcase at the front desk, chances are excellent it might just sail off directly to Guam.

Anyways, worst possible scenario, you arrive in Jamaica to discover your new suitcase with the wheels that roll in every direction has been "taken." Your partner tries to make light of the situation by cracking a little joke about Liam Neeson "saving the day."

You're already tired, jet-lagged, the weather's hot and muggy, and now you've got to buy new clothes and toiletry items in a foreign country. You want to take a shower but have no clean clothes to change into.

So, your partner can have fun cracking little jokes, sure they can! It's not *their* luggage that was lost.

You're about to say something snarky... it's on the tip of your tongue... you really want to... but wait!

Stop and don't do it.

Instead, pause, take a deep breath, and "control thyself." Think of something nice, witty, or funny to say... maybe that Liam was booked, but fortunately, Jason Statham has been dispatched and will roar up in his Lamborghini Roadster momentarily.

# Mothers-in-Law Straight Outta Hell
## Special Bonus Section!

Okay, here we go! This is a sensitive topic, but one that simply can't be ignored.

Ah, the joys of a difficult mother-in-law! Frankly, one could devote an entire volume to this painful, challenging, yet comical and fascinating topic. The mother-in-law and daughter-in-law dynamic is one fraught with the most potential problems and issues. Mothers-in-law usually get along fairly well with their sons-in-law. True, there may be issues, but not nearly so often.

However, mothers of sons... ah, yes, another ferocious beast entirely.

Some girls (DIL – short for daughters-in-law) are unbelievably blessed. God in heaven bestowed upon them a wonderful mother-in-law (hereafter referred to as MIL) who adores them, supports them, truly loves them and doesn't work against them. These lucky gals have got it made in the apple tree shade.

Sad but true, these blessed, charmed, enviable girls are in the distinct minority. In a random sampling of 20 of my married girlfriends, I discovered that only three of them – count them, three – have dream MIL's. All the rest have had serious MIL issues, or at least did at one time.

We've divided this bonus "Mothers-in-Law Straight Outta Hell" segment into distinct categories. There's something for everyone here... the alcoholic MIL, the hostile MIL, the toxic MIL, and the passive-aggressive MIL who deeply resents her DIL for stealing and snatching away her beloved son. This was my reality, and it was sometimes frankly terrifying, as I shall reveal momentarily.

Note: no section whatsoever has been provided for those fortunate girls with the sweet MIL, because we're bitterly envious of them...God bless 'em, they've got it made.

As you may by now have surmised, I myself had a most challenging relationship with my own MIL, Anne. As she's now departed, I feel compelled to add that my husband has given me the go-ahead to share all the following.

My MIL had many admirable qualities. She could be very generous and if you were on her good side, was incredibly fun to talk to. She traveled alone to join a tour group in Europe in the early 70s, which was incredibly far ahead of her time. Robert's friends visited constantly, and she fed many of them dinners all throughout junior high and high school.

Looking back, however, I should have realized sooner the sad fact that ours would never be an ideal relationship. Shortly before Robert and I married, my MIL told me something most revealing. "I do like you, Linda," she proclaimed. "I like you as much as I could like anyone who's taking away my son."

Whew!

In time, my MIL became very displeased with me for a trilogy of reasons. There was the Thanksgiving we spent with my family and not hers, then when we moved two hours away to San Diego, and lastly, when Robert converted to Catholicism.

In fact, for several years, my MIL was so furious with me, I deeply suspected she was actually trying to poison me with her famous red velvet cake.

I wish I was kidding here, folks, but I'm not!

Okay, here goes: the glamor of the red velvet cake.

Before we go any further, let's just say that this cake was very rich, very chocolaty, delicious, and luscious beyond anything you've ever eaten in your entire lifetime. The frosting, a dream come true. Every bite: sheer magnificence. Nothing could possibly equal the decadent splendor of this cake. Once you'd tried it, you were completely ruined for any future red velvet cakes – none compared. You could then spend the rest of your days haunting bakeries worldwide, fruitlessly chasing that first high.

To add to its mystique, my MIL began baking this cake many years before red velvet had even become trendy. Before she decided she loathed me, she trusted me with the secret recipe, which I was strictly forbidden to share.

So, here's where the poison part enters in. Only after I'd fallen sharply from favor, my MIL would meticulously rotate the cake plate with her hands until she got to a certain spot, then announce, "I think this piece for you, Linda."

My heart would race and I would feel kind of panicky, thinking, "Why does she want me to have *this* piece?" I played it safe by always passing it to someone else, usually Robert's little brother Andrew, and gosh, you know, he only lived to be 41.

But as the Irish say, it was the drink that killed him, certainly not his mother's cake.

But just the fact that the thought of poison, like a Criminal Minds episode, even crossed my mind, shows you how fraught with tension the MIL and DIL relationship can truly become.

In addition, such was the sheer fabulousness of this cake, although I suspected those luscious layers might have been arsenic-laced, it's a testament to how marvelous it was... that I still *ate it anyways*!

Oh, happily today, I know my worst fears were unfounded, because I'm still here, and as far as I know, quite healthy, folks!

My MIL was passive-aggressive, a personality trait we shall discuss frequently throughout this book. After we'd moved to San Diego, we sometimes visited her and Robert's dad in Los Angeles and we stayed the weekend.

By then, let's be real: she kind of hated me. When I then took showers at her house for the first time ever, the water would repeatedly, and without warning, blast ice cold.

I never mentioned this to anyone; after all, it was an old house, built in Los Angeles during WWII. Several years passed, in fact, before I even thought to mention this to Robert. One day I said offhandedly, "I just love your parents' house, but they really need to do something about their plumbing."

"What do you mean?" he asked. I explained about the cold water repeatedly blasting in the shower. "No, it doesn't," he replied.

"Yeah, it does!"

"No, it doesn't!"

Oh, geez! Only then, after a period of several years, did I finally realize the horrific truth.

One doesn't need be Agatha Christie to deduce what must have happened. Most likely, my MIL waited patiently, just like a little spider, until I'd gotten into the shower. Then, she'd nimbly dash to the other end of the house and repeatedly flush the "john."

Needless to say, what a *wonderful* feeling to realize this at last. Fortunately, there are countless beautiful and well-appointed hotels in

Los Angeles with steady-temp showers, so, that was my go-to from that point on.

## Victoria's story
### Alcoholic MIL

Victoria and James have been married for 18 years.

Barbara, Victoria's MIL, was fun and charming when they first met. She told Victoria to think of her as a mom. Barbara often took Victoria's side in arguments with James, and they got along exceedingly well. This lasted until 2007, when Victoria and James moved in with Barbara for one and a half years.

Barbara had always had a difficult relationship with her son James. She often referred to him as a "pain in the ass." Despite this, as time passed, she made it clear that she was his number one over her DIL.

Barbara had stopped drinking for years, but then began again after Victoria and James moved in with her. She hid her vodka bottles in the laundry room and front closet. It was often impossible to tell when she had been drinking, as at this point she'd become very sophisticated at hiding it.

Barbara became increasingly competitive with Victoria and boundaries were nonexistent. She borrowed Victoria's clothes, including her underwear. Barbara became irate if Victoria and James didn't want alcohol with dinner. She would awaken her husband when he was sleeping to give him alcohol because she didn't want to drink alone.

As her alcoholism worsened, Barbara became increasingly violent. She hit her husband on the arm and told him their youngest son wasn't his and that another man was the father. When she was sober, she couldn't remember anything she had said or done. Soon after this time, Barbara's husband died in his sleep from asphyxiation due to alcohol. He was only 54 years old.

Barbara both helped and hindered Victoria's relationship with James. She tried to come between them and sometimes it worked. But on occasion, she still supported her DIL.

When asked what advice she'd give to a girl with an alcoholic mother-in-law, Victoria says, "Don't ever think you can get her to stop drinking. If she's going to get sober, that is up to her. Also, keep in mind your MIL wants others around her to drink."

Victoria also stresses emphatically that moving in with her MIL was a mistake of the greatest magnitude. They'd done it to save up to buy a house, but in retrospect, the added pressure on their marriage was not worth the money saved.

Victoria advises new wives when dealing with their MIL's: "Never, ever move in with them, and kill them with kindness."

# Anna's story
## Passive-Aggressive MIL

Anna and Dustin have been married for 28 years. They met in New York City in 1993 and were married in 1995. Anna met her MIL Joanne for the first time in 1994. Joanne was "nice to me at first, but this changed quickly," as Anna recalls.

Joanne treated her DIL with condescension and put her down frequently. To top it off, Joanne was passive-aggressive. She would smile sweetly and lull Anna into a false sense of security, then dish out an insult about Anna's hair or clothes.

It was common knowledge that Joanne had wanted her son to marry her friend's daughter Jessica. She did at one point tell her DIL, "We thought Dustin was going to marry Jessica, and we're not sure what happened."

Anna was 25 and Dustin was 28 when they wed. They planned and paid for their own wedding, but Dustin's parents complained profusely about the food and location. Anna learned to always be on guard with her MIL, who didn't respect boundaries. Her MIL frequently asked personal questions, such as their sex life, how much money they had, and what kind of birth control Anna was using.

Anna gives this advice to other wives: when your MIL asks an intrusive question, smile and don't answer. If she's got the stamina to ask again, reply, "Hey, that's a great question," smile, and *still* don't answer.

Do not ever let yourself be bullied into disclosing something that is very personal.

Anna adds: don't expect your MIL to be your friend. Don't ever let your guard down. Most important of all, don't blame your husband for his mom's creepy behavior. He may know she's difficult, but he will still want to defend her.

## Bonnie's Story
### Wanted her darling boy to marry a Southern girl

Bonnie and Austin have been married for 18 years. They were college students in Detroit when they first met and fell in love. They dated for five years before becoming engaged. When they visited Austin's parents in Savannah, his father Thomas was friendly, but his mother Abigail told Bonnie that her son was expected to marry a Southern girl. She warned Bonnie her prediction was that Austin would dump her and return to his high school sweetheart Ruth Ann, who still lived in Savannah.

When Bonnie's mother called Abigail a week later to discuss the wedding, Abigail claimed to know nothing whatsoever about the engagement.

Several times before the wedding, Abigail called Austin to warn him he was making a dire and colossal mistake, as she phrased it, and that Ruth Ann still loved him desperately. Each time, she hinted that she might be quite busy on the wedding day and would therefore be unable to attend.

Surprisingly, Abigail and Thomas attended the wedding and were exemplary guests. Bonnie and Austin moved from Detroit to Savannah, where their two daughters were born. Abigail and Thomas invited them over frequently, but even after her granddaughters had begun middle school, Abigail still mentioned on occasion that Austin should have married Ruth Ann. The girls visited Abigail frequently, and when they became older they told their parents that Ruth Ann often visited Abigail at the same time. This made Bonnie and Austin very uncomfortable, but when Austin called to ask his mother about this, she denied Ruth Ann had ever visited.

As the years went by, Abigail's poor treatment of Bonnie affected her relationship with her son. Austin grew less and less interested in visiting Abigail or in spending time with her. Bonnie continually pushes Austin to visit his mom. As she puts it practically, "I don't take it personally with my mother-in-law. She is the way she is, and I just think that it's because I'm not from the South that she's never accepted me."

# Anita's story
## Rich, controlling and unpredictable MIL

Anita and Ryan have been married for 15 years. Ryan's parents, Colleen and Blake, are very well-off financially. Colleen is cordial to Anita in front of Ryan, but then insults her when he's not around. She criticizes Anita's hair, wardrobe and shoes in a sweet voice that nonetheless drips with venom. Colleen insisted Anita and Ryan sign a prenuptial agreement, which was not unusual given the circumstances. However, Colleen had a clause inserted which stipulated in case of divorce, Ryan would receive full custody of any future children. The clause was removed, but this made Anita leery of Colleen.

Colleen has three sons; she's accustomed to being in charge of them and her husband as well. She's a powerful force whom few dare to cross. When Anita had first dated Ryan, she'd hoped she and her MIL might become close. She even dreamed her MIL would love her like a daughter. Starting with the clause in the prenuptial agreement, Anita wisely lost that unrealistic expectation.

Colleen can be incredibly generous, but typically, there are strings attached. When Ryan lost his job last year, Colleen called Anita one day to ask if she'd be home for the next hour. Colleen pulled up 10 minutes later, impeccably dressed as always. She left her car motor running and handed Anita a large department store bag. "Just a little something to tide you two over," she called over her shoulder as she walked back to her car. Inside the shopping bag was $25,000 in cash.

This was of course wonderful, but the next month when Ryan planned to accept a great job in another city, one phone conversation with his mother nipped that rose in the bud.

When Anita and Ryan's son Dillon was born the next year, there were many conflicts. Colleen wanted to bring Dillon with her to her ladies' lunches, but Anita refused. This caused a major argument, but Anita stuck to her guns. Colleen drank copious amounts of white wine at these lunches and had received two DUI's within the past three years. When Anita told Colleen "no," Colleen called Ryan. Ryan has been so dominated by his mother his entire life, it's difficult for him to say "no" to her.

Anita was intimidated by her MIL for many years, but has become more adept at speaking up. She believes it's helped her marriage that she sticks up for herself with Colleen and doesn't blame Ryan for his mother's behavior.

Anita is the first to acknowledge that although her MIL is difficult, she has many good qualities and does love her son and grandson. Anita is realistic about the fact that her MIL does not care for her like a daughter; she is her mother-in-law, not her mother.

## Mute It

Sometimes it's brilliant strategy to push your own "mute" button. This means knowing when to talk and when to listen. This is doubly important when you and your spouse are involved in a disagreement.

No one said it would be easy, especially if a) you know you're right and b) you're a good talker. One of our success story husbands says he's learned to not always get in the last word and that as a result, his relationship with his wife has greatly improved.

So, when your spouse is talking, try hitting the "mute" button and just listening. By this we mean really listening... not just appearing to listen while you're actually formulating your reply, and just waiting to jump in with your own argument.

In the end, what really matters is not so much about who is right or wrong, but how you treat one another.

No one likes being interrupted or "talked over."

Particularly if you're more articulate than your partner, perhaps it's become second nature over the years to talk over them, interrupt them, or dominate the conversation. It's a challenge to change this behavior, but the benefits to your relationship can be tremendous.

## Military

There are some real challenges when you're a military spouse:

- Your husband or wife misses out on birthdays, anniversaries, and many holidays.

- They may repeatedly be deployed for six months at a time.

- You most likely will have to move frequently.

- Your spouse can be sent to war. They can also come home with injuries or PTSD.

As one military spouse put it, "My husband's got two wives, me and the United States Air Force!"

A quick side-note: who can recall that classic TV commercial from the 80s? "Army, Navy, Air Force, Marines... we don't ask for experience, we give it!" Gosh, I sure hope I'm not the only one who remembers that commercial!

Following are the stories of three military wives. By the way, Candace and Tom, one of our success story couples at the end of this book, have been happily married for many years. Tom was active duty nearly all of that time.

## Dana and Steve
### Married 12 years

Dana and Steve have been married for 12 years; he's been active duty military the entire time. They've lived in Japan, San Diego, the South and the Midwest. In Japan, they didn't live on base, which she feels was a blessing as she actually became fluent in Japanese. Living in the South was difficult; the Mississippi heat and humidity were very challenging.

On several occasions, Steve has been deployed for six months at a time. Dana has an extensive education and job skills, but due to their frequent moves, can't hold a challenging career. She has, however, become much more resilient in the past five or six years. She finds a way to reach out and stay in contact with family and good friends no matter where she's living. Dana is pragmatic about the fact that she will usually need to restart every couple of years and that her husband will get deployed on a regular basis.

Dana reaches out and develops friendships with other military moms. She goes out every day with the kids to get fresh air, exercise, sunshine and social time. Dana is bubbly with a very fun and outgoing personality. She says that going out of her way to make new friends has helped her adjust when they move.

The biggest challenge with her two small children is feeling much of the time she's a single parent. If her kids are sad and missing their dad she has to console them and cheer them up.

## Annette and Bill
### Married 15 years

Annette and Bill have been married for 15 years and have one son, Wyatt. Bill was in the Navy their entire marriage, but recently retired. Annette is very shy and reserved and this made living on base difficult. For years, she felt isolated and excluded from the other military wives.

Fortunately, Annette cultivated individual friendships, which worked better for her than a group dynamic. She also joined a weekly book club on base. In addition, when Wyatt was little, Annette worked out a babysitting swap with another mom. Each took turns watching both boys, so the other could run errands in peace.

Bill was injured twice during deployments; fortunately not seriously, but this was still very stressful for them.

One of the challenges Annette faced was depression and drinking during Bill's deployments. She felt isolated and lonely; nothing helped like a couple of drinks in the evening. This often turned into five or six drinks and she usually fell asleep in front of the TV.

She didn't believe that this was a problem until her mother suggested she attend an AA meeting. At first, Annette was insulted and furious. But her mother tearfully replied that for several months now, when they'd spoken on the phone in the evenings, she could tell that Annette was inebriated.

Annette then completed an alcohol questionnaire online; she'd answered "yes" to enough questions to indicate she was a problem drinker. She located an AA meeting that was local, but not on base. She didn't want to be the subject of gossip.

After a few meetings, she realized she wasn't a problem drinker, as she'd originally hoped, but was an alcoholic. Her original plan had been to cut back on drinking, but instead she decided to eliminate alcohol altogether.

She waited to tell Bill until four months later when he returned from deployment. He'd been in the middle of the ocean in a submarine, so there'd been no way to tell him anyways. By this time, Annette had been totally sober for almost three months. She felt so energetic in the mornings now, instead of struggling to crawl out of bed hung over.

Now, five years later, Annette is active in AA and sponsors a recovering alcoholic. Her own sponsor has become a close friend. Bill has since retired from the military and is now working at a civilian job, and Annette has a great career at a mortgage company. Wyatt is now in the seventh grade.

# Lila and Ethan
## Married for three years

Lila and Ethan have been married for just three years. Ethan is in the Air Force and both he and Lila are in their mid-20s. Lila says she'd known when they'd married that Ethan was immature, but she hadn't realized the full extent of this. This couple does not yet have children, although that is the eventual plan.

Last year, Lila caught Ethan cheating with one of the wives on the military base. She stresses that since then a lack of trust has been the most difficult challenge in their relationship.

She confronted Ethan about the cheating and he admitted to it. He swore he loved her and that it was just a terrible mistake. He'd been drinking at the time and believes this lowered his inhibitions. He said it wasn't really his fault, since the other woman had pushed herself on him. He promised this would never happen again.

One week after Lila had discovered his infidelity, Ethan had left for deployment. Lila then chose a rather unconventional way to get over her anger.

Lila decided to get over her jealousy in style, and promptly called her old boyfriend Jesse. Jesse had been devastated when she'd married Ethan and had always hoped they'd get back together.

Lila then slept with Jesse quite a few times while Ethan was deployed. She was candid with him about the fact that she wasn't going to leave her husband. She told Jesse it was just because she missed him and it was for old time's sake. She did not divulge that Ethan had cheated on her.

Lila says this was a smart move on her part because it helped her get her "mojo" back so she can now move on and try again with Ethan. She does not plan to tell Ethan what happened with Jesse. As far as she is concerned, it's none of his business.

She's pragmatic about the fact that they haven't gotten off to a perfect start, but feels that if Ethan can stay faithful to her, they have a solid chance of staying married.

# N

## Negativity

Unfortunately, most of us lucky suckers are acquainted with at least two "Negative Nancys." Not to put too fine a point on it, but aren't they spectacularly boring? Particularly when you see that they have so much to be grateful for, yet all they ever do is complain.

Author's note: don't let yourself get trapped listening to a world-class whiner for too long at a stretch, or you might just turn into a dehydrated little mummy or dried-out prune, unable to reconstitute with water or even pineapple-coconut juice.

Nearly 160 years ago, Abraham Lincoln phrased it best, "Most folks are about as happy as they make up their minds to be."

Negative folks see that glass of sweet tea as half empty and they just prefer to (pardon the expression) moan, groan and bitch all the time.

My former co-worker Kate loved to complain, and she did so incessantly. Most folks avoided her like the bubonic plague. Kate griped every single day about the weather. It was either too hot or too cold. I mean, we live in San Diego! San Diego... the weather is fantastic.

If you were unwise enough to actually inquire how Kate was, she'd generally reply, "Oh, you know."

No, Kate, I don't!

Tricia's husband Darren is reliably negative. Over the past 11 years, he's has had six or seven bosses, but never one he liked, or a job that he could stand. He always complains about everyone. You just want to say to a person like this, "Is there *anything* good?"

So, how do you handle really negative people? Unfortunately, if someone past the age of 30 is truly gloomy, they are not real likely to change.

What if that person is your spouse? First off, have they always been this way? Did circumstances conspire to make them more pessimistic?

If you're an upbeat individual, it can be very difficult living with someone who's negative. After awhile, if you're not careful, they'll rub right off on you.

When someone is a positive person, and please keep in mind this explanation is super abbreviated, their brain receptors make them more positive with time. There is an actual physiological component to this. To elaborate, neural pathways in their brain are strengthened into habits through repetition and practice of thinking, feeling and acting. The more positive emotions they engage, the more neurons are activated to form well-worn pathways. This "happy little camper" then proceeds to become even more optimistic and upbeat as the cheerful years go by.

On the flip side of the Morgan silver dollar, when someone's negative, as they continue to complain, they do receive sympathy and attention from others. Now, this may be fake concern, because even those who love the pessimist can grow simply exhausted from listening to them. But nonetheless, the negative person does receive feedback, which acts as a type of reinforcement. So, the gloomy neural pathways of the negative person's brain are reinforced over the years, and this individual becomes even more dreary and downbeat as the sorry years elapse.

If you're reading this and realizing you are little Debbie, not fun mini dessert cake little Debbie, but a little Debbie Downer, remember, self-awareness is crucial. If you've become a pessimistic, complaining, negative person, it's difficult to change, but it *absolutely* can be done.

First off, pause the next time you start griping. If you take the train to work, for example, and it's delayed due to emergency repairs, view this opportunity to talk to another passenger or to catch up on your reading. If you drive to work and there's traffic due to an accident, be grateful you weren't involved in the accident yourself, and be thankful when you arrive at your destination safely.

One way to become more positive is to make a concerted effort to be grateful. This can be verbal or in writing. Earlier, I recommended keeping a gratitude journal. Appreciation and thankfulness are the keys.

Do something to help others, as this is a great way to boost positive energy. Volunteer at a soup kitchen or animal shelter. Go through your closet and find clothes, shoes, and purses to donate. Make food, go out on the street and pass it out to homeless folks.

Here is a trick to stop yourself from complaining: put five dollars into a jar each time you catch yourself griping or making a negative comment.

If your spouse is the complainer, perhaps initiate a competition. Every time one of you gripes, that person has to put five dollars in the jar. When you get to $100, it's time to go to dinner and a movie. P.S. Go see a comedy!

## Never

No pun intended, but the word "never" should never be used in an argument. Budupch!

It's one of those trigger words that elicits negativity.

Louisville, Kentucky couple Samantha and Fred were arguing about money. Fred had just dropped $600 on "bells and whistles" for his Harley. The Harley itself was a sore subject with Samantha as she intensely disliked motorcycles and had never wanted him to buy the Harley in the first place.

When Samantha began accusing Fred by saying, "you never think before you spend money," and "you always blow your pay-check on stuff you don't need," their argument erupted into a full-blown screaming match.

Had Samantha simply stated that Fred had spent more than they could afford, well, that's one thing. But she started heaping on the word "never," including saying "You never think of me or the kids." This made any real communication impossible, as Fred became very angry and defensive.

For one thing, the message she's sending Fred is that she sees him as an eternal screw-up. So then he's likely to think: why even bother trying to please her? Perhaps the Harley is his only indulgence. Samantha's conveniently forgetting the fact that she gets her hair and nails done on a regular basis, and just dropped $280 last week on a pair of strappy summer sandals that she "just had to have" at Nordstrom's.

Now, it's entirely possible Fredster is a "wild child" and is really in the wrong here. In fact, he's always blowing money they don't have, but nonetheless, Samantha using the word "never" just makes him feel insulted and won't contribute to any form of resolution or compromise.

## Neglect the Whole World Rather Than Each Other

If only I could recall which wonderful guest wrote this on our wedding card on June 25, 1988. The card itself is somewhere in our house; God only knows where. At the time, I'd never yet heard this saying. Over the years, I've since duplicated it on countless wedding cards.

Although this concept sounds very basic, executing it is extremely challenging. Multiply this exponentially if you have tiny children.

Let's imagine you and your spouse have been married for ten years and you've got two small kids... does anyone call them "rugrats" anymore?

No matter how much you adore those wee little cupcakes, it is quite possible that your marital satisfaction has simply plummeted since those tiny tater tots made their appearance.

With only so many hours in the day, your sex life, intimacy, sleep, typically all of these greatly suffer. The very idea of quality time with your spouse becomes laughable – all your energy is put toward those tiny little dim sums. You're just trying to pay the bills, and as a bonus, find a way to actually stay awake all day.

Day after weary day you're exhausted, stretched too thin, and maybe for extra fun, you're also broke.

I get it...believe you me, I have been there.

Parents of small children are generally the most stressed-out, exhausted and sleep-deprived segment of our entire population.

So, given all that, how *do* you go about neglecting the whole world rather than your spouse? How on earth can you possibly accomplish this?

Well, for starters, little gestures can make your spouse feel special. Our upcoming post-it notes section discusses how these quick tools provide positive reinforcement and appreciation. You've accomplished this task without investing much time or energy, neither of which you have, since 9-month-old Evan and 3-year-old Amberly are screaming and screeching in your ear. Let's not forget: last night this mini duo "tag teamed" to keep you and your partner awake nearly all night long.

One of our success story couples, Julie and Gary, always made time in the evenings to talk in bed after their children were asleep. They kept their six kids on a tight schedule and were strict about their bedtime. Even 30 minutes of undivided attention in the evenings made the difference in their marriage. That brief half-hour made them both feel loved and appreciated.

This is far preferable to feeling neglected, like old, worn-out tennis shoes, similar to those that evil girl left behind for Carrie at the baby shower in "Sex in the City." Oh, this reminds me, let's insert a quick word about sex. You'll see much more in our sex chapter, but do excuse the bluntness... if you've got small kids, definitely find a way to become an expert at the "quickie."

"Hey, honey, the kids are finally asleep! We've got 14 minutes 'til "Stranger Things" starts! Turn on the Marvin Gaye...Let's get it on!"

The following tips were fine-tuned after repeated mistakes, so please feel free to reap the benefit right here of countless years of trial and error.

- When bringing cookies for the classroom, Girl Scout meeting or soccer game, hunt down that cute little "Chips Ahoy" bag on the shelf. There is only one amazing Martha Stewart on this entire planet. "Good enough" should be your new mantra. Youngsters will gobble down those junky store cookies just as quickly as fancy homemade ones. Trust me on this: impressing those other moms won't mean diddly-squat ten years from now.

- Practice saying, "I'm doing my best." This is more challenging if your kid goes to private school; multiply this by 1,000 if it's also a religious school.

Freely, and without any remorse whatsoever, say "no" when helicopter moms hit you up to volunteer. Say "yes" if you want to, but don't let them guilt you. Often those moms don't have jobs, but guess what? You do. Beware of pushy dads as well. Many dads are now super involved and they don't like to take "no" for an answer.

Most importantly, *never* give a reason when you say "no." Simply smile and reply graciously but firmly, "Thank you for thinking of me, but I won't be able to." If given any excuse whatsoever, the accomplished over-involved parent will immediately devise a clever plan enabling you to say *yes*.

Bonus tip: *never* say "sorry!"

Dr. Linda pointer: if you find it stressful to cart a bunch of kids around, you can cleverly escape this fate by purchasing a small, brightly-colored sports car. As the only "Mustang mom" at St. Kieran's, I smoothly escaped 90 percent of carpooling duties. I then compensated with homemade cookies; sadly, at that time, nobody had yet filled me in on the "Chips Ahoy" trick.

The majority of our success story couples raised small children and lived to tell the tale. During those years, they found ways to make their spouses feel special, although weary and sleep-deprived. As they recalled, this helped maintain or resuscitate their connection as a couple.

Here are a few of their tips:

- Whenever possible, hold hands with your spouse. Make every effort to not drop your baby or toddler when doing so. This was an actual quote, by the way! Holding hands creates a bond and a romantic connection. It's free and it takes no extra time.

- Ladies, it's not forever, but during these years, romance sessions might likely need to be ... well...abbreviated. If you must choose between a "quickie" or nothing, by all means, choose the "quickie."

- When interviewed for this book, men frequently cited the decrease of their sex life as a great source of unhappiness. Initially, they resisted discussing this, but once those floodgates opened, holy guacamole, they vented a *lot*. Incidentally, men complained about this far more often than did women.

- When you shop at the market, buy one or two special items for your spouse. This could be something modest like his favorite candy bar, flowers for her, maybe his favorite beer, or her favorite iced coffee in the can.

- Side note: Get your wife addicted and hooked on La Columbe vanilla draft latte. You'll then look like a real prince when you locate this stuff, because it's not always available.

- Reserve a spot in your home where you leave little gifts for your partner. It could be on the counter next to his wallet. It could be next to her purse.

These are just a few ways to keep your spouse from feeling taken for granted. A prestigious San Diego divorce attorney maintains that feeling unappreciated by one's spouse is one of the issues most frequently cited as a cause for divorce. This appears to be regardless of age, gender, or financial status.

- Just a simple "thank you" is very nice. But if you also toss in a meal, thank-you note, or small gift, your spouse receives tangible positive reinforcement, kind of like a Pavlov dog with meat powder dispensed.

- If your wife endures the kids all weekend long while you ride ATV's with your buddies, buy her some chocolates on your way home. If one of your kids is hyperactive, throw in some flowers too.

- If you have three kids or more, she'll probably need some Prozac as well... most pharmacies stay open late on Sunday nights specifically for this very purpose.

- Acknowledge when your spouse does something extra. Sunday morning he got up early and took Jamison and Ashley to "jungle gym it" at McDonald's so that you could sleep in. Perhaps in return, cook his favorite dinner either that same night, or very soon afterwards.

Now, let's view a scenario where a wife made time for everything *besides* her husband, and the toll this took on their marriage.

Marjorie and Dan lived in Portland, Oregon, and had been married for 13 years. Their daughter Tricia was in the fifth grade. Everyone at Tricia's school adored Marjorie; she was so helpful. The pushy volunteer moms called Marjorie their "little treasure." Marjorie could always be counted on to help with jog-a-thons, school projects, or driving kids all over creation. Even last-minute, Marjorie never, ever said "no."

Marjorie worked a part-time sales job from home. She was only paid for 20 hours a week, but answered the phone whenever clients called. Her phone was "at the ready" every moment of every day. If it buzzed when she was eating dinner or watching a movie, she dropped everything. Her co-workers relied on Marjorie for last-minute emergencies, whether personal or professional.

As she grew older, Tricia began to protest by saying, "Mom, can't you call them back later? We're watching a movie," or, "Mom, we're eating dinner, can't you talk to them tomorrow?"

But Dan rarely complained. Marjorie frequently bragged that he was so easy-going that nothing bothered him. It was true that Dan was laid-back and not a real needy sort. Nonetheless, as the years elapsed, he saw himself slipping lower and lower to the bottom rung of Marjorie's ladder of priorities.

When Tricia began sixth grade, Dan began complaining to Marjorie.

Perhaps most disappointing to him was that their sex life had decreased considerably after Tricia had been born and had never recovered. Eventually, it had dwindled to almost zero. Sometimes Dan and Marjorie scheduled "romance time," but then her phone would buzz or she'd get on Instagram and the time just flew by, so "romance time" almost never happened. During summers, Dan suggested they plan vacations, but Marjorie said she couldn't possibly get away from work. The truth was that she greatly disliked traveling.

Marjorie was very content with their status quo, so she was flabbergasted when Dan informed her one day that he was very unhappy. He wanted to try couples' counseling. His co-worker Brad and his wife had achieved great success with a therapist downtown.

Marjorie felt this was unnecessary, but she agreed to give it a try. However, she no-showed for the first appointment and then canceled the second. The first time she'd been on the phone too long with a client, and the second time had filled in last-minute to drive for Tricia's field trip and got stuck in traffic. Marjorie made it to the third appointment, but she was a half hour late and joked to the therapist that it seemed like a complete waste of money.

Dan was furious. That night at home, he told Marjorie she never made time for him and he was fed up. She promised they'd have more time for each other when Tricia was older. He replied that Tricia was nearly 12, and it didn't seem as though things would ever change.

At that point, however, Dan stopped complaining. Marjorie asked if he wanted to make another therapy appointment, and was relieved when he declined. Things seemed to go back to usual. Marjorie thought that their difficulties were over.

Six months later, however, Dan moved out and promptly filed for divorce. Marjorie was stunned and heartbroken. She told sympathetic friends that he'd blindsided her.

Particularly if your lives are super busy, pause in the middle of it all, sit down with your partner, favorite beverages and snacks in hand, and read this chapter together. See how your partner feels about this subject. They may have complaints they feel guilty verbalizing. Perhaps you both feel neglected, quite possibly in different ways.

Then think together of how you can spend more time having positive experiences as a couple and to make it a goal to put each other first.

# O

## Organization

Years ago, when Robert was still driving his Jeep, the manufacturer did a recall on the brakes. We were promised a $1,000 refund for the brake repairs we'd paid for several months earlier. The only thing we had to do was provide the receipt from the car repair shop.

Forget the fact we'd planned to go to beach that Saturday... we stayed inside and turned the entire house inside out looking for that darn receipt. We finally found it, crumpled up, crammed in the back of a file cabinet. Robert swore I'd put it there and, not to be outdone, I returned the favor by pinning the blame squarely onto him.

So... clutter and disorganization are stressful. I don't claim for perfection in this area, only progress.

Here are some good tips I've read:

If you haven't worked out a system already, get a nice file cabinet and also some of those zipped plastic pouches to store papers.

Important step: toss out things you don't need. Try to handle a piece of mail or other paper just once. In other words, don't do what I still do, which is to "sort of" read it, stuff it in a drawer, and then forget about it until it is way too late.

It's all easier if your household is organized.

This can also tie in with the powerful principles of gratitude and generosity.

Here's how it works. Like many of us, you probably have too much "stuff" lying around your house.

Take some time to clear out excess items. Then, donate as much as you can. My neighbor Valerie did this, with tremendous success. Valerie had been so overwhelmed by all the junk in her house, the last time we had a wildfire scare, her actual statement was, "One way to get rid of the clutter."

To date, she's now donated so much stuff she again worries about wildfires just like the rest of us Southern Californians.

# Optimism
## (see also Positivity)

How does one describe an optimist? He's appreciative. He looks for positives around him. He *wants to be happy.*

To use a well-worn cliché, the optimist sees the tankard as half-full. He believes things will work out well and even if they don't, he will find something beneficial about the situation and is hopeful for the future.

The mirror twin of an optimist is of course the pessimist. When you buy a new car he says, "Oh you know those Teslas get stolen a lot." However, keep in mind the pessimist is great in a pinch. When tragedy strikes, the pessimist comes alive. If your Tesla actually does get stolen, this is the friend who will drive you to the car rental place and will also help you shop for another car.

Perhaps one could call a pessimist a bad news friend. This person may not seem particularly thrilled when things are going well for you; it's not that they are envious, but just that deep down they believe things will eventually always go sour.

You absolutely do not want to eliminate bad news friends from your life; as we said, when you do have an emergency, they will come alive and spring into action for you far better than anyone.

# Over and Over

If you've read our "fatal flaw" segment, this will sound disturbingly familiar.

Now, take a moment, if you will, to picture that mistake, annoying habit, or just plain old dumb thing that your partner has done... over and over and *over* again. If you've been married awhile, most likely you won't have to ponder 'til the alpacas stroll home...nope, you will have a clear scenario "at the ready."

Maybe your husband invariably pays bills late. You've begged to take over this job, but he swears that he's good at it. Meantime, your cell phone and electricity are always on the verge of getting turned off. Maybe your wife frequently forgets to lock the front door of your house. She's clutching her purse, spare shoes, car keys and insulated coffee thermos as she sashays down the front steps. Oh, did we forget to mention? She also usually forgets to activate your house alarm.

Or, possibly your husband blabs confidential information to the wrong person at the worst time and then you have to mop up all the mess afterwards.

Even if you're married to a saint, it's inevitable that there will be some annoying thing they do, over and over and over, and no amount of griping, complaining, crying, screaming, or berating on your part will change it one whit.

Let's add that although they were kind in how they expressed it, and hesitated to criticize their spouse, when pressed, the vast majority of our success story couples did confirm this tragic fact.

Margaret and Sam have been married for 14 years. Sam was generally very responsible, but frequently neglected to lock their backyard gate when he left for work in the mornings. Let's also mention this couple lived in a high-crime area of Chicago. Their gardener had warned them to lock their backyard gate because dogs were getting stolen from their neighborhood on a frequent basis.

Margaret tried nagging, complaining, and yelling, and Sam would remember for awhile, but would then forget again. Finally, she realized there was nothing she could say or do...he was just going to forget. She eventually gave up on Sam being responsible about this one thing. He had many other good qualities... this was just his "over and over" situation.

They never have been robbed, and no one has stolen their terrier Sydney... at least, not yet. Margaret realized she could live with this situation, as tiresome as it was, because Sam's good qualities outweighed his bad ones.

Jacob and Evelyn have been married for 17 years. Jacob was a very successful thoracic surgeon. When they'd been married for six years, she discovered he was having an affair with a nurse. Evelyn immediately had him move out to a hotel. She considered divorce, but her church pastor convinced her to give Jacob a second chance. Raised in a religious household, Evelyn had been taught that divorce was a sin, plus her kids were elementary school-age, so she remained in the marriage.

Fast-forward ten years. In true "Grey's Anatomy" style, Jacob was once again caught cheating, this time with Helena, the wife of his best friend Matthew, also a surgeon. Matthew called Evelyn one day to inform her he'd left Helena and thought Evelyn should know why. Apparently, Jacob and Helena had been carrying on this hoopla for over four years.

Evelyn's pastor once more urged her to stay married, again for the sake of her kids. However, same kids were done with high school by now and Evelyn was fed up, to put it mildly. She told Jacob to move out, and hired herself not just a good, but a *sensational* divorce attorney.

Every married person has individual limits to what they can and cannot accept in a marriage. Only they can determine what they can live with "over and over," and what they just can't accept.

Now, dear reader, we're at least halfway through this book, so you kinda know what's coming next, don't you? It's going be the part where you look at yourself and your own behavior.

In the same way your partner keeps repeating a mistake over and over, yes, you guessed it! You yourself have at least one repetitive mistake which your partner must contend with, and chances are fair you've got more than one.

Though it's a tad embarrassing, I'll now share one of my own "over and over" stories.

Until five years ago, I always paid car registrations late. I did this over and over. Don't even ask me why, 'cuz I don't know! Since the due date was always a couple months out, I'd instead pay a more pressing bill... there always seemed to be a veritable plethora to choose from. I'd tuck the car registration bill aside somewhere, and then just forget about it.

This drove Robert nuts, but I just kept doing it "over and over." I couldn't seem to stop!

However, I've since completely reformed. Nowadays, when a car registration bill arrives in the mail, I pay it immediately. That very same day. Literally at once.

What changed? Why did I reform?

Well, one fateful year, I forgot to send in Andrea's car registration and she was pulled over on the freeway. The police officer pulled her over on a narrow bridge lane, so that cars were whizzing past and almost hitting Ladybug, Andrea's little car at the time. Plus, wouldn't you know, the cop took forever to write the ticket. Talk about feeling like a terrible mom. So... that is what scared me straight!

If your own "over and over" sin is rather harmless, maybe your partner can cut you some slack and just put up with it. But, if it's something that's putting your relationship at risk, or potentially someone's safety in jeopardy, then you may want to change this behavior once and for all.

One of our success story husbands summed this up as follows: is it something you yourself would put up with in a marriage? And if not, why would you expect your spouse to tolerate it?

# Orgasm
## We Saved the Best For Last!

There, I've gone and said it. As I've decided to fight embarrassment by including this glorious topic, why not just go hog wild and repeat this fantastic word...orgasm.

It sounds truly spectacular, doesn't it? It just rolls right off the tongue!

As high school girls, we used this word frequently and with glee, thinking we were so darn cool. We'd say things like, "I'm orgasmically excited about the football game," or, "This chocolate sundae is orgasmic."

This chapter is not just for the ladies, by the way. Men, tune in if you wish...we promise this will be interesting for you as well.

Since a couple's sex life is so important, let's overcome all hesitation and talk extensively about this fun and excellent topic. We shall keep it PG for the most part, but nonetheless, it shall be quite entertaining.

Most folks agree there's really no second best thing to an orgasm, so we can't very well omit the story of O from this book.

So now, for the nitty gritty! When couples stop having sex, or have sex very infrequently, there can be a multitude of reasons. These might be anger or resentment, or perhaps some health issues. But, what I learned from researching this book is there is undeniably an orgasm component as well.

Okay, here it is. We are going to get to the bottom of this ... with no pussyfooting around whatsoever!

When women appear to have lost interest in sex, it goes without saying their husbands are generally not too thrilled. They may very well feel rejected. After all, one of the supposed perks of being married is to be ensured a regular sex life, and so if it peters out as the years go by, men feel kinda gypped. They may feel like they're in a canoe with no paddle.

What happens next is that a couple may lose much of their closeness. They go from F to R to PG and then, if they descend all the way to G-rated, well that's just not so hot at all.

On the other hand, when married couples have a great sex life, they often give off that wonderful "spark." Even if all else is not perfect, they're in sync in a fantastic way. There's that marvelous feeling of having a little secret, perhaps when they just had sex and then go to a party. This is, of course, because they already had their own little party.

Couples may be struggling financially, possibly live in a puny house, have mediocre jobs, their kids are little punks, but, if they're still having great sex, this makes them feel they are living the good life.

Now... back to the orgasm component. Here it is, without further ado... drumroll por favor... if a woman never or very rarely achieves orgasm during lovemaking, eventually she may lose interest in having sex with her partner altogether.

Can anyone really blame her?

You don't need *me* to tell *you* that sex without an orgasm is like a sundae without chocolate sauce and nuts, a rainbow minus the beautiful colors, apple pie lacking cinnamon, or possibly worst of all, lukewarm sparkling water with no ice and definitely no little slice of lime or lemon.

Let's just add here that the gents usually don't have to think too much about coming in for a flying finish, do they now? Those lucky bums, it just happens, most every single time. It's kind of a no-brainer for them, actually.

Not always so easy for the ladies though, now is it?

But, there is a light at the end of the tunnel...a glorious payback for us girls! Ah, yes!

When a lady achieves true proficiency at this, oh, it's a skill like no other. She can land that plane multiple times in a row, and not like it's any big competition, leave any man slightly behind in the dust. It's actually one great side benefit of getting older...years of experience can pay off big-time for a woman at this point. If she's become truly expert, it's easier and better than it ever was in her younger years, and we sure can't say that about everything, now can we ladies?

Dear Gussie, back in my glory days I wore 3-inch high heels all day long; heck, I could even gallop top speed in them suckers! But, as you can plainly see by my "true to life boot camp image" on this book's cover, sadly today, sneakers are "all she wrote." If I tried wearing those heels nowadays, I would lurch around, and then fall flat on my face.

My girlfriend Lydia sobs when reminiscing how she'd once played softball, crashed and landed without injury, well, sadly them days are over. Jeanette used to devour five slices of pizza, three scoops of ice cream, two bags of Dorito's, and that was just a snack! This svelte chickie was so slim you could easily pass a coke can between her tiny little thighs. Now Jeanette must endure low-carb and still must watch every single bite. So, not everything about getting older is a high-heeled walk in the park for us gals.

But, when it comes to this tremendous skill, girls need not be world-class athletes, thank you sweet Jesus! Nope, instead it's an unerring combination of practice, timing, incredible focus and most of all, knowing her body and how it works that are the magic keys to the O kingdom.

But, quite unlike that Indy 500 speed-fest we see onscreen, for most women, it takes a little longer, and timing is crucial. Let's face it: sex scenes on TV and movies are even worse and more unrealistic today than they ever were, and that's saying a lot.

If you believe the baloney portrayed onscreen, women are perpetually 90 seconds away from an earth-shattering climax at any given time of day or night. I don't know about you, but having someone come up behind me by surprise, yank a few of my clothes around, slobber on the back of my neck for less than 12 seconds, then presto, I've gone from one to a hundred in less than a minute?!

Uhhh... yeah, right...guess again.

How about a car analogy? During my teenage years, Zorro, my beloved bright-blue, 1966 Chevy Chevelle was indisputably the love of my life. This car was an absolute white-wall dream. If one girl stretched out across the laps of those in the backseat, Zorro easily accommodated eight of my girlfriends comfortably. The interior was red and the steering wheel was at least 2 feet in diameter...just glorious!

But, before venturing anywhere, Zorro needed some hardcore warming up. I'd often run outside and turn on the ignition, then run back inside to put on my makeup while he "took the chill off." This procedure took at least ten minutes.

Let's now fast-forward to my current car, Scarlett. She's a bright red 2019 Subaru BRZ. Scarlett is undeniably light years ahead of Zorro in terms of technology and manufacture. But even with all her modern advantages, little Scarlett needs warming up too, until that blue light on the speedometer vanishes.

So, we've compiled feedback from some very happy and satisfied women. Their insights are often surprising and most illuminating. Obviously, they've chosen to remain completely anonymous.

Their savvy tips are listed here, in no particular order. Their commentary has been revised to make it just a little more...well, vanilla.

1.  If he's too fast for you, get yourself 80 percent of the way there, and then he can join in. Our house is really big, so I send my husband to watch TV in another part of the house, and then I call him on the phone when I'm ready. We were married for 14 years before I had an orgasm with sex. I finally told my best friend, one of the other moms at my kids' school. She told me to ask another mom for advice. Let's just call this other woman Lisa. Lisa had a reputation for giving good advice and never gossiping. God bless her, she did me such a favor. First thing she asked me was, "Never once, in 14 years?" I had to admit the dreary truth: never. Then she asked if I could fly solo. "Absolutely," I told her, "no problem." That's when she came up with the timing suggestion. Here's how I do it: I light a few candles, and then maybe glance at just a few pictures on my phone of Josh Hartnett or Keanu Reeves. Then, I have my own little party until I'm close to rounding the bend. Only then do I summon my husband. Really, it was just a matter of timing. This has done wonders for our relationship, by the way. I was so damn weary of faking it for all those years. It wasn't his fault and no, I never told him a thing. He just knows that now I'm much more interested in sex. Frankly, he's not too curious to know why; he's just enjoying the change. It would have devastated him to know I was faking it all that time. Face it, I was worthy of a daytime Emmy; my performances were that good. But now, it's great to not have to pretend anymore.

2.  Sometimes you're not in the mood for sex and that's okay. But give it a whirl nonetheless. You're not always in the mood for

Chinese food, are you? But when you get to the restaurant and they set that platter of dim sum in front of you, presto! You realize you're hungry — you end up enjoying everything. Sex is kind of like that... you weren't even in the mood and then you ended up having a great time. I think it's a matter of generosity. I like to make my husband happy and this is a great way to do it.

3.  It's okay to fake it once in awhile; I do if I'm tired. But if you're faking it every time, you're going to get resentful. If your husband is doing something you don't like, tell him about it. He can't read your mind. Speak up, ladies! Not just in the bedroom, but outside it as well.

4.  So, I really need to have two orgasms. They don't have to be exactly in a row. My husband isn't up for it anymore, no pun intended. He's good for once though. So, here's what I do. If I know we are going to have sex later, I bring myself there the first time and then he's there for the second. It's not perfect, but it works out okay.

5.  I grew up in a very religious household. I was 17 and a virgin when I married my husband. I was married for six years before I ever had an orgasm. It would have never happened except for my one helpful girlfriend. One day she asked me if I'd ever had an orgasm and my answer was, "I think so." She said that if I had, there would be no "I think so" about it. She then took me to an adult shop. I was so embarrassed, I'd have walked out if she'd let me. She and the sales guy (it had to be a guy... geez!) helped me pick out a BOB (battery operated boy). Up 'til that point, sex was nice, but honestly, I could take it or leave it. But then, thanks to BOB, I knew what I'd been missing. It took a long time before it happened with my husband also, but it finally did, because then at least I knew what to try for.

6.   Lose the idea it has to happen for you and your partner at the same time. That's usually in the movies. Maybe you're slower than him. Just take your time and go with the flow. If you can be synchronized, great, but if not, it's still going to be good.

7.   If you have trouble getting there with just regular intercourse, you're not alone. Sometimes it takes women years to get to that point, if ever. You may just need to "give yourself a hand," excuse the pun, during regular intercourse. Or...bring out the vibrator!

8.   It's all emotional for me. I have to really be in the mood and that starts early in the day. Obviously, I can't tell my husband this, but there's this smoking hot delivery guy who visits my office once or twice a week. Oh, he's so beautiful. Let's just call him Dominic. Oh my God, his muscles are incredible. Once his watch caught on his shirt and he pulled it up by mistake. When I saw his abdomen, I kept repeating to myself like a mantra, "You're happily married, you're happily married." Yes, he's way younger than me, but still he gives me these smoldering looks. Dang, that's all it takes. So, on those days Dominic shows up, I sign for the delivery, we flirt a little, then I can barely wait to get home to my husband — I practically attack him. My husband loves when this happens; he has no idea why. Thank you and God bless you Dominic. Please, I beg you, don't ever get another job.

9.   Invest in a panty vibrator. You can wear it during the day and by evening you're revved up and ready to go. The great thing is that now you can order these online... you don't even have to go into a store. Invest in a rocking chair to make it super-special.

10.  Go to a sex shop and buy some toys. If you're embarrassed, you can order everything online. Also, turn on some Marvin Gaye. He's in a class by himself. "Let's Get it On!"

11. Men, if you're unsure what to do, just do the alphabet. And please, don't stop suddenly. I think this all is pretty self-explanatory.

12. If there's so much going on in life, kids, work, whatever, that you're losing interest in sex, buy a pair of tight jeans. Okay, I'm just gonna say it: tight in the crotch. It's what I do. I wear them during the day when I'm planning on having sex with my husband that night. They rev me up, what can I say?

13. Be responsible for your own orgasms. Gone are the days when a woman just expected the man to make it happen for her. That's straight out of a Victorian novel. Communicate what you want. Most guys want to please a woman and will appreciate when you let them know. Practice solo, but one caveat: don't use a vibrator every time. If you do, eventually no man will ever be able to satisfy you, because you will have gotten used to just that one rhythm.

14. If you have a particular fantasy that works for you, by all means stick to it, but think of some variations from time to time. Obviously I can't tell my partner this, but when I was in grad school in New York City, I had a passionate affair with Paul, this very handsome older man in my apartment building. For a time, our age difference didn't matter. Without a doubt, he was the best lover I ever had, present company included. He used to kiss me so passionately on my neck when we were making love; I will never forget it. It didn't last; he went back to his wife and I wanted children with someone my own age. But no one else has ever been able to make love to me like Paul did. So when I have trouble getting to Jersey, so to speak, I remember Paul and that "takes me to the limit."

15. This may be a bit unconventional, but I bought this smooth flat polished stone at an exotic shop a few years back. The shop

closed and I haven't seen this anyplace else so I'd better not lose it! I put it inside my panties and sit carefully all day. By the time evening rolls around, I am so supercharged I can have an orgasm in less than a minute. It's just the best thing ever.

16. My first boyfriend Steve was so incredibly bad at sex; just awful: no imagination whatsoever. He was also selfish. Maybe he didn't care if I was satisfied? Sad but true, had I married him, my only orgasms would have been by myself. Once I told Steve to move his hand because it was in the wrong spot altogether, and he actually said, "I like it better here." Wait a damn minute, Esteban! Don't you have that all backwards? Still, with nothing to compare him to, I never imagined why people made such a big deal about sex. Good thing we broke up, because with my next boyfriend, it was a revelation. Oh my God! Sweet Jesus! Now I knew what the fuss was all about. So, I'm just saying girls, test-drive that engine before you get married. They say you only need to kiss someone to see if they're great in bed. Well, that's crappy advice, because Steve was a great kisser, fantastic actually, but he positively sucked in the sack. Girls, I'll say it again, take that car on a nice, long test drive before you ever even consider buying it!

# P

## Peace

There's a wonderful proverb by Lao Tzu: If you are depressed, you are living in the past. If you are anxious, you are living in the future. If you are at peace, you are living in the present.

It's definitely a challenge to be peaceful in today's society. But being more calm and tranquil will extend to all areas of your life and will also benefit other relationships besides your marriage.

Many folks love meditation and hypnosis. Some find that yoga reduces stress while it gets their bodies in remarkable shape. You might want to give these a whirl.

The Prayer of St. Francis of Assisi can be a blessing when dealing with stressful situations or people. You've probably heard it, but just in case, here it is:

Lord, make me an instrument of your peace

Where there is hatred, let me sow love

Where there is injury, pardon

Where there is doubt, faith

Where there is despair, hope

Where there is darkness, light

Where there is sadness, joy

O Divine Master, grant that I may

Not so much seek to be consoled as to console

To be understood, as to understand

To be loved as to love

For it is in giving that we receive,

It is in pardoning that we are pardoned,

And it is in dying that we are born to eternal life.

Amen.

One small habit which can greatly increase peace is to leave the house 15 or 20 minutes earlier than necessary. In this way, you shall have a bay window of time and you can avoid the stress of rushing.

I don't need your pity, but being on time has eluded me for well over half a century. If you're like me, it's easier to show up early than to show up exactly on time.

Kip, a boss in the 80s, yelled at me, "I don't care if you bring a sleeping bag to work and spend the night here, Goddamn it, Linda, be on time tomorrow!"

You youngsters reading this, nothing like HR existed in those days, so bosses like Kip could spout off with utter impunity.

Thus motivated, I left Malibu for West Hollywood the next morning a good three minutes early. Once I hit that remorseless long steak of misery, otherwise known as the 405, I realized in dismay that I was quite nearly out of petrol. There was still a prosciutto-slim chance I might arrive at work on time, so I drove on, praying to God I wouldn't run out.

Well, next thing you know, the mighty and valiant engine of Max, my '69 Camaro, sputtered and then stopped. A man pulled over and told me to hop into his truck to go get gas. He was a UCLA professor and not an axe murderer, as my relaying this story today shall attest.

Now, let's get back to the subject of peace. Within the context of your relationship, it's a conscious decision you make to be harmonious with your partner. Some folks thrive off bickering and drama. However, it's rare that both partners equally enjoy a lot of this. Most people, given a choice, prefer a calmer relationship.

Here are some methods to boost peace in your marriage. Many of these came from our success story couples.

- Extend grace. Give your partner the benefit of the doubt. If they do something you don't like, don't rush to get upset. Take a moment to think about the situation before you respond.

When you do bring it up, speak calmly and give your partner an opportunity to explain. "Splain, Lucy, splain!"

- Use kind words and phrases. Don't use hostile words or yell.

Here are a few examples of kind phrases:

- "I know you didn't mean for that to happen."
- "I understand."
- "I'm here for you."
- "I appreciate everything you do for me and the kids."

Here are some hostile phrases:

- "I can't believe you did that. What were you thinking?"
- "You always such make a mess of things."
- "How do you expect me to believe you did that?"
- "You really screwed up that one."
- "I don't even know what you're talking about."

Pick your battles (this deserves special attention so it's coming up next).

Look beneath anger to pain. When your spouse angers you, perhaps you are in actuality hurt, rather than angry. We're all a sum total of our life's experiences. If your spouse says something you find hurtful, this may be due to your childhood or adolescent experiences.

Joyce and Lance had been married for just four years. When Joyce was growing up, her mother was very exacting and constantly pressured Joyce to stay thin. Joyce struggled mightily with anorexia in college but now has it under control. Last week, she and Lance were at their friend Sue's house for a barbecue. When Joyce picked up a plate of cake, Sue said, "Oh Joyce, you will love that cake." Sue's husband Ted then joked, "Oh, Joyce is so afraid of getting fat, she's only going to eat one bite."

Ted's comment was tactless, but he had no idea she'd had an eating disorder. Nonetheless, Joyce was embarrassed and furious. Her reaction had more to do with her past than with the current situation. Sue apologized a few minutes later for Ted's tactlessness, and Joyce laughed and changed the subject.

However, on the drive home, when she vented to Lance, he shrugged it off, saying, "Oh, he was only joking." Joyce and Lance ended up getting into a massive argument; she felt he wasn't sufficiently upset for her sake.

Does any part of Joyce's story resonate with you? Someone makes a tactless comment; sure, it's tacky all right, but your reaction is completely out of proportion.

Ask yourself this question: are your present reactions to current situations based upon your past experiences? If so, just know that you aren't alone; most people experience this to some extent.

Therapy, journaling, meditation, or hypnosis: all these can help you to deal with bad memories, traumas, or emotional upsets of your past, and ideally help you find more peace in your everyday life.

## Pick Your Battles

There are two distinct methods of picking your battles; both enrich your marriage.

1. Learn to compromise and not always insist on getting your way. Even if your idea is smarter, more cost-effective, and more fun than what your partner suggests, find a way to meet in the middle.

One of our success story husbands phrased it this way: "If you insist on it always being about you, it *will* eventually be just you, and you can do whatever you want, because you will be alone... Elvis will have left the building."

2. Go easy on your spouse when they screw up. Pretend it was you who flubbed up and think how grateful you'd be if your spouse just cut you some slack.

Nicole and Matthew are in their early 30s, live in St. George, Utah, and have been married for four years. Faster than the bus in "Speed," their relationship has careened to a disastrous locale. Matthew says Nicole "bitches all the time." Nicole maintains Matthew "has no respect."

Most of all, Nicole hates it when Matthew's Air Force buddies come over to visit. They mess up the living room and kitchen, are boisterous and noisy, and drink too much beer. She retreats to the bedroom, but their apartment is small. The twice-a-month visits are too frequent for her. Every time his friends leave, Nicole and Matthew argue bitterly.

Nicole thinks Matthew's friends are a nuisance, and doesn't hesitate to say so. But these guys served together and have been friends for over a decade. They're like brothers to Matthew. They're also united over the loss of their mutual friend Stanley, who'd been killed in active duty five years ago.

Last year, Greg, one of these friends, was in a pinch and Matthew lent him $2,000. Nicole was very angry when she learned of this because they were saving to buy a house. Greg paid the money back as promised, but Nicole felt Matthew had gone behind her back.

She insisted he promise to never again lend money without talking with her first. Matthew refused and told her he was sick of her constant griping.

More recently, he'd also bought a motorcycle without telling her. When she'd become furious, he'd shrugged. It appeared Matthew no longer cared if he upset her.

Now, let's investigate a' la' Nancy Drew. Was Matthew like this when they were first married? Absolutely not! He'd worked very hard to make Nicole happy, and was always considerate of her feelings.

Matthew works incredibly hard at his job and does more than his share of housework. He's walked Trixie, Nicole's fox terrier, five times a day since Nicole hurt her ankle two months ago. He's also unfailingly polite to her friends and family, so he particularly resents her rude treatment of his military brothers.

Nicole griped bitterly to her best friend Abigail, who'd been married 11 years and knew the concept of picking one's battles.

Although Abigail sympathized, she warned Nicole that making Matthew feel he had to choose between her and his military brothers could eventually end their marriage.

Abigail suggested that whenever Matthew's buddies visited, Nicole go out with friends, shop or run errands.

So, the next time Matthew's friends visited, there was a lavish spread of appetizers, nachos, and homemade Toll House cookies waiting for them. Nicole visited for about 15 minutes, and was very friendly to all the guys. She insisted that Matthew's friend Bruce spend the night, as he lived over an hour away. Nicole then promptly left the house for dinner and a movie with Abigail.

So, wise grasshopper Nicole listened to Abigail and began to pick her battles.

This exact scenario (well, the recipes changed... next time she made Ghirardelli brownies and avocado egg rolls) was repeated by Nicole twice a month for the next three months.

In the past, Matthew's friends had never once said anything negative about Nicole because they didn't want to embarrass him. Now, however, they all raved about how wonderful she was and how much they loved visiting. Incidentally, when Nicole returned home each time, Matthew had tidied up so the apartment was immaculate.

Girls, as we all know, a guy's friends are sacred to him, and you can multiply that exponentially if they served together in the military.

Now, here's the great part; not likely a huge surprise. During those three months, Matthew's attitude toward Nicole completely transformed for the better.

Without being prompted, Matthew apologized for misusing the house funds and promised to never do it again. He became much more attentive and thoughtful, bringing home flowers and surprises for her, as he'd done in the early days of their marriage. He also gave her wonderful shoulder massages when she returned home from work.

Best of all, Matthew frequently told Nicole how lucky he was to have such a wonderful wife and how much he loved her.

Later that year, Matthew received a very large bonus at work and they were able to make a down payment on a beautiful house.

So, to recap, as the title implies... pick and choose what you're going to fight or do battle over. Sometimes it's far better to say nothing ...and just let it go.

And hey... nobody here said it was easy.

Mark and Elaine lived in Pittsburgh and had been married for nine years. They were excitedly packing for a tropical vacation to Barbados. On their way to the airport, they planned to drop off their little beagle Missy at the "doggie hotel."

This couple did not have children; Missy was their baby.

Mark was hurriedly packing his suitcase as well as Missy's dog toys and personalized lucky food bowl. This bowl was an expensive gift that had been given to them by Elaine's Aunt Lisa.

In his haste, Mark dropped the fancy food bowl and it shattered into a million shards when it hit the tile floor.

Elaine had two choices here: she could carry on about the dish, make Mark feel even worse, and effectively put a dent in Barbados before they even hit that pink sand beach.

Alternatively, she could be gracious, and offer to help clean up the broken glass.

Mark apologized profusely. He knew how much the dish meant to Elaine. He also tactfully refrained from wondering aloud why in hell she'd insisted on bringing the bowl to the doggie hotel anyways, when it was both irreplaceable and breakable.

Elaine made a light comment and helped clean up the mess. She said they'd have time to stop and pick up another bowl, this one plastic.

This may seem trivial, but as we all know, folks divorce over petty stuff every single day of the year, including Sundays, holidays, Easter and let's not forget... Mardi Gras.

As I write this, I hear Robert in the kitchen painstakingly cleaning our oven. Why does he have to clean our oven, you may ask?

Well, this afternoon I made two lasagnas, one for us and one for our next-door neighbors. These lasagnas were beautiful, smelled fantastic, and bubbled over with three kinds of cheese, garlic, basil and oregano. They were virtual Italian masterpieces and they took over an hour to make.

However, when they were done baking, rather than taking 30 seconds to locate two decent potholders, I grabbed one decent potholder and this weird blue square thing... because it was "at the ready."

As I pulled out the first lasagna, it sailed out of my hand, splattering spectacularly into the bowels of the oven. The blobby mess resembled a scene from a B+ horror movie. It truly would have been easier for us to move to a new house than to clean up the ensuing carnage and mess.

The grates at the bottom of the oven were so badly drowned in lasagna sludge, I actually brought them outdoors to hose them off. Since there's a perpetual drought here in California, hey, I did my part! I placed the grates on top of our hillside ice plant and hosed them off. How weird this all must have looked to the neighbors, only the shadow knows.

The majority of the cleanup went to Robert, who had to actually disassemble the bottom of the entire oven. He was such a good sport about it and kept saying it was okay, as I apologized profusely.

Things like this have kept us together for 35 years. Not my spilling the lasagna, of course, but Robert being a prince throughout the whole fiasco.

Two hours later, the oven was finally clean, and Robert walked from our kitchen into our attached garage. Undoubtedly, he was delirious from lasagna superfund fatigue.

Robert opened the garage, completely forgetting our corgi puppy Diana was in there eating her dinner. Diana is always ready for such an exciting opportunity, so within three seconds, she'd torn out of the garage, flown down the hill and into the ravine below our house.

Our ravine is home to a multitude of perils such as snakes and, on occasion, coyotes five times the size of a corgi puppy, plus cars that whiz by at 40 miles per hour on the road below. Luckily, Robert was finally able to catch Miss Corgi. After he was so gracious about my lasagna debacle, I certainly wasn't about to be a jerk about the dog.

So, this illustrates the power of picking your battles. When you cut your partner some slack, chances are better than average they'll return the favor.

## Poachers

What exactly is a poacher? Well, it's not a "huevos rancheros" or "crab benedict" recipe; that's for certain. But now this chapter's making me awfully hungry!

Okay, back to business. Poachers are those folks who don't want the time, expense or work of a full-time relationship. Consequently, their preference is to pursue married individuals. Perhaps their name came about because, in a sense, they are "poaching" a married couple.

Now, listen closely folks, because here is the ultimate rub. If the object of the poacher's affection is unwise enough to actually leave their spouse, quicker than you can say "lickety split," the poacher usually high-tails it right out of there faster than a wild bunny when the hawk flies over.

Let's take a gander at Joan and Ed of St. Louis, Missouri. They'd been married for 12 years, and except for a few minor ups and downs, had a strong and loving relationship. Joan had always stayed home with their three kids, but when their youngest started middle school, she returned to work. Her new job was rather glamorous and entailed a decent amount of traveling. One might then assume that *Joan* would be the partner more susceptible to an affair.

However, Ed, feeling a bit neglected as Joan was so occupied with her new career, became susceptible to his office's resident poacher, Alicia.

Alicia was 15 years Ed's junior, and knew he was married with kids, but that didn't deter her in the least (channel Mia who pursued Harry in the film "Love, Actually"). Alicia greatly preferred older men and suffered no pangs of guilt if they were married. Their unavailable status actually made them more challenging and appealing to her. Only 26, Alicia had already conducted affairs with seven married men to date.

Let's pause for a little joke. Fern announces, "I et seven eggs for breakfast." Will replies, "Why, Fern, you mean 'ate.'" Fern thinks for a moment. "Well, maybe it was eight eggs I et."

Now, is there any way to make your marriage "poacher-proof?" There's no way to guarantee a marriage won't be in danger at some point. Certainly, there are times in a marriage when couples are at higher risk. One of these is after the death of a loved one.

Alan and Frances had been married for 12 years when his mother was killed at age 57. Her car was broadsided by a drunk driver. Alan had been extremely close to his mom and was devastated.

Frances immediately sprang into action, making funeral arrangements and picking up relatives at the airport. She believed she was supporting Alan by taking care of practical matters, which he did appreciate, but Alan also desperately needed emotional support. Frances wasn't great at talking about feelings under the best of circumstances, and she assumed Alan was doing okay.

Prior to this time, if you had asked Alan if he was happy with Frances, he would have unreservedly said, "yes." The two were in their early 30s and neither had yet lost a family member.

After the funeral, they rarely talked about Alan's mom; Frances carefully avoided the subject. When upset about something, Frances didn't need to talk about it. Instead, she kept busy. She was a "pull up by your bootstraps" kind of woman. Frances wasn't being deliberately unkind; she genuinely believed talking about his mom would upset Alan more.

Alan was the opposite; he wanted to talk. When he brought up his mom, Frances briefly replied, and then changed the subject. After awhile, he felt that she just didn't care.

After a few months, Alan became very resentful as he felt Frances was indifferent to his suffering. He was experiencing tremendous guilt and regret, as he'd planned to visit his mom two weeks before she died, but then had canceled the trip last-minute.

Missing that last chance to see his mom was devastating. Most of all, Alan was angry that his young mom had been taken so suddenly at the hands of a drunk driver, who incidentally had fled the scene and had still not been caught.

Enter Paula, Alan's single co-worker. Paula was 12 years his senior; the two had already worked together for five years. Paula could see that Alan was heartbroken, but attempting to hide it.

Paula went out of her way to talk to Alan about his mom and the two began having lunch frequently. She helped him accept that it wasn't his fault he'd missed seeing his mom that last time and that he'd always been a good son. This friendship really helped Alan, who began to slowly bounce back from his loss.

In the beginning, Paula was merely a good friend to Alan. She was absolutely not a poacher and had never been involved with a married man. Neither of them had any intention of becoming more than friends.

Alan, who had never strayed, eventually became involved in an intense emotional affair with Paula, which deepened into a physical one as time went on.

Could this situation have been avoided? Yes, possibly. Alan might have gone for counseling at this difficult time. He could have tried talking to his wife more and let her know he was feeling neglected.

## Post-It Notes

This tip is simple, but very effective. Buy some post-it notes at the drugstore. Every so often, leave one on your spouse's computer screen, wallet, inside their purse, or in their briefcase, with a tiny note saying something like:

- I love you.

- Great job at work.

- I'm proud of you.

- Thanks for being such a great husband (or wife).

- Thanks for being such a wonderful mom (or dad).

- You were fantastic in bed last night.

- Last night's dinner was wonderful.

- Good luck at work today.

- Thanks for running out to the market last night.

These simple messages represent two things which all human beings crave: appreciation and affection.

For the few measly bucks you shell out for the post-it notes, plus a miniature investment of time, you can make a positive difference in your relationship. Sure, it's cheesy and a little corny... but couples who do this say it's a small thing which actually makes a very big difference.

To reiterate, this activity costs virtually nothing, takes just a few moments, but might just create a wonderful difference in your relationship.

It may seem silly, but hey, if it works, what the heck.

Here are some clever ideas found online. Tape an actual matchstick to the note saying, "We are a match made in heaven." Or attach an actual sugar packet to the note and write, "You're my sugar." You can even write out "I love you" on a mirror, with each letter being its own post-it note.

Your spouse has a 50/50 chance of either loving this or finding it dumb... only one way to find out!

Reminders such as "drop off the laundry," are perhaps best used sparingly, or not at all. Truthfully, this takes all the fun out of it. The post-it note then becomes a chore, and there's no less sexy word in the entire English language than "chore," except the bleary and dreary "budget," or, worse yet, "portion control." Bleh.

By the way, if this seems silly to you, but you know your partner will love it, give it a whirl. Keeping one's spouse happy is a goal for any smart married person.

## Prayers

Many married folks consulted for this book believe that praying together makes them stronger as a unit. Incidentally, some aren't church-goers or of the same faith as their spouse.

Other couples love attending services together and find that this builds cohesion in their marriage. They have close friends and a support system through their church, parish, synagogue, Kingdom Hall, or other place of worship.

Quite a few folks interviewed prefer sleeping in on Sunday mornings and efficiently praying from the comfort of their home, wearing a robe and booties, and sipping a cup of joe.

They have a very strong relationship with God that doesn't involve churchgoing.

Not me, of course, oh no, I'm there for seven a.m. mass, five days a week, rain or shine. If that sounds kosher to you, why, I've got this beautiful beachfront mansion in Indiana that's just gone on the market. It's got its own boat dock with three towering palm trees and a heated Spanish tile jacuzzi.

Marla lived in Atlanta, Georgia, and was a believer, but didn't attend church. However, she donated an inordinate amount of time each week helping animal rescues and tutoring foster kids.

Every Sunday, jogging at the park, she ran into her married acquaintances Winston and Beth. Winston was a pastor at her parents' church. Each time, without fail, Winston energetically scolded Marla for missing church.

"Why, young Miss Marla, you *need* to go to church," he always cried out in an impassioned tone.

You've got to wonder, says who?

Each time, Winston fervently added that churchgoing would enable Marla to walk in the path the Lord had created just for her. He'd then toss in a few psalms to give his micro-sermon some extra punch.

Winston stated all this with absolute conviction as he raised his fist heavenward. Perhaps God had phoned him that very morning to say, "Hey, Winston, here's what's up with Marla."

One Sunday morning, Marla jogged through the entire park with no sign of Winston or his mini sermon. She later discovered he'd been busted for massive criminal tax evasion... why are we not surprised?

Geez Louise, Winston!

"God is calling out to embrace you. I want y'all to reach deep into your hearts and your pocketbooks, and take God's hand."

## Please

How often do we say "please" or "thank you" to co-workers, friends, waiters and waitresses, but then neglect to do the same with our spouse?

Santa Barbara couple Lisa and Grant had been married for nine years; theirs was an unhappy union. Lisa did most of the cooking; when she handed Grant a plate of food, he always accepted it without comment. She'd then state loudly, "You're welcome," and thus prompted, Grant would mutter "Thanks," but there wasn't exactly a mother lode of sincerity there.

Lisa also did most of the cleaning and kept their house immaculate, but Grant never commented. As a result, she felt unappreciated and resentful.

But this highway apparently ran in two directions. Grant washed both of their cars, took out the trash, mowed the lawn, and did the gardening, but Lisa never thanked him. So, he was resentful as well.

As this couple's tale shall illustrate, a lack of appreciation is often the surface symptom of a much deeper problem.

Initially, Lisa and Grant had been incredibly happy. They had adored each other, they had laughed and joked around; both felt so lucky to have found one another.

Two years into their marriage, Grant had abruptly quit his job as an attorney and began teaching. He lost a lot of income, true, but he'd hated being a lawyer and he absolutely loved teaching. Lisa angrily told him he'd never earn a substantial income as a teacher and they'd still have to pay back his student loans from law school.

Grant countered that if Lisa loved him, she wouldn't want him to spend his entire life in a career that made him miserable.

Seven progressively unhappy years have since elapsed, until now these two are a miserable couple. Now, here's an interesting tidbit: over the past seven years, Lisa has regularly protested they'd never get ahead financially, but she herself was unwilling to find a full-time job.

This couple had no children; therefore, nothing prevented Lisa from making more of a contribution to their income. She had a college degree and decent work experience, but chose to work part-time at a local bookstore for meagre pay.

Although Lisa's chief complaint was Grant being under-employed and underpaid, this was rather like the pot calling the kettle black.

So, for the past seven years, rather than loving and appreciating one another, this couple has been utterly miserable. They only spoke when necessary, rarely laughed and avoided each other whenever possible.

Now, here is the two million dollar question. Wait a minute! With the price of gas so high, two million dollars just don't go that far anymore. The three million dollar question is: how can Grant and Lisa turn their marriage around?

These two have now nearly descended to the Freddy Kruger basement of mutual regret, blame, and disappointment. Out of the corner of his eye the other day, Grant thought he saw a very attractive red sweater with green stripes, and folks...that definitely ain't a good sign.

This couple may never actually divorce. But, will they spend the rest of their lives being miserable, or can they turn things around?

How's about Lisa breaks the ice and tells Grant she's proud of him for being a teacher, and apologizes for not being supportive earlier. To top it off, she adds that she'll immediately start looking for a full-time job.

So, let's just say Lisa is obstinate. This woman is *very* stubborn. Why should *she* be the one to apologize and make changes?

But, what if by making that one initial statement, then coming through with a full-time job, Lisa turns around the negative trajectory of seven long years?

Although we've criticized overuse of the phrase "just communicate," here *indeed* lies a situation where communication would be an invaluable first step. At that point, it's likely that Grant in turn would apologize and try to make amends for his staggering law school debt.

This couple could potentially transform their miserable relationship back to a happy one very quickly.

So, to recap, using words such as "please" and "thank you" help your partner feel respected and appreciated. Most importantly, this prevents them from feeling taken for granted, which, as we've already determined, is a major kiss of death for a relationship.

## Positivity

It's no great secret that a positive person is generally easier to live with than a negative one. My English friend Tracy has a funny saying: "I avoid negative people like the plague, Covid and herpes all rolled into one fine Cuban cigar."

Negative folks, aka "gloom and doomers" can slurp the life right out of ya like maple syrup out of a tree ... *if you let them.*

Audrey lives in Seattle and has been wed for over 21 years to "moaner and groaner" Tad. Never mind that Tad's in good health, has a nice house, wife and job, he's going to find something to gripe about... no matter what.

Tad is always disgusted with his boss. We've all had some crummy bosses in the past. But in the 21 years Tad's been married to Audrey, he's had seven bosses, and couldn't stand a single one of 'em.

There's no easy way to phrase this: Tad's expression usually looks like he's been staring down into open caskets all day long.

Waiting in line at the supermarket is annoying to Tad and he sighs loudly and repeatedly. Tad complains when eating out at restaurants. Even if the food and service are impeccable, he will find something to harp about, because of course, *it's all about him.*

All of this is clearly embarrassing to Audrey, who often must apologize to friends for his behavior.

If you're laughing by now, it's probably because you know someone who's eerily similar to our pouty little poster boy Tad.

So, worse yet, what if you've got a spouse like Tad? First, determine if this is new behavior, or if they've always been this way. If the negativity is fresh, perhaps it's in response to an event, such as the loss of a loved one. If so, perhaps therapy or group support might help. If it's chronic, like Tad, who's been super negative for decades, it's more challenging. When others have pointed out to him that he's difficult, Tad emphatically disagrees. It's always the fault of someone else, the slow waitress, the lousy boss, the awful traffic. Tad truly believes that events conspire against him.

So, there's a bit of the victim mentality here as well.

What do you do if you're saddled down in holy matrimony with a constant complainer?

Tad's wife Audrey handles it quite well. She makes light of his complaints and even jokes to him about it. Her main weapon in the battle against gloom and doom is unfailing humor.

With typical optimism, Audrey is quick to point out Tad's many great qualities. He works hard and is generous with her and the kids. He's reliable and faithful, much like those dependable little mules carting tourists down to the bottom of the Grand Canyon. Speaking of tourists, even though Tad whines incessantly while on holiday, he, Audrey and the kids do travel and eat out quite frequently.

Audrey gives herself "space" and breathing room. She socializes frequently with her girlfriends, who, it may come as no surprise, are all very positive and upbeat ladies. Audrey thus escapes Tad's negativity on a regular basis.

Audrey is pragmatic about the fact that Tad will quite likely never change. He will probably complain until he gasps his very last pessimistic breath.

Now, if your spouse is negative, such as Tad, perhaps, like Audrey, you've concluded this is how they'll stay. But, as in the case of Tad, perhaps their fine qualities compensate, so you remain married to them.

Perhaps you recognize yourself in Tad; *you* are that pessimist.

*Ergo*, how can you foster that elusive quality of positivity in yourself? Here is a list of just a few ways:

- Every day write in a gratitude journal.

- Give to those with less than you. Walk dogs at the shelter, volunteer at a soup kitchen, make food at home and pass out to your local homeless.

- Get regular exercise. Just getting out of the house and taking a walk is a great mood lifter.

- When something disappointing or upsetting occurs, think of something positive about the situation and state it out loud.

- Instead of cursing the traffic on your daily commute, think how lucky you are to have a job. Rather than complaining about the slow service at a restaurant, take this opportunity for more conversation with your dining companion. Acknowledge that perhaps the restaurant is short-staffed and that the employees are doing their best.

- Always try to find the humor in an unfortunate or difficult situation.

- Write positive messages on post-it notes and put them around the house. "Embrace Change" is a great one.

- Come up with a personal, self-affirming mantra: "I'm fierce and I've got this." "Suck it up buttercup." "If it's to be, it's up to me." "Progress, not perfection." Repeat throughout the day as needed.

- Go through the alphabet from A to Z and say out loud (or to yourself if in public, so people don't think you're weird) one positive adjective for each letter. For example: Amazing, Beautiful, Courageous, Determined, Energetic, etc. This also works great if you have insomnia. Just say it over and over on auto-loop until you bore yourself to sleep! Don't do it out loud, by the way, if you're trying to doze off.

- Spend time in nature, preferably with the pets you love best.

- When you see guys out on the street doing manual labor, particularly on a hot day, go buy them icees at 7-Eleven. They will be stunned and thrilled ... nobody does this.

- Laugh at yourself. It makes life easier and so much more fun. We have three new rescue horses at our house: Mirlo, Malibu, and Jasmine. We call them the Three Musketeers. Recently, I was pushing an empty trash can and tripped, fell and went sailing over the can. The horses seemed to be very amused. It really hurt, but I laughed thinking how silly I must have looked. Too bad I didn't get it on video to be a YouTube sensation.

If you're more positive, this may rub off on your marriage partner. Then again: maybe not. In the final analysis, we're only 100 percent responsible for our own behavior.

## Prom Vortex

This uncanny syndrome typically afflicts more brides than grooms, although men as well can become sucked up into the terrifying "prom vortex."

What on earth, you may ask, is a prom vortex? It sounds rather like a teenage "slasher" movie. You know the kind: 90 percent of the characters die within the first 20 minutes, but the last two survive, dehydrated and unkempt, never needing to eat, drink, sleep or use the restroom, it must be noted, all the way to the gruesome finale.

Ladies, it's rather like hair ties! They all break within the first month except for one, which then lasts for three years.

Let's now illustrate a real couple caught up in the unique and compelling "prom vortex."

Annette and Daniel dated for nine months before becoming engaged; their wedding took place eight months later. This couple adored the idea of a perfect dream wedding. Their big day included great excitement and joy, huge expense and planning, and was an unequivocal success.

Their guests all agreed it was the most beautiful wedding ever. Annette's parents took out a second mortgage so they could afford the lavish celebration for 300 guests. Years after the event, friends and relatives still fondly reminisced about the all-you-could eat sushi bar, the glorious prosecco bar, and the five separate wedding cakes.

Annette and Daniel's two-week honeymoon in Bora Bora was glorious, first class baby all the way. Annette and Daniel went scuba diving, took helicopter rides, glorious sailing trips, went horseback riding, snorkeled with the dolphins, and enjoyed shopping and dining.

They returned from their honeymoon in an ecstatic glow and set up house, as Annette put it. Both were thrilled to be married and looked forward to spending their lives together.

But only one year later, Annette confessed to friends that she was very unhappy, bored and restless.

Annette had been so captivated with the idea of their wedding being one huge, fantastic, sensational prom, and then their perfect honeymoon the glorious after-prom, but then she had difficulty with everyday life.

The majority of Annette and Daniel's relationship had been talking about and planning their wedding and honeymoon. When everyday life set in, well, no other way to phrase this...it was humdrum.

So, herein lies the harsh, whirling reality of the prom vortex. When some folks prepare to get married, they're so excited about THE DRESS! THE RING! THE CATERER! THE RECEPTION! THE HONEYMOON!!

It's like a giant, fun, exciting, beautiful, stupendous party, and they are the stars of the show. But that's the best part. The "being married" part, unfortunately, quickly becomes disappointing or dull to one or both parties.

What, then, is the unfortunate result?

Sadly, prom vortex couples often break up after just one or two years of marriage.

One would imagine this scenario only besets young couples, but "prom vortex" can afflict older folks as well.

Face it, it *is* fun being engaged, showing off the ring, and planning the wedding and honeymoon. But some couples completely focus on these and not the reality of day-to-day life together. This is where premarital counseling can come in handy.

Another strategy is making time for fun things after the wedding, such as trips. If money is tight, it might take ingenuity to plan inexpensive getaways. Most of our success story couples mentioned trips or quick holidays to keep a sense of fun and unity as a couple and to keep it all from getting too humdrum.

A quick aside: when I see the glorious, slinky creations girls nowadays wear to their proms, I cannot help experiencing some bitterness when recalling the prim get-ups we girls sported back in June of 1980. Let's face it: my dress was the floral equivalent of those black dresses with white collars that the Pilgrim ladies were forced to wear "back in the day." I must add that on prom night, when I told my date I had to remain a virgin to keep from disappointing my mom, he accepted this without question. My "Little House on the Prairie" garb undoubtedly gave my excuse total validity.

## Proud of You

The phrase "I'm proud of you," carries tremendous impact. We human beings are sensitive creatures (yes, men, too...sometimes even more so than the ladies!).

If we were fortunate enough to hear "I'm proud of you," or other supportive comments in our formative years, well, we love hearing them again. These words evoke wonderful memories of kind, loving parents, encouraging siblings and teachers, and coaches who saw our potential.

Sadly, however, many children and adolescents grow up with criticism and negative comments from parents, siblings, teachers, and coaches. This sends them a clear message during their formative years: no matter what they did, it was never good enough.

Therefore, giving your spouse this kind of positive statement is a beautiful gift. You can also text your spouse these words, or put them onto a tiny but powerful post-it note. It's also nice to compliment your spouse to your kids; for example, "I'm so proud of your dad."

## Picking Up The Slack

Robert and I recently ate lunch in Los Angeles with a friend who left the restaurant before us, accidentally leaving her phone on the table. Robert drove clear to the other end of town in terrible traffic to return the phone to its owner. This took three extra hours of driving, and he never complained or made a big deal about it.

"Picking up the slack" for your partner is best done like this: no complaining and with a giving heart. This is particularly crucial when you have small children. One partner might take the kids to the park on a Saturday morning so the other can get some much-needed sleep. Or, one might keep the kids entertained while their spouse is on an important phone call.

One frequent complaint from wives is their husbands don't pick up the slack around the house. They mentioned emptying out the trash, the dishwasher, putting away laundry, washing dishes in the sink.

Important note: there are two ways to make "picking up the slack" most effective. First, think of something helpful to do without being asked. Second, go out of your way for your spouse *without complaining*.

## Procrastination

Ahh ... the simple joy of futzing around. Not to brag excessively, but I myself procrastinate at a truly Olympic level. I am the Nadia Comaneci of putting things off!

At this precise moment, I'm simultaneously fighting the urge to a) call a high school friend to chat b) make yet another boba iced coffee, although now, at 10 a.m., I'm already completely cracked out on caffeine c) check my Facebook or d) stroll outside to see if it's raining. Bear in mind that it's May and I reside in San Diego, where the odds of winning the lotto are substantially higher than those of experiencing actual rainfall in May.

Yes, I'm royalty, a bonafide Queen or Duchess of Procrastination. Putting things off is truly one of my greatest talents, and partially why this book took so darn long to complete. It's also in some measure why my PhD took nine years....count 'em, nine excruciating years from start to bone-crushing, weary, haggard finish!

I hereby expose my shortcomings in this milieu from the get-go, lest I seem superior doling out advice.

Okay, if your spouse delays completing jobs around the house, this admittedly can drive you bonkers. If they're a legitimate procrastinator, your nagging or reminding them has a 110 percent chance of prolonging the misery.

Let's just say your husband is supposed to clean out the garage. He promised to do it over six months ago. He works weekdays, so he will have to do the job on the weekend. It should only take five or six hours — tops! It shouldn't be all that big of a deal, now should it?

Nonetheless, for the past six months, every weekend has gone by, and the garage stays nasty and messy. Hubby watches the ball game, drinks beer and eats snacks, and hangs out and chats with the neighbors. He's having a sensational time, while your blood pressure shoots right through the roof. You've nagged him, reminded him, and finally, gotten mad and yelled at him. You offer to do it yourself...he refuses. You offer to hire someone... he refuses again, because *he's* going to do the job.

He keeps vowing to do it, but sunshine, it ain't happening!

The longer you put something off, the harder it gets, until it's nigh as insurmountable as climbing Mt. Kilimanjaro wearing flip-flops and nonchalantly sipping a dirty martini.

So, if your spouse is driving you nutso in this manner, you have to get clever... *real* clever.

Here's a bizarre but useful scheme: instead of scolding or nagging your spouse, thank them as though the job were already completed. They will be stunned, because of course they are painfully aware that the garage is still full of dust, junk, spiders and cobwebs, but here you are, actually thanking them!

This is a strange and most peculiar trick, but one that's oddly effective.

Now, for a live re-enactment of this exact process: Rudy and Evelyn lived in Phoenix and had been married for eight years. Rudy had been promising for *27 months* that he would re-grout their kitchen counters. Their kitchen was small, so at the very most, the job would take one day.

Over two years ago, painfully conscious of the fact that Rudy put things off, Evelyn had offered to hire someone, but as he breezily assured her with supreme confidence, "Why pay someone all that money when I can do it so much better and for free?"

Now, it's two years later. Picture if you will, the narrator in "Sponge Bob Square Pants." *Two years later.*

Evelyn has nagged Rudy, gotten mad and yelled, but the kitchen counters still sit there, double-ugly and stained. Each time she's brought it up, he's promised to do the job, but it's never actually quite happened.

About a year and a half ago, Rudy voyaged to Home Depot, where he bought all the materials for the job. These items have since solidified in their hot garage during the course of not one, but two sweltering Arizona summers.

What choices does Evelyn have? She could do the grouting herself. She could hire someone to do it next time Rudy goes on a business trip. Or... she could be ingenious, by implementing the following strategy.

Bright and early the next Saturday morning, Evelyn grabbed her purse and prepared to leave the house. "I'm going to be gone all day running errands and so forth," she told Rudy. "Thank you so much for doing the grout in the kitchen while I'm gone. I'm taking you out to dinner at Casa Escobar tonight for crab enchiladas and strawberry daiquiris to celebrate!"

Evelyn gave Rudy a big hug and kiss, thanked him again, called him "the best," and dashed out the door before he could even reply.

Rudy was totally perplexed as he watched Evelyn's blue Kia back down their driveway. She didn't seem mad at all, and this had been a really touchy subject with them for well over two years. The most confusing part was that for reasons unknown, Evelyn truly seemed to believe that it would happen that day.

Rudy settled in to watch Pepperdine versus LMU, his favorite snack in hand. But for the first time in his life, he couldn't focus on a basketball game. Despite himself, he began daydreaming about the sensational blue crab enchiladas and guacamole at Casa Escobar. This joint also served hot, homemade corn tortillas with melted queso, plus fantastic strawberry daiquiris, made with fresh, ripe strawberries and just a touch of lime.

That did it! Rudy just couldn't take it anymore! 15 minutes later, he somehow found himself in the grout aisle of Home Depot, where he bought all new supplies for the job. Later, he couldn't even remember driving there... it was almost as though he'd been hypnotized, but in a good way.

By the time Evelyn returned home at about seven, Rudy had already finished the grout. She thanked him and gushed over the beautiful counters and said he did a fantastic job.

They had a delicious dinner at Casa Escobar, complete with strawberry daiquiris, and Evelyn proudly bragged to their waitress about her gorgeous new kitchen counters.

Okay, folks, I freely admit this is a weird method; some might even call it bizarre. However, I've recommended it to quite a few friends over the years, and its success rate is just about 53 percent.

## Positive Template

This wonderful technique was taught to me by my amazing therapist, Laurie. In 2015, I was rather emotional because Andrea was planning to study abroad in France. Laurie asked when Andrea would be leaving, and I told her that it would be in five months. Laurie replied, "Okay, good, this gives us time to get you emotionally prepared."

I recall thinking, "What the heck is this?" I'd never before prepared emotionally for anything in my life. This concept was completely foreign to me. Things just happened, and then I dealt with them, often rather poorly.

Here's how the "positive template" works. Let's imagine your only daughter Tiffany is leaving for six months' study abroad in Italy.

You've seen the movie "Taken" four times, and well-meaning friends remind you what a dangerous place Italy can be. Isn't Italy where that American college student was wrongfully imprisoned for so many years? What if Tiffany loses her passport? What if she takes the wrong train and ends up in Milan instead of Florence? What if Tiffany's purse gets stolen in Rome? What if Tiffany becomes seriously ill or accidentally falls into a canal in Venice? Tiffany will be thousands of miles away, and will travel so much, some days you won't even be sure what country she's in.

Okay, here's how "positive template" works: you close your eyes (this works great just before you fall asleep) and visualize Tiffany getting on the plane, enjoying a delicious meal, encountering friendly flight attendants, a smooth flight, and an uneventful cab ride from the airport to her beautiful, clean, safe apartment in Italy.

You then envision Tiffany meeting her mature, sober and responsible roommates. You picture Tiffany happy and smiling, taking car trips, train trips, flights, even boat rides that are smooth and uneventful. You visualize Tiffany happy, healthy and safe.

And here is the key: you do this over and over again, at least ten times a day, for several months. This technique works somewhat like brainwashing, but in a really good way.

Then, when Tiffany actually does leave for her study abroad adventure, you're not in tears, you're not sad or worried. Instead, you're calm, happy for her, and cool as a little cucumber.

I personally attest to the power of this simple exercise. When Robert and I dropped off Andrea at the airport, I went in with her but was only allowed as far as the ticket counter.

Presto! No tears, no drama, nothing to make her feel guilty about leaving. A half hour later, I arrived at work, and several sympathetic co-workers stopped by my cubicle. They all hugged me and one actually patted the top of my head. They all were amazed I wasn't crying and how well I was handling the whole experience.

Imagine you and your husband must relocate from California to Missouri for his work. You've never lived in cold weather and are anxious about the change. You have never before driven in snow. Plus, you're leaving behind family and lifelong friends.

By utilizing the "positive template" technique, you become emotionally prepared for this major change in your life. It then makes the entire process easier and less of a strain on your marriage.

## Pull Your Share of the Load

This is kissing cousin to "picking up the slack." We recently rode the stagecoach at Knott's Berry Farm. I finagled a seat next to the driver to chat him up about – you guessed it – the horses. They were both beautiful; one a grey and the other a black bay. The driver pointed at the grey horse and said he was lazy and "never pulled his share of the load."

You knew I'd throw in an equine scenario someplace in this book, didn't you?

Much like two horses pulling a stagecoach, minus the hooves and tails of course, you and your spouse should ideally function as a team. Therefore, if one of you doesn't pull your share, it's unfair to the other partner and both of you ultimately suffer.

Let's now take a gander at two prime examples: money (dear Gussie, why is it always money?)... and that most gruesome of topics: housework.

Carol and Alan lived in Joplin, Missouri, and had been married for ten years. They had two children, Abby, age five and George, age nine. The agreement was that Carol would stay home to raise the kids, but when Abby began kindergarten, Carol would return to work.

Carol and Alan were not well-off by any means; countless sacrifices had been made to survive on just one income. Alan was thrilled that soon Carol could begin pulling a share of their financial load; they were barely managing on his assistant restaurant manager salary.

Alan felt keenly, as Carol did not, the absence of niceties such as dinners out and real vacations. He was tired of camping trips. He wanted to go to Hawaii. He wanted to eat out more often. Most of all, he was tired of juggling bills and barely getting by.

Unfortunately, there arose a major drawback: Carol avoided going back to work. She loved being a stay-home mom. She claimed to be looking for a job, but said she couldn't find anything. By the time Abby had finished her first semester of kindergarten, Carol hadn't even begun sending out resumes. Alan was very disappointed, and the two had several fruitless arguments.

Right about this time, Carol suddenly began talking about wanting a third child.

Alan didn't want more children. He might have, had they been able to afford it, but he and Carol had discussed this many times and both had agreed there was just no way.

It wouldn't require Sherlock Holmes to deduce Carol's sudden motivation for a third child. Alan felt betrayed that she wasn't "pulling her share of the load." It would be glorious to report this couple worked out their issues, but Carol is now very insistent on having another baby. Alan recently confided in his older brother that he feels deceived and for the first time is considering divorce.

Let's now view housework. Nobody *really* wants to do housework, now do they? But if you do, please move in with us Watsons. Robert knows I'd agree to a second wife *under the condition* she was a genuine Martha Stewart doppelganger and kept our house sheer perfection, plus of course those glorious recipes.

Grace and Joanne were in their late 20s, had only been married for one year and lived in Manhattan, New York. These two co-parented a small cinnamon poodle named Frida Kahlo. Their work schedules overlapped; when Grace returned home from her office, Joanne was scooting out the door. At her bougie restaurant server job, Joanne earned a minimum of $500 a night in tips. She generally returned home well after midnight, stayed awake until 2 a.m., then slept until noon the next day. She then spent most of her daytime hours gaming or watching movies on DVD or Netflix. She also took the fluffy Frida for short walks three or four times a day.

This "poodle parade" was the full extent of Joanne's contribution to the housework.

She never made the bed, took out the trash, or brought dirty clothes down to the corner Laundromat. When Grace returned home each evening, the kitchen was always a mess with dishes piled in the sink. Grace especially resented Joanne "forgetting" the laundry, since the corner Laundromat was kind of sketchy at night.

Prior to getting married, Joanne had lived with an older cousin, her brother and some guy from the restaurant. Their place had been a spectacular pigsty; all four had relished a kind of "disastrously messy" prestige. So, Joanne neither noticed nor cared if her living area was a complete disaster.

However, Grace cared very much about having a nice, tidy and clean apartment. She loved having things in order. So by Joanne ignoring the housework, she wasn't "pulling her share of the load."

What's a possible resolution for these two couples? Since theirs is an easier fix, let's first address Grace and Joanne. One possible solution would be to list all the tasks on a small paper on the fridge, then rotate these weekly.

I recall my college apartment: my three roommates and I divvied the drudgery into four sections: 1) vacuum 2) dust 3) scrub bathroom and kitchen and 4) oh, God only knows what four was!

I mean, this was the mid-80s, so you know it's been *a minute*. We used to play "Dynasty," that game where you take a swig of your drink whenever your character does. I always dreamed of being Linda Evans with the glorious big hair and shoulder pads, but every dang time I got stuck being John Forsythe. During commercials, we'd dance around to "Der Kommissar" and "She Blinded Me With Science." Perhaps it's best that the complete lack of technology back then made videos or snapchats impossible.

Now, back to the future!

For Grace and Joanne, let's just say job number 4 is laundry. If they rotate these jobs - remember we never use the word "chores" as it's so dreary - this makes it a little more equitable and hopefully less boring.

If Joanne won't pitch in no matter what, Grace might hire a cleaning person and find a laundry service, although this does cost. But hey! Joanne is making bank at her restaurant job, so hopefully, she'll be happy to kick in.

As for Carol and Alan, their situation is much more difficult. Even with all our sterling advances in technology, it's just not yet possible to give birth to only one-half of a baby. Perhaps couples' counseling will help as Carol is likely quite anxious about returning to work; addressing this issue may be beneficial.

# Passive-Aggressive

What are some of the top hallmarks of the passive-aggressive spouse? For starters, if you're married to one, you sure as heck won't know for certain if they're mad at you. You may have a tiny inkling, because out of nowhere, they may suddenly become extra nice. Often, it's a fake nice, kind of like saccharin or nowadays, maybe stevia.

The passive-aggressive spouse will avoid direct conflict at all costs. But eventually they'll say or do something on the sly to let you know they're unhappy. They're masters at the art of concealed aggression.

It's very difficult living with a passive-aggressive spouse. You may conclude you cannot trust them, and you're probably right.

By contrast, if you're married to someone who's direct, they may be really crabby from time to time, but at least you know where you stand with them. As Ben described his wife of 12 years, "Christina is a real bitch sometimes, oh my God she is, but I always know where I stand with her. She won't smile in my face and then stiletto me in the back."

Stanley and Annabelle live in Natchez, Mississippi, and have been married for 19 years. Annabelle is always agreeable, with a pleasant smile on her face. But it's all a big act. Inside, she's fuming. Stanley's inconsiderate and consistently takes her for granted. He frequently answers his phone right before dinner, so all her hard work goes to waste as their food gets cold. She especially fumes when he spends time on the phone with his brother. Stanley rarely remembers their anniversary, and he's painfully stingy to boot.

Annabelle has been furious about these and other transgressions since 2007, three years after they got married. So, she's been irate for about 16 years. That's nearly two decades, folks! Stanley treated her well at the beginning of their marriage, but when he realized she wouldn't speak up for herself, he became progressively lazier as the sorry years passed.

But she never says a word, not one word.

You guessed it: passive-aggressive and martyr-like behaviors often walk hand in hand.

No doubt Stanley's behavior is inconsiderate. But if Annabelle actually called him out, perhaps he'd improve. But she just gets back at him in sneaky ways. For example, instead of telling Stanley to get off the phone so they can eat dinner, she makes a lot of noise in the background. This was more of an issue before cell phones, when Stanley couldn't escape. Nowadays, he goes out onto the front porch so he can talk uninterrupted. However, since this couple lives in Mississippi, summers are 100 degrees with 90 percent humidity. June through August, Stanley can either sit on the front porch and swelter, or go inside and deal with Annabelle.

Often after he gets off the phone, there's an argument and Stanley berates Annabelle for embarrassing him during his phone call. This is when she "plays dumb."

So, how does one deal with a passive-aggressive spouse? Unfortunately, if called out on their behavior, they will nearly always deny it.

Why is Annabelle this way? Possibly, she doesn't have the confidence to confront Stanley directly. Perhaps, like many women, she was raised to be polite and pleasant and was made to feel that expressing anger is unfeminine.

This personality type is unlikely to change because behavior like this is very ingrained, often since childhood. If one looks back at Annabelle's upbringing, not surprisingly, she was raised in a household where she wasn't permitted to speak up when upset.

Therapy might help someone like Annabelle find her voice. Couples therapy would be beneficial as well. The therapist would likely tell Stanley to encourage her to speak up and communicate with him.

## Pretend it's 1985

You may be asking yourself, "Just what in the heck is she talking about? Why 1985?"

1985, it ain't no jive! Oh wait, jive was from the 70s! Well, too late now, it's already out there!

In 1985, I graduated college, met Robert, and began a career. Can we even call it a career? Frankly, it was a mediocre job for $1,200 a month with no benefits, but hey, it was in the entertainment industry, so glamour outweighed any need for groceries. Plus, gas was a dollar a gallon... I am bitterly sobbing as I write this! $1,200 sure went further in those days!

In 1985, technology as we now know it did not exist. Sure, there were computers, but they took up an entire city block, and virtually no one could operate one. Also, there were no such things as cell phones, social media, texting, emails or cameras on phones.

You've got to wonder how we even survived!

For you youngsters who weren't even alive then, or were just tiny little cupcakes back in 1985, I'm gonna tell you how it was.

If you planned to meet a friend at the movie theatre at 7 pm, you just had to show up.

Unless you were dead or in a coma, your friend expected you to be there. No way to reach them to say you were running late. No texting to say you had just parked the car, and were heading over. If your friend didn't show up, you just assumed they were stuck in traffic and you people-watched while waiting.

But we did it. As Robert's amazing cousin says, "Somehow, we made it work." It was great back then, absolutely it was, but most folks wouldn't want to go back to that time 100 percent, myself included.

Nonetheless, there's something to be said for spending a day every so often minus technological distractions of any kind.

Let's just say like most folks, you work full-time. Your normal job entails sitting in front of a computer eight or nine hours a day, every day.

Unexpectedly, you get a rare day off during the middle of the week.

In the past, on your precious days off, perhaps you spent time on Instagram, Facebook, and also checking emails and text messages. So, it wasn't really a true day off, was it? Your little face was still peering at a screen.

Maybe next time, instead relax at the beach or sit in a chaise lounge in your backyard with a nice iced tea and a good book. Or, perhaps watch a movie at a theatre or at home. Or meet a friend for lunch; your primary activities are the food and conversation. If you must wait for your friend to show up, or they leave the table for the restroom, instead of making an immediate grab for your cell phone, just sit there. What a concept! Just sit there! Maybe chat with your waitress, enjoy a little people-watching, or just relax.

I've recommended this to several stressed-out friends over the years. They thought it was weird, but they gave it a try, probably just to humor me, but then were surprised how much they loved it. They felt very weird doing it, but in a good way. Everyone admitted to a brief cheat here or there throughout the day; sometimes it was unavoidable, such as checking their phone because their friend was texting a time of arrival.

So how does one "Pretend it's 1985" for a day? The concept is quite simple. For just one day, perhaps even once a week, literally pretend you are living in the dark ages, aka the year 1985 (by the way, please feel free to substitute another year if you so prefer).

Stay off your computer, stay off your cell phone, don't check the stock market, and wait until tomorrow to check your emails or social media.

Easier said than done, I know!

Now, let's reveal an additional benefit. If you're in the dating world and your boyfriend is rather apathetic about your relationship, just see how truly powerful it can be when he hears not one single peep from you all day long. If you normally text or message him regularly, then for an entire day he hears "nada," this may just get him off his duffy. He'll wonder where you've gone to, and that's not necessarily a bad thing.

Maybe this will even force him to go "old school" and drive past your house even though he knows you're not home.

A brief warning: if you're normally very active on social media, a few friends may reach out to you by the end of the day. They may fear you've been abducted by aliens, or unexpectedly hospitalized.

Bonus points if you also listen to 80s tunes on this day: Cyndi Lauper, Billy Idol, Spandau Ballet, Annie Lennox, Simple Minds, Tears for Fears, Sade, Bryan Adams, Boy George, Springsteen, Scorpions, U2, just to name a few.

To toss a little 70s into the frozen yogurt, let's just say it again: "1985, and that ain't no jive!"

## Positive Affirmations

Here are a few positive statements you can make to your partner:

- "I appreciate you so much."
- "I'm lucky to have you in my life."
- "It's so great having such a smart husband."
- "Our kids are lucky to have such a smart mom."
- "I appreciate that you work so hard at your job."
- "Thank you for the excellent dinner."
- "Our kids have such a great dad."

These all sound cheesy, don't they? But folks rarely complain when they hear something complimentary. Au contraire, most people simply *adore* the recognition.

Unhappily married folks generally complain about feeling unloved, unappreciated, and taken for granted.

Most of us love hearing positive affirmations. Try a couple on for size with your spouse and see the results.

# Q

---

## Quality Time

It's tough for parents of small kids to get "couple time." Gary and Julie, our success couple who raised six children, say it's best to give kids a firm bedtime and make them stick to it. Otherwise, those little dynamos are still awake at 11:15 p.m., chock-full of energy. Of course they are! It's that electric youth.

How can a couple get quality time? Here are some suggestions from happily married folks:

- At home: after the kids are asleep, talk in bed for a few minutes uninterrupted. Try to stay awake long enough to finish two entire sentences. Cook dinner together unless you get on each others' nerves sharing the kitchen.

- Out of the house: seeing movies, dinners out, hotel getaways, car shows, art exhibits or museums. Walks on the beach or at the park don't cost a cent.

- Getting stoned together and watching a funny show on Netflix came up more than a few times.

- Note: running errands together in the car while one looks at Tik Tok and the other curses the lousy traffic ain't exactly quality time.

Bo and Geoff, a success couple who raised two daughters, always made time for date nights, romantic dinners out, and even when they had to scrimp, trips back to their beloved Ireland. Pamela and Craig took fun trips to Disneyland and Southern California with their kids, plus frequent date nights. Both couples attribute these outings to their current success with "empty nest" status.

Even just 15 minutes sitting on the couch in the evening, holding hands and talking can keep you close.

## Queen

This chapter was created to give all you men out there some sure-fire ammo on how to butter up your wife and keep her a happy lady who's fun and easy to live with. So stay tuned, don't change the channel, you're going to get some real insider tips!

Simply stated, a woman loves feeling like a queen. No doubt about this whatsoever.

Gentlemen, if you treat your wife like royalty, she's more likely to be content. Now it doesn't take a rocket scientist to ascertain that happy women make married life smoother and easier for their lucky husbands.

Guys, let's just cut to the chase: I am going to tell it like it is. If you make her feel like a queen, chances are simply excellent she's gonna want to have sex with you *much more often*.

There, I've gone and said it! That right there is the bottom line.

So, how do you make your wife feel like a queen? Here are some tips provided by happily married women who claim these work like magic.

1.  Buy her flowers. In a word, women love them. If you're married to that very rare woman who truly does not appreciate flowers, surely you will think of a substitute, such as candy. But, by and large, you cannot go wrong with flowers.

2.  Open doors for her...lots of doors, including the car door. We realize this is a dying art, but it's a terrific show of gallantry. Rise above mediocrity and graciously open doors for your lady. Help her bring in the groceries and take the initiative! Don't wait to be asked.

3.  Frequently compliment her beauty: use the actual term "beautiful." Not "pretty," not "cute," sure you can toss these in sometimes, but *beautiful*. There is no substitute for this word. Trust me on this. Dr. Linda knows women, so believe me when I say this: ladies love to be called beautiful. You almost cannot overdo this. Think of it this way: if those lucky gals who are legitimate knockouts still sometimes feel homely, chubby, or bloated, just imagine how average women feel. We still live in a world where women are judged on their appearance. It sucks, but that's the way it is. Gifting her with this compliment will make her feel wonderful. In summation, the word "beautiful" is just a glorious thing for a lady to hear.

4.  If you and your wife are at the cinema, and someone is being rude and loud, or shining their cell phone right in your face, do speak up. Do not wait for your wife to be the one. If she has to do it, she will look at you as being less manly and you will lose respect. We realize this is not in keeping with today's mores, but the fact is women like a man who's going to speak up when necessary, and not be a "little wussy."

When you treat a woman with love, gallantry and respect and shower her with little gifts and compliments, true, you're doing this for her, but kind of more importantly, for yourself.

This is because a woman who feels cherished and adored will generally be warmer and more affectionate toward you, and therefore — presto! Your life just got a whole lot easier.

## Quickie

This topic is so crucial it's featured in several places throughout this book. Let's just sum it up in one sentence, shall we?

"Honey, Trevor and Adelaide are finally asleep and we've got 22 minutes until "Criminal Minds" starts! C'mon! Let's do this!"

For couples with small children, finding the time and privacy for an extended lovemaking session may seem well nigh impossible.

Therefore, let us present here the delightful and agreeable "quickie."

As Johnathan, who has a nine-month-old son and a two-year-old daughter explains, "My wife and I both work full-time, plus we have a baby and a toddler. Oh, and did I neglect to mention, our baby gets colic frequently. Gone are those days when we actually had leisurely sex. Nowadays, the best we can hope for is 14 minutes. And even then it's only if by some miracle, both kids are asleep at the same time. But this keeps us close and it's a thousand times better than nothing."

So, although the quickie is not always ideal, it does maintain the physical connection which is so important for a couple.

If sex only happens when the stars align, when the romantic backdrop is perfect, well then, maybe it will never actually occur. Maybe not until the kids hit middle school!

It should be noted that unhappily married men complained about a lack of sex far more frequently than did unhappily married women.

Here's what happens when a couple stops having sex *at least* once or twice a week. When we say "stops," we are talking about more than a few weeks going by without. A couple begins to lose that romantic connection and morphs into business partners.

Rarely does this affect both partners equally. One spouse generally takes this harder and feels rejected, slighted or ignored. Perhaps the other partner misses sex, but has found a way to turn it off, or was less interested to begin with.

So, after awhile, the rejected one starts humming this song, "We've lost that loving feeling, oohh that loving feeling, we've lost that loving feeling now it's gone gone gone... whoooo."

Okay, enough singing! I'm so sorry! No quitting my day job... I promise!

Beth and Jayden had been married for five years with an energetic three-year-old son, Oliver. After the birth of little Oliver, their sex life had dwindled sharply and had never revived. Nowadays, Beth and Jayden rarely, if ever, had sex anymore. Sometimes two months went by without. When Jayden made overtures, he was usually turned down. Beth always had an excuse; by the time Oliver was four, Jayden had almost given up initiating romance.

Beth's stated reason was she just couldn't find the energy. She told her girlfriends there was just no time for sex. Her girlfriends sympathized, because that's what girlfriends do best.

As for Jayden, he felt increasingly frustrated and neglected. When he complained, Beth said she was just too tired. Now, we get it, Beth! You have a small child. But you also only work part-time. Do you mean there's really no way you can't squeeze an extra hour or two out of your *entire week*? *Really?*

Beth maintains there will be time for sex later. Well, when will that be, Beth? Later may never come. Or if it's 40 years later, Jayden may not be quite up for it, no pun intended, even with the sterling chemical enhancements the world of science surely will have created by that time.

I will just put it out there by saying married individuals who feel neglected in the sex department sometimes do stray. This is not to condone infidelity, by the way. But the marriage package is supposed to include sex. When someone gets married, one of the perks is supposed to be lots of intimacy.

At least, the expectation is that there will be a *decent amount* of sex. If a married person doesn't even get that, and this holds true for either gender, eventually they feel gypped, kind of like that proverbial boat without a paddle.

Now, let's get back to the topic of the "quickie." Imagine you're not really in the mood. Maybe you've got indigestion, your boss was in a foul mood at work and you're stressed out. But remember, maybe this is for your partner. You may not *really* be in the mood, but perhaps just give it the "old college try." You may find that you get into it after a little while; maybe not, but you've made your partner happy.

Not to detract from romance, but there's a practical aspect to all this. If you can become a "quickie" expert, oh Lordy, this is a skill like no other.

Learning to get into the mood rapidly and focusing on results may sound unromantic and businesslike, but this benefits your marriage in a multitude of ways.

I'm no longer mortified by the story which follows because so many years have passed, so what the heck, I'll share it here.

In 1997, Robert and I were out on a date. I'd recently read a magazine article which described couples with small children whose romantic lives had gone kaput.

Therefore, on our way home from the movies, I suggested a quickie in the car. Robert mentioned it was freezing, as it was December, which here in San Diego means it could have even been as cold as 60 degrees, but I was undeterred. I kept thinking about that depressing magazine article.

No one thinks it gets very cold here in Southern California, but in actuality, it was only *58 degrees* that night and very dry. It was the pinnacle of static cling season. I mention the weather only because it's an integral part of the story.

I was wearing a Christmas sweater, black leggings, black pointy flats and pale-green, knee-high stockings. How do I say this, but afterwards, I couldn't find one of my knee-high stockings anywhere in the car. The next day was a Saturday and Robert said he could wash and vacuum the car and would find the stocking.

When we returned home, as I was paying our red-headed babysitter Jessica, she wore the oddest expression on her adorable little face and kept glancing over my right shoulder. I had no idea why.

Robert was driving Jessica home, and after they'd left, I went to the bedroom to get undressed. Presto! There was my pale-green stocking, clinging for dear life to the back of my sweater.

"Wee ginge Jessica" was only 14 at the time, plus a church kid, but after all, she was an A student and therefore what the Germans call "no stupnackel."

To say that I was mortified is putting it mildly; of course, Robert thought it was just hilarious.

So, don't discount the idea of a quickie in the car, but do beware of static cling season!

# R

## Respect

Listening to your spouse is one way to display respect. My friend Clare created a private buzzword to get her busy husband's full attention. This worked so well for Clare I copied this. You can invent your own buzzword or borrow mine, which is "pomegranate."

Privacy is another way to show respect. Plenty of husbands and wives read each others' emails and text messages. This can spell doom, as the following story shall illustrate.

Ben had a gorgeous fiancée named Melissa. The two had just moved in together and were planning their wedding. Ben had been crazy about Melissa from the moment they'd met. But six months later, his feet were freezing faster than if he'd been ice fishing in Alaska.

The reason was that Melissa was spying on him, and didn't realize he was on to her. Ben frequently changed the password on his phone and the combination on his briefcase, not because he was hiding something, but because Melissa was – pardon the expression – really starting to piss him off.

Folks, unless your stealth and espionage skills rival Liam Neeson's in the movie "Taken," your partner likely has known for quite awhile you've been poking around their things.

One day, Ben came into work extremely aggravated. He'd walked in on Melissa fiddling with the combination on his locked briefcase. While they were arguing, she accused him of changing the combination on the case. The only reason he'd done this was because he was sick of her riffling through his things.

Ben told us, "Since she already thinks I'm cheating on her, maybe I should just go ahead and do it."

This is not good, folks. And Ben immediately said he didn't mean it. But perhaps it's human nature to feel like if someone doesn't trust you, after all, what have you got to lose?

Ben and Melissa married anyways, despite his misgivings. He hoped that once they were married, she'd feel secure and know that she could trust him.

Melissa was so beautiful she took your breath away, and Ben was completely in love with her. But sadly, she had so many insecurities, and their getting married didn't alleviate these in the least, as Ben had hoped. A mere four months into their marriage, she accused him of sleeping with one of her single girlfriends.

Melissa and Ben divorced less than one year later.

Here are some ways happily married folks show respect for their partner.

- Never spy through your partner's texts, emails, wallet, purse, or briefcase.

- Listen when your partner speaks and be a good audience.

- If your partner tells you something in confidence, don't repeat it. Do not tell "just one person."

- Compliment and appreciate your partner for the person they are, not just their accomplishments.

- Don't compare your partner to other people unless it shows them in a favorable light. Your husband can easily live without the knowledge that Sally's husband earns twice what he does and rises each day at four a.m. to hit the gym.

- Tell your partner you're proud of them and praise them in front of others (your children especially).

- Okay, ding ding ding! This one is huge. Avoid nonverbal signs of disrespect such as heavy sighing and rolling of eyes. This is even more horrific and horridious, as the Brits say, when done in front of others, most particularly your children.

- Don't interrupt your partner when they're telling a story. Of course, this can be deeply challenging if they're repeating themselves, or just plain boring you.

- If your spouse is repeating a story, even though you've heard it countless times, avoid pointing this out. If you've been married for over five years, chances are excellent you've heard all their best stories a minimum of 471 times.

Robert has probably heard 201 times how my friends and I got suspended from our religious college and booted off campus for three days. He's likely petrified with boredom, but I must say, does a sensational job of concealing it. I've heard 202 times how a customer threw a chocolate shake at him at his Baskin Robbins job, but I love the story and so haven't really gotten tired of it yet.

As your spouse drones on, just smile and think of Mother England. Remember Mother England? We touched on her in the orgasm section. If your spouse is relaying a story you've heard two million times, just remember that you can always create a Trader Joe's list in your head as you appear to be listening intently.

## Rough Spot

During the 12 years I worked for the same company, here's what I told my newly married co-workers. In a year or two, maybe five years, you'll hit a rough spot. It happens to *every* married couple at some point.

In the beginning, you were so in love, so completely enraptured that you couldn't even sleep at night. How wonderful your partner was! They were sheer perfection. Just being with them was like oxycontin flowing gloriously throughout your veins. They were your dream come true. No one had ever been in love the way you were. This angel was put on earth just for you.

Well, now, a little time has passed. Maybe something big and bad went wrong, or perhaps it was just the grubbiness of everyday life.

Whatever it is, you were living the dream, but baby, now you're wide awake.

You may even feel kind of betrayed because you're just not that crazy about them anymore. Worst of all, maybe you're not even sure why. Perhaps they did something stupid, or it's just that their creepy little habits are working your last nerve. You're beginning to wonder what you ever saw in them in the first place.

For whatever reason, they're driving you absolute bonkers. Or, maybe you're just now realizing...they're kind of boring. Perhaps you made a colossal error marrying them in the first place.

But...know that you are not alone! This ties in closely with the "alien" chapter, by the way, and happens at some point to *every single* married person on the planet.

When this sad and harsh reality smacks you right in the face, I beg you, please, please, please talk to someone who's been happily married for a long time. They'll empathize with you, listen to you, sympathize with you, but are very unlikely to tell you to give up.

One quick disclaimer: if one partner is being physically abused by the other, this advice to hang in there during a rough spot flies right out of the window.

## Resilience

By the time a couple reaches their 50s, they've usually overcome some major misfortunes such as job losses, health issues, passing of a parent, and so forth. Resilience is defined as "the capacity to recover quickly from difficulties; toughness," and also "the ability of a substance or object to spring back into shape; elasticity."

So...how exactly does one acquire this invaluable resilience? For starters, confiding in one's spouse, friend, or trusted relative can be essential.

This is the polar opposite to how many of us were raised. My parents' generation tended to "suck it up" and keep problems to themselves. After all, they lived through the Great Depression. They weren't accustomed to having things easy.

But stuffing down stress and unhappiness often leads to substance abuse, emotional eating, and alcoholism. So, for most folks, reaching out for help and support is crucial.

Many happily married folks describe themselves as possessing a resolved mindset; they're determined to overcome difficult situations.

It's far easier to remain positive when the job's fantastic, the kids are a breeze, you and your spouse are simpatico, and life's going just swimmingly.

It's entirely another matter when you've lost your job, the car breaks down and you've no cash to fix it, your punk-ass kid is flunking out of school, and your spouse is driving you nuts.

Here are some tips from happily married couples:

- Write down your thoughts and feelings in a journal. Vent about what frustrates you, either your spouse or life in general.

- Jot down a few notes in a gratitude journal every day.

- Write a letter when you're angry with someone; perhaps rather than mailing it, shred or burn it later.

- See a therapist if needed.

- Forgive yourself when you screw up, brush yourself off, and move on.

In the late 80s I worked in real estate and had a very smart boss named Ron. One day I made a colossal mistake, and kept kicking myself. Ron gave me advice I still remember to this day. He told me, "Stop blaming yourself, and move on. Dumb people make the same mistakes over and over. Smart people make mistakes, but they learn from them. Don't stay mad at yourself; but don't make the same mistake again."

Forgiveness and resiliency are very tightly enmeshed. Sometimes it's easier to forgive others than it is to forgive yourself.

But, no doubt about it, forgiveness of others can certainly be challenging as well. Let's say your spouse does something really foolish, the consequences of which can last for many years.

Pittsburgh couple Joanie and Peter were in their late 30s and had been married for seven years when Peter received a DUI. The irony was that Peter wasn't even a drinker. The most he normally consumed was a beer or two on the weekend. Peter received the DUI driving home from happy hour with his co-workers. Several were heavy drinkers; their favorite beverages were tequila or bourbon shots.

Peter rarely joined them, but since Joanie was away on a business trip, he thought he'd have dinner and maybe just one beer.

Unfortunately, the bar was packed, and the wait for food was very long. While waiting for his dinner, Peter somehow got talked into doing three Patron shots. He hadn't eaten anything since noon. Since he wasn't used to drinking, he didn't realize how hard the shots had hit him. On his drive home, when a cop pulled him over for an unsafe lane change, Peter failed a breathalyzer test, was put into handcuffs and arrested.

In Pittsburgh, penalties are severe for a first DUI. Peter faced a possible six months' jail time, a maximum $5,000 fine, and potential loss of his driver's license for one year. This last would have been catastrophic, as he worked in outside sales and drove all day to see his clients.

Peter and Joanie found an attorney who prevented jail time and loss of Peter's driver's license, but the total cost was over $7,000.00. This completely drained their savings account and they had to put the last $2,000 on a credit card.

Peter was also required to attend alcohol safety classes and have a breathalyzer device installed in his car.

Joanie was absolutely furious. She pointed out to Peter that he'd been making judgy comments about his hard-drinking co-workers for years, but now he was the one with the DUI.

Two things turned their situation around for the better. First, Peter found a second job on the weekends working at a sporting goods store.

Thanks to this extra job, within five months he had replenished their savings account. Secondly, Joanie was able to accomplish something extremely difficult, which was to truly forgive Peter. She told him she wouldn't ever bring it up again, and she kept that promise.

When asked how they got through tough times, our success story couples listed qualities such as gratitude, humor, forgiveness, and drawing strength from their partner.

It's noteworthy to add: maintaining a sense of humor was mentioned by almost every couple.

## Religion

I already touched on this subject in the "faith" segment, so this will be brief.

Some couples find harmony and greater closeness through their church or religion. Those who are very involved with their church say this gives them a spiritual base as well as social connections. Our success story couple Lynn and Larry are very involved in their church and have made many wonderful friends there.

Church membership can certainly be a positive, but can also have disadvantages. Some couples felt judged by fellow parishioners when their teenagers became pregnant or got hooked on drugs. However, other friends in similar circumstances received overwhelming love and support from church friends.

Like any friends, church pals can be kind, loving, and supportive, or two-faced, disloyal and "judgy."

Don't let anyone bully you if church isn't your bag, or you aren't part of an organized religion. Faith is very personal and it's not for one person to impose on another.

If your marriage is in trouble, or you're going through any type of struggles, praying together can strengthen your bond.

Note: if your spouse is driving you nuts, don't be surprised to hear yourself devoutly and fervently praying, "God, give me strength."

# Romance

My first two horses, Terra and Shiloh, have now both galloped over that rainbow bridge to greener pastures. While they were with us, for years I'd joke that the most romantic thing Robert did was get up early every morning to feed them. Particularly when it was cold or raining, this meant more than flowers, candy or jewelery...although face it, those things are nice too!

Romance means different things to different folks. To her it might mean flowers, candy, or a nice dinner out. Baseball games, fishing, or a big steak dinner might spell romance to him.

But of course, we can't assume just based upon gender what spells romance to someone.

On his third date with Sheila, Steve thought it would be romantic if they walked on the beach and saw the sunset. It was what he imagined a woman would enjoy. After they'd walked for ten minutes or so, she wanted to turn around. When he asked about the sunset, she shrugged. He realized pretty fast his idea of romance did not coincide with hers. But incidentally, this couple is still married; they just don't often walk on the beach.

Think of ways to spoil your partner and bring more romance to your relationship. Don't make the common error of spoiling them with things that you yourself would enjoy. Instead, do things for them or buy presents that *they* will love.

Does your partner prefer gifts or experiences? If they don't much care about material things, you may want to save your hard-earned cash.

When Susan and Blake had been married for three years, she surprised him with a Rolex watch for his birthday. Susan was a San Francisco realtor and the watch represented half the commission from a house she'd sold. She herself absolutely loved expensive watches and jewelry.

Blake, on the other hand, didn't much care about fancy things. Material possessions meant almost nothing to him. What he really enjoyed was traveling.

Blake thanked Susan politely for the watch. He wore it every day for awhile, but thereafter, forgot to wear it unless reminded. When his brother kidded that Blake and Susan could have visited Europe for three weeks with the $10,000 the watch had cost, Blake laughed and agreed.

Poor Susan had made the unfortunate mistake we've all made with gifts. She bought her husband something *she* liked and *she* wanted, but it wasn't something he particularly cared about. He would have far greatly preferred a trip.

## Restless

Much of this topic was already covered in our "bored" section. But restlessness is a real thing with countless married folks, so I'm going to address it here just a little further.

Here in San Diego, a new billboard recently popped up on the 8 freeway, promoting a prominent local divorce attorney. The billboard was most attractive. The caption read, "Baby I'm sure bored," and it included the attorney's toll-free number and website address.

Here's some food for thought: if you're single, who is there to blame if your life is a - pardon the expression - crashing bore? Short answer: you can only really blame yourself. But if you're married, ah well, that's different... now you've got someone to point the finger at.

If you're restless, dissatisfied or just plain old bored, perhaps it's not because of your spouse. Well, maybe it's partly them. But, it's possible you're also experiencing *ennui* with yourself.

If you get no time away from your partner, after awhile you may feel really stifled. We shall address the all-important issue of space in our next section. If you're not pursuing your dreams, or at least keeping them alive until you're able to bring them to reality, you may feel dissatisfied and unfulfilled.

Quick note: 99.9 percent of married folks have felt restless in their marriage at some point. If a "married forever" pal feeds you a line of baloney that they've never felt antsy, ha! They are fibbing! They are, "Liar, liar, pants on fire! Hanging from a telephone wire!"

Now, let's take a look at some common signs you're feeling restless in your marriage.

- You feel like you're trapped or bored.

- You pick fights with your spouse.

- Little things your spouse does *really* bug you lately.

- Oddly enough, these same things never used to bother you.

- You begin reminiscing fondly about your ex, even though he or she was an absolute schmuck.

- You feel irritable for no reason.

- You fantasize about another life, or about being single again.

- It seems life is passing you by.

- You feel old before your time.

- Many of your friends or acquaintances seem to be having more fun than you.

- You feel you could do more with your life if your spouse wasn't tying you down like some big old albatross.

- You develop a crush on a cute friend or hot co-worker.

- You fantasize about getting down and dirty with that same cute friend or hot co-worker.

If you're experiencing any of these symptoms, please wait before calling the doctor. You can probably remedy this current "itch" on your own.

Max and Annabelle had been married for four years. They had a one-year-old son named Gunner, owned their own home and both had great jobs. Max worked in sales and Annabelle worked from home; in this way, Gunner didn't need day-care.

Max had so much to be thankful for; everyone liked Annabelle and said he was the luckiest guy. He loved Annabelle so much and knew he was fortunate to have married her. Therefore, he felt horribly guilty how restless he'd become after just four short years of marriage. Max spent all his spare time fantasizing about his gorgeous, sexy, vivacious co-worker Gina. Gina was 27 and single, spent most of her time skiing, bungee jumping, zip lining, and taking frequent weekend trips. Although he was only five years older than Gina, Max felt like an old man by comparison. Gina loved to visit him at his cube in her short skirts and four-inch heels and she sat on his desk, twirling her long blonde hair.

Prior to Gunner's birth, Max and Annabelle had both loved traveling more than anything else. Europe had been their top destination. In fact, Max had proposed to Annabelle on the Eiffel Tower. Planning trips had once been one of their favorite activities. They also loved poring over their photo albums and reminiscing about their trips.

Now however, their biggest excursions were Chuck E Cheese on the weekends for pizza, screaming kids and the same exhausted parents at every single party. It had been at least a year since they'd cracked open one of their travel photo albums.

Max and Annabelle perfectly illustrate the strain experienced by young couples when they spend no time without their kids. Like many young parents, their entire lives revolved around their child. Most of their friends operated this way, so they hadn't really made a conscious decision. It was just a lifestyle they'd fallen into.

Fortunately, Max spoke up to Annabelle and confided his feelings of restlessness.

Luckily, Max's mom didn't raise no dummy, as he wisely omitted any mention of Gina, his office crush.

To his surprise, Annabelle said she'd been feeling much the same way.

After a long discussion, they realized their number one priority was to return to Europe. They were realistic, however, that this could not happen immediately.

Annabelle and Max then came up with a firm plan to return to Europe in three years. They opted for fall, their favorite time, since Gunner wouldn't start kindergarten until the following year.

They then opened a special savings account just for the Europe trip and planned to save enough money so Annabelle's older sister could accompany them to help watch Gunner.

From that point on, they had a "bon voyage" party once a week after Gunner was asleep. Annabelle and Max drank a glass of their favorite French or Italian wine, planned their upcoming trip and looked at photos from their two other European holidays.

The death of a dream is unutterably sad, but rebirth of hope is beautiful and miraculous. Now that Max and Annabelle had revived their dream of travel, this completely transformed their marriage.

This couple did a lot of things right. Number one, Max communicated with his wife. Mind you, he didn't over-communicate by spilling the beans about his office crush, which turned out to be fleeting anyways, as it was just a symptom of the larger issue. Annabelle listened to him and made him feel heard. Then, they both worked together to find a solution.

Parents of small children may often feel restless with their spouse. They may think they chose the wrong partner, when in fact it's much more complicated. Instead, they may be sentimental for their youth and carefree "good old days."

Don't assume your restlessness is the fault of your spouse or that you married the wrong person.

## Regret

Half the proceeds from this book are to help horses, but you may have noticed there's actually very little mention of horses here. Muy poquito!

This is due to the "golf syndrome." What, you might ask, is the golf syndrome? Well, let's just say I ask someone, "Do you like horses?" If their response is half-hearted, my blabbering on about horses to them would be like them talking golf to me all day long.

We both would be crashing bores and putting each other to sleep.

However, let's toss in a quick horse story as it beautifully illustrates the concept of regret. Our two wild horses are Malibu, age 4, and Mirlo, age 8. Our third horse, Jasmine, age 2, is a paint.

So, our "Three Equine Musketeers" are all youngsters. Nonetheless, if they all live to be age 40, not one single minute of their lives would have been wasted on regret. It's simply not any part or parcel of their makeup.

The other day, Malibu was eating some carrots out of my hand; I wasn't paying attention, and he almost bit my finger.

Luckily for me, Malibu realized in time, and avoided biting me. However, let's just envision a grim scenario where I'd been badly injured, as in going from ten fingers to nine. Malibu likely would have experienced momentary concern, but ten minutes later, would have been munching hay in the pasture with blissful abandon.

But we humans, ah, we're another species entirely. Most of us live with regret, often over mistakes made aeons ago, and many folks spend their lives virtually crippled with remorse.

How does this translate to your marriage?

Well, let's just say you made a decision which "f'd up" things for the both of you.

Sheila and Bruce have been married for 13 years. Three years ago, Sheila's company relocated to Arizona. Bruce disliked the Arizona heat, and their sons Sam and Jackson didn't want to leave their friends. Nonetheless, the company offered Sheila a hefty moving allowance and a decent promotion, so she convinced Bruce to move.

After selling their San Diego townhouse, Sheila and Bruce bought a house in Phoenix three times larger, with a huge backyard and the obligatory swimming pool. Everything was peachy for eleven months, though the boys disliked their new school and Bruce hated the heat.

Then, without warning, Sheila's company did a massive layoff and she lost her job. She was absolutely devastated. She'd worked there nine years, ever since finishing grad school. She and Bruce tried to return to

San Diego, but found they couldn't afford it. Townhouses similar to their old one had increased $140,000 in value; not to mention, Sheila was no longer employed.

Sheila regretted everything: leaving San Diego, selling their townhouse instead of renting it out, and most particularly, relocating without an employment contract.

Before they'd moved, Sheila's brother Phil had told her flatly that she was foolish to relocate without an employment contract. Sheila had been complacent, so sure the company couldn't live without her, that at the time, this had seemed like paranoid thinking.

Now, of course, she realized her brother had been absolutely right.

They were stuck in Arizona, for the foreseeable future at least, and it was all her fault. Bruce did not blame her, but Sheila just kept kicking herself.

We've all been there, haven't we? We know we ought to dust ourselves off, forgive ourselves and move on. But we keep kicking ourselves about our dreadful mess-up.

Fast-forward three years. Sheila found a job she actually liked far better than the first. Their sons had made solid friends and had adjusted; Phoenix was now their home. Bruce had persuaded his mom to relocate from Pennsylvania to Phoenix, and the hot, dry weather had completely cured her bronchitis.

In the end, this was a good move for them all. But the years Sheila had spent blaming herself and regretting everything were years she could never get back.

If there's something you've done, some mistake you've made, forgive yourself.

Life is short; too dang short for regrets.

Of course, like many things, this is easier said than done.

What are some methods to eliminate regret from your life and become more carefree?

The first step is self-forgiveness. Think of something you've really bungled; if you're like me, there have been several things over the years. Look at yourself in the mirror and say out loud, "I'm moving on." Keep reminding yourself that it's ancient history. Say this often enough and you'll start to believe it.

Even if you're not a churchgoer, if you believe God loves you and can forgive anything, this can take a big weight off your shoulders.

This is cheesy for sure, but when I'm being hard on myself, I stroke my arm and say out loud, "I'm doing the best I can." Also perhaps try a "cutting the cord" guided meditation; there are several fantastic ones on YouTube to choose from.

Our Watson family motto is: "Never look back, always look forward." I don't kick myself anymore about mistakes I've made, because it accomplishes nothing.

If I kicked myself for every dang dumb mistake I've ever made, I could flamboyantly propel myself from San Diego, California to Milwaukee, Wisconsin and then I could regret eating one single piece of cheese.

# S

## Space

This isn't the slightest bit sarcastic, but who here has experienced the unbridled joy of a clingy, possessive, and insecure partner?

What are some hallmarks of this personality type? They likely resent your hobbies and become jealous when you spend time with your friends. They may lurk in the background eavesdropping when you're on the telephone. When you run errands, they insist on accompanying you although you really just wanted to go alone.

The partner who "steals your space" is going to smother you worse than Hollandaise sauce on eggs Benedict, with or without capers. This can be sheer misery, particularly if you cherish friendships and your alone time.

Now beware! If you allow them to, the partner who steals your space will suck the life right out of you just like air from a helium balloon.

But don't forget: you have control over this.

How does that saying go? "Don't blame someone for sucking the life out of you when you keep giving them the straw."

Valerie and Wayne lived in Philadelphia and had been married for just two years. When they'd first dated, she'd congratulated herself on finding someone who loved spending so much time with her. It was flattering and made her feel cherished. If perhaps Wayne was a teeny bit clingy, Valerie assured herself it was only because he was so crazy about her.

When Valerie's best friend Wendy predicted Wayne would smother her, Valerie assumed Wendy was just the tiniest bit jealous.

Once they were married, however, Valerie did begin to feel stifled. Wayne wanted to do *everything* together. He brought lunch to her office several times a week. If she went shopping with a girlfriend, he insisted on dropping her off, and then he ran errands. Sometimes, he'd even wait for her in his car outside the Shops at Liberty Place mall.

When Valerie's sister asked why Wayne didn't spend some time with his own friends, Valerie never replied. The truth was that Wayne had no real friends of his own.

Things quickly became worse. Wayne then accused Valerie of sleeping with her boss Steven. Never mind that Steven was 23.5 years Valerie's senior and happily married to boot. Wayne was convinced that wild hanky-panky was going on at Valerie's job. He began showing up at her office with little gifts. Sometimes, between bringing her lunch and a gift, he visited twice a day. This mortified Valerie, although several female co-workers thought she was lucky to have such an attentive husband.

Wayne fussed whenever Valerie went places without him, and this rapidly grew worse.

She grew weary of his questions and their arguments; she saw her friends less and less as time went by. She declined being matron of honor for Wendy because she missed the Las Vegas bachelorette party. Wayne had been terribly concerned about her safety, whether or not there would be a male exotic dancer, and so forth. They had argued and argued until he'd finally gotten his way, and she'd skipped the party.

Wendy was heartbroken when Valerie declined to be her matron of honor. The two had been best friends since the 9th grade. Valerie and Wayne still attended the wedding, but afterwards, Valerie and Wendy began drifting apart.

Six months later, Valerie planned to attend a reunion and didn't invite Wayne. He wanted to go, but as she told him, no other guys were invited. Valerie and her three college roommates planned to shop and see the sights of New York City.

Valerie was still upset about Wendy's wedding and decided she was done having Wayne tell her what to do. This time she put her foot down... she was going to New York, and she was going alone.

During the three weeks prior to her trip, Wayne was so upset, they argued constantly. Valerie went anyways, but her mobile phone mysteriously stopped working once she arrived at the hotel. Apparently, Wayne had actually put a tracker on her phone to see if she was really in New York, which caused a glitch in the phone's functioning.

Valerie was livid and also very embarrassed, because her college friends found out what had happened.

When she returned home, she gave Wayne an ultimatum: either he agreed to therapy, or she'd file for divorce.

Initially, Valerie and Wayne attended therapy together, but after a few sessions, their counselor told Wayne he needed individual help.

Wayne finally now began to understand the source of his insecurity. When he'd been eight years old, his mom had left Wayne and his dad. She'd moved out of state, married another man and had two other children. Wayne never could understand, even as an adult, how she'd left him when she had claimed to love him.

In his early 20s, Wayne had visited his mom, seeking some answers. Her explanation was she hadn't needed reminders of her unhappy first marriage, and that included him.

Wayne's abandonment issues ran deep; but he bravely continued with therapy for four years.

During this time, he told Valerie it was as if a huge weight was being lifted off his shoulders. Wayne also joined a hiking club, something Valerie didn't enjoy, but that he loved. This meant he had an activity of his own every Saturday, while Valerie enjoyed shopping and lunches with her girlfriends. Wayne made several friends through this group, which helped his self-esteem and independence.

Through therapy, he learned to trust Valerie and stop fearing that she'd suddenly leave him. This was difficult given his past, but not impossible.

Wayne stopped trying to control Valerie and no longer minded when she saw her friends and took vacations without him. He now has several good friends and interests of his own.

Wayne and Valerie are still together; she credits therapy and his willingness to admit he needed help and to work on his issues with saving their marriage.

# Shelf It

This novel psychological technique was lovingly hand-crafted by yours truly, moi. The Dr. Linda "shelf it" technique, although deceptively simple, can, in a word, be transformative. It benefits you individually, and it benefits your relationship.

So, what exactly is the "shelf it" technique?

Boston couple Clare and Adam were watching TV on a Saturday night. They'd just returned home from a lobster roll dinner double date (how's that for alliteration?) with their best friends Anita and George. Clare was thoroughly enjoying her weekend. As she strolled into the kitchen to microwave some popcorn, Adam called out from their adjoining den. "I forgot to mention, Lisa called earlier; she needs a ride to the airport Monday morning. I've got an early work meeting, but I said you could probably drive her."

Clare was instantly annoyed. Her sister frequently asked for favors, but never reciprocated, so Clare had no intention whatsoever of rising early on Monday.

She knew Lisa was pushy, and that Adam had been caught off guard. But this couple has frequently dealt with his need to be "Mr. Nice Guy," and his inability to say "no." It was too late to call Lisa now, as she went to sleep early on Saturdays.

Clare's good mood completely evaporated. There was no way to immediately resolve the situation. So, this relatively minor issue could have easily ruined the rest of their evening.

Instead, Clare took her annoyance and she "shelved it." She placed it on an imaginary ledge in back of her head, to be left there until the following morning.

Tomorrow morning she'd call Lisa and say she couldn't drive her. At that time, she could also ask Adam yet again to not answer for her.

What's the alternative? Clare gets angry at Adam and bitches about Lisa all evening long, and their nice evening is ruined.

Here's the beauty of the "shelf it" technique: by giving yourself the gift of temporary amnesia, you can fully enjoy the present moment. If you can live in the present, without fretting about the past or worrying about the future, you'll be in a very rare minority in this country.

It takes time, practice and self-control, but proficiency at this "shelving technique" enables you to avoid useless arguments with your spouse.

It's a sunny Saturday morning in San Diego; Joy and Ted are leaving for breakfast. They're visiting a new eatery where diners flip pancakes on a special griddle right on the table. All week long, Joy has fantasized about red velvet pancakes with white chocolate chips and vanilla drizzle.

On their way out the door, Ted spots Friday's mail on the kitchen counter. On top of old Smokey is an envelope from their car insurance company; he opens it to find a grim cancellation notice.

Joy, who pays their bills, is astonished. She's positive that she paid it. She rummages around, but can't locate the bill. It's possible the company called or emailed Joy, but she rarely checks her voice mails or emails.

The premium must be paid by the following Friday, or their insurance will go bye-bye.

Although Ted is annoyed, he has a crystal-clear choice. Does he – pardon the expression – bitch and gripe at Joy, who clearly feels bad about her screw-up? Or, does he "shelf it," setting the insurance situation aside so they can still enjoy their gourmet pancakes?

Nothing can be resolved until Monday morning, so how about Ted just "shelves it?" He simply tucks this car insurance worry onto an imaginary ledge in the very back of his skull. They can have a good time at breakfast and benefit from a relaxing weekend; Joy can deal with the insurance company on Monday.

By the way, when you perform this technique, don't worry about looking silly, but actually take your hand and physically pretend to shove something onto a shelf on the back of your skull. Trust me, I've done this now for over a decade, and no one, as far as I know, has ever even noticed.

Both of the above examples illustrate minor issues. But what if you're dealing with more serious concerns, like poor health or serious financial problems? What if you're forced to deal with these *all the time*?

It takes practice to employ this technique with large, ongoing situations, but I can personally attest to its effectiveness.

It can actually save your freakin' sanity.

# Stop Talking
## (or Shut the Fuck Up)

Please do pardon the language!

Ah... talking too much! I've been terribly guilty in the past. But really, haven't we all?

Both genders can be guilty of this, by the way.

We've all known someone who is in love with the sound of their own voice. They talk and talk, and won't listen, then repeat everything.

Wouldn't it be glorious fun to say to them: "Would you just shut the fuck up?"

All joking aside, relationships involve give and take, and letting your partner get their two cents' in is no exception.

Women are often "better talkers" than their husbands, meaning they speak faster and can devise clever rebuttals more quickly in an argument.

The problem is they can talk themselves right out of a relationship.

My wonderful friend Louise, who's an incredible talker, but an even better listener, says, "No matter how funny or entertaining you are, if you're doing all the talking, you're boring *someone*."

Here are a few of Louise's tips for communicating during an argument: 1) Stop talking! 2) Give him a chance to say his piece. 3) Really listen. 4) Don't interrupt. 5) Even if you know better, and as a woman, you surely do (just joking, guys!), let him finish his whole thought before jumping in. 6) Wait until he completely stops talking before you begin.

Let's now review step 6 for a moment. It's called "not tailgating" on someone's conversation. This means: don't pounce on the end of their sentence. Wait a moment before saying your piece.

Most challenging of all: don't pretend to be listening, while in actuality formulating your own reply.

By the way, I'm not just picking on the ladies here; some of you men out there are the culprits.

When someone begins talking before you've completed your train of thought, it's like that pushy person behind you in line at the market. You're just trying to put your tomatoes, peaches and Ben and Jerry's on the conveyor belt, and their little shopping cart is just creeping right up your arse.

## Stubbornness

If an individual is obstinate, needless to say, it ain't no picnic being married to them.

The "stubborn as a mule" personality does things their own way.

They generally believe they know best.

And hey, maybe they do! Perhaps that stubborn individual is way smarter than their partner and knows it.

Here are some statements exemplifying stubbornness:

- "It's my way or the highway." This one would be hilarious if it wasn't so awful, but apparently, it's still quite in vogue.
- "You're wrong."
- "You're crazy if you think I'll apologize."
- "You know I'm right."
- "I'm always right."
- "I refuse to discuss it."
- "I'm telling you, this is how we'll do it."

- "I know better than you!"
- "We're doing it my way!"

It all comes down to that old adage: do you want to be right, or do you want to be married? This corny saying is actually quite spot on, as the Brits would say.

The following are some stubborn statements, and next to them, more flexible alternatives.

| Stubborn | Flexible/Reasonable |
|---|---|
| "My way or the highway." | "Your opinion is important to me." |
| "No way will I consider your viewpoint." | "Of course your viewpoint has merit also." |
| "If you think I'll apologize, guess again." | "I do apologize." |
| "I know I'm right. Of course I'm right." | "We're probably both right when it comes down to it." |
| "I refuse to discuss it." | "Of course, let's talk about it." |
| "I don't care what you think." | "Of course I care what you think; let's talk about it." |
| "I'm not interested in what you have to say." | "Of course, I care what you have to say." |
| "I'm not interested in your opinion." | "Please tell me what you're thinking." |

What if you're nodding grimly, as you recognize your bullish partner throughout these examples?

Try to get them to read this section. Couples' therapy can also be quite helpful.

Also, maybe your partner isn't always stubborn. Perhaps it's your approach, or your timing.

For example, if your husband gets "hangry," do avoid important topics if he's so starving he could tear wallpaper off your walls and shove it down his own gullet. Wait until after dinner when he's full, and therefore, more receptive.

Perhaps your wife is not that stubborn, unless you're really bossy. Then she can switch into mulish mode and dig in her heels. Maybe a lighter approach would work better.

## Selfishness

"Selfish people always end up alone."

We've all heard that saying many times, haven't we?

If tracked over the course of many years, sadly, selfish, self-absorbed folks often do end up alone, not just without a relationship, but with few, if any friends.

To a certain extent, we all are selfish. Even Mother Teresa likely hogged the covers or the TV remote sometimes.

But to remain happily married, you must regularly place your own egomania on the back burner of the stove.

Perhaps this means attending baseball games petrified with boredom; thank you sweet Jesus for the Dodger dog and peanuts. Or it's seeing soppy romantic movies, although the only thing keeping you awake is steadily munching popcorn and swilling Pepsi.

This section was originally quite brief.

But one of the most frequent explanations folks give for divorcing their spouses is they were just so "God-dang selfish."

So, let's jump off the high dive here like Chris Hemsworth in the film "Extraction," and delve into this just a little bit deeper.

This reminds me: my happily married friend Diana dislikes violent movies, but sat through "Extraction" an impressive *six times* during Covid, because her husband Brent absolutely loved it. She also watched "Den of Thieves" a total of seven times.

By the end, she'd become completely immune to bloodshed, but also secretly relished the films because of Chris H. and Pablo Schreiber.

Now that Covid's over, it's payback time. Diana and Brent are actually visiting Paris, even as we speak. He's a motorsports and truck kind of guy, so croissants and museums are not his favorites by any stretch of the imagination. So this perfectly illustrates how the unselfish thing works.

Now, let's get back to those self-absorbed spouses. They think primarily of their own comfort, likes and dislikes. They've been this way forever and probably are blissfully unaware. If someone pointed out to them that they're selfish, they would be indignant and genuinely baffled.

Maybe mommy spoiled them too much. Or perhaps mommy never cracked down when she darn well should have.

It's not just their insistence on their favorite restaurant, travel destination or movie. It's that they also rarely do things for others. They're not givers, not by any stretch of the imagination ....but you can bet your bippie that they *love, love, love* to receive.

The fact that they don't realize they're "takers" makes the possibility of change even more challenging.

Here's a "potluck example." For nearly 12 years I worked for a very large company; during this time, there were literally thousands of potlucks at our office.

I'd usually bring lasagna, my manager would make enough nachos for 50, and one amazing co-worker would design an entire taco bar.

A few individuals showed up empty-handed, every potluck. No one noticed the first 80 or 90 times... but over the course of several years?

Finally, it becomes impossible to ignore.

Susie never contributed a single thing... for three years! You'd think she'd be embarrassed, but oh no! She'd load her plate three or four times, relishing each and every bite. Ingenious little Susie even brought plastic containers from home to squirrel away leftovers.

Oh, help yourself Susie! By all means! Nobody wants you going hungry!

Finally, at the three-year mark, Susie's manager informed her she couldn't attend another potluck unless she *actually brought* something. Susie appeared flabbergasted by this insane request; apparently, she believed her attendance was quite contribution enough.

But next time, Susie did actually bring something: a single one-liter bottle of soda.

Way to go, Susie!

So, you say these people are just stingy...well that's often a part of it, but not all. Extreme stinginess with money is, of course, another form of selfishness.

The self-absorbed person generally expects others to make much more effort, such as with friendships. We've all had pals like this. They don't keep in touch, but they're sure happy to hear from you.

The acid test is to completely stop reaching out to this friend. Oftentimes, you'll never hear from them ever again. They're truly puzzled as their friends drop off over the years; they don't realize it's due to their own inaction.

Selfishness can also be exhibited by preventing one's spouse from seeing their friends.

Alan and Martha have been married for 22 years. She's become quite adept at intercepting his friends. When Alan and his buddies plan a fishing trip, Martha points out jobs around their house needing completion. Even when Alan fixes everything, she picks huge fights, which leaves him upset the whole trip.

Martha frequently makes such a fuss that Alan cancels his plans last-minute. She has almost no friends of her own, so tries to stop him from seeing his. Sadly, for the most part she's been successful...and he's miserable.

Now, on the other hand, unselfishness is a trait shared by successfully married people. They're willing to leave their comfort zone and compromise to make their partner happy.

They'll watch the tearjerker romantic movie, because their spouse wants to see it. They'll attend the football game in freezing cold weather, though they don't know a touchdown from a forward pass. They'll support their partner in their interests, because they want them to be happy.

Our success story couple Juliette and Daniel are much like this. As Daniel often says, Juliette is his best friend. She encourages him to spend time with buddies and with his brother on boating trips. This couple has been happily married since they were teenagers.

## Stick Together

If a couple sticks together through thick and thin, they earn that wonderful feeling of having each other's backs.

This was a common theme with many of our success story couples. They emphasized that they were a united front and they stuck together, no matter what. "It's got a lot to do with loyalty," as one of the husbands explained.

Here are some ways to stick together as a couple:

If your mom (substitute brother, sister, aunt or friend) is "talkin' smack" about your spouse, defend them, and do so quickly. Even if what you're hearing is painfully accurate, make sure the person speaking knows you're loyal to your spouse.

Exceptions to this rule do apply. You can agree if someone points out that your partner is violent, abusive, misuses drugs or alcohol, or doesn't replace the toilet paper roll with a fresh one, instead placing the new one on top of the empty, just *waiting* for the next person to do it.

Ladies, perhaps your husband kills every plant in your yard, and wouldn't you know, your father just happens to be chairman of the local camellia club. If your dad criticizes your paltry garden, promptly spring to your husband's defense.

Gentlemen, if your mother is Martha Stewart incarnate, but your wife's top culinary achievement is well-done microwave popcorn, speak up if your mom makes little digs.

Loyalty is one way to forge a strong unit as a couple. If you just sit there like a "bump on a pickle" when someone trash-talks your spouse, first of all, it shows a lack of loyalty.

"Well, I just ignore what they say, it's not like I actually agree with them" you may protest. Well, that's not quite enough. You want to actually stick up for them as well. This is regardless of whether what's being said is true or not. Just that someone has the dang nerve to gossip about your spouse right in front of you should make you want to support them. Once you defend your spouse a couple times, that person won't criticize your partner... at least not in *your* presence.

If you're at a party or dinner, and your spouse is telling a story or anecdote, listen and act interested, even if the story is boring and you've heard it trillions of times.

Be patient with your spouse and be especially kind to them when they're having a rough time. Examples of a rough time: he's been laid off from his long-time job, she wasn't invited to the girls' weekend in Palm Springs, he sprained his ankle and can't go fishing, her thyroid supplements went haywire and she gained 20 pounds in three weeks. Cut your partner some slack. Go out of your way to be especially devoted when things suck for them, because that's when they'll need your support the most.

If your spouse loses their job, this is often very challenging.

Possible reactions to a job loss vacillate wildly. Your partner might immediately transform their resume and within two days have five interviews lined up. Or, just as likely, they'll lie on the couch wearing a robe, eating top ramen with Cool Ranch Doritos on top and watching Drew Barrymore and Kelly Clarkson shows nonstop for two weeks.

It will take all your self-control, but resist attempts to "manage" your spouse's job search, unless they specifically request your help.

Bud and Sue lived in Indianapolis and had been married for 21 years when he suddenly lost his job as a department store manager. Although the layoff was unexpected, Bud was optimistic. He was certain he'd quickly clinch another position. To his surprise, due to his lack of a college degree, he had trouble even getting job interviews. Sue, a high school teacher, tactfully refrained from mentioning even once that she'd been encouraging him for many years to get his degree.

Bud spent several weeks on the couch, eating chips and salsa and watching sitcoms. Sue wisely kept silent. Their teenage son helped Bud with his resume and LinkedIn; although he went on some interviews, no job offers came his way. Younger candidates with Bachelor's degrees could always be hired for cheaper.

Bud speculated about opening his own fishing supply store, a dream of his for many years. During this time, Sue listened when he vented, cooked a lot of his favorite meals and surprised him with a month-long road trip across the country in July, since she had the summer off.

This was something they'd never done in all their years of marriage, as Bud had never had more than two weeks' consecutive vacation. Sue also frequently initiated romance with Bud because she'd read that men doubted their own attractiveness after a job loss.

Bud and Sue struggled financially for two years, but also took some wonderful trips. His unemployment elapsed after six months; they refinanced their house and burned through their savings. Bud was finally hired by a small company which valued his experience and gave him a flexible work schedule. His new employer even partially reimbursed him for school, so he finally took Sue's advice and earned his college degree.

Now, five years later, Bud credits his wife for being so loyal during a rough time. He brags to friends that she is his hero, his rock. He tells their son that his mother is the best woman on earth. Bud maintains that Sue's being strong for him was the most wonderful gift she could have ever given him.

## Separate Bedrooms

Many couples who are otherwise very well-matched suffer for years or even decades because unfortunately, they totally lack compatibility in just one place, and that's the bedroom.

We're absolutely not talking about sex. Rather, a lack of harmony in sleeping styles and habits. How do *you* spell snore...S...N...O!

Tremaine and Samantha were in their 40s and had been married for 12 years. They had no problems sharing a bed when they first wed, but as they aged a wee bit, they began to suffer from sleep incompatibility, which rapidly grew worse.

Tremaine was a light sleeper and woke frequently because Samantha snored (Okay ladies! I know none of us out there has ever snored... only Samantha!). She tossed and turned throughout the night. She kicked off her covers and she talked in her sleep. Consequently, Tremaine awakened countless times throughout the night. Many evenings, he never once fell into a deep sleep, and then he was always tired and drowsy the next day.

Their cat Luna also ambushed their bed several times each night. This would awaken Tremaine, but since Samantha could sleep through anything, Luna could jump right on top of her and Samantha would "saw on" with abandon.

Sometimes, when the roar of Samantha chopping down the redwoods grew so deafening Tremaine couldn't take it anymore, he would nudge her to roll over. This then woke Samantha, who became very irritated if she couldn't fall back to sleep.

Consequently, both Tremaine and Samantha would frequently awaken tired, cranky, and seriously annoyed with one another.

Samantha knew that she snored. She'd tried everything from breathing strips to super-gluing a tennis ball onto the back of her nightgown. Nothing whatsoever helped.

"Timber!" Hey!! Those redwoods are becoming extinct! Come on, Samantha! Think what you're doing to the environment!

Poor Samantha...we're just kidding. Besides, it wasn't just the snoring. Her talking in her sleep and kicking off the covers also kept Tremaine awake.

So, one possible solution: separate bedrooms for this weary twosome. They might have a little romance time or watch TV in their shared bedroom before one exited to sleep in the spare bedroom. In this way,

Tremaine and Samantha would ideally maintain closeness as a couple, but also actually get some sleep.

In the morning, if there was time, or perhaps on weekend mornings, the two could reunite in their shared bedroom.

The idea of different bedrooms isn't very romantic, is it?

Oh, heck, no. Especially when you see couples on TV, talking and cuddling in bed, looking so cute, so lovey-dovey, so...*cozy.*

Let's all remember the phrase: "compare and despair."

If the pathetic reality is that one partner sleeps like a baby, whilst the other tosses and turns all night, or if both of them miss out on sleep, well, that's not so romantic. Not by a long stretch.

Some couples resist separate bedrooms, even if their sleeping situation has become horrific. They fear they'll lose their closeness as a couple. So they continue sharing a bedroom, and as the years go by, night after bleary night, their health can often suffer.

Now, if you travel back through time, you'll see that many couples, particularly well-to-do or the nobility, never actually shared a bedroom full-time. Each had their own bedroom, usually with an adjoining door or suite in between. Castles in England, France and other European countries had separate bedrooms for the Mr. and Mrs.

Take heart in the knowledge that many, many couples encounter this same difficulty. Particularly as we get older, it becomes challenging to sleep well even under optimal circumstances. Folks who effortlessly shared a bed in the past, sleeping like logs in their electric youths, often encounter major insomnia as they age.

Miles and Beatrice have been married for five years; both are in their mid 30s. Miles absolutely cannot fall asleep without the TV going. Beatrice, on the other hand, needs quiet. He's tried accommodating her by wearing headphones, but they pull out of his ears and awaken him when he rolls over. If he skips the headphones and falls asleep with the TV on, she's unable to drift off. If she turns down the TV, this wakes him. She then sleeps soundly, but he lies awake staring at the ceiling until his alarm buzzes at 6 a.m.

Miles is a UPS truck driver and Beatrice is a nurse. Both have very demanding professions which have become even more challenging due to daytime weariness.

Twice in the past year, Miles dozed off behind the wheel of his truck while he was waiting at a red light. He only awoke when the driver behind him honked their horn repeatedly. As for Beatrice, she's normally very calm and collected, but when sleep-deprived, she becomes easily annoyed by demanding patients.

So, what's this couple to do? One possible solution is for them to "turn in" together in their bedroom at the start of the evening, but then when Miles is ready to fall asleep, he could go into the family room and turn on the TV there. They could both watch TV together in their bedroom, and then when she's ready to nod off, Beatrice could go sleep in the spare room. In this way, he gets his background noise and she gets her peace and quiet, but they still have a little cozy time at the beginning of the evening.

They could possibly alternate nights for leaving their shared bedroom; yep, there's that good old cherished standby, *compromise*. Compromise... ta daaa!

What, you say? This all seems kind of sad and unromantic? Yes, truthfully, it kind of does. We've all grown up with the rosy TV image of a loving couple, sleeping peacefully beside one another all night long.

But, for many couples, this glowing image is light years from reality. Perhaps an alternative setup is not as sad and unromantic as being sleep-deprived night after night, week after week, month after month, year after weary mother-f'n year.

Alan and Jessica have been married for only two years; both are in their early 40s. This is a second marriage for them both: unfortunately, they already feel like they're incompatible. Differing sleep patterns comprise a large part of this disharmony. Both Alan and Jessica had been divorced for over a decade before remarrying and both have well-established sleep habits.

Jessica enjoys reading in bed for an hour before falling asleep. She's always done this; in fact, she cannot fall asleep otherwise, but the light bothers Alan. If he manages to fall asleep while she's still reading, when she turns out the light, this then wakes him.

Alan rises one hour before Jessica on weekdays; she's a light sleeper, and since he's a big guy, about 240 pounds, he wakes her when he gets out of bed. This has been a source of arguments because Jessica can't understand why he must get up so early. The truth is that Alan enjoys leisurely drinking his coffee, reading the newspaper and not feeling rushed. His morning routine is the only time of day he has peace and quiet.

Jessica, on the other hand, can roll out of bed just like a little pill bug, hop in the shower (does anyone here ever actually hop or jump when they enter the shower?), gobble some toast, and scurry out the door. She can accomplish this in an impressive 20 minutes or less. Therefore, she resents Alan's waking her up an hour earlier than she would otherwise, just because, as she puts it, he dawdles around in the morning.

On the weekends, there's no issue at all. Instead of reading, Jessica watches the late show with Alan, and then they both awaken the same time. Not surprisingly, they get along much better on the weekends than during the week.

Ergo, one possible solution might be for Alan and Jessica to share their bedroom on the weekends, but sleep in separate bedrooms during the week.

## Single Friends

Craig and Talia had been wed for about 12 years and were in their early 40s when Talia began working for a new company. There, she became friendly with her glamorous co-worker Jasmine, age 33. Jasmine was obsessed with health and fitness. This quickly rubbed off on Talia, who began visiting the gym at least four times a week.

Jasmine was newly divorced and had been single for less than a year.

Craig and Talia got along quite well, but currently, their relationship was in a bit of a rut. Craig was a very decent individual and had always been a good husband to Talia. This couple did not have children; Craig's 16-year-old daughter Annette lived an hour away with her mother, and she despised Talia. This had unfortunately made Craig's relationship with Annette very difficult.

When Craig returned home from work, he would slump in front of the TV, falling asleep on the couch nearly every night. He could barely be roused to get up and go to bed. Craig used to be in good shape, but had put on a great deal of weight since his mom had passed two years earlier. His restaurant manager job was stressful, as he dealt with many demanding customers. It bothered Talia that he wasn't taking better care of his health; her own father had died from a heart attack at age 57.

Talia was finished with work by six o'clock, but Craig didn't generally return home until nine-thirty or later.

Talia's pal Jasmine began dating a handsome new guy named Armando who spent at least two hours a day at the gym. Armando had several single buddies who were also into health and fitness. Jasmine encouraged Talia to join them all for happy hour after work, which they did at least twice weekly.

Eventually, Talia spent more time with Jasmine, Armando and his friends than she did Craig. Armando's best friend Steve energetically flirted with Talia and told her she was beautiful and desirable. Jasmine had never yet met Craig but made little "digs" when she compared him to Steve, who lifted weights at the gym every day.

Will this spell trouble for this couple? While a large section of this book is devoted to the importance of space, some friendships can hurt a marriage.

Either way, this is kind of a "danger baby" situation. When Andrea was a toddler and reached for something dangerous, I would yell,"Danger, baby!"

# Stalemate

Maybe it is money you're arguing about. Or, perhaps it's the annoying in-laws. Possibly your neighbors mow their lawn at 6:55 a.m. on the weekends, and your spouse refuses to speak with them.

Quick interjection: this may sound sexist, but I'm gonna throw it in anyways! Men, if this is you, step it up. Go on out there and speak to the neighbors. For the love of God, do not make your wife do it. I'm just saying....

Guys, I do not utter this lightly because many women friends were consulted on this and 100 percent confirmed it.

Okay, now back to our topic of a stalemate in your marriage. What if it's not something simple? What if there's a large impasse? What if there's a jumbo disagreement going on, with no easy solution in sight?

Perhaps your spouse convinced you to move to Tennessee for the cheaper cost of living, but unfortunately you both hate the climate...and frankly, you're blaming your partner. After all, it's *their* fault you're living in a place with 95 percent humidity and bugs the size of hummingbirds.

You moved everything, changed jobs and now you're stuck – at least for the foreseeable future. So, what good can it possibly do to keep bickering, grumbling, or, pardon my Italian, bitching? Short answer: none whatsoever.

And so...drumroll please...without further ado, presenting the truce. Neither partner acknowledges defeat or admits they are in the wrong. Instead, both take a much-needed break from squabbling, arguing, or just plain being angry with one another.

Annoyance can rapidly escalate when there's a stalemate, and, in turn, relationships can break down very quickly. That's why calling a truce can be so beneficial. You're stuck in Tennessee; nothing changes that, but you're giving the argument a break.

And here's a potential plus: maybe after some time passes, you've made new friends, you've fallen in love with the fall weather and the food, and you've come to feel like Tennessee is your new home. You wouldn't want to live anywhere else.

Or, if after some time you still despise it, at least you and your partner haven't been bickering the whole time.

Here's an example of both a stalemate and a truce. It's a story with a very unlikely happy ending.

Several years ago, my former colleague Bruce was so unhappy with his wife Charlotte that he regretted having ever married her in the first place. They'd been wed for only two years. Bruce told our mutual co-worker Adam that he planned to move out of their condo in a month, and would file for divorce shortly thereafter.

I'd only met Bruce once, very briefly, as there were thousands of employees at our company. Adam told him to come see me before doing anything drastic. "Linda might be a little hard on you," Adam told Bruce, "but listen to what she has to say."

When Bruce and I met at the coffee cart downstairs, I asked why he wanted to end his marriage after such a short time.

"She's a huge nag," he started with. "She barely ever wants to have sex, and never during the week. I'm only 30 and I didn't get married so I'd only have sex on the weekends. I feel like I've gotten gypped. She hates my friends and she leaves a mess in the bathroom and the kitchen. We lived together before we got married, but she's a much bigger slob now that I'm stuck with her. She seems angry with me most of the time."

I must say, the nagging and no sex during the week seemed to be bothering him the most, so I zeroed in on that. It must be added that Bruce was very handsome, well-educated, had a good job; in other words, he was a "catch." But he was kind of arrogant; he didn't appear to take any responsibility for the state of his marriage. He rolled his eyes when I said it was never all one party's fault when a relationship was deteriorating.

I then asked Bruce two questions: what did Charlotte nag him about, and what were their schedules like during the week.

Apparently she nagged him to do more around the house. Bruce didn't really see why he should. His mother had done everything around their house when he was growing up; his dad hadn't lifted a finger. Bruce described his mother as being some kind of a "wonder-woman;" however, further investigation revealed his mom had never worked outside of the house, whereas his own wife worked full-time.

As for their schedules, Bruce arrived home almost two full hours before Charlotte, due to their differing work schedules and her longer commute.

This couple did not yet have children, by the way.

Our office was less than ten minutes away from their condo; Bruce sashayed home most days by 5:30 p.m. He sometimes stopped by the gym for an hour, and in that case he arrived home by 6:30 at the latest. He'd grab a beer and some snacks and watch TV on the couch until Charlotte came home. She usually arrived after 7:30 p.m., due to her hour and a half commute.

At this point, dinner needed to be cooked, the trash taken out, and the kitchen cleaned up from last night's mess (they both left early so neither had time to clean up in the mornings). Charlotte was expected to do all the housework and cook dinner, even though she returned home two hours later than Bruce.

I suggested it was only fair that he cook dinner Mondays through Thursdays and they could eat out the other days. Bruce was not receptive to this in the least. He joked that he had no idea how to cook, although he just loved to barbecue. I suggested he pick up one of those pre-cooked chickens and a "salad in the bag" kit one night, order pizza another, and possibly take-out the other two nights.

Bruce's assignment for the next week was to tidy and clean up the condo when he got home, especially the kitchen, and to take out the trash. He was also to set the table so that it was completely ready when Charlotte got home. I added that it couldn't hurt to also put a little bouquet of flowers on the table.

Bruce then rolled his eyes heavenward, and he blew air out of his mouth exactly the same way my horse Malibu does when he's extremely bored.

At that point I became annoyed and I told Bruce tactfully, "If I were your wife, I wouldn't want to have sex with you either. You're kind of arrogant and spoiled."

Well, it didn't quite take a crystal ball to see that by this time, Bruce was really sick of me. He maybe kind of even hated me. He joked resentfully that of course I'd side with the other woman. Suddenly, he was in an enormous rush to get back to his office. But too bad for Bruce, and fortunately for me, there was a long, winding line of caffeine addicts ahead of us at the coffee cart. He was virtually trapped.

I then decided to channel the incomparable Judge Judy. "JJ" cuts right through the mustard. She asks smart questions and doesn't pretend to sympathize when people make dumb-ass excuses.

So, I proceeded to ask Bruce lots of questions, "Judge Judy style." After all, he'd come to me for advice.

I began with, why should Charlotte do all the cooking? Is it just because she's the woman? It would be unreasonable to expect this even if she were a stay-home mom; everyone needs a break from the kitchen now and then. But, as I reminded Bruce, Charlotte was working full-time and was gone from their home at least three hours more than him, every single day of the week.

Bruce shrugged and laughed. I said his thinking was right out of 1959, the year my parents married. At this point, Bruce began to joke around and didn't seem to have absorbed any of what I'd said.

To be honest, it didn't appear that I'd chalk this one up as a success story. But, as we all know, people can really astound you.

Five weeks later, Bruce unexpectedly invited me to lunch and insisted upon treating. He suggested the Butcher Shop, the nicest restaurant in the area. Much to my surprise, Bruce told me over lunch that he'd done everything I'd recommended. He'd cleaned and tidied their condo every day when he got home from work and he'd had dinner and flowers on the table every night except Fridays and weekends.

Bruce confided that the first night Charlotte had returned home to see flowers and dinner on the table, she had burst into tears. She had sat at that table and cried for about 10 minutes.

She'd told him she'd known their marriage was failing and hadn't known what to do. The one simple act of his cooking dinner and cleaning the condo turned things around completely for this couple. Because, you see, Bruce really did love his wife and he'd felt terrible when she'd cried, because only then had he realized how selfish he'd been.

Granted, it wasn't a great dinner by any stretch of the imagination. Bruce had carefully pre-mixed the salad at about 5:45, so when Charlotte had arrived home at 7:30, the lettuce and dressing had become one. They were inseparable soulmates. Bruce had also repeatedly nuked the chicken until it resembled chia seeds married to rubber, but still, it was the first dinner he'd cooked for her himself.

From that day onward, Bruce transformed from a little boy to a very fine man. He went out of his way to help his wife, and he anticipated things that needed to be done, rather than waiting to be asked. Bruce and Charlotte now began to truly operate as a team.

Not surprisingly, their sex life improved rapidly and dramatically. For one thing, Charlotte was not so exhausted all the time, but even more importantly, her husband was making her feel adored. And ladies, I'm sure you'll agree with me here, when women feel cherished, they are much more likely to want to have sex, and it's as simple as that.

Men, please feel free to re-read the above paragraph.

Charlotte also made compromises of her own by becoming neater in the kitchen and the bathroom. She picked up after herself in the kitchen and no longer left makeup spills on the bathroom counter. She also stopped complaining about Bruce's friends, whom she'd never actually disliked. Griping about them had just been her way of expressing her dissatisfaction with Bruce. Both Charlotte and Bruce began going out of their way to please one another and to continually do kind, giving, and thoughtful acts for one another.

By the time Bruce treated me to our fancy lunch, he and Charlotte had rekindled their relationship to the extent he felt they were actually more romantic than they'd ever been.

A nice footnote is that this couple is still very happily married, with two beautiful children.

So, in summation, the conventional advice for Bruce and Charlotte would have been to talk and communicate. And isn't that what we hear all the time? Communicate, communicate, communicate! We've all heard that word until our eyeballs are just about ready to fall out.

Communication without action would have resulted in arguments and not much accomplished. Instead, when Bruce, the partner who was causing more of the problem, abruptly improved his behavior, this turned things around very quickly. Bruce also displayed humility, and showed his love for his wife through actions and not just words.

## Sometimes the Trash Takes Itself Out

No doubt you've seen this clever saying on social media. Its various interpretations include: "It's great when toxic people stop talking to you... it's like the trash took itself out," or "after it expires, it's no longer good for you, and this ain't just about food."

Let's imagine there's someone, perhaps a "frenemy," or a "user and abuser" in your life. In particular, the "user and abuser" can drain you financially, emotionally, time-wise, or for bonus points, all of the above. Because they're clever and know you well, they may likely have become experts at manipulating you.

Particularly if they're your relative, or if you've known them most of your life, even if you're normally a sharp cookie, they can take gross advantage.

Ironically, this toxic individual may dump you just like a pair of old sneakers if you call them out or stop allowing them to take advantage.

Now, how does this apply to your marriage? In particular, those charming and delightful "users and abusers" can simultaneously suck the life out of you and strain your relationship.

Santa Ana couple Joshua and Stephanie had been married for just five years and were in their early 30s. Joshua's best friend Steve could be charming and fun, but tended to use others and rarely reciprocated. Steve always had a plausible reason why he was fired from his latest job and therefore needed to be rescued. Over the years, he'd alienated nearly all of his friends, with the notable exception of Joshua.

Joshua and Steve had first become friends in junior high. Joshua had been extremely introverted back then, a self-proclaimed math geek. He'd been very overweight, with braces and zero confidence. He was still this way in high school. Steve, on the other hand, had been quarterback of the football team, good-looking, outgoing, beloved by girls, and by far the most handsome and popular boy in school. Everyone liked Steve - and Steve liked Joshua. Steve included Joshua in everything, and on a few occasions when another student tried to pick on Joshua, had defended him vigorously.

Steve had peaked in high school, but then never lived up to his "glory days" potential. He'd dropped out of college after one semester, and then bounced from job to job and relationship to relationship. He'd begun drinking heavily and had stopped working out.

However, at their ten-year high school reunion, nobody recognized Joshua, who had completely transformed for the better. He was no longer heavy, his braces were gone, and he'd finished both college and grad school. He now had a huge career in finance and to top it off, his beautiful wife Stephanie.

Initially, Stephanie had liked Steve, but over the years, she'd seen how much he used Joshua, and so now she referred to him as "that user and abuser." Every few months Joshua bailed out Steve; usually by paying his rent or overdue bills.

Joshua and Stephanie seldom argued, but their disagreements were usually about Steve. Stephanie felt Steve was using Joshua, but Joshua always defended him. Had Steve not made high school bearable for him, Joshua would have dropped out, would have never gone to college, or had a successful life.

Joshua felt he owed so much to Steve; his whole life really. Once Stephanie truly understood this, she wisely backed off and they stopped arguing about the subject.

By this time, Steve owed Joshua more than $25,000.00. Perhaps it was best that Stephanie didn't know the total. One time she had asked, and Joshua told her he wasn't sure, but he was a mathematical genius, so of course he knew the exact amount. He'd never pushed Steve to pay him back because Steve rarely had two dimes to rub together, as the saying goes.

One day, driving home from the beach, Steve was rear-ended by another driver. He suffered whiplash and some minor back injuries. A friend recommended a local chiropractor who worked in conjunction with a personal injury attorney; this attorney acted upon Steve's behalf.

Eleven months later, Steve received a $47,000.00 settlement check in the mail. He was beside himself with excitement; he had never before possessed anything approaching this much cash.

Steve immediately splurged on a dirt bike, a custom stereo system and a Chanel purse for his new girlfriend Mallory. He did treat Joshua and Stephanie to a nice dinner out at Outback Steak House and a one-pound box of See's nuts and chews.

After three months, Joshua finally asked Steve to return just a part of what he owed him. Steve agreed to pay back $10,000, while cracking a joke that this must be chump change to someone like Joshua, who earned over $200,000.00 a year.

Steve then dropped out of sight and Joshua didn't hear from him, but did see on social media his lavish trips to Costa Rica, Paris and Jamaica. Joshua texted Steve a couple of times, but never heard back.

Six months later, Joshua had at last become seriously annoyed. He'd bailed out Steve literally dozens of times; two years ago, in fact, he'd paid three months of Steve's back rent, or Steve would have been evicted and left homeless.

And now Steve was ghosting him.

Now that Steve could actually pay him back, at least partially, he was completely avoiding him. But, as Joshua reminded himself, it wasn't as if he actually needed the money.

This could have driven Joshua and Stephanie apart, but Stephanie refrained from reminding Joshua how she'd told him many times to stop lending money to Steve.

A couple months later, Steve had blown through every red cent of his settlement money. Mallory and her Chanel purse had both moved out in a huff once he'd asked her to begin pitching in for rent.

When Steve finally called Joshua, he made countless excuses, implying that Mallory had stolen most of his money. Joshua said that he was disappointed, but that he wanted to let bygones be bygones.

He didn't even call Steve out for the excursions to Costa Rica, Paris and Jamaica. He knew Steve was downtrodden over being broke yet again.

Again, Stephanie showed remarkable self-control by keeping silent on the topic. She told Joshua it was between the two of them and she wasn't getting involved. She said she was there to support him.

So, how does this all tie in to the success of a marriage?

In an instance such as this, a spouse must exercise exceptional self-control. Stephanie was a real champ; few could "stay in her lane" the way she did.

Joshua was ordinarily very savvy and didn't allow himself to be taken advantage of; Steve being the notable exception. Since Joshua believed he owed everything to Steve, no one, not even his wife, could have persuaded him to end the friendship.

Surprise, surprise, Steve began regularly calling Joshua again, asking for loans and bailouts. Incredibly, amazingly, Joshua went right back to helping out, just like the good old days.

The guys continued to get together regularly for fun outings. Joshua told himself, "This is my best friend. Steve is my brother; money cannot come between us."

One day, Steve called and asked if he could borrow Joshua's spare truck for his new construction job.

Joshua agreed to lend the truck, which was almost brand-new, for as long as Steve needed it. Joshua only used the truck for desert season, still six months away. The two guys were already planning their next desert trip.

Five and a half months later, Steve returned the truck and parked it on the street in front of Joshua's house. Joshua had asked him to be sure to leave the truck on the driveway, but Steve seemed to have forgotten this detail.

Joshua and Stephanie were out of town, so two weeks elapsed before Joshua saw what remained of what had once been his beautiful truck. There was a dent in the front left panel and a section of the back passenger door had been scraped clean of paint. One rear headlight was broken. The back bumper was completely missing. There was also a small dent on the driver's door. Inside, the once-beautiful upholstery was badly stained.

Steve completely denied having damaged the truck. When Joshua called him, he said that maybe one of Joshua's neighbors had run into it. He also wondered aloud if perhaps Stephanie had driven the truck and neglected to tell Joshua.

This was, at last, the final straw.

Joshua was furious. He told Steve he couldn't believe he'd trashed his new truck and was now lying about it. Steve apologized, and then quickly hung up the phone.

Two weeks later, Steve phoned Joshua to ask for a loan. He'd been fired from his construction job and needed to pay his rent. For the first time ever, Joshua refused to help.

Steve then called Joshua twice in the next month, asking to be bailed out, and was again turned down. Steve seemed absolutely astonished that his decade-long gravy train had screeched to a complete halt.

After the third time Joshua refused to lend him more money, Steve deleted him from his social media accounts. When Joshua called to check up on him, Steve shouted that he was blocking his phone number.

Joshua tried to reach Steve awhile longer; he felt sure that Steve wouldn't end their friendship after nearly 20 years, but ultimately he gave up. Steve told mutual friends Joshua resented him and had been jealous of him since high school.

So, as the saying goes, sometimes the trash takes itself out. Joshua was taken advantage of by Steve for well over a decade. When he finally put a stop to this, he was unceremoniously dumped. This was painful for Joshua at first, but he eventually realized this wasn't such a bad thing after all.

His wife was wise in this situation by exercising an incredible amount of self-control and not interfering.

## Seether

Well, yes... Seether is a band and quite a talented one at that.

But, what we're referring to here is the unique experience of being wed to that individual we shall dub the "silent seether."

The "seether" may range from annoyed, somewhat angry, to downright furious with their spouse. This is not unique; at times, every married person becomes angry with their spouse.

What distinctly separates the "seether" from the pack is their husband or wife is always the last to know. The "seether" will hold it all in... no matter what. Their partner lives with them day in and day out, and perhaps has a gut sense things aren't exactly as they should be, but nothing's ever discussed.

Even when asked, the "seether" will smile and say that everything is fine. They're like the Big Island's Kilauea volcano. It wouldn't take

King Kamehameha to predict that this sucker could literally erupt at any given moment.

The "seether" might possibly give off non-verbal cues such as rolling their eyes and sighing heavily. They might complain to friends or co-workers, but never, ever their spouse.

How can you maintain an authentically happy marriage with a "seether?" Well, short answer: you cannot.

To a large extent, it's a fake relationship. Although smiling and outwardly cheerful, the seether is quietly churning with rage. It sounds like a B+ horror movie, doesn't it? Seether! Muahaha!

It's tough being around a couple with this dynamic. Perhaps it's not as embarrassing as hanging out with married folks who yell, but when you can cut the tension with a butcher knife, it still makes for a pretty stressful environment.

Now, what are some hallmarks of the silent seether? I shall warn you, a few of these are pretty wild!

- They mumble under their breath when you talk.

- They are overly nice; they use a fake sweet tone and synthetic smile.

- They cross their arms when you're talking to them (note: some people do this and it doesn't mean they're angry...it's just their particular body language).

- They don't look at you when you're talking, or they ignore you altogether.

- If you ask what's wrong, they will invariably say that everything is just peachy.

- This one is wild! When cooking for you, they deliberately make the food too spicy, too bland, or however you don't like.

- Okay, this one's a real zinger and starts verging on the world of creepy: they leave something out on the floor or steps of your house that you could actually trip over.

Some of these, particularly the last two, are quite nasty and extreme. This person is churning with rage, but can't or won't express it through normal channels. They then commence overtly hostile or passive-aggressive actions, such as spicy food or items on the staircase.

By the way, the last two examples are stranger than fiction and were relayed to me years ago by my acquaintance Frank. Frank and his soft-spoken wife Lydia were married for nearly a decade until they divorced.

For their entire marriage, Frank had believed Lydia was just forgetful when she put too much spice and hot seasonings in his food. He also chalked it down to accidental carelessness when she left things lying around, such as her tiny little high-heeled shoes on their basement steps.

Lydia was always ladylike, soft-spoken and never seemed the least bit angry. Butter, margarine or even Parkay wouldn't melt in her mouth.

Frank had no clue their marriage had ended until one lovely Sunday springtime morning; he and Lydia were in bed together watching TV. The doorbell rang, and Frank got up to answer it. There, on his front porch, stood a strange man who handed him divorce papers.

Let us not ever forget that Lydia herself was there in the house, in bed, in her attractive floral lace nightie, watching TV as divorce papers were being served to her husband.

Okay, if this isn't a little bizarre, I don't know what is!

Two years after their divorce finalized, Frank heard from a mutual friend that Lydia had seasoned his food too much on purpose. Apparently, she'd been very angry because he was stingy and didn't like her mother. Turns out, that had also inspired the creative Lydia to leave her cute little high heels lying on their basement steps. She claimed she hadn't been trying to injure Frank, but just thought it would be amusing to see him trip. Oh, wow. I don't know about you, but Lydia's kinda scaring me. *Yikes!*

If this behavior seems extremely bizarre to you, well, you're not alone.

So, why is someone like this? Well, psychology teaches us to look at the childhood. Perhaps the "seether" grew up in a household where they weren't allowed to express anger or frustration. They grew up unable to convey their hostility, so they became accomplished at holding it in.

What do you do if you suspect you are married to this person? You can try to get them to open up. Be truly interested in what they have to say. You can even ask the type of questions that in research are called "provocative questions."

Nope, these aren't questions like, "What shade of underwear are you wearing?" No, by provocative, I am referring to questions that can be somewhat challenging. For example, if you suspect your "seether" wife is mad because you forgot her birthday, ask, "Hey, Wilma, are you mad because I forgot your birthday?"

Now, keep in mind, as an accomplished "seether," Wilma is highly unlikely to come clean. She'll probably assure you that everything's just fine, as she's simultaneously giving off subtle clues, such as dumping copious amounts of cayenne pepper onto your spaghetti bolognese.

If your spouse actually tries to communicate when they're upset, perhaps you can help. Truly listen if they say something's bothering them; don't change the subject or brush them off.

Even the most hardcore "seether" might possibly reform if their spouse starts making them feel heard. It all just depends how many years this behavior has gone on.

If you're the one holding in all your frustrations and suspect you're a "seether," ask yourself some questions. Were you able to express anger or other negative emotions as a child or adolescent? Chances are excellent you weren't.

Holding in anger is exhausting and draining. Stuffing down anger leads to problems such as drug or alcohol abuse or emotional eating.

What can you do as an adult to turn this around?

Talking to a therapist or trusted friend can be very helpful. This isn't the same as simply venting about your spouse and not telling them. If you're married to someone who doesn't allow you to express your emotions, couples' therapy can be a lifesaver.

Individual therapy can also help you find the source of your anger, which likely occurred many years before you even met your spouse.

Physical exercise can be a great outlet when you're angry.

If you try talking to your spouse and they refuse to listen or acknowledge your feelings, at least you're making an attempt to speak up. Your spouse may not understand your feelings no matter what you do. However, if you speak up at last, they are likely to respect you more. At least try. You may be pleasantly surprised to find they're more receptive than you'd ever thought possible.

What if your spouse has no interest in your feelings and refuses to get therapy? Well, although this book is about staying married, let's just say thank God we live in a time where you can escape if you're miserable.

Tina Ann was an accomplished, world-class "seether." She'd been married to Jeff for 12 years when she received a wake-up call from her best friend Emily. Emily was that sweet, agreeable friend who always spoke kindly and rarely challenged anyone.

One day, Tina Ann was venting to Emily "per usual" about how Jeff was inconsiderate and sloppy. Tina Ann had a full head of steam as she was relaying for the 12,000th time how Jeff always left his wet towel strewn on the bathroom floor, when Emily suddenly interrupted her.

Perhaps Emily had eaten a bad burrito that day, or maybe she was just worn out from hearing the "same old, same old." Possibly, the oft-repeated tale about the wet towel had petrified Emily with boredom at long last.

For whatever reason, when Tina Ann launched into her usual tirade, Emily became impatient for the first time ever in their long friendship. She made an unprecedented statement: "Next time, tell him it bothers you when he leaves his towel on the floor."

Tina Ann insisted that wouldn't do any good. At that point, Emily retorted, "Tell him because I'm sick of hearing about it."

Well, maybe this breaks the girlfriend code of sisters always sticking together. And coming from the uber-patient Emily, it was a super-shocker, to say the least.

Tina Ann was stunned, but somehow kept her composure. The next morning, Jeff predictably left his wet towel on the bathroom floor. She left it there, and waited until he was dressed. She then said firmly, "Jeff, please hang your towel on the towel rod; it's bad for the tile." Jeff nodded and shrugged, looking at his cell phone.

Gary and Julie, one of our success story couples, have a tried and true method. If your partner isn't paying attention when you're relaying something crucial, courteously ask for their full attention. Don't begin speaking until they've put their phone away, or at least turned it over.

Tina Ann then spoke very clearly and she firmly added, "Jeff, this is important. I want to tell you something that has really been bothering me." She told him she felt like she was his mother, cleaning up after him. She added that it was driving her nuts.

Jeff nodded, looked at his watch, kissed her, and hurried out the door. However, the next morning, he hung his towel on the rack. The next morning, will the Saints preserve us, he repeated this entire amazing performance. The *third* morning, he forgot, but Tina Ann left the towel on the floor, and he picked it up when he got home from work. Thereafter, he remembered every day.

The towel shenanigans were now firmly a thing of the past. Apparently, something that had been – pardon the expression – pissing Tina Ann off for nearly a decade turned out to be an easy fix. All it took was for her to actually speak up.

## Shared Project

This section ended up being a last-minute addition to this book, due to the news of an impending divorce of a beautiful celebrity couple. Let's just call this couple Sofia and Jack. They seemed to have it all: money, looks, fame, and success. They were just really one of the cutest couples I've ever seen, and I've seen a lot of 'em. Of course, I didn't know them personally, but when I heard the news, I admit I was kind of shocked. I mean, they were just such a gorgeous couple and seemed to be so in love.

So, this got me to thinking: what could have kept this couple together? It was a second marriage for them both, by the way. If you look at the rate of divorce for second marriages, it is, of course, staggering.

The concept of a "shared project" for a couple is something which links them together and which makes divorce more difficult or unlikely. In the case of many couples, it's their children: kids are the ultimate "shared project."

But what about a couple who marries later in life and does not share children? What could their joint project be?

For inspiration, let's look at radio disc jockey Howard Stern and his wife Beth. This couple could just spend their days enjoying their fame and money and not doing much else. Instead, they share a passion for rescuing and rehabilitating cats. They both invest a great deal of time, money, energy and compassion toward this shared project.

What if "Sofia and Jack" had entered into a shared project, such as an animal rescue, or a home for unwed teenage moms, or a project to help the homeless? Would this shared venture have kept them together? Hard to say, but it gives us some food for thought.

# Sex
## Again, We Saved the Best For Last!

Okay, here goes! We promise this will be fun!

This is the last part of the S section – and without a doubt, we saved the best for last!

No preambles here, no foreplay, we shall just cut to the nitty gritty!

For this section, we sought advice from three amazing goddesses: Evelyn, Candace, and Sasha. These three ladies are fun, uninhibited and how do we say this: sex is a major priority for all three.

Evelyn, Candace and Sasha are specifically dispensing advice to the ladies, but gents, please tune in as well! We promise it will be most intriguing.

Language has been toned down to make this a little more vanilla, but you'll still get the general idea!

Now, put on your seat belts, not your chastity belts, as our merry trio, Evelyn, Candace, and Sasha take you on an adventurous ride and spill their top-secret tips for an amazing sex life!

Okay, Evelyn first!

Evelyn's suggestions for fantastic intimacy:

1. The best sex toy you'll ever have is your imagination.

2. If you're creative, you can find sex toys all over your house.

   Here's a couple: neckties or scarves for a quick tie-up. Ice cubes for an unfamiliar yet burning sensation.

3. Your feather duster to tickle *anywhere*.

4. Pizza paddle or spatula if someone's been very, very bad.

5. If you do it right, you can blur the lines between pleasure and pain.

6. Become a fan of the "double egg" vibrator. You can put them *anywhere*. One for you and one for your partner, or you can keep both.

7. If you want to join the mile-high club, grab a blanket and a partner. Best time is during take off...enjoy the ride!

8. Liquid latex is so fun and you can just wear it around the house if you feel like it.

Expert number two: Candace!

Candace's tips for a stellar booty experience:

1. If you have a man who knows what he's doing, you know what I mean, it's indescribably glorious. He'll drink from that fuzzy cup all night long.

2. Ladies, you can have a great climax without a man. Toys are wonderful for your "romance library." Put on some soft music and get yourself in the mood. May I introduce the "CalExotics"

toy. It has two motors with twelve functions... go for it girls! There is also the incredible "rose."

3.  Now, those times when you're with a man, tell him exactly how you want him to perform on you! If he's not doing it right, show him!

4.  Remember, it's all about foreplay to get you hot and bothered. Without this, making love is not as good. You must get each other all hot and bothered.

5.  Adult stores have wonderful products like kama sutra lovers' paint boxes. There are white chocolate, milk chocolate and dark chocolate. This even comes with a fun little paint brush!

6.  A great book to buy with pictures is "The Joy of Sex," by Alex Comfort, PhD. It's a classic — still one of the best! An international best-seller since it was first published.

7.  Experiment with edible oils like pleasure balm by kama sutra. Spearmint sensations, oh, heck yes!

8.  Lastly, there are some great edible oils a man can use on you. Salted Caramel is delicious.

Now, our third adventurous lady shares some fun ideas: go Sasha!
Sasha's tips for fantastic hanky panky:

1.  Buy that oil that gets hot when you breathe on it. Use sparingly. Always read labels because if you use this incorrectly, things can go so wrong, so fast.

2.  Ladies, don't feel guilty using outside inspiration to warm you up in advance. Maybe look at photos of hunky actors on your phone. Alain Delon is still quite handsome; back in the day, he was indescribably beautiful. There's also Pablo Schreiber, a true work of art. Men enjoy looking at gorgeous women, so ladies, don't feel a bit guilty if you do this as well!

3.  You are the star of the show. Don't get hung up about a few extra pounds or whether you're getting too noisy. Just enjoy yourself and live it up.

4.  Teach your man how the hit the right spot. He may be off base but he needs to know how to hit that right spot.

5.  Spur-of-the-moment sex is a good thing. Sometimes it happens too quickly for you to have an orgasm. That's okay; it's not every time.

6.  Sex on the beach is fantastic. No other word for it. If you haven't done this yet, put it at the very top of your bucket list. Plan ahead if possible by bringing a towel, but if you're hot and bothered, you won't care if sand travels "where the sun don't shine!"

7.  Don't fake it. Be honest if it's not going to happen that night. My husband and I have been together for quite awhile, so at times I've told him, "Don't try too hard, I've got gas."

8.  Whatever it takes to get into a sultry mood: candles, soft music, or a massage. Think of your partner often and with lust.

9.  Pretend you're a character in a romance novel. Get noisy, get down, whatever you feel like. Don't be lukewarm and boring about sex.

10. Ben wa balls and panty vibrators are the best. Look online how to use them. Use two hours before sex for the fastest and best orgasms imaginable. Between the ben wa balls and the panty vibrator, you can become so sexually charged you'll want sex every day. My husband loves sex, especially when I initiate it.

11. When it comes to a man's anatomy, don't ignore those stepchildren. Enough said!

12. Buy some overpriced raspberries. Organic is best. Wash and dry them well. Your partner can place these luscious berries

anywhere on your body and eat them off. Raspberries do leave stains, so put down some towels. Can't hurt to be romantic and practical at the same time.

Now, here are some tried and true methods that couples say have kept their sex lives interesting and fun. Some of these will be surprising. They're only slightly edited, so some comments will be blunt. Some of these tips come from men and others from women.

1. Couples swapping. We've got another couple whom we've "dated" for the past 20 years. We call them our partner couple. Believe it or not, we all attend the same church. Nobody knows; not our kids, and not friends. People would be stunned because we don't give off an image of swingers in any way, shape or form. But we love our partner couple and they love us. They've helped us fight off boredom for over two decades. We eat out and travel frequently together.

2. Meet at a hotel and pretend to be strangers. Pick up one another in the bar and go back to a room which one of you booked earlier. Get really dressed up for this. Order room service afterwards.

3. When it comes to oral sex, don't be stingy. If your partner's like most people on the planet, they love it. Ladies, use your hands a lot, and practice. There are even great classes for this. Men, if in doubt, just start with the alphabet. And remember, in giving, you are far more likely to receive.

4. When my husband wants to have sex, he texts me an emoji of an eggplant, even if we're sitting in the same room. It is fun and I love it.

5. If I need some warming up, I heat up a little coconut oil and my husband gives me a massage. You can always put down extra towels to save your sheets.

6. Go on vacation together because it's easy to want more sex without the grubbiness of everyday home life. But that being said, don't use this as an excuse to avoid sex when you're at home.

7. My ex-wife always had excuses. She either was pre-menstrual, post-menstrual, or tired. Or it was a headache or cramps. Only three or four days a month did she actually have the green light. We had other problems in our relationship, but the lack of sex really wore on me. I'm glad I remarried. My new wife loves sex and doesn't come up with constant excuses.

8. Buy Halloween costumes and keep them around all year. She dresses up like a naughty nurse and I dress up like a Warlock. It's a silly kind of fun. It gets us in the mood.

9. Vary the time and place. If you only do it in your bedroom on Wednesday and Saturday nights, it's going to get boring. Maybe the den, the bathroom, the hallway, the kitchen, and also different times of day.

10. Kindness means a lot. If your partner is acting like a jerk to you, then expects you to be a dynamo in bed, well, it's unrealistic. Romance happens outside the bedroom, too.

11. Bring food into the bedroom, whipped cream in the can, strawberries, honey, chocolate syrup, ice cream, yes, it's a little messy but it's fun. Then jump in the shower together afterwards.

12. Do it in your jacuzzi or pool. Ignore snoopy neighbors. They might just learn something from you.

13. Do it in the car. You can park by the side of the road like a couple of teenagers. Or go to the drive-in movie and park in the back row.

14. Give each other long massages. It gets you in the mood.

15. Anything to shake it up. If you usually have the room quiet, play some romantic music. Even rock or heavy metal has its place.

16. Initiate sex with your partner more often. Don't always wait for them to make the first move. You can even have a little signal or a code word you use to let them know you're in the mood. Something like "Maltese Falcon" or "Greta Garbo."

17. Go to a sex shop together and buy some stuff. Maybe that oil that gets hot when you breathe on it. But read labels. Make sure neither of you is allergic to the stuff. My husband got a terrible rash "you know where" from this love potion I bought. He was too embarrassed to go to the doctor and walked with a dreadful limp for three weeks.

18. Go someplace in public where you can make out like teenagers but can't go any further. Maybe like a park bench.

19. Bring out the vibrator!

20. Once in awhile, spend the entire day in bed. Watch a couple movies and get food delivered. Take a long shower together.

21. Cook a meal together in the nude or wearing really skimpy outfits like chef aprons.

22. If you have little kids, put a lock on your bedroom door. Make sure the kids get plenty of exercise so they'll sleep soundly and give you some privacy.

23. Sex at least twice a week; three times is better. If one of those times is kind of rushed, well what can you do?

24. Spur-of-the-moment is the greatest. I text my husband at work and tell him to get home fast because I'm waiting for *love.*

25. Couple swapping is fun. Don't make it more than what it is: a way to have sex with another couple and have a good time. There's always the risk of getting emotionally involved. But

that's a chance you may want to take once you see how enjoyable it is spending the afternoon or evening with someone *new*. My wife and I have done this for three years, and we like it a lot. We even went on vacation with another couple and traded hotel rooms. My wife got a little uncomfortable at first and jealous of some of the other women, but she's past that now.

26.  Above all, remember there are 24 hours in each day and 7 days in every week. If you cannot make time for sex at least a couple times a week, your relationship will suffer. Unless you are doing marathon sex, this only takes up a few hours per week total.

# T

---

## Therapy

Many folks swear by couples' therapy; others claim it was a waste of time and money.

Salt Lake City couple Bella and Warren saw a marriage therapist for over a year. Ultimately, it saved their marriage. Bella found it hilarious that she, an attorney, and Warren, a stockbroker, both of them mature, accomplished adults, completely regressed during therapy. During early sessions, the two became like little kids "tattling to mommy," as she put it. Both Bella and Warren wanted their therapist to see just how awful and guilty the other kid was.

But through therapy they both learned to temper their strong personalities and stop competing. Their therapist was impartial and they both felt they were being treated fairly.

However, a frequent complaint is that the therapist appears to take sides. Either the husband or the wife is chosen as "favorite kid." Perhaps the therapist scolds or corrects the other spouse more frequently.

Or, it's a matter of personality. Perhaps you just don't "jive" with a particular therapist.

Kari and Marlon saw a therapist who had helped their friends resolve some issues. Unfortunately, Kari and Marlon's experience with the same therapist was rather poor.

Kari's personality is forceful even under optimum circumstances, but when upset, she becomes particularly strident, one might even say rude. Marlon, on the other hand, was Mr. "Personality Plus," very likeable and easygoing.

Marlon may come across as charming, but in actuality, he's an extremely selfish man and very difficult to live with.

On rare occasions, perhaps once or twice a month, Kari had dinner with a few girlfriends or co-workers. When she'd return home around nine pm, their two little girls, ages six and eight, would still be running around in their dirty school clothes, their "dinner" having consisted of junky snacks, and with none of their homework done. When Kari confronted Marlon on these occasions, he made excuses and complained it was just too much to keep track of the girls and their evening routine.

Marlon supervised close to 250 people at his company, so it's difficult to fathom he couldn't handle taking care of his two small daughters for just a few hours. To top it off, Marlon was also a careless driver, had received many speeding tickets and had been in several accidents.

Therefore, Kari had legitimate grievances, but when she expressed herself in such a strident manner, the therapist became annoyed. By contrast, Marlon was smooth and charming, and the therapist seemed to find him delightful.

Kari believed therapy was making their situation worse. She felt the therapist was thinking, "You have a nice husband and should be grateful, instead of complaining all the time."

Now, this was possibly just Kari's perspective, but for couples' therapy to succeed, both spouses must feel supported.

Kari then found another therapist, a man this time, who immediately caught on to Marlon's "BS." To Marlon's credit, when he found himself no longer teacher's pet, the therapist was able to rapidly "cut through the mustard," and Marlon shaped up fast. His driving immediately improved and he became much more accountable with his daughters.

# Travel

Saint Augustine phrased it best: "The world is a book and those who do not travel read only one page."

Here's a great saying: "There are two types of people, those who love to buy furniture and those who love to travel."

Excluding rich couples who can afford to do everything, most do fall into one of these two categories.

If one partner loves to travel and the other has no interest, and also possibly resents the other traveling without them, this can be a colossal problem.

Whenever my old boyfriend got a hankering to go somewhere, for example Europe, he went to the library and looked at photos of Europe (this of course was in the 80s and pre-internet). By looking at the photos, he'd then be quite satisfied and thus felt he didn't need to *actually visit* Europe. Though I was quite smitten with him at the time, I recall thinking to myself how odd this all was. A modern-day equivalent would be someone looking online at photos of holiday spots rather than actually ever traveling there.

Heavens to mergatroyd, if travel is your jam, this is *not* the person to marry.

However, if you adore traveling and are already married to someone who has no interest, please revisit chapter C (compromise). One possible solution is traveling with a friend.

Hopefully, you can work out a plan that suits you both. One couple contributing to the "Do's and Dont's" section mentioned that long weekend getaways revived their relationship.

One last note about travel: don't miss out altogether if you've got little money or time off from work. Even a quick getaway for two days can give you a welcome break from everyday life. Camping is generally less expensive than staying at hotels, and hotels are less costly on weekdays.

# Tailgating
## (see also envy)

Tailgating, envy's bitter little cousin, definitely merits some special attention. What exactly is tailgating? Well, this evil syndrome occurs when one couple deeply envies another, and tries desperately to keep up with them. We've all been there!

Perhaps the other couple is younger, better-looking, has nicer clothes, more sparkling personalities, or appears to have an enviable sex life.

But, in no instance is tailgating so detrimental than when the other couple has more of that glorious green stuff...you guessed it! Moola ... aka money. Money, money, money, money, money! As I'm warbling away, I deeply assure you, I've no plans whatsoever to quit my day job for a singing career. Of course, I hope and pray Demi Lovato, Celine Dion or Adele listens and offers me a backup singer job, but deep down I realize this isn't too likely.

I touched upon this nasty little subject earlier in the "envy" section. It's important to recognize when you're tailgating, as this habit can deviously sneak up behind you just like Joe in the show "You," preferably Season One.

Seattle couple Candy and Ted were in their late 30s, had been married for five years and were best friends with Sue and Jeff. Candy was a schoolteacher and Ted worked for the post office. They had decent jobs; nothing extraordinary. On the other hand, Sue was an attorney and Jeff was a cardiologist. Candy and Sue had been roommates in college and best friends ever since. Money had never been an issue in college, since neither girl had much back then. They'd even joked about how poor they were. Somehow, this had been so much more amusing "back in the day."

There was never an issue with money when Candy and Sue socialized, but when the two husbands were involved, their differences became glaringly apparent. While Jeff was certainly not a snob, his idea of a Saturday night dinner wasn't exactly Applebee's. As Jeff earned approximately 23 times more than Ted, he was more than happy to pick up the tab at restaurants. However, Ted found this humiliating, and he and Candy had frequently argued about it.

One possible solution would be to eliminate double dates, but the four of them had a really great time together. Fortunately, they created a plan. Sue and Jeff visited Candy and Ted at their home for dinners, and then when they all ate out, Jeff picked up the tab. This compromise worked out beautifully; Ted was an excellent cook and loved showing off his culinary expertise.

By the way, Candy and Sue decided upon this solution, and then both of them later spoke with their husbands. Money can be such a touchy issue, especially when pride is involved.

Now, tailgating becomes the biggest mess when the poorer couple actually goes massively into debt in a vain attempt to keep up. This happens far, far more frequently than you might ever imagine.

Frances and Sterling and Alice and Mike lived in El Paso and had been best friends for nearly 20 years. During this time, they'd taken over 15 wonderful vacations together. This would have been sheer perfection except for one snag: Frances and Sterling were richy-rich, and Alice and Mike were not. Alice and Mike had actually refinanced their home three times to pay off debt from these trips.

This was causing much stress, as their mortgage had become as ginormous as a sasquatch footprint.

The foursome took two big trips each year; spring and fall. Alice wanted to curtail the travel; Mike did not. He felt keenly that they weren't getting any younger and he feared the day when travel might become impossible.

After much discussion and frankly, a few arguments, Alice called Frances and said candidly that she and Mike wanted to take the next trip, but needed to cut costs. To her surprise, Frances was extremely accommodating and suggested a road trip to the Sedona desert in Arizona. This holiday was very affordable and turned out to be one of the best trips the four had ever taken.

If your friends are the genuine article, they'll want to spend time with you minus lavish settings. But no doubt, money's a touchy and often embarrassing topic, and maybe that's why folks can get into such scalding water "keeping up with those darn Joneses."

# Thank You

These two simple words are among the most powerful in the English language. They rank right up there with "I'm sorry."

Interestingly, the lack of a simple "thank you" from their spouse is one thing unhappily married folks complain about most frequently.

When you say "thank you" to your spouse, they feel appreciated. When someone feels appreciated, they don't feel taken for granted. Feeling taken for granted is rarely good and contributes to resentment. Resentment leads to deterioration of the relationship and perhaps an eventual phone call to "Divorce R Us."

Some folks *never* give their partner the gift of a simple "thank you." Why is this? Possibly, it's just a bad habit and they've always taken their spouse for granted. Maybe after so many years of marriage, they feel a bit entitled.

Perhaps the "bread winning" spouse feels their pay-check is quite thanks enough.

Quick quiz: if you suspect you're guilty of this, does your spouse ever blurt out "You're welcome," when you haven't actually uttered the words "Thank you?"

If you haven't expressed gratitude in a long time, it may feel awkward, fake and phony.

The more you do it, however, the easier it becomes. Don't get fancy, either. Just a simple "thank you for taking out the trash," is admittedly mundane, but a good start nonetheless.

Perhaps shake up the method of delivery. Perhaps even write an old-school snail mail "thank-you" note from time to time. Put a stamp on it and mail it to your spouse! They likely will be stunned, as possibly 15 years have elapsed since anything besides magazines, bills and junk have arrived in the mailbox.

There's always the good old faithful "post-it" note. Maybe stick the note on top of your partner's favorite snack or candy bar.

# Try

By now, most of us have heard the famous Yoda saying: "Do. Or do not. There is no try."

Or, my personal favorite: "Give it the old college try."

If, like me, you're a virtual genius at making excuses, when you do finally embrace the concept of "just do it," it's a mind shift. You'll look at things in a completely new way.

But first, let's take a look at that perennial favorite: the concept of "to try."

It starts early. We're taught as kids to "try our best." Just the sound of it is fantastic, so all-American. You get Ghirardelli brownie points when you say you're going to "give something a try."

Let's now view the excruciating topic of weight loss. How many of us (myself for sure!) have proclaimed, "I'm going to *try* and lose weight."

And honestly, we really do mean to try. We have the absolute best intentions. But often, nothing truly changes.

We embark on yet another reducing plan, very determined, and then we go through all the motions, but deep down, we are skeptical.

We know very well that Toll House cookies, Dorito's, and sinister macaroni and cheese are evilly lurking everywhere. Baskin-Robbins and wicked Ferrero Rocher are hiding in the alleyway behind a dumpster, just waiting to jump us.

So, when we cheat on the plan, maybe don't lose much, or like many sad sacks, and I've been part of this elite group more times than I can count, actually lose the weight, then gain it all back, and then some, we can at least say, "Well, I tried."

We definitely garner sympathy from friends and loved ones, but nothing has really changed, has it? The tragic result is our plump little booties have not substantially reduced in size.

So, how does all of this apply to your marriage? Well, if your marriage has sadly deteriorated, but is still salvageable, perhaps don't just say you're going to try.

Just do it.

I know, I know...easy for me to say "just do it."

Therefore, to provide more oomph to this section, I shall hereby share an embarrassing personal story "straight outta 1990." Some of you cute little youngsters weren't even a gleam in mama's eye way back then.

Ok, here goes: I myself have had to improve my bad temper. I'm not proud to share this example, because it's mortifying, but worthwhile to relay.

When Robert and I had been wed just two years, we went through some issues with his mother. There was a huge conflict over Thanksgiving plans. My MIL wanted us to spend Turkey Day in Los Altos with her side of the family, but my dad felt rather neglected.

For the past three years, I hadn't seen my dad on Thanksgiving Day. So, we decided to spend the holiday in Los Angeles with him that year. Seems reasonable, right? But my MIL was furious and making my life miserable. Or, I should re-phrase this: I was *allowing her* to make my life miserable. Robert and I were arguing about this as I was setting the dinner table. To be accurate, I was doing most of the talking, ranting about how his mom was driving me nuts.

In all fairness, I was only 27. Some girls are quite mature at this age; I was still rather childish. Nonetheless, of course, I "knew it all."

Trying vainly to appease me, Robert said I shouldn't let his mom bother me. At this, I completely lost my temper and yelled, "Your mom is driving me nuts!" At the same time, I deliberately dropped the plate I was holding onto the floor.

It shattered into a gazillion pieces.

Robert was horrified and said, "I can't believe you did that!" By this time, I had a full head of steam, and I yelled, "You want another one?" before dropping a second plate.

I'm not proud of this incident; it's actually quite humiliating.

But it's worthwhile to share because I don't ever want to sound like, "Ooh, look at me, I've been married 35 years, what an expert! I'm so good at marriage!"

By the way, who can recall that show, "Crazy Ex-Girlfriend," where the instructor sings, "I'm so good at yoga!"

Robert was clearly disgusted with me; he grabbed his car keys and left the house. I'm sure he feared he'd married a complete nut job.

I grabbed some things and stayed the night at my girlfriend Lisa's house. If I'd been expecting girl-to-girl solidarity, well, I was sadly mistaken. Lisa agreed my MIL was a royal pain in the arse, but as she put it, Robert was a really nice husband and I was way out of line dropping not just one, but two plates.

The next day after work I slunk home with my tail between my legs, so to speak. Robert said we had to talk, so we sat on the den couch. I cried a lot and apologized. "I didn't grow up in a house with violence and I'm not going to live that way," Robert began. I should point out here that I had not either. My parents had yelled at one another, but nothing had ever gotten broken.

Until this time, my flimsy excuse for my bad temper was that I was Italian. Now, I must add here that my mom was actually 100 percent Italian, yet had somehow managed to keep from breaking a single plate in her entire lifetime. As for me, I'm actually less than half Italian - so I must abandon that excuse.

Although I've been told my being half Eastern European and half Italian makes me a volatile mix, darn it, much as I'd love to shove the blame onto my folks, it wasn't really genealogy.

Robert then added the perfect thing to "scare me straight." He said, "What if we have a child someday and they're in the room when you're breaking plates and a piece of broken glass flies up into their eye?"

Of course, I was bawling by this time.

I can't pretend to have never yelled since 1990. However, since the "plates fiasco," I've never thrown or broken anything, and I've been angry plenty of times in the past 33 years.

I knew Robert wouldn't tolerate that behavior, and honestly, why should he? Why should anyone? Losing your temper is not a great place to be emotionally. Learning to control this is a learned skill for many; it certainly was for me.

So, although this particular story is mortifying, it does illustrate a point. If you're doing something your spouse can't tolerate, and you know you're in the wrong, don't "try" to improve. *Just do it!*

Ironically, the two innocent plates that died such a tragic and violent death that day were part of a set given to me by my (now deceased) MIL. They were quite beautiful, and I use the remainder of the set to this day... the eight dinner plates, *six* salad plates and so forth.

As luck would have it, I have searched everywhere but have been unable to replace the two salad plates.

So, think about something you can do to improve yourself, or to better your relationship.

Are you just trying? Or are you ready to just do it?

## Timing

Skillful timing is crucial to any good relationship. While all of us can probably agree with this statement, if you're like me, your timing often kind of...well, sucks.

Here's one example. Your spouse comes home after a long, stressful day at work, tired and cranky from dealing with difficult co-workers, a demanding boss, and terrible traffic. All they care about is taking a load off, watching some TV and getting some peace and quiet.

Ergo, now is *not* the ideal time to pounce on them with the jolly news that your checking account is overdrawn, the kitchen faucet is dripping, or your next-door neighbors have once again griped that your Boston terrier Alfie barks energetically under their window.

One wife mentioned that when her daughter was being obnoxious, she'd "fire off like a cannon" to her husband the moment he walked through the door. He wasn't receptive, and so she realized her timing was off.

Since then, she's learned to wait. Perhaps she takes a brief walk before he gets home from work, so she's a bit more relaxed when he arrives. She greets him in a positive way and waits until later to tattle about their daughter.

Incidentally, a 1970s marriage advice book suggested that wives greet their husbands at the door enveloped head-to-toe in saran wrap. Just wondering if anyone else recalls this? No judgement whatsoever...so long as the plastic gets recycled later.

Again, let your spouse unwind a bit before leaping on top of them with problems. Perhaps broach the subject after dinner, or once the kids have been put to bed.

The same goes for good news, unless it's the "scream it out loud" variety. With moderately good news, wait until the timing is right before mentioning it. Otherwise, you may be setting yourself up for failure. If you spring good news on your partner when they're distracted, their reaction may be lukewarm, and you'll be disappointed.

Lexington, Kentucky couple Candy and Jim had been married for six years and had two small daughters. Candy was a stay-home mom and Jim had a high-pressure sales job.

One day, Candy was furious about an upsetting confrontation with Judith, an overbearing mom in her younger daughter's class. Judith had rudely called Candy out for not helping enough with art docent. To add to the charm of the situation, Judith did this in front of their kids' teacher, Miss Davison.

Candy was infuriated and she couldn't wait to tell Jim. This wasn't the first time she'd had problems with that bossy, fake boobs, fake blonde, know-it-all Judith.

But Jim's day had been even worse. He'd painstakingly created an ingenious plan to streamline production at his company, but his evil, sneaky co-worker Hudson had gone and stolen all the credit.

That morning, Jim had described the plan to his buddy Tom; walking out of the break room, they'd encountered Hudson, lurking and creeping in the hallway. Devious little Hudson had been blessed with supersonic hearing, and at their department meeting that very same afternoon, had introduced Jim's idea as his very own.

Their boss had absolutely loved the plan. Jim was furious. He'd waited too long to tell their boss, and now it was too late.

Jim and Hudson were competing for a promotion, and it now appeared that the slimy scoundrel Hudson had the edge.

So, by the time he stomped through the front door, Jim was in a lousy mood. Before he'd even set down his briefcase, Candy had launched into a tirade about annoying, bitchy, know-it-all Judith.

The normally patient Jim rolled his eyes and said Candy's problem was minor compared to his. The two ended up having a full-blown argument.

After the crummy day they'd both had, instead of comforting one another, both went to bed angry.

Had Candy waited just a bit to tell Jim her story, she undoubtedly would have gotten a better response.

Good timing is like any other skill...it can improve with practice.

Perhaps this falls under the category of "adulting." (Who else isn't crazy about this word?) It takes patience and self-restraint to wait until just the right time to communicate with your spouse.

Perhaps they handle bad news best after a meal. If so, make sure they polish off a full bowl of pasta carbonara before dropping the bomb that 16-year-old Jamison dented the Rav 4. For bad news prep, you absolutely can't go wrong with pasta for a woman and a big steak for a man. This may sound like a cliché, but frequently, this seems to hold true.

Again, be clever...wait patiently until the last of the top sirloin with A-1 sauce has been consumed to ever-so-casually mention that a parking pole ran into your Jetta at the mall, and that 14-year-old Chelsea will need braces costing seven thousand dollars.

# Truce

One definition of "truce" is "an agreement between enemies or opponents to stop fighting or arguing for a certain length of time." You can also call it a "ceasefire."

Well, hopefully you and your spouse aren't enemies. But if you're perilously close, please do circle back to the "Dr. Linda Boot Camp" section.

Even if your relationship is healthy overall, when you're in the middle of a fight, you may feel like enemies.

So, on those occasions when you're really just "stuck" and can't agree, perhaps a truce is in order.

How you handle the truce is entirely up to you. Either partner can be the first to suggest it. If that's you, don't feel like you're capitulating. You're merely being practical by saying that - just for now - you are putting a halt to the bickering.

You're also evading the dilemma of who's right and who's wrong.

You're always at liberty to resume the argument later. However, you may be pleasantly surprised that after the truce, you both lose steam and forget why you were angry in the first place.

If it's a larger issue, the truce gives you some time to regroup and regain energy.

Robert and I have "called a truce" more times than I can count. We even have a hand motion we do to signify this; we touch thumbs and we both say the word "truce." This physical action is valuable because it gives concrete motion to begin the ceasefire.

Don't feel that you're "caving in" if you're the one suggesting the truce. You're simply weary of arguing, and you're being practical.

If your spouse argues and debates more than is healthy and it's driving you bananas, suggest they volunteer at an animal shelter. While walking the dogs, they can debate to their heart's content. Dogs love conversation and are great listeners.

## Tactless

How does one define a tactless person? For starters, they are usually prone to make insensitive or insulting remarks. Often they cannot resist commenting on someone's race, religion, appearance, or age. Their observations are often delivered "in fun," but it's always fun at someone else's expense.

It's difficult to truly relax around an insensitive person, as there's no telling what cringe-worthy comment they may blurt out next.

When confronted, this individual typically protests they were only joking.

My high-school classmate Michelle always made tactless jokes at someone's expense. You never knew when you'd be the unlucky recipient of one of her "zingers." One day, some of us kids were sitting on the quad at lunch and our friend Angela was eating cottage cheese. Michelle said to no one in particular, "Hey, did you know cottage cheese was fattening? Yep, because only fat people eat it."

Angela had recently slimmed down, but like many high-school girls, myself included, was super-sensitive when it came to her weight. So, as one might imagine, Michelle's comment went over just like a two-ton load of bricks.

Michelle paid a steep price for her tactlessness; she had few close friends.

Here's another retro tale from the big 80s about Robin, aka "frozen yogurt girl" at my dorm freshman year at Pepperdine University.

Robin had a special talent for cutting others down. If a girl wore new jeans, Robin would charmingly comment they made her butt look big. She once advised me, "Your new haircut is unfortunate, Linda, but it will grow out."

In those pre-cell phone days, if we wanted frozen yogurt, we'd stick our heads out into the hallways and yell, "Frozen yogurt, five minutes." Everyone then gathered in the dorm lobby below, piled in a few cars, then headed down the hill to town. Robin never missed an outing, and each time she managed to insult someone. The girls got sick and tired of her in record time.

By Thanksgiving, we'd cleverly revised our frozen yogurt regime. Rather than yelling down the halls, we'd phone one another, sneak quietly down to the lobby, and make our escape. Often, Robin was the only one left behind.

After awhile, I pitied her. I insisted we invite her next time. So one evening, we were all sitting at the "Thinnery," a frozen yogurt joint in Westwood, when a man entered wearing overalls and work boots. Robin, whose father was a very prominent attorney, made an observation about blue-collar workers who couldn't speak English. My father had sacrificed a great deal to send me to this fancy college, was blue-collar all his life, and spoke perfect English. I said something in defense of the guy to Robin, and she just laughed. I instantly hated her guts. I told my roommate later at the dorm we could never invite Robin again.

There are two categories of tactless folks: the truly clueless, who say insensitive things without true malice, and those individuals who are more deliberate in their actions. Those in the second category say cruel things in an attempt to feel better.

If you're nodding your head by now, is your spouse tactless?

If so, it's inevitable that they'll embarrass you and cause you stress. Here are three possible choices: get your spouse to change, endure the mortification, or socialize without them as much as humanly possible.

Or, perhaps it's you who is tactless. If, after some soul-searching, you realize that you actually enjoy upsetting and embarrassing others, congratulations on facing your flaw. A next step could be to get some counseling to see where this stems from and then work on changing it.

## Toot Your Own Horn

This was one of my mom's very favorite sayings. When I was in elementary school, someone had hurt my feelings and I didn't stick up for myself. I can't remember all the details, but I do recall my mom telling me to speak up next time.

The part I remember best was her saying, "Linda, if you don't toot your own horn, no one will do it for you."

So what does this mean for building a good marriage? Well, for starters, it's got a lot to do with speaking up and being true to yourself.

*Speak up* when you feel your partner isn't treating you well. This isn't the same as endlessly griping and bitching, by the way. Instead, it's being loyal to yourself and having a voice in your marriage.

If you've spent many years in a relationship where your input is not heard, this will be a challenge. Baby steps may be the best way to go. Therapy can also be invaluable. If you've never really "tooted your own horn," try giving it a whirl. You may love it.

## Teenage Date Night

Okay, this one is goofy and fun.

Here's how teenage date night works: you and your spouse create a fun date you would have absolutely loved as 17-year-olds. If, like me, you were a "dateless wonder" in high school, this will be particularly gratifying.

Here are some suggestions:

- Get Sonic or Jack-in-the-Box and go see a drive-in movie.

- Go to a pier with a Ferris wheel. Ride on the wheel and eat corn dogs and cotton candy.

- Visit an amusement park and go on all the rides.

- Rent bicycles and ride at the beach.

- Roller blading or ice skating.

- Go see the submarine races. At Westchester High, this was a euphemism for "make out" in the car.

# U

## Understanding

Understanding is empathy's kissing cousin. Realizing what makes your spouse "tick" and what's important to them is crucial.

But often we barely understand ourselves...!

George and Lisa lived in Charlotte, North Carolina, and had been very happily wed for seven years when they hit a very large snag. Before marrying, they'd discussed the subject of children and agreed that neither wanted any.

Having already done the "kid thing," as he phrased it, George had absolutely no desire for more children. His 12-year-old son Matthew lived nearby with George's ex-wife Bonnie and had almost no relationship with George. Lisa had only been 31 when she'd married George, loved to travel, and was a free spirit. She absolutely didn't want kids of her own.

Seven years elapsed, during which time several of Lisa's friends became moms, including her best friend Carla. Lisa attended multiple baby showers, was present for the birth of Carla's baby Daniel, and also frequently babysat Daniel.

Eventually Lisa realized she'd been mistaken; she very much wanted to be a mom after all.

George and Lisa had several fruitless conversations which always culminated in her crying and him feeling resentful. Lisa felt George was being inflexible. George felt deceived, because they'd been in perfect agreement, and now she was "changing the playbook," as he phrased it.

Lisa was now 38 and believed that her window of opportunity to be a mom was rapidly closing. She decided to leave George and find another relationship. She also contemplated hiring a surrogate father, and becoming a single mom.

Lisa packed her bags and prepared to move in with her sister. George was frantic; he didn't want to lose his wife. Fortunately, in an attempt to find some common ground, this couple tried marriage counseling.

During counseling, some crucial facts arose. George had endured a horrific experience as a parent. He and Bonnie had been teenage parents. Bonnie was bipolar, had refused to take her medicine, and had lashed out in unpredictable rages. She had done terrifying things such as trying to shove George out of moving vehicles.

George and Bonnie had split up when Matthew was three; sharing custody had been a living nightmare. Bonnie used Matthew just like a pawn in a chess match. Whenever she was angry with George, she pretended Matthew was ill so he couldn't visit his dad. Bonnie also fabricated outrageous stories to turn Matthew against George.

George had vowed to forget that awful time, so had never shared with Lisa the miserable crazy train parenthood had been for him.

During therapy, George realized he wasn't opposed to having more children, as he'd previously believed. He actually liked the idea, but had feared that his marriage to Lisa might take a horrifying turn, such as with his ex-wife. Their therapist helped George realize he was comparing apples and kumquats, as Bonnie was destructive, dishonest and bipolar, and Lisa was stable, truthful, and emotionally healthy.

George and Lisa went on to become parents to a son and daughter. They are still very happily married to this day. George's son Matthew is now a college student, and over the years, the two have become extremely close.

## U-turn

Imagine this: you and your spouse are planning to attend a fabulous, momentous event. This might be a European getaway with another couple, your nephew's college graduation in New York, or a destination wedding in Provence.

You normally would be anticipating this event with all the eagerness of a crooked politician on Election Day, but sadly, you're tempted to abandon the whole enchilada.

Why? I'll tell you why, it's because you and your partner can't stand one another right now. You hate each other's guts. You're fighting just like a micro-pack of rabid, snarling little hyenas.

Pardon the expression, but no matter what you do, you're screwed. You'd rather die than miss this event, but it doesn't take a Magic 8 ball to predict that you'll have a ghastly time. Right now, every time you look at one another you grimace and show your teeth.

Might we introduce, drumroll please: the simply divine, the glorious U-turn. This strategy is so simple in its concept and execution that skeptical friends who've tried it are utterly amazed how beautifully it actually succeeds.

Put simply, the "U-turn" works this way: when you and your partner are *really* not getting along, in fact can't even tolerate the sight of one another, you abruptly change your attitude and convincingly deceive yourself you're no longer angry.

Here's the crucial part: you give *zero advance notice and no explanation whatsoever* to your partner.

It's exactly as the name implies.

You're driving down Wilshire Boulevard in Beverly Hills in your bright blue Jetta with the moon roof, the sun is shining, Tom Petty's playing on the car stereo, there's not a cop in sight, so you gleefully pull an outrageous, abrupt U-turn, right out of nowhere.

The best way to explain this strategy is by giving an example.

My former co-worker Patricia was not getting along with her husband Brad. The two had been married for about five years. Normally, they had a very solid and loving relationship, but recently were going through a decidedly rough patch.

There hadn't been any one major incident, but rather instead, many small annoyances had built up until the two had begun arguing nonstop. This had been going on for about a month.

One Friday, Patricia mentioned to me that they'd planned to visit Palm Springs the next day, but she'd decided to cancel the trip. The flights and hotel had been booked and paid for some time ago.

Patricia and Brad both simply adored Palm Springs, but in their current state, she predicted the trip would be a disaster.

Particularly since the trip had already been paid for, I suggested Patricia give the "U-turn" a whirl. Her instructions were to return home that evening bearing Brad's number-one favorite food, Thai curry. She wasn't to mention their ongoing argument or display any "attitude" whatsoever.

Instead, she was to dish up the Thai food and talk excitedly about Palm Springs and all the fun things they'd do there together.

After dinner, Patricia was to then immediately begin packing for their flight and to not indicate by any word or gesture they'd been arguing.

Patricia agreed to give the "U-turn" her best shot. She was somewhat skeptical, but as she put it, "What have I got to lose?"

When Patricia returned to the office a few days later, she said it was one of their best trips ever. Brad had appeared stunned on Friday when she dished up his favorite food and acted like nothing was wrong. He looked at her quite suspiciously as she was packing for the trip, but made no comment.

He'd seemed relieved that she'd somehow developed a very weird case of total amnesia.

Patricia and Brad went on to have an absolutely wonderful time. The plane rides, weather and hotel were all perfect. Brad had said on the flight home he'd thought she would cancel the trip, and was so glad she hadn't.

Added bonus: when they returned home, Brad and Patricia were still in sync. They then resumed their normal relationship dynamic, which was positive, cordial and loving.

Whatever they had been fighting about was forgotten because it was small beans. And face it folks, divorce attorneys deal with couples splitting up over mini frijoles every day of the week, including Sundays.

The unpretentious yet glorious U-turn accomplishes this: when you're at a stalemate like Brad and Patricia, number one, you don't miss out on an important event, and number two, your relationship might miraculously improve to boot.

To recap: with no warning whatsoever, completely change your attitude for the better, carry on as if nothing were wrong, then proceed to thoroughly enjoy the trip or other event.

Then, at the conclusion of the event, you can decide whether to stay in denial or pick up where you left off with the arguing.

Particularly if you weren't in conflict over something crucial, such as he wants to move to Alaska and you want to stay in Hawaii, you may then just choose to keep the denial going. Perhaps if it was merely a bunch of petty annoyances which had built up, then how *sensational*, to paraphrase Hayley Mills in the original "Parent Trap" film, if you can just drop it and forget the whole conflict.

In the case of Patricia and Brad, the "U-turn" accomplished exactly what was intended: they had a wonderful, romantic trip, and didn't lose any hard-earned money from cancelled reservations. Best of all, like hot fudge, nuts and two cherries on a sundae, their relationship took a miraculous turn for the better.

During their Palm Springs mini-break, Patricia and Brad rapidly evolved from cranky, crabby and sick of one another, to refreshed, renewed, and rejuvenated.

## Unity

Another title for this section could be "united front." No one can deny that unity is so important for a couple.

Of course, we all want to succeed in achieving this unity. I myself often fall short, very short; sadly, even shorter than my actual height of 5'4" and ¾ inches.

In 2003, when Andrea was just eight years old, our little family visited Hawaii. At the time, Andrea loved nothing more than jumping up and down on her bed at home. No surprise, when we got to our room, she immediately started hopping up and down on the bed. Robert told her it was rude to jump on the hotel bed and he made her stop. Honestly, I didn't see what the big deal was. After all, half my childhood was spent jumping on beds.

So, I stage-whispered to Andrea, "Wait until daddy gets into the shower, and then you can jump on the bed as much as you want."

Well, this would have worked out splendidly, except that at age eight, Andrea was far too young for this type of collusion. She had a simply fantastic time jumping on the bed, but then when Robert got out of the shower, she tattled on me first thing. Consequently, Robert was quite annoyed with me for the first three days of the trip. He said I didn't have his back, and he was kind of right.

So...how exactly does a couple foster this unity? One way is by displaying solidarity. For example, I should have backed Robert on the "no jumping on the bed" thing.

In a perfect world, disagreements take place in private, and couples "have each other's backs" at all times when dealing with children, family and friends. For example, one parent thinks it's fantastic if their nine-year-old son attends summer camp for three weeks, but the other thinks it's insane. One parent wants their college-age daughter to study abroad in a third-world country, while the other parent finds this absolutely nuts.

Couples with children should discuss important matters privately before making announcements to their kids. The kids then realize, darn it! They cannot pit one parent against the other. Children are sheer geniuses at doing this, by the way. They can work parents at both ends with a combination of persuasion and "guilting." It takes both skill and cunning to outsmart the little rascals.

Plus, parents must never, ever forget for an instant that the average child is a world-class eavesdropper. They are marvels at lurking around — their tiny bodies enable them to listen at closed doors like miniature 007's.

If you and hubs are in the bedroom discussing Aunt Pamela's steamy affair with her church pastor, rest assured that little Gunther already knows every scandalous detail. Of course he does! His 40-pound frame expertly creeps down the hall just like a mini ninja.

Displaying unity is also important with the in-laws. Here's one tale how this can go awry. Judy and Dustin had been married for 15 years and had one teenage son, Eddie. Two years ago, Dustin had quit his job working for a large public relations firm, and had opened his own small PR firm which represented athletes.

Dustin and Judy had both agreed this was the best thing for their family. The firm he'd worked for had gypped him out of several substantial bonuses over the years. The new plan would enable them to live a much better life. But in the meantime, and Judy had absolutely agreed to this: Dustin would need to put in a lot of hours.

When Dustin began staying late at the office, Judy complained to her parents that he was never around. She could have vented to her girl-friends, the mailman, even her cleaning lady. Even the person standing in line behind Joan at Trader Joe's, like it or not, would have been a captive audience. Instead, by unloading to her parents, she put herself back in the position of being their little girl.

Up to this time, Judy's father, Ron, had been very close to Dustin. The two had taken monthly fishing trips for the past 14 years. Dustin especially valued his relationship with Ron as his own father had passed away when he'd been in college. As for Ron, he had two daughters and so regarded Dustin as the son he'd never had.

Now, however, Ron increasingly heard from his daughter how lonely and neglected she was. Judy did have some valid complaints; Dustin frequently promised to be home by a certain time and was often quite late. But no matter how busy he was, Dustin did manage to get home for dinner at least two weeknights. He also spent time with Judy on the weekends. But Judy played the victim and chose to vent to her parents.

After about a year, at dinners or holiday occasions, Ron began commenting to Dustin, "You're never there for my daughter." Judy would just sit there and she never stuck up for Dustin. Incidentally, Judy had been an excellent 3rd grade teacher back in the day, but had let her teaching credentials expire. So, her not being busy enough possibly contributed to her feeling of being abandoned.

We all have dreams in life; things we wish to achieve. Whether or not our partner encourages us and supports us in those dreams brings us either a sense of unity or division.

I formed Nimchuk Equine Foundation the summer of 2021. My original dream was to open my own horse rescue. But since we live in San Diego, California, where an acre of land costs more than an acre of gold, it was more practical to build a fundraising organization to help existing horse rescues.

Robert encouraged and supported me throughout the entire process. He spent countless hours packaging caramels for our fundraisers, working at events, and giving me advice.

So...back to Dustin and Judy. Over the next two years, Dustin worked incredibly hard and became more and more successful. Judy continued to vent and began to exhibit signs of being a martyr. She complained that she was forced to raise their son Eddie all on her own. This was not exactly accurate: Eddie was now a sophomore in college, plus Dustin and Eddie had a very solid, close relationship.

Dustin and Ron no longer took fishing trips together because Ron blamed Dustin for his daughter's unhappiness.

During this time— no surprise— Dustin and Judy lost nearly all their unity as a couple. Dustin cared less and less about pleasing her because no matter what he did, she was still unhappy. Their relationship continued to suffer, and a year later, Dustin filed for divorce.

Now, what could have kept this couple together?

Judy had continued describing herself as a "full-time mom" even after Eddie started high school. She could have renewed her teaching credentials, but never galvanized herself to make this happen. She'd had very little going on in her life; rather than working to change this, she'd blamed her husband for her unhappiness.

This brings up a key point: it's far easier to point the finger at your spouse for your unhappiness than to make positive changes in your own life. We addressed this earlier, but it's good to reiterate, as this happens frequently.

Dustin gave up on their marriage because no matter what he did, Judy was just going to complain. He felt she didn't value anything he did. The concept of "value" comes up later in this book... stay tuned, folks!

## Ultimatum

Is it a mistake to give your partner an ultimatum? Well, the short answer is: yes and no. There are two kinds of ultimatums, the way we see it, little ones and big 'uns. While both can be perceived by your partner as threats, little ones can be effective, given certain circumstances. Big 'uns, on the other hand, can backfire like those cannons they fired in the Revolutionary War.

Let's just say your partner has acted like a real jerk all morning. He or she has snapped at you several times, and is just being plain rude. There's no other word for it. Now, imagine you two had planned on having lunch that same day at the beach. How about you tell your partner: "If you keep acting like a jerk, I won't go to lunch with you."

So, while this *is* an ultimatum of sorts, it's not exactly like you're threatening divorce here. You're merely acknowledging that you have a choice whether or not to go to lunch, and you're warning your partner that you may decline.

Now, how about a "big 'un" ultimatum? This would be threatening to move out, or dial the number of "Divorce Attorneys R Us." While this may shock your partner into improving their behavior, it can also – pardon the expression – really piss them off.

Dish out too many ultimatums and this may irk them to the point of saying, "Okay, go. Don't let the swinging saloon door hit you on the way out." Then, where does that leave you? You either move out at that point, or if you don't, you kinda lose face. You become the King or Queen of empty threats.

While one might view ultimatums as a manipulative technique, in certain circumstances, they can actually save a relationship.

Kaitlin and Liam had been happily married for four years and were in their mid-30s. They resided in the grand historical "ye olde" town of Boston. Their goal was to start trying for a baby, but Liam's drinking had recently become an issue.

Liam worked as the manager of a gastropub. His usual schedule was the lunch shift, and he never drank on the job. However, he'd begun socializing frequently with his hard-drinking co-workers who frequented the Red Lion, a bar down the street.

Liam's shift at the gastropub ended at about three p.m., and then he hung out at the Red Lion until six p.m., returning home the same time as Kaitlin, who worked at a nearby insurance office.

Liam typically consumed no more than three drinks over the course of three hours, and always ate a big bowl of "clam chowda," or even a little "lobstah," so that the liquor didn't hit him so hard. One night somebody bought rounds of drinks for everyone and Liam lost count; he'd had about seven. He also hadn't been keeping track of how much he'd been drinking at home, and this amount had increased in the past few years.

Kaitlin was cooking dinner in their kitchen when she heard a crash down the street. Liam's blue F-150 truck had smashed into the Winthrop's beautiful gray birch tree. The Winthrops were not home at the time and were remarkably gracious the next day when Liam told them he'd swerved to avoid an oncoming car.

Kaitlin, who had several alcoholics in her family, knew he'd been drunk, and she was livid. She told Liam the Winthrops weren't upset because they hadn't seen him until the next morning, when he'd sobered up.

In ensuing months, Liam continued to visit the Red Lion, but always returned home sober. However, he began drinking more at home. Kaitlin discovered empty beer bottles he'd hidden in their trash can. She then gave him an ultimatum: he either quit drinking entirely, or they wouldn't try for a baby.

Kaitlin's ultimatum accelerated the process of Liam's becoming sober. He wanted to be a father more than anything. The very next evening after work, he attended an AA meeting. Once he began the meetings, Liam realized he was a problem drinker and needed the group support that AA provided.

The happy result is this couple is still married, with two young daughters. Interestingly, Liam still works at the same gastropub and is still quite close with the Red Lion group. He credits Kaitlin's ultimatum for his sobriety. He drinks Dr. Pepper or a lime fizzy they make for him especially at the Red Lion, in this way getting his social time without alcohol.

## Unconventional Advice

The following advice comes from friends who've been happily married for quite awhile. I've mixed it all together like Tollhouse cookie dough, hoping the end result will be fun and delicious.

- Tell your wife she's more beautiful than her friends. Name a specific friend... let's say it's Cassandra, who's actually much better-looking than your wife. Say, "Cassandra is a dim bulb compared to you."

- Buy plane tickets and have her best friend pack her suitcase. Surprise her with a trip...maybe someplace tropical.

- Put a blindfold on her and tickle her all over with a flower or a feather, whatever's handy. If she doesn't like blindfolds, you can skip that part.

- Pretend to have a bad dream and mumble loudly in your sleep about how you want to visit Jamaica, Barbados, or wherever you want to go. Don't try this more than once...twice tops.

- If your husband's ex-wife calls him too often, set her up with one of your single guy friends. Worked for me! My husband's ex has been happily remarried for four years now; it was all my doing. Now she's too busy and happy to bug my husband.

- Send your kids away to summer camp and have sex in every room of the house, just like you used to do before they came along.

## Unsexy Phrases

So, you and your partner are a sexy, fun and exciting couple! You want to keep that romantic vibe alive! With that fabulous goal in mind, we hereby list some of the most *unsexy* words and phrases on the planet, so you can avoid them, or better yet, completely eliminate them from your repertoire. Okay, let's go:

- "We're on a strict budget."

- "You want sex too often."

- "Let's practice portion control."

- "You look great in that flannel nightie Aunt Betsy gave you."

- "I'm pre-menstrual."

- "I'm post-menstrual."

- "Have you seen my toenail clippers?"

- "I've got massive indigestion... can I tell you *all* about it?"

- "Let's clip coupons together."

- "Have you done your household chores?"
- "I'm too busy to shave my legs."
- "I can't see spending money on flowers for you when they'll just die."

# V

---

## Value

This info comes from Larry, one of our success story husbands. Larry has been happily married for 60 years.

Larry relayed the following: you need to place a high value on the relationship. Your marriage needs to be something you consider to be very important and thus, you treat it accordingly. If you do not place a high value on the relationship, you are showing that it's not meaningful to you, and that it's not something worthy of a lot of effort and work to make great.

Larry added that if you are in a marriage where you feel your partner does not place enough value on the relationship, resist the urge to play the victim. Take a long, hard look at yourself and what you bring to the table.

Undeniably, this is difficult. It's human nature to take the gravel path of least resistance. That's what we earthlings are hard-wired to do. It's why fishing nets were invented. But by pushing ourselves to excel, we can then set a better example for our spouse. This also gives us more leverage if we insist they improve in some way. Now, it could be that you're married to a selfish person, and that of course brings its own set of challenges. However, perhaps one of you is pulling less than your share.

I mentioned this earlier in the "pull your share of the load" chapter, but as it's such a common complaint, I'll revisit it briefly.

A spouse might shirk their share of responsibility with housework, kids, or money. Quite often, as our next example will show, the big bamboozler is financial responsibility, aka money. Not a romantic topic at all, but one which came up repeatedly.

Carl and Melissa had been married for 16 years with two young sons. This family lived in San Diego, a very, very, *very* expensive place to live. Lordy, I should know! I live here myself. This family adored the warm weather and casual beach lifestyle of Southern California. Both Carl and Melissa had grown up in Detroit and had hated the snow and cold, so they now felt they were living in paradise.

Carl had a good job – not great, just good – as a construction supervisor. Melissa was a stay-home mom. This had made sense when their boys were little, although financially it had been a struggle.

Carl and Melissa barely made ends meet on just one salary. After paying their mortgage, utility bills, food and gasoline, there was nothing left over for travel, entertainment or savings.

The plan was "when the boys were older" Melissa would return to work. She'd had an excellent job in property management back in the day.

The statement "when the boys were older" was subject to interpretation. Carl felt this meant middle school, but when their younger son reached this stage, Melissa argued it meant when both boys were done with high school.

One of Melissa's stated reasons for remaining home was to keep their boys out of trouble after school. Carl pointed out that both boys played sports and were rarely home before dinnertime. Also, both were serious students, so this seemed to Carl as Melissa's excuse to avoid going back to work.

As the boys grew older and entered high school, Carl became more and more frustrated as Melissa continually resisted all attempts to find even a part-time job.

Melissa argued that she was good at managing money and they were able to live "just fine" on one salary.

So, folks, this is how divorce attorneys get really rich. Top divorce attorneys can earn over one million dollars per year. Those who own law firms, a whole lotta Rosie more.

Melissa and Carl now faced an enormous issue every single day. Her image of "living just fine" contrasted sharply with his. Carl disliked pinching pennies and juggling to make ends meet. He enjoyed the finer things in life, like nice restaurants and travel, and had always dreamed of visiting Ireland.

You'd be amazed how frequently this exact same dynamic occurs with couples. It's an enormous source of stress which frequently leads to divorce.

This impasse continued for two more years, as Carl grew increasingly annoyed with Melissa. For the most part, however, he didn't say anything. He wanted peace and quiet in his life, not arguments. But he steadily grew unhappier and more disappointed in his wife.

Melissa's best friends, all stay-home moms themselves, sympathized and told her she was doing the right thing. They said Carl was being unreasonable. Now, it should be mentioned that Melissa had met these women when her sons were in private elementary school. The majority of them were married to doctors, dentists, lawyers or business owners. Whether or not these women worked, there was still plenty of money for travel, eating out and so forth. Their situations were nothing like Melissa's.

Quite possibly, Melissa feared returning to work after being home for so many years. I can certainly relate. I took just three years off with Andrea and still recall my panic when first returning to work just part-time.

Candace, Melissa's older sister, was an architect and took an entirely different view than Melissa's girlfriends. She tactfully informed Melissa that she was lazy and should "get off her ass" and get a job, or would end up divorced.

After her initial resentment, Melissa realized her bossy sister was right. She quickly found a good job working in property management. To her surprise, she absolutely loved working again. Not to mention, the extra income was a godsend. Melissa experienced deep satisfaction when informing her family, "I'm taking you all out to dinner." Their sons now listened when she told them to clean up after themselves. Their younger son began cooking dinner several times a week, saying, "I'm so proud of you, mom."

Not surprisingly, Melissa and Carl's relationship improved tremendously. After she'd been working for a year, she surprised him with a birthday trip to Ireland. She paid for everything. It was the first trip the two had taken alone since their honeymoon.

This tale of Melissa and Carl definitely included that good old standby: compromise. Another key was Melissa's willingness to overcome her stubbornness and listen to the sage advice of her big sister.

## Vacations

Some couples enjoy camping or hiking. Others relish road trips. Some prefer tropical destinations such as Hawaii or Jamaica, and staying at luxury resorts. Still other couples love cruises.

Now, what if a couple can't afford the time or money for a real vacation? Here is where creativity can come in handy.

The following are either free or very inexpensive:

- Drive to a town about two hours away; walk around and sightsee like you're on a real holiday. If you don't have kids with you, go to a park and make out on a bench.

- Drive to the beach, mountains or lake and bring a picnic lunch.

- Go to a local museum (there are many free ones) or someplace like a mission or historical building. Our missions here in California are truly spectacular. Most cities have historical buildings or monuments. Pretend you're on a real holiday; read the display placards and take photos.

- Go to a really fancy hotel or resort and hang out. Bonus points for pretending that you're staying there. Extra bonus points for faking accents, but beware! If you're pretending to be from Toronto and someone from Winnipeg overhears you and initiates conversation, it can be a trifle awkward, eh?

- Get creative! The point is to do something, *anything* out of the ordinary to avoid a rut.

# Valentine's Day

Time for one of the most controversial topics on the entire planet!

One hardly goes out on a limb when estimating that perhaps only one husband in twenty really cares two figs about Valentine's Day.

But we women... ah well...most of us do love it. Many of us simply adore it.

Gentlemen, if you couldn't care less about Valentine's Day, but know your wife does, do yourself a favor... spoil her with chocolates, overpriced roses and pushy crowds at dinner.

The reason this is doing *you* a favor is that by extending yourself on this special day, your wife, whom after all you have to live with each and every single day, shall be a happier lady all year long.

This way she won't be – pardon the expression – pissed off until *next* Valentine's Day.... and that's a whole year away!

Guys, 364 days can be a really long time.

Ladies, don't let him off the hook unless you truly, genuinely don't care about Valentine's Day. Don't ever pretend something important doesn't matter, then act like a martyr later.

Beautiful married ladies out there, let's repeat this crucial statement.

Don't ever, *ever* pretend something important doesn't matter, then act like a martyr later.

Without further ado, let's relay a true story from 1989. You young-uns, try and picture if you will, the giant hairdos and enormous shoulder pads. We all looked this way back then, so no one grasped how truly weird it all was. With my perm updo, I gained at least 2 inches in altitude, so, that combined with my 3-inch pumps, made me at least 5'11" tall in those glorious "ye olde" days.

Speaking of hair, in those days women used "Dippity Do," men used "Brylcream" and "Grecian Formula 15," and the punk rockers used "Tenax." We're just keeping these cool words in rotation!

Now for our story: I was 26 years old and worked in outside sales. My co-worker Suzanne was about 45; she and Scott had been married for

19 years. The day before Valentine's Day, instead of her usual happy and bubbly self, Suzanne was quiet and very subdued.

When pressed, she confided that Scott did nothing for her on Valentine's Day, no card, no flowers, no chocolates, no nothin'. He'd spoiled her when they'd been dating, but for 18 years now, laziness had taken its sorry toll.

Get this: Scott even expected Suzanne to cook dinner for him par usual. He couldn't deal with the crowded restaurants... how many times have we heard *this one*?

Let us not overlook one fact: this couple resided in Los Angeles. The City of the Angels is a heavenly place, but residents must deal with crowds from the day their very first diapers are placed onto their tiny gleaming little booties.

So Scott, that excuse just won't fly.

Each Valentine's Day like clockwork, Suzanne's girlfriends and co-workers were spoiled, and she was always disappointed. Invariably, she and Scott would get into a huge argument, so the day was always crummy for them both.

Scott knew very well Suzanne would be upset. Each year was the same dreary story. But he stubbornly clung to his refusal to support a fake Hallmark holiday solely designed to make money.

We've all heard this excuse before...what does this even mean? Scott, this has nothing to do with the Hallmark Store. It's got to do with making your wife feel special.

Ahh...I've got to calm down!

Anyways, the next morning on Valentine's Day, I told Suzanne there'd be a surprise at her house that night, and to act innocent. She pressed me, but I refused to tell her what was up.

Right before lunch, I stopped at "Sav-On's" (we all remember "Sav-On's," don't we?) and bought Russell Stover chocolates and a frilly romantic card. See's chocolates would have been preferable, but I was short on time. I signed the card left-handed with a masculine flair.

I parked at the far end of Suzanne's street, since all of us sported identical Dodge Dynasty company cars. Scott worked from home, but fortunately their house was large, and his office was at the rear of the house.

I left the goods on the front porch, rang the doorbell and dashed down the street as fast as my 3" high heels could carry me. As you may recall, I was 5'11" back then, so I could run just like a gazelle.

I jumped in my gold Dodge Dynasty and took off fast, tires screeching. If Scott had seen me, it would have ruined everything. It wasn't even noon yet, so Scott still had time to "make it rain, baby!"

The next day at the office, Suzanne was absolutely beaming. On her left wrist, she sported a gorgeous new diamond tennis bracelet. Apparently, Scott had suspected the card and candy were from one of our drivers (we worked for a trucking company, by the way).

Jealousy had galvanized Scott into lavishing Suzanne. Oh, it was glorious! Champagne, chocolates, roses, dinner out, and - bonus points for Scott, the lovely diamond tennis bracelet. When I left the company three years later, Scott was still pampering Suzanne on Valentine's Day each and every year.

# W

---

## "We've all done it" versus "What were you thinking?"

The first statement promotes harmony, and the other serves mostly to alienate.

As of this writing, Robert is at the desert riding quads with his buddies.

Let it be known that I'd baked a huge and fabulous batch of my very best brownies for him to bring to the desert. They're made from scratch, extra-special...Ghirardelli chocolate chips, Madagascar vanilla, pecans... in other words, the Rolls-Royce elite of the brownie multiverse.

On the morning Robert was going to the desert, I left the house first. As I was dashing out the door, I said, "Don't forget your brownies, Robert," and he swore that he wouldn't. I even offered to put them in his truck, but he assured me that he'd remember them. When I got home, those gosh darn brownies were still sitting on the counter. What the actual heck... he forgot them!

But when Robert phoned that night, I strictly refrained from ever mentioning the brownies. This takes such self-control, folks. Of course, of course, you want to mention the brownies. Might I also add that those blasted "brownies ultimo" then cruelly taunted me all weekend long, screaming viciously at me from their kitchen-counter perch, "Eat me, eat me now, Linda!"

By the way, my gracious M.O. was quite a departure from when we were first married. Back then, I would have griped at him immediately. "Geez, Robert, you forgot your brownies!" I would have guilted him, blah blah blah.

Fortunately, I've gotten smarter over the years. I didn't even bring it up. Right before we hung up, he said, "Damn it! I forgot the brownies! I can't believe I forgot them."

What was my nonchalant reply? "No worries...we've all done it."

"We've all done it" is an incredibly powerful statement. It assigns no guilt and graciously lets your spouse off the hook. Let's face it: we all know when we screw up. It could be minor, like brownies, or huge, like crashing the Audi.

When we "f" up and our spouse extends us grace, we love and appreciate them.

Next: the alternative. Life is certainly tough enough without hearing, "What were you thinking?"

This is the flip side of the coin from "We've all done it."

Imagine for a moment that your partner has messed up something. If you've been married for awhile, you won't likely need to expend a huge amount of energy to recall an incident.

When your partner screwed up, was your attitude "We've all done it," or was it "What were you thinking?"

Did you berate your partner? Did you bring up their mistake repeatedly, perhaps for weeks, months, or even centuries?

Did you convey the message that your spouse is a real "dumb ass?"

This scolding, scornful and critical behavior is a very powerful component of an *unhappy* relationship.

Back in the early 90s, we socialized with a couple named Isabella and Santiago in Los Angeles. Santiago was very agreeable, with the greatest sense of humor. We would have loved to spend time with him minus Isabella.

Isabella was funny and could tell a good story, but she put down Santiago relentlessly. It wasn't always what she said; it was also nonverbal toxicity. When Santiago talked, she often rolled her eyes and sighed heavily.

We all met for dinner one evening when Santiago had just received a speeding ticket. In front of everyone, Isabella berated him in a "what were you thinking?" type of way. We all heard how their car insurance would increase, and that he should slow down etc., etc.

Another night at happy hour, Santiago revealed that he had just been passed over for a promotion. Isabella just couldn't help but mention in front of us all that if he hadn't been late to work so often, the promotion would have been his.

What Isabella said about Santiago being late deeply resonated with me, but not to the extent that I'm on time anywhere, even to this very day.

Everyone pitied Santiago, but he never stuck up for himself. Once, just once, it would have been simply glorious to hear him tell her to shut up.

We then moved away to San Diego, but over the years still heard from Santiago occasionally. Then the day came that their only son Cesar left for college. Cesar had just finished unpacking his foot locker at his dorm room when Santiago informed Isabella he wanted a divorce. After 22 years of wedded bliss, he was dead-set on ending their marriage. We heard through the citrus grapevine, aka L.A. gossip, that Isabella had begged him to try marriage counseling, but Santiago said no. He was absolutely done.

So, here's your mission, should you decide to accept it. Next time your partner bungles something, even if it's horrendous, communicate that you yourself could easily have messed up things just as badly. You'll earn extra bonus points if their "screw up" is something that you yourself would never, ever in a million years have been dumb enough to do.

Let's stop for a moment to think about why "we've all done it" is music to our ears.

It's because we're not feeling judged by our partner. Unfortunately, we live in a world where we're judged for pretty much everything: our age, our weight, how much money we have, how attractive we are, what kind of car we drive, our wardrobe, how well-educated we are, and so forth.

I don't know about you, but that feeling of always being judged is exhausting.

In her beautiful book, "Listen Like a Horse: Relationships Without Dominance," author Kerri Lake explains why it's so wonderful to be in the company of horses. When you are around them, you can remember how it feels when you're not being judged. She says, "Horses don't need you to be different than you are, in fact, they just want to know who you are in your heart." (Lake, K, 2013)

And of course, dogs, cats and even bunnies give us that wonderful feeling as well.

## Will It Matter One Year From Now?

This clever strategy first came to me ten years ago from a very smart co-worker, and it really impressed me. The concept is simple: if something upsetting, inconvenient, or annoying happens in your life, stop and ask yourself this one very important question: "Will it matter one year from now?"

If the answer is no, don't sweat it - not one single drop. Move on. Shrug it off and forget about it.

This is very powerful. It can apply to all aspects of your life, not just your marriage. You're refusing to get all worked up over something that won't matter one year from now. It's a wonderful concept to live by.

Fred and Sarah have been married for five years. She's a decent driver, but goes way too fast. It's been over a year since her last speeding ticket, but lately Fred has noticed she's been driving faster again, and he recently warned her she could get another ticket. One day shortly thereafter, Sarah did indeed receive a speeding ticket on her way home from work.

Fortunately, as it had been over a year since her last infraction, Sara was eligible for traffic school.

Fredster can then react in two distinct ways.

The more common response would be to nag and criticize, saying something like, "I told you so. You've been driving way too fast lately; now our insurance rates will go up!"

This will likely precipitate an argument, and certainly won't cause Sarah to drive any slower.

Sarah might actually begin driving even faster, since Fred, aka "Captain Obvious," has kinda pissed her off.

Now, here's the alternative. When Sarah comes home complaining about the ticket, Fred can say, "Wow, I'm so sorry about that. But after all, you can always go to traffic school." Presto! This works like magic. Sarah feels comforted because Fred is supporting her, and very importantly, she doesn't feel criticized.

Most importantly, Sarah feels that Fred is on her side. All of this was accomplished by Fred using the principle of "Will this matter one year from now?"

This practice takes a lot of self-discipline, but like many challenging habits, becomes easier in time.

## When a Man Marries His Mistress

"When a man marries his mistress, he creates a job opening." This wise phrase is generally attributed to the French. Why *are* the French so darn clever? Well, it's probably because they've been around for thousands of years. Not the same exact ones...oh, you know what I mean!

Now, let's relay the tale of Gavin, hailing from Laguna Beach, California. Gavin was 35, incredibly handsome, with movie-star hair. He was successful, charming, always big man on campus; in short, a real catch. Gavin and his first wife Elizabeth were married for two blissful years when he fell hopelessly in love with his co-worker Julia. Elizabeth was heartbroken, and wanted to stay together. But Gavin couldn't possibly live without Julia and he begged Elizabeth for a speedy divorce. Elizabeth was remarkably gracious, and their parting was quite amicable.

Gavin and Julia's lovely wedding took place seven months later, the precise moment his divorce finalized. Most of his friends had forgiven him sufficiently to attend. Gavin and Julia were wed for three delightful years and had a baby boy named Aidan when Julia received an anonymous letter in the mail.

The Papyrus card revealed Gavin was dating their cul-de-sac neighbor Vanessa on the sly. Julia deeply suspected Vanessa herself had sent the note; Julia's rage was tempered by grudging admiration that Vanessa had selected such beautiful stationary. There was even the requisite gold hummingbird sticker adorning the envelope. Julia and Gavin briefly reconciled for Aidan's sake, but split up when she discovered his credit card bill with stupendous charges for gifts for Vanessa.

Gavin, why on earth didn't you replace the shredder when it finally broke down from sheer exhaustion? Ah, well, too late now for regrets!

Gavin married wife number three, Vanessa, one year later. Amazingly, the turnout for their wedding was substantial, but truth be told, 90 percent of the attendees were Vanessa's friends. Fast forward: two glorious years of marriage have elapsed. Miraculously, the two are still wed, but only because Vanessa finds a way to turn a blind eye to Gavin's mistress Cassandra.

Vanessa found out about Cassandra six months ago. Understandably, there was drama, but Vanessa is sticking it out, at least for now.

She realizes, as perhaps the first two wives did not, that Gavin will always have someone "on the side." Moreover, he's sharply detoured from his previous M.O. Gavin's not insisting on marrying Cassandra; instead, he deeply wishes to remain with Vanessa.

Even a true romantic like Gavin must be practical sometimes. You see, he brings in a massive income, but shells out hefty alimony to not one, but two ex-wives. To top it off, whenever Vanessa suspects he's been seeing Cassandra, she energetically hits the mall for another round of her favorite new sport: revenge shopping.

Gavin's only saving grace is that Vanessa heartily detests computers. As of this telling, she hasn't commenced that hobby which outrivals everything for highest dollar expenditure per hour. That, my friends, is online shopping. Your average resentful woman can only travel so quickly at the mall, and fortunately Vanessa wears extremely high heels, so she tires easily.

Regardless, at this rate, poor Gavin won't be able to retire until age 97.

Que' lastima!

## What Motivates Them

Here's where I get to put on my "Dr. Watson" psychology hat. By the way, it's a peach-colored baseball cap which reads, "Charleston, South Carolina," one of the best and most fun cities out there! If you haven't been, I highly recommend it. Beautiful architecture, stupendous seafood, haunted tours, the harbor, the pineapple fountain, the Battery! And Savannah is only about an hour away.

So, back to our topic: what motivates them?

Here's the situation: if your spouse doesn't go out of their way to treat you well, stop and think carefully about what motivates them.

The following are some rewards which motivate both men and women to do more for their partner.

- Recognition
- Physical affection/sex
- Respect
- Appreciation
- Compliments
- Gratitude
- Second-hand compliments

Stella and Jack have been married for over 30 years. He still buys her flowers regularly, opens her car door, and holds her hand in the movies. He brings her coffee in the mornings and tells her every day that he loves her. He doesn't criticize her or embarrass her in front of others. He washes her car for her, and waxes it too.

What inspires Jack to keep doing these wonderful things for his wife, especially after so many years? Well, for starters, Stella always thanks him. She compliments him to their children and refrains from telling them when he messes up. She doesn't criticize him or embarrass him in front of others. She invites his brother and father over for dinner at least once a week. She fixes lots of his favorite foods. He likes O'Henry candy bars, so she often buys him one at the market.

In other words, Stella makes Jack feel like he's ten feet tall... and in fact, Jack stands at only 5'7". He says he's the luckiest guy on earth, because Stella makes him feel appreciated and loved. And isn't that what we all want?

In turn, he makes her feel beautiful, loved and appreciated. She says she's the luckiest woman on earth.

Jack and Stella are fictional, but were inspired by two of our success story couples. The noteworthy thing about the success story couples is how many nice things they do for one another. They make one another feel loved and appreciated and they go out of their way for each other. They view their spouse in a positive light, choosing to focus on their good qualities, rather than dwelling on negatives.

The things they do for their spouses are frequently small: but these add up to a lot. Little treats such as buying their partner's favorite candy bar, warming up their car, bringing them coffee in the morning, fixing wonderful lunches for their workday, donating to their pet charity, the list goes on and on. Add your own creative ideas! Your spouse will appreciate it.

## Workaholic

Remember those quizzes in women's magazines which determined your personality type? You'd circle A, B, C or D, then tally your answers at the end to determine if you were co-dependent, insightful, insecure, and so forth. Who here can recall the "Irma Kurtz Agony column," which was painful to read but also massively entertaining?

Now, there's no need for a magazine quiz to determine if you're married to a workaholic. By the way, in this section, we shall alternate the pronouns "he" and "she" for balance.

Let's not deny that there are phenomenal advantages to being married to this personality type. Here are just a few:

1.  You rarely get sick of the sight of your partner's face, as you would with a more leisurely partner. On the contrary, *your* better half is spotted around the house so infrequently you may find it necessary to rely upon photographs to keep their beloved image fresh. Life-sized cardboard cut-outs are quite popular with spouses of workaholics, and these can easily be ordered online.

2.  The workaholic is very seldom around, so they have less time to get on your nerves. It's unlikely you'll catch them lounging around the house eating Doritos, spilling crumbs and binge-watching Netflix. They may actually do this "crash and burn" on an occasional day off, but very, very rarely.

3.  Let us never forget that the workaholic spouse is far more likely to pull in a nice, fat, juicy, hefty income. *Yes!!* In addition, they're typically passionate about their career, which can make them interesting to be around.

Okay, the party's over. Now, it's time to chat about some drawbacks. The workaholic's passion for their career might make them interesting, but there's an unholy flip side. Of course there is. Maybe *all* they want to talk about is their work. Listening to them was interesting for a few years, possibly for even a decade, but now, today, no words could adequately describe how sick and tired you are of hearing about your spouse's job.

Or here's a scenario: you labored for an entire afternoon to create Gordon Ramsay's luscious beef Wellington with all the trimmings for your husband's birthday. You and "workaholic hubster" watched the show together only last month. How could you forget? It's the only TV show he's watched from beginning to end in the past three years. He claimed he'd absolutely love to try the Wellington, so you secretly practiced the recipe twice... you want it to be perfect.

You explained repeatedly that this special dinner would need to be eaten promptly, and "overachiever hubs" convincingly swore that he'd be home by 7:30 p.m. at the absolute latest.

Countdown to dinner..."Welly" emerges from the oven in all its glory. It's beautiful, divine, a work of art. It is sheer magnificence. The pastry is light, flaky, golden and crispy. The inside: utter perfection. Your entire house smells heavenly. Your glorious Wellington could win any cooking contest on the planet.

It's actually 8:45 p.m., because you fibbed about the time to allow hubby an extra hour and 15 minutes. But by 9:15, he's still not home. You peer out the window, obsessively check your phone, you call and text: no answer.

By 9:30, "Welly" is now rather lukewarm, it's a bit soggy, a little dispirited, true, but still salvageable. You shove it in the microwave to avoid food poisoning. You ring hubsters again; finally, he answers. He's not in his car, he's nowhere near home. God bless it, he's still at the damn office. He swears he's getting in the car this very minute, but who can forget that his office is a 40-minute drive from your home.

At 10:15 p.m., he rushes in, so apologetic, chock-full of excuses. It's his birthday, so you can hardly bitch at him, but as you inwardly curse savagely, you wearily reheat and then serve the shrivelled, sad, greasy, pathetic, and ancient Wellington.

One can only imagine the dismay and fury on Chef Ramsay's face if he were to behold the soggy, disgraceful, sodden excuse for his beautiful recipe you've dished up tonight. You're furious with your husband, but most of all with yourself for actually believing for even one single moment he'd be home in time for dinner.

Or, imagine this: the other parents at your son's school assume that you're a single dad since they've never once met your wife...and it's now May. You both promised your son a day trip to Disneyland, but your wife cancels last-minute due to a client emergency. You're stuck faking it to your kid all day long at the happiest place on earth, even though you're pissed off and disappointed. You're so sick and tired of taking him places by yourself.

Without further ado: drumroll please, here's some insight from spouses of total workaholics. These savvy individuals stay happily married, even though their partners typically log anywhere from 70 to 100 hours per week.

- Keep busy with friends, activities and interests besides your spouse. Have your own stuff going on, so you aren't always sitting around waiting like a nerd. My husband brings work home every weekend and I used to complain, but now I accept it. In the past, we argued because I wanted to go places together on the weekend. He just doesn't have the time. So now, I spend Saturdays shopping and having lunch with girlfriends. Or I run errands – either way, I stay out of the house. I do insist on dinners together Saturday and Sunday nights; during the week he gets home too late for us to eat together.

- Accept that your partner will miss social functions or be late to them. My wife manages a busy restaurant. Although she complains when she has to fill in for sick employees, I know she secretly loves it. It's a second marriage for us both and we don't have children. I've got a group of buddies; we go fishing on the weekends and we also take deep-sea fishing trips. Hey, I feel lucky compared to the guys whose wives always complain and make a fuss when they take fishing trips.

- My husband's a textbook workaholic. He hits the gym every morning, and then spends ungodly long hours at the office. Even his rose garden is perfection. No matter how thin he spreads himself during the day, damn it if he doesn't make love to me like a maniac at night. He only requires six hours of sleep. If I ever begin to resent his long hours at the office, I recall my first husband. He was so damn lazy he never held a job for more than a few months. He was fun, but we were always broke. My ex contributes almost nothing toward our two daughters' upkeep or education. My new husband provides everything for them without complaint. They love their dad, but they respect their stepfather.

- Pick carefully which events you insist your spouse attends. For example, my wife never makes it to the birthday parties of our kids' friends. You both don't really need to be there. My wife is there for our son's birthday parties and soccer games. Aside from that, she has a huge job in retail and she travels often. I know she's tired a lot but she loves what she does.

- My husband is a very successful attorney who works at least 85 hours per week. He will always be a workaholic. I have my own career, friends and activities. You need your own interests such as friends, your job and maybe volunteer work. You just can't sweat the small stuff. If I just waited on him all the time it would cause a real rift. I know how important his career is to him. In recent years, he's cut back on his schedule a bit for the sake of his health. I'm proud of him and appreciate how hard he works. He's incredibly generous and so good to me and the kids. He loves what he's doing and wants us to have a good life, so I'm very grateful for that.

- Don't whine to your kids and act like a martyr. My wife is a stockbroker and is always on the computer or on the phone. I knew she was a workaholic when I married her, so none of this came as a surprise. Thing is, I'm insanely proud of her and her work ethic. Most of all, I support her to our two young daughters. I pick up the slack with cooking and housework. I also tell our daughters, "Look at your mom. Look how hard she works."

# X

---

## X-husbands and X-wives

Your evil ex is a living nightmare, the worst person in the world, the bane of your entire existence. Encounters with "evil x" resemble mucking through all nine levels of Dante's Inferno hell whilst sporting old ratty rubber flip-flops. After last year's custody battle, the strap on one of the flip-flops snapped, and now you trudge along with an odd limp, wearily plodding through the squelchy, muddy abyss.

Your ex takes sadistic pleasure in making your life utterly miserable. Even when it isn't deliberate, they still screw things up for you. They never return the kids on time. They can't or won't hold a job, so they can't pay child support. Or they don't pay their share since they're spending all their cash on dating. Which brings us to: your ex recently began seeing someone who appears to be a lunatic, or possibly even a serial killer.

They lie to get their way or to make you look bad. They wickedly manipulate your kids like pawns in a chess game to enact their spiteful revenge. Your ex hasn't found a new relationship, so they bitterly fabricate stories to torture your new spouse. The level of stress your ex produces in your life is not just through the roof; it's through the stratosphere.

In an alternate universe, your wonderful ex is your most trusted confidante and cherished friend; you seamlessly share custody of your beloved children. You didn't stay married, but you work just beautifully as friends. Your ex is that steadfast individual who's always there for you. You are joined by mutual history, love and respect for one another.

No one understands you better than your ex. They support and defend you to the kids; you both agree on the kids' schools, tuition, camp, activities, sports, and hobbies. Now that you're both remarried, you are on such exceptional terms that last year you all vacationed together in Bora Bora. It was a glorious, fantastic tropical melding of two couples, five kids, plus one great-Aunt Bethany thrown in for good measure.

How many times have you heard someone say, "We are much better friends than we were a married couple?"

After a divorce, particularly a nasty one, it's understandable to wish you could erase that person completely from your life. "I don't ever want to see my ex again, so long as I shall live, until death do us part."

If you don't have children together, that's a distinct possibility. But if you do, you must then interact with your ex for an eternity, otherwise known as the day your youngest child finishes college.

A crucial secret shared by individuals who maintain good relations with their exes is that at some point, they both humbly apologized to one another. They attempted to reconcile past differences by saying, "I'm sorry for my mistakes and the part I played in our marriage ending."

Milwaukee couple Jennifer and Clyde were in their early 30s and were parents to two small children, Amelia, age four, and Braden, age six, when they very suddenly split up. They'd been married for eight years.

Jennifer had absolutely wanted to stay together; Clyde had initiated the separation.

Last year, he and Jennifer had attended his 15-year high school reunion. Clyde had spotted his high-school sweetheart Amanda across the room; the two instantly fell back in love.

Amanda was newly single, and Clyde told friends he'd never stopped loving her since they'd broken up two years after high school graduation.

When Clyde packed his bags three months later and moved in with Amanda, Jennifer had been shocked and heartbroken. At first she'd thought this was some kind of ghastly early midlife crisis.

Is anyone else out there wondering what kind of weirdo school has a 15-year reunion, anyways?

Clyde told Jennifer he cared for her and the kids very much, but Amanda was the love of his life. Jennifer was devastated. Their two children were sad and bewildered. They were too young to really understand; they just knew their dad was gone.

Clyde promised Jennifer he would always make their children top priority and he was very fair with custody and finances. He felt horribly guilty, but maintained that life was too short to not spend with the person he was meant to be with.

The moment the ink dried on the divorce papers, Clyde whisked Amanda away to Jamaica, a spot Jennifer herself had incidentally never visited, for a romantic destination wedding on the beach.

Isn't this the crummiest situation imaginable? Well, it is, and sadly it's a true story, although details have been altered.

So, how does Jennifer handle this admittedly wretched, horrendous situation?

Does she stay angry at Clyde forever and make his life miserable? No one can dispute he did her dirty. Ditching her and the kids like that was lousy, no denying it. But Clyde loves his kids and wants to do right by them.

Clyde took full responsibility for what he'd done, and apologized repeatedly to Jennifer. She wasn't ready to hear it yet, but he was sincere in expressing his regret over the pain he'd caused her.

So, let's give Jennifer some advice. Divorced friends who've created solid, positive working relationships with their exes were consulted, and they shelled out some great suggestions. Beware! Some of these are rather unconventional.

1. Jennifer, separate your emotions at feeling betrayed by that "shmucko" Clyde from the logical process of creating a working relationship with him. A good therapist can help you channel your anger into healthy outlets, such as exercise.

2. Jennifer, put yourself and your children first. You're the most important person here, certainly not your rotten ex. Every day spoil yourself, get your car washed, get a massage, get your nails done, maybe a long hot bath, a Starbucks, whatever. Jennifer, pamper thyself. Become your own love object.

3. Jennifer, you must fly straightaway to New Orleans, buy one of those little cloth dolls from a reputable voodoo shop, name it "Miss Amanda" and then stick pins into it. Lots of pins. Within a few months, your anger will cease and you can get along with your ex. Always remember: act surprised and genuinely sympathetic if your ex references any mysterious aches and pains experienced by the hapless Amanda.

4. *Author's note: I was a wee bit surprised to hear this voodoo advice coming from my soft-spoken acquaintance Erica. Frankly, I was also deeply thankful I have never angered Erica, at least not to my knowledge. I don't recommend Jennifer take this voodoo doll step, no matter how tempting it may sound. It may be just too much bad "joo joo."*

5. Though it would make you feel better momentarily, strictly refrain from insulting Amanda. But, if you're discreet about it, Amanda need never know that there is a dartboard hung on the inside door of your closet with an unflattering photo of her face plastered to it.

6. Jennifer, without delay, go get some, girl. Be careful and use condoms. We aren't talking about a serious relationship here. After what you've been through, you deserve it. You're entitled to a distraction. While you're at it, find that "ride or die" single girlfriend. The two of you can go out on the town, meet guys, have fun, and this will keep your mind off your ex. He doesn't deserve one single instant of your mental time.

7. Here's a Dr. Linda tip: Jennifer must locate that priceless individual who's known in inner circles as "transition boy." He's perhaps younger than her, someone fun for her to date, engage in passionate kissing, but she must never, ever sleep with him. If she does, she runs the risk of leaping into rebound zone. "Transition boy" will boost her ego and help her realize that

there are other guys out there. He's an amusing distraction, nothing more. He'll help her forget her ex and prepare her for another serious relationship one day. When my heart was broken by a college boyfriend, my "transition boy" Marco was a godsend. Jeepers, was he ever cute and fun. He quickly got me out of my slump.

8.  Jennifer, don't badmouth Clyde or Amanda to your kids. You'll want to, of course, particularly as they get older, but just remember that movie, "Stepmom," with Julia Roberts and Susan Sarandon. In this film, when referring to his stepmom, Susan Sarandon's son says, "I'll hate her if you want me to."

9.  Jennifer, do eat healthy, get enough sleep, and maybe indulge in a dash of marijuana. Just a tad, though. Don't try to mask your pain with drugs or alcohol. It will help at first, but then you'll have to deal with an addiction.

# Y

## "You're Probably Right"

No need at all to overuse this phrase. It is best used sparingly, kind of like that kickass red pepper hot death sauce in the tiny glass bottle.

But, once in awhile, give it a whirl. Trot out these three magic words just like a show pony: "You're probably right." Then, sit back and witness firsthand the veritable cornucopia of joy which this unassuming phrase creates for your partner.

This holds particularly true if you both have strong – or, shall we say- stubborn personalities. If each of you has a powerful need to be correct, chances are better than average you frequently butt heads over – pardon the expression- dumb and trivial stuff.

If so, "you're probably right" is the magic phrase for you. Your partner will likely be so shocked, so overjoyed to hear this captivating triumvirate of words they may in fact be struck dumb.

Quick disclaimer: this author assumes no responsibility. If fully five minutes have elapsed and your partner is still speechless, do call urgent care. They may have suffered mild cardiac shock.

Imagine this: you and your spouse are both packing suitcases, because in less than one hour, you're headed for a glorious Hawaiian vacation. You're staying at one of those gorgeous resorts where they give you the little wristband good for meals, drinks, the pool, the waterslide, the gift-shop, everything. It's your first holiday in over two years. You can already taste the chocolate macadamia nuts, the coconut sweet bread, and smell the blooming plumeria.

But, for reasons unknown, you and your partner are now squabbling about something completely inconsequential. Somehow, this minor issue has taken on life or death significance.

Hello, how do you say "power struggle?"

Here's the silly way it all started. Whilst packing your swimsuit and beach clothes, you'd begun reminiscing aloud about your Uncle Albert. He's long since departed this green earth; in fact, he passed away nine years ago. Somehow, Uncle Albert's classic 1968 Cadillac enters in the conversation. Your husband fondly recalls the Caddy's pristine gray leather seats. No, you say casually, they were beige. Your partner replies, nope, they were gray.

Now, you're getting a bit irritated.

You recall unquestionably that Uncle Albert's prize Cadillac had a *beige* interior. Your husband stridently replies those seats were *gray*. You know you're correct. And why is he being so pushy anyways? After all, Albert was *your* uncle! Goddammit, why does your husband keep insisting when he knows you're right! Of course you're right!

Next thing you know, the two of you are embroiled in a massive argument. It's incredibly poor timing, since your plane departs for Maui in three hours. Will your first getaway in over two years get off to a crummy start when maybe even Uncle Albert in heaven can't quite recall the shade of his Cadillac's seats?

What the sugarcane boils down to is this: 24 hours from now, who will even care?

If you cut the upholstery argument off at the pass by saying, "Maybe the seats *were* gray," there's a 99 percent probability your spouse will drop the entire argument. Then, next thing you know, you've got a lei around your neck and people are shouting "Aloha!"

Now, some couples engage in this type of fruitless argument on a continual basis. It's basically a power struggle and no one wins.

Catherine and Steve had been dating for many years, so their friends were overjoyed to see them finally tie the knot. In a town of dazzling wedding rings, Catherine's ring nonetheless stood out. It was unbelievably beautiful. You could have framed that ring and hung it on a wall.

Catherine and Steve had been married just one year when they began remodeling the den of their San Francisco home.

Great so far, right? However, both of them possessed extremely strong personalities and they butted heads every day over colors, patterns and styles.

As this was Steve's house before the wedding, he felt this gave him more sway. But Catherine said since it was no longer a bachelor pad, she knew just how the den should look.

If only Catherine had told Steve, even just once, "You're probably right." If only Steve had told Catherine, just one single time, "You may be onto something." But neither was willing to compromise, or to give an inch of ground.

In ensuing months, Catherine told friends she and Steve weren't getting along. She made it seem funny, but as the months dragged on, their relationship deteriorated at a breakneck speed. Catherine and Steve were both so hard-working and prosperous, so much in love, lived in an already beautiful home, but none of that saved their marriage. They bickered over the remodel until their relationship fell completely apart and they divorced right after their two-year anniversary.

Was it really worth it? Maybe the den won't be exactly to your liking, but after all, it's just a f-ing den. You can always hang out in the living room.

Or it's just the beige seats, or maybe they were gray, in Uncle Albert's Caddy.

So, take a minute and visualize you and your spouse arguing about something silly, maybe dining room wallpaper. Stop, take a deep breath, because of course, you have the perfect wallpaper all picked out. But just give it a whirl.

Graciously inform your partner, "You're probably right. Let's just go with that bright green and yellow 70s-style Paisley."

You may then be pleasantly surprised that this magic statement completely defuses the situation. Your partner admits that they don't care and *you* can pick out the wallpaper.

Or, saints preserve us; they may be overjoyed and proceed to order the Paisley straightaway. If that's the case, wait a year, during which time, eat out whenever possible, and then throw a "Swingtown" party where everyone gets drunk, rips off the wallpaper and draws pictures on the wall.

This all ties in closely with our theme of picking your battles. Incidentally, this strategy is employed by several of our success story couples. They believe in being smart and not wasting time arguing over trivial stuff that won't matter two days from now.

## Youth

It's often been said that "youth is wasted on the young." Some say that marriage, as well, is wasted on the young. Before age 23 minimum, you're really just a kid and don't even know who you are yet. You're still in the process of growing up to become the person you will be. That's one of the reasons why marriages of the very young fail at an alarming rate.

Chances of staying together if a couple is under age 20 are spectacularly low. However, there are exceptions.

It's wonderful to see couples who were high school sweethearts and 30 years later still adore one another. But, far more common are couples who grow apart as they become adults.

Bonnie and Warren have been married for 15 years. How does one describe Warren... can we say *jerk*? He's rude, chronically unfaithful, and just plain nasty to Bonnie. Bonnie married him at age 22. At the time, she told friends she wasn't sure he was right for her, but she was worried she wouldn't meet anyone else. So in essence, she sold herself short out of fear.

Bonnie's friends would cheer and celebrate if she finally kicked Warren into a muddy curb. Bonus points if Pennywise was lurking below with his evil grin and red balloon.

There's no guarantee that Bonnie would have met someone else. But by tying herself down to Warren at an early age, hoping for some sort of security blanket, she pretty much guaranteed she wouldn't end up with someone nicer.

Experts suggest young folks under age 23 consider an engagement of two years' duration. If he or she is right for you, they still will be in two years.

## Yellow

This is a super brief section! And it is quite random information. Here it is: if the walls of your home are painted yellow, you are far more likely to argue and bicker as a couple. Strange, but true!

So, in short, don't paint your walls yellow!

If they're already this shade, unless you two get along like peaches and cream, head on out to Home Depot for another hue. There are, of course, literally thousands to choose from.

## Yelling

Some folks believe that yelling clears the air. Others maintain that shouting exacerbates an already crummy situation.

If occasional yelling works for you, who are we to step on it here?

Embarrassing but true: once in a while, Robert and I yell. Yeah, we do. But it's like a short burst of energy and then pouf! It's gone.

We've gotten lazier over the years, lacking energy to prolong arguments like we did in our electric youth. Also, my temper has dramatically improved through maturity, therapy and self-discipline. I'm Italian and Ukrainian; just look at the movie gangsters! I am a volatile mix. In the past, I'd blame my temper on being Italian, but after doing ancestry, well, I'm not even as Italian as I thought!

Generally, I shout one dramatic statement such as, "Robert, you're driving me nuts!" He usually yells back, "Believe me, you're driving me nuts, too!" Often, that's all she wrote.

One-sided yelling relieves tension for the person doing it, but can also really – pardon the expression – piss off the other party. If one partner is doing all of the shouting, the word "bully" comes to mind.

Generally, the same rules apply for yelling as for arguing: no name-calling, no swearing and no personal insults. Otherwise, things descend more rapidly than cave explorers in one of those subterranean horror films.

Sally and Dan lived in Maine and had been married for four years. Dan was quiet and reserved; Sally was definitely the spark plug in their engine when it came to personality. On an everyday basis, they got along great; their opposite personalities made life interesting.

Normally easygoing, during arguments Sally lost her temper and shouted. Dan would then completely shut down. So, to provoke a response, Sally yelled more, and Dan increasingly tuned her out. In her family, everyone yelled: screaming was an everyday occurrence. His family ignored issues, and there were never arguments.

So, Sally's clan of shouters wasn't ideal, but Dan's family dynamic wasn't so hot either. The two were polar opposites when dealing with conflicts.

Since Dan didn't fight back like her siblings had, Sally carried on unchecked. Recently, she'd become more verbally aggressive. She wasn't basically unkind, but all her bullying tendencies had come to the forefront.

Their conflicts got uglier as time elapsed. When she began calling him names, this was the last twig. One Saturday morning after an argument, Dan packed a bag with blueberries and snacks and moved into a hotel.

He then texted Sally he was filing for divorce.

Needless to say, this was a colossal wake-up call. Perhaps Sally's calling Dan a "stupid asshole" hadn't gone over so great. Please pardon the Canadian, folks; just paraphrasing Sally here!

Dan refused to move back home, but fortunately he and Sally began seeing a marriage therapist named Christy.

Christy saw right through Sally's excuses and told her she was verbally abusive. Christy also helped Sally and Dan improve their poor communication skills and do role-plays of conversations.

When Sally raised her voice or interrupted Dan, Christy promptly called her out. Sally always made excuses for her behavior, but Christy was tough on her, which was ultimately a blessing.

Dan was encouraged to speak up, and Sally learned to listen without interrupting.

Over time, Dan became more adept at speaking his mind. He'll always be quieter than Sally, but the two have found a healthy balance.

This couple resolved their issues a decade ago, and are still happily married.

## Your One Precious Gift

So, hopefully, most of this book has been funny, or at least mildly amusing. This next topic, however, is a little more serious.

We're all given a limited number of days on this earth. Some folks linger until they're practically prehistoric, while others get gypped and die young – they don't get much time at all.

Why do so many wonderful, amazing, beautiful people get such a short time on this earth? It's something I've struggled mightily to understand.

I used to think how wonderful it would be if every human being lived for 85 years, with no illness or injuries of any kind. Initially, this sounded fantastic. Imagine never worrying about cancer or disease, because you couldn't get sick. And if you got injured, presto! Your body would heal itself overnight.

The "no cancer or disease" part still sounds *superb*. But knowing exactly when you'd die would actually be horrific. Your whole life would resemble one giant countdown. Imagine the grim check marks on everyone's wall calendars!

Since we have no idea how much time we have on this beautiful planet, how then can we more fully embrace life? How can we be happy, even if our spouse is driving us nuts? What if we don't love or even like our partner anymore? What if they're kind of selfish or dumb or they endlessly disappoint us?

Current philosophy says if you're trapped in an unhappy marriage, life is short, get a divorce, and get the heck out of there.

But what many people say after divorce is that their life didn't really get much better. Many say they now wish they'd tried harder to make their marriage work.

So, let's replace some thinking.

What if you told yourself: "I'm in an unhappy marriage, but I'm going to turn it around?"

"I shall find a way to be happy with this person; after all, I chose them in the first place. Maybe I think they're creepy now, but how can I go backwards to when I thought they were awesome?"

"Also, I'm going to do everything I can to change and better myself. I'm going to get rid of the thinking that I want to end my marriage, and I will find a way to improve it. I'm not going to give up. I want to stay married, and my time on this earth is my one precious gift, so I'm not going to squander it by being unhappy."

# Z

---

## Our last section is "Do's and Don'ts."

*These wonderful tips have been shared by long-time happily married folks. This is our printed book bonus, only available here.*

Please note: these intentionally have been minimally edited to show the original words of those who contributed.

## Do's and Dont's

## Arguments

Do kiss each other goodnight, even if mad at each other.

Calling names hurts and you can't take it back. Be kind. Look at their point of view; you don't always have to be right. When you say you're sorry, mean it! Let him win an argument sometimes.

Don't belittle one another; treat each other as equals.

Occasionally, we do have disagreements and have learned how to deal with those. Mostly we let things cool down before talking about it. This keeps emotions to a minimum and helps resolve issues. For me, I just tell my wife she's always right! Never go to bed mad. I'm sure everyone says that, but it's true.

Don't sweep it under the rug for it to come back up later.

Know when to hold 'em, know when to fold 'em (more folding than holding).

Forgive a lot – people are human (especially your spouse).

Don't go to bed angry; always resolve your issues to your best ability.

Don't argue when you are hungry, tired or stressed for other things (work etc.). Don't blame or take out your stress on them just because they are there to love you, not be yelled at.

Don't stay mad if arguing; get it out and take some space, but then be forgiving of each other.

Don't keep bringing up past issues unless it is done in a healthy way; for example, counseling.

I know some folks who complain and fight in public and it makes me feel so uncomfortable. Keep your dirty laundry to yourself. It is the golden rule for me; treat your partner the way you would like to be treated.

Even if you are hurting and he doesn't apologize, if you know his heart is good, forgive him anyways. Being right isn't always the most important thing in a marriage, but being humble is.

Avoid being passive-aggressive (just say what you want) and holding on to anger for too long (you can go to bed angry, but don't let it go more than 24 hours).

## Hobbies, Recreation and Fun

Pursue your own interests as well as things together.

Find something you enjoy doing together. The creative outlet will propel times of growth as a couple and a common bond when reconciliation is needed.

Go on walks together after work to talk about your day or plan the upcoming weekend.

Laugh, laugh and laugh some more.

Find ways to do novel things that break up your routine.

Find one or more "third thing" - this is something that the poet Donald Hall talked about. A third thing is something you both love with a passion that is beyond the two of you, so it could be your kids at first, then a hobby like golf. It could be travel. For my husband and me, it is yoga, it is travel, building our house, and hiking.

Do things you don't necessarily want to do - and realize if it's important to him – even if it's "stupid," it's still important.

Do your best to make your significant other laugh.

## Travel

Go on a random trip.

Try new adventures together. We like to do things like ride electric scooters around L.A. and San Francisco which is fun.

Go outside your comfort zone if possible to visit someplace your spouse really wants to see, even if it's not your first choice.

Our biggest one and most important for us is to take a night or two get-aways. It's hard to be intimate at home with problems swirling around. A night in Temecula does wonders!

## Faith

Pursue God with all your heart, mind and soul.

Realize that God put you on this earth for a reason. These are challenging times we live in and God put you here now so you can make a difference, even if it is a small difference.

Don't just opt for faith; faith and works is the combination. If you just pray for those less fortunate than yourself that is not works. Feed the homeless, help out at an animal shelter, and show God you are working to help others.

## Cooking

Cook together and eat at the dinner table as a family. Or, if you are like me and your amazing hubby does 95% of the cooking, sit in the kitchen with him while he cooks!

Take a cooking lesson. Ok, I admit, I'm a lousy cook, but I've learned so much by watching someone who knows how to cook.

Once in awhile, bring home his favorite treat; treat him to dinner next time you go out.

Food equals family. My grandma and grandpa bonded over feeding themselves and their family. I remember them both because every meal gave us a time to bond and share about our day. Going out and sharing food together creates food for life.

## Children

I think when you raise children together there is a time you need to be on the same page and a united force; that is important.

Do make time for dates, whether you have kids or not.

## Alcohol

Don't drink too much or other bad habits that cause issues in your relationship. If your wife or husband is asking for you to stop or do less, that's a big sign to take action.

Don't say nasty things to your spouse or act snotty to them when you've been drinking, then blame the alcohol.

## Sex

Have your husband take you on trips so you have more sex on vacations. But do it at home, too!

Don't make excuses; just keep having sex and lots of it.

Keep wooing your partner and keep having sex.

Always try to find time to have intimacy as much as possible.

Don't get into too much of a routine. Do it in different rooms of the house, at different times of day. Keep it fun and sometimes spur of the moment, but there's nothing wrong with planning "sex dates" as well.

## Space

We give each other space; we have our own time doing our own things. Also, if you really aren't getting along, find the root cause of the issue, and if that's been done try a year of separation to give space and see if it can help because most times it's an issue with one person not knowing who they are anymore or someone may have changed. Also try couples' counseling.

Do give each other their own space. As we age, peace and tranquility mean more. He golfs for his outlet; I go to the gym.

You don't have to spend all your time together; enjoy alone time and allow yourself and your partner to do things they enjoy on their own (hobbies, being with friends, going out, etc.).

Make a book of coupons. Coupon for a massage or car wash (you wash the car). Coupon for a week of the remote (you let them have the remote for a week).

## Miscellaneous

My husband and I have a great relationship because we both respect the fact that we have to fill up ourselves before we can pour into anyone else, including each other. You can't pour from an empty cup; self-care is not optional.

Never talk down about or criticize your partner to other people.

Love your partner enough that you listen, you can be flexible because you care what they think and feel, and try to find your way together when making choices in life.

I would say try not to embarrass each other, try to go out of your way for each other, try to really listen to the other person. Try to show appreciation and gratitude.

Always be respectful of each other. Once you lose that, there is no turning back.

Patience (of course), lots of "I love you's" and "thank you's" and lots of hugs and kisses. My husband works longer hours than I do, so I wash and put away his clothes and do more around the house. I never "nag," I just do it for him. I don't mind and he always thanks me.

Just do what your wife says and all will be fine.

Put each other first before friends and family.

Accept your partner for who they are. Don't try to change them. Marriage is not easy and takes a lot of work to make it last. You have to believe in your vows and not think divorce every time there's an issue. Lastly, you have to be willing to compromise. Never take things too seriously. Keep life in perspective. Things could always be worse.

Look for the good in others. My dad used to tell me, "If you see something good in someone, let them know. Everyone needs encouragement." This is a jewel.

Do not lose sight of who you are, and allow him to grow with you.

Don't try and change someone. Accept them for who they are.

Marry a guy who says things like: I'm proud of you, I can't believe you're mine, you can do it, baby.

Don't expect your husband to be your girlfriend. Things get a bit messy when you expect to have the same conversations/reactions with your husband as you would with your girlfriends. Some of the chitchat with my girlfriends would be tedious but something my women friends would just get and want to discuss in depth. This shows the uniqueness of the husband/wife relationship and value of great girlfriends.

Say, "good morning," "good night," "have a wonderful day," and "I love you" every single day.

Always kiss and say "I love you" when they leave, whether to work or store.

Mine might sound cheeky, but we joke about giving each other the illusion of control. Also, I think that we've tried to live by this: only one of us gets to fall apart at a time. We always kiss each other goodbye before we leave to go somewhere and before we go to sleep.

Limit technology (especially TV).

Do brag about your spouse. Don't talk bad about your spouse. Do flirt, show affection and especially in front of your children, be a positive role model on affection. Don't be critical of your spouse. Do be patient. Don't cut off your spouse while they are talking, because you already have a defense comment. Do find time to do fun things together. Don't wait for the perfect moment to be intimate, act now. I know these are common, but they work.

Always push them to do their best in life, work, or university.

Cleaning is a two-partner job.

Don't belittle one another, treat each other as equal.

Never forget that marriage is not 50/50. It's 100/100. Both need to give their all.

Be the partner you'd like to have.

Do be their biggest fan. Allow one another to keep reinventing themselves and do the same. Support their dreams.

## Communication

Communicate – even when it's inconvenient.

Communicate clearly (especially not making assumptions or expecting your partner to read your mind).

Make an effort to connect with each other, whether it's a quick kiss on a busy day, and have some laughs before falling asleep.

Only one word of advice: Listen and hear your significant other without judgement or trying to be right with no expectations.

We've always felt the most important thing is respect and communication.

Be committed to the framework for working things out, which is based on not getting sucked in too deeply to the surface issue of whatever is happening at the moment. Be committed to working things out, which is based upon give and take and mutual respect.

Talk through every issue, even if you think it is small. Getting it off your chest is the best release and allows everyone to move on.

I have learned through trial and error to be nice about the way I discuss things with my husband. Timing and a respectful delivery are huge. Every human being wants and deserves respect.

Okay this one is hard but so important. When your spouse is talking, try repeating what they said and ask if that's what they meant. This will mean a lot to them.

Do…communicate. Do…talk about everything before marriage…kids, finances, expectations etc. Don't….put your partner down.

If there is a problem, do not communicate it by writing a letter. Only communicate about it face-to-face. Too many things can be misinterpreted and the tone is missing in the written word. Things can escalate too quickly that way, whereas talking in person with ground rules and listening to one another is much better.

My only tip is open communication and being honest. Even if that means you need to take time by yourself before communicating your thoughts and feelings.

Don't forget to say, "I love you." You may say it multiple times a day and even randomly, but always say it out loud.

Know when to listen and when to help or "fix."

Be patient; let your partner speak their whole thought before you jump in with your own comments.

Don't keep secrets.

## Timing

Timing is everything; you have to find the right time to discuss issues. It can make a huge difference in the outcome.

When challenges arise, give yourself a time-out before reacting. We've faced a great deal of difficulty with our daughter. When my husband comes home I would immediately fire off like a cannon with all that is wrong and what she's done… I've learned to go for a brief walk before he comes home and bite my tongue when he arrives as that is not how he wants to be greeted.

Do find a way to talk about uncomfortable things like going on a walk together or sitting down together for a meal without distractions such as television.

## Empty Nest

The empty nest is when many marriages fail; you have grown apart and the easy thing to do is to walk away. The hard part is to stay and work it out and truth be told there have been times I have had a foot out the door; what brings me back in is the history and the family we have built together.

Keep up the sex life and date nights when the kids are small. That way when your kids move out someday, you will still feel like a twosome.

## Holidays

Celebrate holidays in a way that is meaningful to you both.

Don't let family guilt you too much over the holidays. Do only as much as you comfortably can.

## Money

Consult each other before you make big purchases.

Have and spend your own money.

Don't talk about money or spending at all; it's unromantic. I realize this may seem like strange advice but it works for us. If it's a matter of less than a few hundred dollars, we never even discuss it.

## In-laws

Don't hate the in-laws just because they are different from your parents.

Back your spouse if your parents are making their life difficult.

## Dates

Date! Go out on playful dates where you don't have to take yourselves too seriously... like bowling, karaoke, an arcade, or mystery dinner theater!

Have date night regularly.

Even if all you can afford is a movie and fast food, get out of the house and away from the kids a minimum of once a week.

## Romance

Life is very busy – hold hands, share desserts, sing in the car, shower together – do things that keep you connected.

Laugh together and get little gifts to show you were thinking of each other.

Never let the honeymoon end. If it does you will never recapture the magic that it once was.

Remember why you fell in love.

Selfless love. Love selflessly.

Build shared connections, even small ones so that you can express love throughout a regular day. This can be things like phrases, inside jokes, songs, physical actions like two quick squeezes of the hand, things like that.

Once in a while, bring home his favorite treat. Treat him to dinner next time you go out.

Put your partner first. Make sure that is for both big and small things. Give your partner the bigger piece of pie, the window seat, etc

Make sure you are the person you would fall in love with. If you cannot see your inner/outer beauty, your compassion, sexiness, etc, you can't expect others to either.

Kiss each other, for no reason at all.

## Unconventional Advice

Just keep from killing each other (this from a happily married wife and mom of 5 kids)!!

Do have romantic dates regularly, do find time to talk and check in, do say I love you… hug, snuggle, and kiss.

If you do have an affair, never, *ever* admit to it. Your partner will never trust you again. You will have to carry the burden of that secret, but if you unburden yourself, your partner will just end up getting hurt. Keep it to yourself.

## A few last pearls of wisdom

Don't pick on them for their hobbies or insecurities; you are the one they trust indefinitely.

Don't assume you know what the other is thinking or wants, don't hold grudges or make unilateral decisions without the other's knowledge.

Don't leave, stick it out; fight for your marriage unless you are not in a safe place. Throughout the years we do grow apart but in the end, it is worth the work.

Don't focus on the frustrations of today.

Don't let work or other distractions consume your relationship.

Don't criticize your partner to others.

Don't compare your relationship to others. Don't take your partner for granted.

Don't push them outside their comfort zone — things like going out or swimming if they aren't comfortable.

Don't go to bed angry. It's a cliché, but that energy can cause you to lose sleep, which is never good!

Don't cheat or lie or give up on your partner. Don't blame or accuse. Don't have kids play a parent.

Don't forget to say "I love you" every time you think of it. You may say it multiple times a day and even randomly, but always say it out loud.

# SUCCESS STORIES

---

The following are personal success stories of beautiful couples who've defied the odds by staying happily married for at least 25 years. Hopefully, some of their tips for success may help you with your own marriage!

## Lynn and Larry
### married for 60 years

If you're in your 20s or 30s, reading "married 60 years" probably seems incredible.

Lynn and Larry are so fun, outgoing and positive they're like kids in their 20s.

They first met in 1959 in Illinois; both were working for Sears, Roebuck and Company. Lynn was 18 and had just graduated high school. Larry was 21 and had just graduated from General Motors Institute of Technology in Flint, Michigan.

Larry invited Lynn for coffee on their break the following day, and she said yes. The next day, he was working in the paint department and didn't correctly replace the lid on a paint can. The paint sprayed all over him and he had to postpone their first date. The two dated for a year and then he proposed; they were engaged for one year before marrying. Larry and Lynn had three children, Amy, the oldest, Connor the middle child and Annie the youngest.

They faced some challenges as a young couple. For one thing, they had no money. He was just beginning his career and she was still in college. Their first apartment had just one room, with a bedroom and kitchenette in one. They shared the bathroom with four other people. The apartment was so miniature that Larry, who is 6'5" tall, jokes that he could lie in bed and fry an egg on the stove at the same time!

Amy arrived a little more than nine months after they were married; Larry then got called in to the Berlin crisis. This changed everything, as Lynn recalls.

Lynn couldn't join him at Fort Polk in Louisiana because her first pregnancy was difficult. For six months she needed to stay near her doctor in Illinois. When Amy was six months old, Lynn joined Larry at Fort Polk. Their military housing was very primitive with no inside restroom. With customary good humor, they made the best of it.

After Larry was discharged from the military, Lynn became pregnant with their son Connor. Their youngest daughter Annie was born a few years later.

Lynn and Larry say that challenging times have drawn them closer together. In 2011, they lost their beautiful daughter Amy to cancer. She was only 48. Their strong commitment to one another got them through this terrible loss.

They never go to bed angry with one another and both have a great sense of humor which unifies them.

They are both devout Catholics and credit their spiritual life for their successful marriage. They attend church regularly and also have a large circle of good friends. Communication and commitment are their top relationship strengtheners. "If things get tough, you stick together," Lynn says.

Lynn's advice for young couples is to attend premarital counseling for a clear understanding of each other's views on money, how to raise kids, spiritual values and so forth.

They both remind one another not to interrupt when the other is talking if they are upset. Neither of them yells or screams; Lynn believes that this contributes to a peaceful relationship.

Larry and Lynn have been happily married for over 60 years and anyone who spends time with them can see their mutual love and respect.

# Bill and Mary
## married for 55 years

Bill and Mary met at a party in 1962 in San Diego, just after he'd graduated high school. Mary claims her only interest in Bill was friendship, but her mother recalled that Mary returned home from the party mentioning a boy with blue eyes.

Bill had been dating another girl, but after she moved to Oklahoma, they eventually broke up. A few months later, Bill and Mary began dating.

When Mary was 16, Bill said he loved her, which, as she recalls, was a little much at that age. Mary was a student at Grossmont College and Bill went into the National Guard.

After they'd dated a couple years, Bill surprised her with a visit to a jewelery shop, where he slipped a ring on her finger. They were engaged for eight months and married when she was 19 and he was 22. The year was 1967.

Mary and Bill were married for four years before starting a family; they have three daughters, Margaret, Jenny and Cathy.

Both Bill and Mary maintain the biggest secret of their successful marriage has been their friendship. "Friends before lovers" is Bill's slogan.

The biggest issue for this couple has been money; Mary is much more of a spender than Bill. She loves to travel, and over the years she has converted Bill so he now loves to travel as well. One favorite destination is England; Mary's family is from England and she lived there until age five.

Mary and Bill were able to "come to an understanding," as they put it, so far as the spending went. Mary once threw out a bunch of credit cards; Bill made a collage out of them, framed it and has it to this day.

Bill and Mary have a very different style of handling disagreements. Mary yells and then starts crying. Bill doesn't say much. But they use their humor and friendship to come to an agreement when there are disputes.

There was a crisis in their marriage when their two oldest children were small. Mary was furious with Bill because he was working so much and getting home late. She decided to divorce him. She called her parents, who quickly came over and talked her out of it. They reminded her how great Bill was and so forth. Mary recalls that several of her friends were getting divorced at this time, which may have been an influence.

Mary's advice for young couples is to maintain a friendship. Treat one another as you would treat a cherished friend. Be patient with yourself and your partner. You need to have this patience, all day, every day. For example, Mary wants Bill to get projects done around the house. She now realizes he will do these as he schedules them, and to not be a nag. Mary says it's important to accept that your partner is a different person than you and to be patient.

Bill says to always keep your sense of humor. He adds, "You can't get divorced over the toothpaste tube!" Little things matter a lot; for example, Bill brings coffee to Mary every morning with a nice comment such as, "For you, my love."

Mary says it's crucial to have humility in the relationship and to not think of one's self as being perfect. It's also important to know how to apologize; this is a skill that can be improved. Bill never could apologize in the early days of their marriage, but has become good at it now.

Bill and Mary joke around and are so warm and comfortable with one another. They have been happily married for over 55 years.

## Candace and Tom
### married for 42 years

Candace and Tom met in 1975 in Massachusetts as junior high school sweethearts. Interestingly, Candace didn't like Tom at first; plus, Candace's sister thought that Tom was interested in her rather than Candace. After awhile, Tom and Candace began to like one another. They dated all through her high school years and his college years and never broke up.

Candace recalls that Tom was the nicest guy in their school; always opening doors for girls and such a gentleman. Tom's mom was a single mom; his dad had passed away as active duty military. She'd raised Tom to have good manners and to cook and do his sisters' hair. He was considered a good catch.

They married in 1980 when Candace was 18 and Tom was 22. He proposed by asking her, "What do you think you'll be doing for the next 50-60 years?" He then added, "Would you marry me?"

They married on June 26th of 1980. It was a big wedding with about 400 guests, 370 of whom Candace recalls she and Tom didn't even know.

Tom surprised Candace with a romantic honeymoon in Bermuda. She'd thought they were going to Florida, but then he surprised her with two plane tickets labeled "Mr. and Mrs. Plebe."

They had two children, Andy, born in 1984, and Bobby, born in 1987.

Their main challenge was that he was active duty military, so he was gone all the time. For example, they married in June and he was deployed that September for six months' duration. Over the years, Tom was usually gone for at least half of the year.

Tom and Candace coped by staying in close communication. They wrote letters and numbered them, so that the sequence wouldn't be confusing in case a letter was lost. Tom's first duty location was Newport, Rhode Island. They also moved to California in 1999. Altogether, they moved 29 times in 37 years.

Candace advises young couples to have persistence. She feels marriage is not to be taken lightly, and couples who tend to glamorize it and then bail out at the first difficulty do not last.

Candace says that couples need to go into marriage with the thought that it's for the rest of their lives and to remember the vows say "Til death do us part." Candace adds that Navy life isn't for everyone. One thing that helped Candace and Tom over the years was to not go to bed angry. No matter how annoyed they are with one another, they set this aside at bedtime.

She adds that it's important to see the other person's point of view and to not alienate one another.

Candace and Tom have been happily married for 37 years. They still enjoy one another's company and they love to travel, take cruises, eat out and visit with friends.

## Susan and John
### married for 40 years

Susan and John met in 1980 as college students. John and a friend walked in late to a class Susan was attending. As Susan jokingly puts it, she initially wasn't that impressed. The girl sitting next to her said that one of the two boys was the student body President; Susan pointed to John and said she knew it wasn't him. Who would have thought from this inauspicious start that these two would turn out to be happily married, as of this writing, for over 40 years?

After class, John approached Susan and asked her out. She said no. He asked why not, and she said she had to work that evening. He then asked where she worked, and Susan replied, "Mervyn's." That same evening, John actually showed up at Mervyn's to see if Susan was really working.

The two then began dating. After some time had passed, John decided to go to Germany and work there for a year. Before he left, he had spoken to Susan about marriage, but this subject was left up in the air.

However, John became homesick and especially missed Susan, so he returned to California after just three months. At this time they got engaged and set a date; Susan also bought her wedding dress. Right before the invitations were printed, John got cold feet and called it off.

As Susan describes it, she picked up her dress at the shop, since it had already been paid for, and then "did a Mexican hat dance on it on the street." After trampling her dress, Susan realized she was a bit relieved herself. They didn't break up, but their relationship changed a bit during this time, as John had to earn back Susan's trust. One year later, on February 19th the two were married. She was 22 and he was 28.

One of the biggest adjustments Susan and John had to make was living together. This was harder for him as he's six years older than her, so had been single longer.

Their son Jeff was born in 1986 and their younger son Tim in 1991. Susan and John agreed on childrearing, so this was never an issue for them. They were both children of divorce and didn't want to put their kids through the same. They both felt they had learned from their parents' mistakes, and made sure not to repeat those errors. Waiting a few years to have their first son was a wise choice, as they wanted to make sure their relationship was stable. The gap in ages between the boys was also a positive factor.

According to Susan, there are three things she and John never discuss, because they will never agree: the Middle East, dancing, and hanging wall paper! Susan and John are well-matched as a couple because they seldom argue. They believe in letting things go and not sweating the small stuff.

One very important part of their lives is their faith. Susan and John are Jehovah Witnesses and they credit this as a very strong contributor to their marriage. Their religious beliefs aligned later in their relationship and brought them closer together. They've had challenges raising Tim, who is special needs, and their faith helped give them strength and patience as parents.

Susan explains that in their faith, they are taught to be kind and loving and think of one another not just as husband and wife, but as spiritual brother and sister. Becoming Witnesses bound them closer in their relationship. They see their marriage as a vow, so they take their marriage commitment very seriously.

As Susan describes it, they would never speak harshly to their brother at Kingdom Hall, so they would never speak harshly to their spouse either. Susan and John make it a point to always treat one another with love and kindness.

Susan advises young couples to take your time dating and be sure this is the person you want to spend forever with. Make sure they are someone you can trust.

Choose wisely. If warning bells are going off, don't ignore this big red flag. It is better to not be married than to be in a relationship that is destructive or hurtful.

Here is this couple's advice: be careful in choosing a spouse and don't rush into it. Once you're married, do everything to keep the relationship healthy and positive. You're always going to need to be the bigger person and work to figure out how you can improve your marriage.

Susan and John have given their sons a stable, loving home and foundation and have become closer over the years, due to their shared faith and commitment to one another. They have been happily married for over 40 years.

## Karen and Brad
### married for 33 years

Brad and Karen met May of 1989 at the swim-up bar of a hotel in Puerto Vallarta, Mexico. Karen had just graduated college and Brad was due to return home to San Antonio, Texas the next day. If they hadn't met at that exact time, it's unlikely their paths would have ever crossed again.

Karen recalls that she liked Brad right away but she didn't believe she'd hear from him again. For one thing, they lived so far away (she was in Denver), and they'd just met that one time. But Brad called her soon afterwards, and they exchanged phone calls and letters until he moved to Colorado November of 1989. He proposed December of 1989 and they were married on June 16, 1990.

Both sets of their parents are still married, so divorce was something neither of them saw as a concern. Unfortunately, many of their friends have divorced over the years.

Both Brad and Karen were raised in the Catholic Church, so religion was never an issue. They attended premarital counseling sessions through their church, and met regularly for five months with Pete and Gina, another couple who had been married for 15 years.

These premarital counseling sessions gave them wisdom about things like finances and how to handle disagreements.

Karen was 23 and Brad 27 when they married. They have four children: Tanner, David, Emily, and Brendan.

The work and responsibility of four children was a challenge, but Brad did his part with housework, diapers and so forth. Their motto was "divide and conquer," with, for example, one parent watching David play football and Emily play lacrosse, then switching off.

Karen worked full-time when they had the first two kids which was challenging; she worked part-time when Emily was born, then became a stay-home mom when their youngest Brendan was born.

An early challenge was starting out with no money, but there were many fun memories. For example, Karen and Brad's first home had just one kitchen drawer. This had to hold silverware, utensils – everything. They made Christmas ornaments to give away instead of spending money on gifts. In later years, another big challenge was paying college tuition for three kids at once.

Karen and Brad get along well as both are easygoing and rarely disagree. Of course there are arguments, but they are both "in it for the long haul."

Karen and Brad feel it was a huge benefit for them to be raised in a home with their parents together and they wanted the same thing for their kids.

They take their vows very seriously and encourage new couples to do the same. There are going to be ups and downs in any relationship and it's necessary to get through the bad times by enjoying the good times.

Now that the kids are older, Karen and Brad are thoroughly enjoying their "empty nest." They can relax more and enjoy each other's company, whether it's eating out, watching "Game of Thrones," or doing puzzles. They love to go on dates and made sure to do this when the kids were younger, which helped keep their relationship strong. They were fortunate to have family nearby to help babysit until they felt comfortable hiring non-family members.

When asked the top advice for young couples, Karen quotes her grandma Ada who said, "You only want to marry a person you can't live without."

Karen and Brad never go to bed angry. They are close to their families and love travel, restaurants and movies. Even when a little peeved with one another, they still kiss goodnight and say, "I love you."

Karen and Brad are an energetic and positive couple; they love to spend time with each other and their family and friends. They have been happily married for 33 years.

## Jessica and Mattson
### married for 34 years

Jessica and Mattson first met when she was in the fifth grade and became friends with his older sister. Jessica later met Mattson's mom, who was their Girl Scout troop leader. Mattson was one year older than Jessica; both attended the same high school.

Jessica and Mattson's first date was when she was 15 and he was 16. They dated all through high school but then broke up right after she graduated.

They then got back together at the end of the summer. In retrospect, Jessica believes because they were so young when they'd first begun dating, it was beneficial that they took some breaks before marrying.

When Jessica turned 21, Mattson asked her to marry him. After dinner at the Redondo Beach Charthouse, he proposed on the beach, and she said yes. Since they'd looked at rings together, it wasn't a total surprise.

They had another break-up the next summer; again, both sowed some wild oats. It was a rather odd phase of their relationship, because this time, Mattson took the engagement ring back.

Jessica was devastated at first, but then enjoyed what she now calls their "summer of craziness." After three months they reunited and Mattson wanted to return the ring to her, but she "strung him along," as she puts it, for awhile.

One night in 1988 at Gulliver's restaurant, as Jessica recalls, Mattson filled her up with Long Island iced teas. After dinner, she was desperate for the ladies' room. As she got up to leave the table, he pulled out the ring and told her, "This is the last time I am asking you."

Jessica recalls it was quite comical; as Mattson got down on one knee, all she could think about was how urgently she needed the ladies' room. Mattson began a very lengthy and romantic proposal. Jessica said a hasty "yes!" then made a mad dash for the ladies' room.

They were married February of 1989 and had a beautiful wedding with four bridesmaids and four groomsmen. The wedding was at University Synagogue in Brentwood and the reception was at Mission Hills.

For their honeymoon, they'd originally planned to go to Jamaica, but a hurricane took down the resort, so they spent a week in Puerto Vallarta.

Jessica dealt with fertility issues for awhile; she'd gone off the pill at age 25, but for the longest time her body did not learn to ovulate.

Fortunately this situation resolved itself; their beautiful daughter Josie was born in 1994 and their son Derek was born in 1997.

This couple has faced some challenges over the years. Sometime after their wedding, Mattson was laid off from his job, and to make ends meet, took side jobs and odd jobs.

He was not at home as much, which was stressful to their relationship.

Just eight weeks after the birth of Josie, Jessica went right back to work. Although her teaching job was part-time and her grandparents helped babysit, it was still a very rough and exhausting time. So when their son Derek was born three years later, Jessica didn't return to work for nearly six months.

One challenge they have faced is money issues. Jessica likes working and earning her own money; she doesn't wish to be dependent on Mattson.

Jessica and Mattson have always been invested in staying together and maintaining a solid relationship. Her own folks divorced when she was four years old and she didn't want her children to go through a divorce. Mattson's parents were together until his dad passed away.

Power struggles and communication issues can be challenging, but this couple works together to stay in sync.

Mattson becomes quiet when he's angry or upset, and doesn't want to talk. After awhile he will be fine. Jessica, on the other hand, likes to discuss things when she's upset.

So, this couple does what so many other successful couples do: they compromise. At times when she's upset, Jessica also confides in a couple of trusted girlfriends.

Jessica and Mattson are comfortable with one another and enjoy each other's company. They are proud that they've built a fine life together and know one another so well; after all, they grew up together.

They are both grateful for their two beautiful kids. They respect and love one another, which is very evident to anyone who spends time with them. Jessica stresses that the respect in their relationship is the most crucial part.

They were so young when they met, so of course both have evolved dramatically, but they've remained close over the years. They have worked hard to make their relationship a success.

Jessica puts it this way: sparks can come and go, but if you respect and like one another, your relationship will last.

The top advice Jessica and Mattson give a young couple is to respect the person you are with, and give them room to grow. Keep your girlfriends, and let him keep his buddies.

Here is some more advice from this successful couple:

- Take fun "girl" and "boy" trips and don't prevent your spouse from spending time with their friends.

- Maintain a separate life outside of your couple life.

- Do fun things together as a couple, but also make friendships a high priority.

Jessica and Mattson have been married for 34 years. This couple has a high level of love and respect for one another. They also have a wonderful sense of accomplishment and pride that they've maintained a happy marriage and a fine life together.

## Victoria and Joe
### married for 30 years

Victoria was 23 when she first met Joe. She and her best girlfriend Kat visited a tiny pub called Camel's Breath Inn located behind Black Angus restaurant in El Cajon, California. Victoria wasn't interested in Joe at first; she knew Kat liked him, but she did think that he was cute. Later that week, Kat was supposed to meet Joe at Black Angus, but sent Victoria instead. As it turned out, Joe had been interested in Victoria the entire time.

From that night on, they were a couple and things progressed very quickly. Two weeks later, they met each other's parents. Six weeks into their relationship, Joe proposed to Victoria. Two weeks later, they eloped to Las Vegas. Eight months after that, they had a big Catholic wedding.

In 1993, when they were married, Victoria was 23 and Joe was 25. Their first daughter Colleen was born in 1995 and their younger daughter Elizabeth was born one year later. Their son Joe Jr. was born in 2000.

Joe and Victoria have faced many challenges together. In their earlier years, finances were an issue. When their kids came along, spending on them became top priority. Joe and Victoria invested in private Catholic school for all three kids, which was a huge expense.

Joe worked for many years as a police officer and was involved in a shooting and pursuit. The long hours he was working, combined with the dangers of the job were very difficult. Victoria thought at one point, "I can't do this anymore; this is too much." However, she eventually got used to it.

When their kids were still very young, Joe was badly injured when his partner accidentally ran him over with her car during a pursuit. This was very frightening for both Joe and Victoria. Another day on the job, Joe was in his car doing paperwork when a driver pulled up, shooting at him. Luckily he wasn't injured, but it was an extremely traumatic incident.

Joe once had to shoot and kill someone in the line of duty. This was an ordeal for them both; but by now Victoria was able to accept that this was his job. At times he would get hot and cold from the stress and Victoria was always there for emotional support.

All three of their children were born prematurely; after each birth, Joe took time off from work to help Victoria.

Joe then had his biggest case; a man who had killed his own child. This was highly publicized and very difficult for Joe, particularly since his own son had just been born. Victoria supported Joe during this difficult time, and they became even closer as a couple.

Joe and Victoria credit the success of their relationship to spending quality time together and talking about everything. They frequently say, "I love you," and "you look nice today." Joe often tells Victoria she looks beautiful, which she really appreciates after all their years together. He opens doors for her and makes her feel special. Victoria does a very careful job with Joe's laundry and gets his lunch ready for him when he's going to work. "He's spoiled," she says.

Joe and Victoria always hold hands when they go out. Their work schedules are different, so she runs errands for him. Doing little things for one another is very important to this successfully married couple.

When asked to give one piece of advice to new couples, Victoria said that good communication and honesty are both key.

Joe and Victoria keep their marriage romantic and special after many years and three children. They've been happily married for over 30 years.

# Juliette and Daniel
## married for 32 years

Juliette and Daniel were military brats living on the same street at Tierrasanta, California navy housing. When Juliette was 11 she saw Daniel for the first time; shortly thereafter, she declared over the middle school intercom that she would marry him. Juliette was 14 when Daniel first noticed her; they began dating summer of 1989.

Juliette and Daniel married on July 12, 1991. She was 16 and he was 18. Their son Daniel Jr. is 35 and their daughter Izzie is 27.

Juliette says the success of their marriage is due to good communication. Since, as she puts it, they were "super young" when they married, they bickered and got nowhere during disagreements or important discussions.

However, Juliette realized at an amazingly young age something married folks of all ages may have difficulty grasping. When she was spiteful and angry, they got nowhere at all.

Juliette thought, "Is this how you want to come across?" She also thought, "If you were gone tomorrow, is this how Daniel would remember you?"

By age 16, Juliette had figured it out. From then on, they both continued improving their communication skills. Instead of yelling or acting spitefully, Juliette would say calmly, "I'm hurt by what happened and would prefer that it not happen again."

Juliette's motto was to wait and think carefully what to say. This couple does argue sometimes, and occasionally voices can be raised. But the overwhelming majority of the time they communicate in a respectful, thoughtful and loving manner.

There's no formal or set way they do it; they just talk. When their kids were little, if they planned to discuss something they didn't want the kids to know about, they went into their bedroom.

Juliette says that from the very beginning, their bedroom has been their fortress. She says it is their safe place. Once they walk past that threshold, this is their cue they will talk things out. For example, if one is really upset, they might go into the bedroom alone, and the other one gives them space. But this is only for 15 minutes or so. They check in with one another every 15 minutes. This gives the angry one time to cool off before they communicate.

Juliette and Daniel don't bicker over silly things, and really listen to one another.

She believes to make a marriage last, you need to truly be in love with that person and love them inside and out. You need to accept their flaws and work to improve your own flaws whenever possible.

Juliette made the statement, "I always do for Daniel, and Daniel always does for me." It is this sense of being a team, united in their lives, that has most contributed to their closeness.

When asked if they ever had a very challenging time, Juliette said that at one time she had a personal tragedy and was grieving. She felt lost and looked for Daniel to solve everything. She thought he should have been more upset. She then realized he was grieving as well, just in a different way and that he was trying to be strong for her. It took about three or four months before they once more began communicating well.

They've always stayed active in their kids' lives and cracked down on them when necessary. Once their daughter got older, she actually appreciated this very much.

Juliette says they never fight about money or bills. When things are tough, they delegate so that each has responsibility for something. At times they've made mistakes (Juliette jokingly mentioned getting suckered into Amway and other "get rich quick" schemes), but didn't run to their family for help. They solved the problem themselves.

Juliette and Daniel also make sure to show gratitude for one another. When one does something for the other, even a small thing, they always thank one another and show appreciation.

Juliette and Daniel beat the odds by marrying young but having a close, happy marriage for over 32 years. They're a fun, engaging couple who always go out of their way for friends and family.

# Madeleine and Thomas
## married for 30 years

Madeleine and Thomas met in 1992. At the time, she was principal of a Catholic elementary school in El Cajon, California and he worked for the husband of a teacher at this school. They first met at dinner at this couple's house.

Madeleine and Thomas started out as friends and found they enjoyed one another's company. Something "clicked," as she puts it. Their relationship grew over time, as did their feelings. Thomas asked Madeleine if she'd seen the monument at Point Loma; she had not. That became their first date, with dinner out at Smuggler's Inn in Mission Valley (Smuggler's Inn is now P.F. Chang's).

Madeleine and Thomas dated for two years and then were married in 1994. It was her first marriage, his second. Madeleine was 48 when she married Thomas; he was 63.

Madeleine was a nun for 22 years. She's also a twin; actually a "mirror twin." This is like looking into a mirror reflection. For example, if Madeleine has a birthmark on her right arm, her mirror twin's birthmark will be in the same spot on her left arm.

An interesting aside: one year when Madeleine was a nun living in the convent, her twin sister was pregnant. One evening, Madeleine fell asleep as usual. She woke up in terrible pain and agony. The sisters at the convent thought it was an appendix attack, but Madeleine's appendix had been removed in the second grade.

Madeleine's niece wasn't due for nearly two months, so Madeleine could not know that her twin sister was in labor. Although completely exhausted, Madeleine finally managed to get back to sleep. The next day at lunchtime, Madeleine's mother called to say that her twin had labored all night and had given birth to Madeleine's niece Connie. So, in essence, Madeleine had gone through the same labor experience as her twin.

By the way, this has nothing to do with the marriage success of Madeleine and Thomas, but it's one of the most amazing twin stories, so I wanted to share it here.

One challenge faced by Madeleine and Thomas was language. Although Thomas is fluent in English, his primary language is Spanish and Madeleine doesn't speak Spanish. For many years, Thomas was very involved with the House of Argentina in San Diego. He attended their events once a month, sometimes more frequently. At first Madeleine joined him, but she didn't really "click" with this group, particularly since events were conducted in Spanish. In addition, Thomas wasn't very interested in her school events.

For this couple, communication was how they resolved this difficulty. Therefore, each picked just a few activities to attend. The key was their ability to compromise.

For many years, Madeleine worked extremely long hours and commuted an hour each way. Thomas supported her 100 percent. He never made her feel guilty when she returned home late and he never pressured her to alter her routine. He realized she was a workaholic and he respected this. Thomas did nearly all of the cooking and housework to help Madeleine; in this way, they forged a strong partnership.

This was all discussed and agreed upon before marriage.

Madeleine and Thomas enjoy socializing with friends and doing fun activities together. They have always reserved Saturday nights for "date night." No matter how busy things were, they have always had their "date nights" together.

Madeleine's number-one advice to young couples is to respect each other for where you are in life and who you are. You don't need to give up everything of yourself to be successful in a marriage partnership. Respect all of it – the good qualities as well as the faults.

Madeleine and Thomas identified areas that might have been issues and they dealt with them. Her faith was very important to her and wasn't such a big part of his life. However, they both respected this difference, so it wasn't an issue. Communication and respect were vital to their success.

Madeleine and Thomas truly enjoy each other's company and their differences in personality (Madeleine is very outgoing and bubbly and Thomas is rather quiet). They married later in life and were able to join their lives and different cultures to form a close and loving partnership. Madeleine and Thomas have been happily married for 30 years.

# Bo and Geoff
## married for 34 years

Bo was born in Waterford, Ireland and came to the U.S. when she was 21. Geoff was born in Belfast, Northern Ireland, and came to the U.S. when he was 17. They met in 1983 when she was 21 and he was 20 at a Westchester, New York bar called BJ Moran's.

At the bar, Bo and her girlfriend heard Geoff and his cousin talking and realized they were Irish. Bo recalls she noticed him before he saw her, but Geoff now claims that he spotted Bo first. Geoff quickly made it clear he was interested in Bo and asked her out.

For two months she turned him down, as she'd just moved to the U.S. and wasn't looking for a serious relationship. She also planned to return shortly to Ireland. However, the two began dating and became close before she flew back home. She returned to New York a couple months later, as by this time she and Geoff were crazy about one another.

Bo and Geoff dated for six years and were married in 1989. They have two daughters: Hannah, born in 1993, and Jodie, born in 1995.

This couple faced some challenges in their early years. Geoff, a carpenter, had bought an old log cabin in Westchester County and had transformed it into a beautiful house. Living there was difficult for Bo as she found it quite isolating. Previously, she was accustomed to living in the Bronx, where there were lots of people and constant activity.

Geoff had come from a large family and wasn't used to doing much housework. Bo worked longer hours than he did, so Geoff adjusted by helping out more. Geoff also had a hot temper and could get angry and yell, and as Bo describes it, the two could have a screaming fight, but then would make up easily. Neither tended to hold a grudge, but both could sulk if the argument was a bad one. However, as Bo puts it, she likes to talk, so she never cared to keep up the silent treatment for long.

This couple has gotten better at taking things in stride as the years have passed. They realize what is really important and "don't lose their mind over the newspaper." Both feel they have grown older and wiser with time and experience.

Divorce is relatively new in Ireland, only becoming more prevalent in recent years, and Bo observes that couples today give up rather quickly on their marriages. "Marriage is work," she ascertains. "You have to work on it all the time." She states that if the love is gone you may want to give it up, but if the love is still there, keep working on it.

Bo credits the success of their relationship to being crazy about one another. Loyalty is also important to both Bo and Geoff. They also believe it's smart to be honest with your partner and say frankly at times, "You're really annoying me today."

One of the most important aspects to their successful relationship is giving one another space. Geoff spends time with buddies from time to time, and Bo loves taking trips with girlfriends. They've never stopped each other from doing the things they love, and always put trust and faith in one another. A marriage breaks down quickly if trust is not there, according to this couple.

The number one piece of advice Bo and Geoff give newly married couples is this: Don't sweat the small stuff. Give each other space to do things you both enjoy. Trust your partner, and let them enjoy time with friends or hobbies.

If you love and trust one another, you simply cannot spend your time worrying about your partner having an affair. Bo has known wives who constantly check up on their husbands, never letting them out of their sight, but as she says practically, "An affair can be at lunchtime. He doesn't have to go out at night to have an affair."

Bo adds: make sure you are truly ready to settle down; you can still do so much fun stuff when married, but things do change. Be kind to each other, don't forget the flowers or the sexy lingerie, keep the spark, and stay interesting and interested. Enjoy the life God gave you. Love one another deeply. Above all, forgiveness is so important. Forgiveness is the biggest thing you may have to do someday. Enjoy your children if you have any.

This festive couple has been married for over 33 years. They make the most of life and enjoy eating out, traveling, and spending time with their two daughters and with friends.

## Pamela and Craig
### married for 31 years

Pamela and Craig met the summer of 1990; both were living and working in Oregon. She worked at a real estate office and he worked for an electrical contracting company. He sometimes visited her office in order to get keys.

Over time, they began talking and found they enjoyed each other's company. A couple of months later, he invited her out to lunch. Lunch was a comfortable first date and felt more casual, like friends.

Pamela and Craig dated for one and a half years before they married. She was 24 and he was 34. The difference in their ages didn't matter; they got along so well and had lots to talk about. They discussed everything, including religion and money, so nothing was unresolved by the time they wed.

Pamela and Craig lived together for about six months before marrying in August of 1992.

They have two children: Brandon, born in 1994 and Jessica, born in 1997.

One of the challenges Pamela and Craig have faced is communication. Pamela jokes that Craig thinks she can read his mind, or thinks he's already told her something, or that she should know by osmosis. She laughs that he is a typical guy this way.

It's clear that Pamela loves and accepts Craig as he is, and he does the same with her. She's more in touch with any issues, and he prefers not to know about problems. So in this way they complement one another.

Another challenge this couple faced was when their daughter Jessica was born with a minor birth defect; her tongue was slightly enlarged. For years they didn't know if she'd need surgery. The uncertainty was very stressful, plus having to make special trips to Children's Hospital in Portland.

During this time, Pamela and Craig helped one another cope. When Craig is upset he shuts down and doesn't want to talk. Pamela, on the other hand, must talk things out when she's upset.

Fortunately, everything worked out fine; Jessica is now a beautiful young lady and a college graduate.

Pamela and Craig are now empty nesters as both Jessica and Brandon live in Los Angeles. Pamela says enthusiastically that they love the empty nest. She and Craig consistently made it a point over the years to do fun activities together, so they kept their "couple vibe." They take long walks together and go out to dinner and the movies; this keeps their close bond and friendship going.

When they argue, Pamela usually gives Craig the silent treatment for a little while. This is beneficial because it gives her a chance to think of what to say, and time for him to notice she's upset. He generally goes on with his life and she has to ask for an apology. However, they never let a small argument turn into a big thing.

When asked what she credits toward the success of their long and happy marriage, Pamela says that she and Craig love to laugh and have a good time. She also mentions long walks as being one of their favorite activities.

Craig has a motorcycle and on occasion goes on rides with friends. Pamela has a close circle of girlfriends and enjoys "girl time" activities, plus going to the gym.

Pamela says that Craig is more optimistic than her and that she's generally the worrier in their relationship. Craig is always confident that things will be great, and sometimes Pamela needs to be the voice of reality if there's a problem.

They both agreed how to raise and educate their kids and both wanted to attend their kids' sports events and other activities.

The number one piece of advice from this couple: try to be each other's friends. Don't ever let that go away. The love will always be there, but it ebbs and flows. The friendship always needs to be there. Laughing a lot and being giddy like little kids is great as well.

Pamela and Craig have been happily married for over 31 years. They've built a very strong partnership, friendship and life together.

## Claire and Sam
### married for 28 years

When Claire and Sam first met in 1992 at her neighbor's house, she'd been exercising her leased horse and was covered in horse hair. Claire found Sam intriguing, but thought her friend was interested in him, plus he was younger. Claire was newly separated, working at a luxury hotel, and renting a Pasadena bungalow. Sam was so quiet Claire joked, "Sam, can you please be quiet so someone else can get a word in edgewise?" Claire and Sam eventually went out for lunch; their relationship slowly but steadily gained momentum.

Claire was going through a divorce at the time and Sam was working on his Master's degree and building his career. They shared a love for animals and nature, and she admired his forthrightness and loyalty; after about 18 months, they moved in together. Their relationship was progressing too slowly for Claire however, so she decided to move out. But then Sam proposed on Valentine's Day, 1995; he brought home a little kitten wearing Claire's engagement ring on a ribbon necklace.

They were married on a beautiful, sunny day in September of 1995.

Early in their marriage they had a number of heated fights about money. The year they got married they bought a home which had attached back taxes, which they got stuck paying. But they were determined to dig out of that hole, which gave them both a sense of unity and accomplishment.

They moved to Oregon at a time when they were battling financial pressures and infertility. Claire returned to school and graduated with a double major; she then became a grant writer. In October of 2009 they moved back to California. They were dealing with several obstacles, including infertility. The whole process of testing and procedures was discouraging and at times humiliating.

Claire says it's important to realize that there will be times of conflict, but with cooperation these can be overcome. She adds that couples can get tired and burned out on each other. These things, combined with media representations of "happily ever after" and the "perfect marriage" are misleading.

Claire's says it's important to not throw away what's truly good because it doesn't look like what we've been told it should be. The mundane events, days when you're annoyed by your partner or not "on the same page" are part of the total package, but not the defining moments. Make sure to carve out time for fun and adventure. Remember the qualities you loved about your partner and why you decided to choose them.

Claire feels their relationship is better than ever with time and victory of overcoming roadblocks. She adds that it's important to say "I love you" often and sincerely.

Sam believes destiny caused him to ditch class that summer night of 1992. When Claire showed up at his co-worker's house, dressed in her English horseback-riding outfit, Sam was too shy to introduce himself, but as he puts it, was "struck by the thunderbolt" and totally smitten.

"I had no moves," he recalls, but mutual friends helped orchestrate encounters until he finally got up the nerve to ask her out.

Sam recalls challenges of their age difference and the biological time clock for a woman who wanted children.

Sam believes one secret of success is to be grateful for what you have. When money was very tight one Christmas, Claire made homemade gifts for friends. Sam's gift to Claire that year was to take her to an old-time movie theatre for her favorite movie, "Breakfast at Tiffany's."

Sam says it was difficult seeing Claire go through infertility, especially when he knew what a wonderful mom she would have been. However, he believes they have a wider circle of friends and more freedom to be spontaneous than couples with children. He sees this as an example of when one door closes, another opens. They've also had incredible opportunities to travel, including a two-month European holiday where they visited Italy, Croatia, Slovenia, Austria and Germany.

Sam says you need patience, gratitude and selflessness, and must always remember you committed to spend your life with this person. Claire and Sam are thankful to be together when so many of their friends have divorced. For many years, Sam has been in a fantasy football league with 11 other guys; half of them are now divorced.

Claire and Sam have been happily married for 28 years. They are a fun, caring and energetic couple, interested in others and passionate about animal rights and the environment.

## Julie and Gary
### married for 35 years

Julie and Gary met in 1982 as sophomores at the University of San Diego. They were living in adjacent on-campus apartments, the university's alternative to dorms. One day Julie's little red Fiat convertible wouldn't start, so she asked Gary's roommate for help. The roommate said that Gary raced cars and knew quite a lot about them. Gary was able to get the Fiat started, and he and Julie became friends.

Julie began to like Gary, but by the time finals were over, he hadn't yet asked her out. She'd already moved home for the summer but knew Gary was still on campus, so one day she put her tennis racket in her Fiat, then drove to campus on pretext of playing tennis. She fortunately saw Gary, and invited him to her cousin's wedding at the Bahia hotel; this was their first date.

Julie and Gary began dating regularly their junior year. They also developed a strong friendship, which Julie believes contributed to the success of their relationship.

Both graduated in 1984; Gary then moved to Los Angeles to attend dental school at USC. Julie stayed in San Diego and earned a Master's degree in Marriage and Family Counseling. This education later stood her in good stead when raising six children!

Julie and Gary continued their relationship long-distance, seeing one another on weekends whenever possible. They dated for seven years before they were married.

They were engaged on New Year's Eve, 1986, while skiing at Lake Tahoe. Gary at first envisioned asking Julie to marry him on the ski lift, but feared he'd drop the ring in the snow. Instead, he located a perfect little restaurant called the Soule Domain. As all tables were taken that night, Gary had to bribe the hostess. Once she saw the ring, however, she let him pick the best table. So, seated by the crackling fireplace over a delicious spaghetti dinner, Gary proposed and Julie joyfully said "yes!"

Julie and Gary were married on August 20, 1988 at the University of San Diego's Immaculata and they honeymooned in the Bahamas. At the time, Gary was in his third year of dental school.

Julie and Gary have six kids. There are two sets of twins: Kevin and Ryan and Lucas and Tyler. Their fifth son is Rhys and the youngest is their daughter Sophia.

One great challenge was that Julie was pregnant with the second set of twins when the first two were just toddlers. By this time, Gary was working as a dentist.

Julie and Gary have always given 110% to their kids. At one point, their two newborn babies and two toddlers were all wearing diapers at once. Julie and Gary became experts at teamwork.

Here's Julie's advice: pick the right person and take your time getting to know them. Talk about career goals, raising kids, core values and faith; take time to understand each other's views.

Never underestimate the power of open, honest communication. Be a good listener, but also share your side. Get your partner's full attention by saying "let's talk," and mean it. If they are looking their phone, remind them you need their full attention. Timing is everything; pick a good time to talk.

This couple shared responsibilities in everything, including their kids' soccer, football, Tae Kwon Do, gymnastics, piano, horseback riding and school activities. After the kids were in bed, Julie and Gary made time for one another to decompress and talk about their day. Julie made sure the kids stuck to a schedule so they wouldn't stay up too late.

When their kids were growing up, they occasionally left them with their nanny and visited Palm Desert or Las Vegas for weekend getaways. Gary and Julie often say little things to one another such as, "I love you mostest."

He fixes smoked salmon Eggs Benedict for her on Mother's Day and buys her Reese's peanut butter cups. She surprises him with peanut M & M's on his birthday because they're his favorite.

Together with their six children, Gary and Julie have built a wonderful life. They have been happily married for 35 years.

## Kathy and Kevin
### married for 30 years

Kathy and Kevin met for the first time in a jetway in Phoenix, Arizona, on April 13th, 1987. She was a flight attendant and he was a pilot.

They didn't start dating at once; she had a boyfriend and he was living with a girl. However, they kept in touch through work, and over time became friends.

Kathy was living in the Florida Keys, doing a lot of diving, and also flying and enjoying life as a single person; then someone recommended her to Kevin to decorate his house.

Kathy decorated Kevin's entire house in 3 months; he loved what she had done. The color scheme of the house was royal blue and yellow. By this time, Kevin's girlfriend had moved out.

One day Kevin called Kathy and asked, "What are you doing?" It was perfect timing, as she had just broken up with her boyfriend. Kevin invited her to Cozumel with his brother and his brother's wife.

This was fall of 1989; from that time on, they were a couple. They dated for three years before they were married. She was 30 and he was 33.

Their first big challenge came in October of 2001 when they'd been married for eight years; Kevin had a flying accident at the Grand Prix of China. His plane crashed into a river when he lost control of the plane. Kevin hit his head badly and had multiple injuries, but fortunately he eventually made a full recovery.

Also in 2001, Kathy had a molar pregnancy and lost the pregnancy, which was a very sad and stressful time for them both. This situation was even more difficult because Kathy was pragmatic and felt it was meant to happen; Kevin was not okay with it. This experience changed Kathy's perspective; she believes that it made her much tougher mentally.

They had been married for 12 years when their daughter Kelby was born March of 2005. Kathy was age 42 when Kelby was born; she left her career as a pilot and stayed home full-time. Kevin returned to Arizona frequently, but was on the road much of the time; this was a big adjustment for Kathy as she felt somewhat like a single mom.

When Kelby was one year old, Kathy began traveling with Kevin to races. Fortunately, this allowed Kathy and Kelby to be on the road most of the time with Kevin.

Kathy also built her own very successful skincare business while working for their family aerobatics company. She continues to be very active with both companies.

This family loves to travel together and is planning a big Central America trip for later this year. They all also enjoy flying in the wind tunnel.

Kathy and Kevin are now in a new phase of life with Kelby getting ready for college soon, and there will be another adjustment as well when Kevin retires from flying. They are a fun and active couple who enjoy spending time with friends and with one another. Kathy and Kevin have been happily married for 30 years.

## Mae and Shane
### married for 25 years

Mae and Shane met in November 1995; he was 38 and she was 39. They dated for a few years and then were married February of 1999. He proposed at the top of the Sea World tower; he bought her a pearl and dolphin ring that day and she later picked out her engagement and wedding rings. They were married outside at the Birch Aquarium at Scripps on a warm February evening; the reception was inside.

This couple enjoys traveling, gardening, wine tasting, shopping, walking, boating, snorkelling, especially in Hawaii, and going on cruises. They've been on eight cruises in all, mostly to the Caribbean. They love live music and outdoor concerts as well as theatre performances.

This couple exemplifies many benefits of a lifestyle without children, as discussed in the "child-free" section of this book. They spend lots of quality time with one another and have more disposable income than couples with children. They also take advantage of many fun activities in their town of San Diego, such as outdoor concerts, parks, the beach, outdoor shopping and restaurants.

Shane built a pond for their koi fish and he also built waterfalls. He and Mae adore everything tropical; including their garden and vacations, and Mae loves wearing tropical-themed dresses.

They also enjoy entertaining and have friends over frequently. Mae and Shane both make a point to be kind and patient with one another. This is a second marriage for them both, so they don't wish to waste time arguing about money, restaurants, travel, working or commuting.

One difficulty this couple experienced was Shane's mother. Shane had originally lived in Virginia, but after moving to San Diego, loved everything about Southern California and never wanted to return to the East Coast. Unfortunately, his mother never accepted this and blamed Mae for Shane's not returning to Virginia. As Mae puts it, Shane's mother always blamed her and hated her. Shane's mother has now accepted that San Diego is his home but for many years went out of her way to make unkind comments to try to make Mae's life miserable. Shane was very supportive of Mae during this time and this created an even stronger bond for this couple.

Mae and Shane exemplify the concept of "carpe diem," or "seize the day." Travel and fun are priorities and they make sure to enjoy their free time. This couple married later in life and so they make the most of each day and are always sure to show appreciation for one another. They have been happily married for 25 years.

## Lori and Eugene
### married for 37 years

Lori and Eugene both worked at a store called Fed Mart, near Helix high school in San Diego. They met in 1980 when she was 22 and he was 28. Eugene had two kids and was divorced. He'd been single for four years and was very serious about his faith, so he wanted to be very careful before remarrying.

Eugene's sister worked at the Fed Mart also. Eugene noticed Lori and asked his sister to help him get a date with her. Eugene and Lori's first date was at the pizza place next door to Fed Mart, so all their co-workers seemed to know about the date. Lori liked him right away.

They dated for four years before they were married. Lori wanted to finish her college degree first; she feared she'd quit school if she married before graduating.

Lori took the initiative on their engagement. Once she'd finished college, she asked Eugene, "When are we going to get married?" His only reservation was his kids, but they got along well with Lori. He and Lori were engaged in July of 1985 and married April of 1986. As both were big Padres fans, they coordinated their honeymoon so they could attend baseball spring training as they'd done for years.

On their honeymoon, Lori and Eugene road tripped to Zion and saw Lake Powell and Sedona, Arizona. They got stuck in a sandstorm in Paige, Arizona; the wind was so bad it peeled the corrugated metal roofs off of buildings.

Eugene's two children Amy and Ted lived with their mother, but spent summers with Lori and Eugene. They were kind to her as Lori recalls, and since she'd had a stepmom of her own, she knew not to push too much. Lori and Eugene vacationed with the kids every summer, plus their own vacation every April to their honeymoon spot of Sedona. Bonding with the kids brought them closer as a couple.

One of the biggest challenges in their early years was that Eugene worked the graveyard shift for a grocery business.

Also, both Amy and Ted were on drugs during their teen years, which was an enormous strain. Lori and Eugene used lots of "tough love," and both kids are now doing well.

Another huge challenge for this couple has been money. They had no problems until the financial crash of 2008, but like many others at that time, had to file bankruptcy and lost their house. This was partly caused by the food worker's strike which lasted five months, during which time Eugene had no income. They used their home's equity to pay bills, and like many others at this time, had a predatory home loan. They now rent their home, but feel it's freeing to rent as there's no home maintenance, which neither feels is their strong suit.

Instead of driving them apart, financial strain made their marriage stronger. Lori and Eugene each felt they'd played a role in what had gone wrong and didn't blame one another. Even when going through bank-ruptcy, they continued to tithe ten percent to their church.

Lori believes every young couple should receive a solid education on finances. She and Eugene made financial mistakes in part because they'd never been taught how to manage money.

Eugene and Lori feel their commitment to one another is so solid that nothing could ever come between them. They always put each other first and feel fortunate to have one another. Lori says her successful mar-riage is the gift she treasures most in life.

Lori and Eugene are a great example of a couple who overcame great challenges and stayed close throughout it all. They have been happily mar-ried for 37 years.

# FOOTNOTES:

---

"The Cheerleader," by Ruth Doan MacDougall. Printed by permission of Ruth Doan MacDougall.

"Listen Like a Horse: Relationships Without Dominance." Printed by permission of Kerri Lake. www.kerrilake.com.